Lecture Notes in Computer Science   14185

Founding Editors

Gerhard Goos
Juris Hartmanis

Editorial Board Members

The series Lecture Notes in Computer Science (LNCS), including its subseries Lecture Notes in Artificial Intelligence (LNAI) and Lecture Notes in Bioinformatics (LNBI), has established itself as a medium for the publication of new developments in computer science and information technology research, teaching, and education.

LNCS enjoys close cooperation with the computer science R & D community, the series counts many renowned academics among its volume editors and paper authors, and collaborates with prestigious societies. Its mission is to serve this international community by providing an invaluable service, mainly focused on the publication of conference and workshop proceedings and postproceedings. LNCS commenced publication in 1973.

Nicolas Tsapatsoulis · Andreas Lanitis ·
Marios Pattichis · Constantinos Pattichis ·
Christos Kyrkou · Efthyvoulos Kyriacou ·
Zenonas Theodosiou · Andreas Panayides
Editors

Computer Analysis of Images and Patterns

20th International Conference, CAIP 2023
Limassol, Cyprus, September 25–28, 2023
Proceedings, Part II

 Springer

Editors

Nicolas Tsapatsoulis (iD)
Cyprus University of Technology
Limassol, Cyprus

Marios Pattichis (iD)
The University of New Mexico
Albuquerque, NM, USA

Christos Kyrkou (iD)
University of Cyprus/KIOS Center
of Excellence
Nicosia, Cyprus

Zenonas Theodosiou (iD)
Cyprus University of Technology/CYENS
Center of Excellence
Limassol, Cyprus

Andreas Lanitis (iD)
Cyprus University of Technology/CYENS
Center of Excellence
Limassol, Cyprus

Constantinos Pattichis (iD)
University of Cyprus/CYENS Center
of Excellence
Nicosia, Cyprus

Efthyvoulos Kyriacou (iD)
Cyprus University of Technology
Limassol, Cyprus

Andreas Panayides (iD)
CYENS Center of Excellence
Nicosia, Cyprus

ISSN 0302-9743   ISSN 1611-3349 (electronic)
Lecture Notes in Computer Science
ISBN 978-3-031-44239-1   ISBN 978-3-031-44240-7 (eBook)
https://doi.org/10.1007/978-3-031-44240-7

This Springer imprint is published by the registered company Springer Nature Switzerland AG
The registered company address is: Gewerbestrasse 11, 6330 Cham, Switzerland

Paper in this product is recyclable.

Preface

CAIP 2023 was the 20th in the CAIP series of biennial international conferences devoted to all aspects of computer vision, image analysis and processing, pattern recognition, and related fields. Previous conferences were held in Salerno, Ystad, Valletta, York, Seville, Münster, Vienna, Paris, etc.

The scientific program of the conference consisted of plenary lectures and contributed papers presented in a single track. A total of 67 papers were submitted and were reviewed single blindly by at least two reviewers per paper. A total of 52 papers were accepted. The program featured the presentation of these papers organized under the following eight Sessions:

SESSION 1: Deep Learning
SESSION 2: Machine Learning for Image and Pattern Analysis I
SESSION 3: Machine Learning for Image and Pattern Analysis II
SESSION 4: Analysis Object Recognition and Segmentation
SESSION 5: Biometrics/Human Pose Estimation/Action Recognition
SESSION 6: Biomedical Image and Pattern Analysis
SESSION 7: General Vision/AI Applications I
SESSION 8: General Vision/AI Applications II

Furthermore, CAIP 2023 featured a contest on "Pedestrian Attributes Recognition with Multi-Task Learning (PAR Contest 2023)", organized by Antonio Greco, University of Salerno, Italy and Bruno Vento, University of Napoli, Italy.

In addition, the CAIP 2023 program included distinguished plenary keynote speakers from academia and industry who shared their insights and accomplishments as well as their vision for the future of the field. More specifically:

Keynote Lecture 1:	**Semiconductor Chips in the Center of Geopolitical Competition** **Chrysostomos L. Nikias, *Ph. D*** *President Emeritus and Professor of Electrical Engineering* *Malcolm R. Currie Chair in Technology and the Humanities* *Director, The Institute for Technology Enabled Higher-Education* *University of Southern California*
Keynote Lecture 2:	**Improving Contour Detection by Surround Suppression of Texture** ***Prof.* Nicolai Petkov** *Bernoulli Institute of Mathematics, Computer Science and Artificial Intelligence* *University of Groningen, The Netherlands*

Moreover, CAIP 2023 included four tutorials, as follows:

Tutorial 1:	A tutorial on multimodal video analysis for understanding human behaviour *Estefanía Talavera Martínez, University of Twente, The Netherlands*
Tutorial 2:	Stochastic gradient descent (SGD) and variants: Evolution and recent trends *Paul A. Rodriguez, Pontifical Catholic University of Peru, Peru*
Tutorial 3:	Video Analysis Methods for Recognizing Multiple Human Activities *Marios S. Pattichis, University of New Mexico, USA*
Tutorial 4:	Using digital tools for health and improving digital skills of health professionals in oncology - Needs assessment for clinical and non-clinical professionals Efthyvoulos Kyriacou, *Cyprus University of Technology, Cyprus*

We want to express our deepest appreciation to all the members of the CAIP 2023 organizing committees and technical program committees, the associate editors, as well as all the reviewers for their dedication and hard work in creating an excellent scientific program. We want to thank all the authors who submitted their papers for presentation at the meeting, and all of you for being here to take part in CAIP 2023 and share your work.

Moreover, we would like to express our sincere thanks to Easy Conferences personnel and especially Christos Therapontos for their excellent and continuous support throughout the course of organizing this conference. In addition, we would like to express our sincere thanks to Elena Polycarpou for her excellent secretarial support.

September 2023

Nicolas Tsapatsoulis
Andreas Lanitis
Marios Pattichis
Constantinos S. Pattichis
Christos Kyrkou
Efthyvoulos Kyriacou
Zenonas Theodosiou
Andreas Panayides

Organization

General Chairs

Nicolas Tsapatsoulis   Cyprus University of Technology, Cyprus

Andreas Lanitis   CYENS & Cyprus University of Technology, Cyprus

Marios Pattichis   University of New Mexico, USA

Program Chairs

Constantinos S. Pattichis   CYENS & University of Cyprus, Cyprus

Christos Kyrkou   KIOS CoE & University of Cyprus, Cyprus

Efthyvoulos Kyriacou (Tutorials and Special Sessions)   Cyprus University of Technology, Cyprus

Zenonas Theodosiou (Contests and Awards)   CYENS & Cyprus University of Technology, Cyprus

Andreas Panayides (Industry Section)   CYENS Centre of Excellence, Cyprus

Honorary Chair

Nicolai Petkov   Univ. of Groningen, The Netherlands

Local Organizing Committee

Constantinos S. Pattichis   CYENS & University of Cyprus, Cyprus

Constandinos Mavromoustakis   IEEE Cyprus Section & University of Nicosia, Cyprus

Alexis Polycarpou   IET Cyprus Local Network – Frederick University, Cyprus

Toumazis Toumazi   Cyprus Computer Society, Cyprus

Steering Committee

Constantinos S. Pattichis (Co-chair CAIP 2021)
Mario Vento (Chair, Chair CAIP 2019)
Gennaro Percanella (Co-chair CAIP 2019)
Michael Felsberg (Chair CAIP 2017)
Nicolai Petkov (Permanent Member)

Awards Chairs

Zenonas Theodosiou   CYENS & Cyprus University of Technology,
                               Cyprus
Christos Loizou   Cyprus University of Technology, Cyprus

Contests Chairs

Antonio Greco   University of Salerno, Italy
Bruno Vento   University of Napoli, Italy

Tutorials Chairs

Efthyvoulos Kyriacou   Cyprus University of Technology, Cyprus
Kleanthis Neokleous   CYENS, Cyprus

Student Activities Chair

Andreas Aristeidou   University of Cyprus, Cyprus

Industry Liaison Chair

Andreas Panayides   CYENS Centre of Excellence, Cyprus

Publicity Committee

Nikolas Papanikolopoulos	Univ. of Minnesota, USA
Andreas Spanias	Arizona State Univ., USA
Marios S. Pattichis	Univ. of New Mexico, USA
Stefanos Kollias	NTUA, Greece
Andreas Stafylopatis	NTUA, Greece
Xiaoyi Jiang	Univ. of Münster, Germany
Enrique Alegre Gutiérrez	Univ. of Leon, Spain
Alessia Saggese	Univ. of Salerno, Italy

CAIP 2023 Reviewers

Athos Antoniades	Stremble Ventures Ltd., Cyprus
Zinonas Antoniou	University of Cyprus, Cyprus
Andreas Aristidou	University of Cyprus, Cyprus
Aristos Aristodimou	University of Cyprus, Cyprus
Alessandro Artusi	CYENS, Cyprus
Vincenzo Carletti	University of Salerno, Italy
Chris Christodoulou	University of Cyprus, Cyprus
Constantinos Djouvas	Cyprus University of Technology, Cyprus
Basilis Gatos	National Center for Scientific Research "Demokritos", Greece
Antonio Greco	University of Salerno, Italy
Minas Karaolis	University of Cyprus, Cyprus
Savvas Karatsiolis	CYENS, Cyprus
Efthyvoulos Kyriacou	Cyprus University of Technology, Cyprus
Christos Kyrkou	KIOS Research and Innovation Center, Cyprus
Andreas Lanitis	Cyprus University of Technology, Cyprus
Christos Loizou	Cyprus University of Technology, Cyprus
Alberto Marchisio	Technical University of Vienna, Austria
Mariofanna Milanova	University of Arkansas at Little Rock, USA
Andreas Neocleous	University of Cyprus, Cyprus
Costas Neocleous	Cyprus University of Technology, Cyprus
Kleanthis Neokleous	CYENS, Cyprus
Athanasios Nikolaidis	Technological Educational Institute of Serres, Greece

Andreas Panayides   CYENS Centre of Excellence, Cyprus
Harris Partaourides   CYENS, Cyprus
Constantinos S. Pattichis   CYENS & University of Cyprus, Cyprus
Marios S. Pattichis   University of New Mexico, USA
Ioannis Pratikakis   Democritus University of Thrace, Greece
Benjamin Risse   University of Münster, Germany
Antonio Roberto   University of Salerno, Italy
Theo Theocharides   KIOS Research and Innovation Center, University
                                 of Cyprus, Cyprus
Zenonas Theodosiou   CYENS, Cyprus
Nicolas Tsapatsoulis   Cyprus University of Technology, Cyprus

Keynote Lectures

Semiconductor Chips in the Center of Geopolitical Competition

Chrysostomos L. Nikias

President Emeritus and Professor of Electrical Engineering, Malcolm R. Currie Chair in Technology and the Humanities, Director, The Institute for Technology Enabled Higher Education, University of Southern California

Abstract. Semiconductor chips are the "brains" behind everything in today's economy. They have become the world's most critical industry. The single most important factor affecting semiconductors is a "cold war-type tension" that has slowly developed in recent years between the USA and China that is rooted in the starkly different systems of governance of the world's two largest economies: democracy versus autocracy. We will address the current geopolitical tensions that are disrupting the crucial global semiconductor industry even as artificial intelligence applications and the cloud computing revolution fuel a surge in demand, the complexities and multinational nature of the supply chain, the challenges with 5G telecommunications hardware, the importance of educating this industry's highly skilled workforce, and the role that democratic societies around the world can play, and make some predictions on what the future holds.

Short Bio: Dr. Chrysostomos L. Nikias is currently President Emeritus and Life Trustee of the University of Southern California (USC), Professor of Electrical Engineering, and the holder of the Malcolm R. Currie Chair in Technology and the Humanities. He has been at USC since 1991, and in addition to his work as a professor, has served as research center director, dean of engineering, provost, and president of the university. Dr. Nikias is a member of the National Academy of Engineering, a fellow of the American Academy of Arts & Sciences, a charter fellow of the National Academy of Inventors, an associate member of the Academy of Athens, a foreign member of the Russian Academy of Sciences, and a life fellow of the Institute of Electrical and Electronics Engineers (IEEE). He is the recipient of the IEEE Simon Ramo Medal for exceptional achievement in systems engineering, the Academic Leadership Award from the Carnegie Corporation of New York, the Ellis Island Medal of Honor, UNICEF's Spirit of Compassion Award, and six honorary doctorates.

Improving Contour Detection by Surround Suppression of Texture

Nicolai Petkov

Bernoulli Institute of Mathematics, Computer Science and Artificial Intelligence,
University of Groningen, The Netherlands

Abstract. Various effects show that the visual perception of an edge or line can be influenced by other such stimuli in the surroundings. Such effects can be related to non-classical receptive field (non-CRF) inhibition, also called surround suppression, which is found in a majority of the orientation selective neurons in the primary visual cortex. A mathematical model of non-CRF inhibition is presented. Non-CRF inhibition acts as a feature contrast computation for oriented stimuli: the response to an edge at a given position is suppressed by other edges in the surround. Consequently, it strongly reduces the responses to texture edges while scarcely affecting the responses to isolated contours. The biological utility of this neural mechanism might thus be that of improving contour (vs. texture) detection. The results of computer simulations based on the proposed model explain perceptual effects, such as orientation contrast pop-out, 'social conformity' of lines embedded in gratings, reduced saliency of contours surrounded by textures and decreased visibility of letters embedded in band-limited noise. The insights into the biological role of non-CRF inhibition can be utilised in machine vision. The proposed model is employed in a contour detection algorithm. Applied on natural images it outperforms previously known such algorithms in computer vision.

Short Bio: Nicolai Petkov was full professor of computer science (chair of Parallel Computing and Intelligent Systems) at the University of Groningen from 1991 till 2023. From 1998 till 2009 he was scientific director of the Institute for Mathematics and Computer Science. He has done research in parallel computing, pattern recognition, image processing, computer vision and applied machine learning. His current research interests as emeritus professor concern predictive analysis of financial time series.

Chair: Andreas Lanitis, *CYENS & Cyprus University of Technology, Cyprus*

Contents – Part II

General Vision - AI Applications

Contents – Part I

Machine Learning for Image and Pattern Analysis

Object Recognition and Segmentation

Biometrics - Human Pose Estimation - Action Recognition

A Systematic Approach for Automated Lecture Style Evaluation Using Biometric Features

Eleni A. Dimitriadou[1,2]($\boxtimes$) (iD) and Andreas Lanitis[1,2] (iD)

[1] Visual Media Computing Lab, Department of Multimedia and Graphic Arts, Cyprus University of Technology, Limassol, Cyprus
ela.dimitriadou@edu.cut.ac.cy, andreas.lanitis@cut.ac.cy
[2] Centre of Excellence-CYENS, Nicosia, Cyprus

Abstract. An integrated system that provides automated lecture style evaluation, allowing teachers to get instant feedback related to the goodness of their lecturing style is presented. The proposed system aims to promote quality improvement of lecture delivery, that could upgrade the overall learning experience of students. The proposed application focuses on specific measurable biometric characteristics, such as facial expressions, body activity, speech rate and intonation, hand movement and facial pose, extracted through video and audio. Measurable biometric features extracted during a lecture are combined to provide teachers with a score reflecting lecture style quality both at frame rate and by providing quality metrics for the whole lecture. A pilot evaluation of the application was conducted with chief education officers, educators and students to obtain feedback on the proposed application. Initial results indicate that the proposed teacher evaluation system is innovative, and it has the potential to become an invaluable tool for educators who wish to maximize the impact of their lectures.

Keywords: Lecture assessment · Lecture style quality · Biometric features

1 Introduction

Automated lecture quality assessment tools can provide objective and timely feedback on the quality of lecture delivery, leading to an improved learning experience for students. In this study, we aim to develop an integrated application that provides automated lecture delivery quality assessment using measurable biometric characteristics extracted through video and audio recordings in real time. Although there are some existing tools that use automated methods to assess lecture quality [11, 18], they have limitations in terms of the accuracy and range of attributes measured. The proposed application estimates lecture quality based on specific measurable characteristics defined through the systematic multi-phased process outlined in Fig. 1. The main steps in the process include literature review, interviews with stakeholders, the definition of biometric features associated with lecture delivery quality, feature extraction from video, and the estimation of an overall lecture delivery quality score.

Previous approaches for developing lecture evaluation systems include the work of Zhao & Tang et al. [24] who proposed an automated classroom observation system to

N. Tsapatsoulis et al. (Eds.): CAIP 2023, LNCS 14185, pp. 3–12, 2023.
https://doi.org/10.1007/978-3-031-44240-7_1

Fig. 1. The systematic approach for developing a lecture assessment.

evaluate teacher performance based on teacher's speaking rate, student engagement and teacher's body language. Gao et al. [11] analyze lecture videos and extract features such as the speaker's posture, movement, eye contact, and facial expressions. In relation to the works reported above, in our approach we adopt a systematic approach for obtaining the profile of a good lecturer and then derive an integrated set of features associated with a good lecture rather than choosing features arbitrarily. Furthermore, the combination of quality scores from all features both at frame rate, and for the whole lecture, allow the lecturers to get useful feedback regarding the lecture delivery quality.

In the remainder of the paper, we present a literature review on the topic of educator performance assessment and present the methodology adopted in our study. In Sect. 4, we present the measurable characteristics and in Sect. 5 we present the evaluation of an integrated system. Section 6 includes concluding comments followed by a discussion and plans for future work.

2   Literature Review

Traditional teacher assessment methods are usually based on the observation of course delivery by experts during course time something that can be expensive, not accurate and usually the feedback provided is infrequent and related to the performance and not on how teachers can enhance their techniques [3]. To overcome this crucial impediment in teacher development, new technologies could be used to produce high quality and meaningful automatic feedback for the educators.

Bhatia et al. [7] use IoT systems in classes to collect information regarding students and educators in order to identify their progress. Utilizing the Bayesian modelling approach, the collected information is assessed through a fog-cloud computing device with the aim to determine a quantitative description of success likelihood. The results of this method are viewed through the experiments conducted using four datasets and prove the efficiency of the method. Srivastava et al. [21] also use IoT systems that collect data during class hours and process them by utilizing Machine Learning (ML) models and cloud computing.

Jensen et al. [13] propose a method that allows teachers to effortlessly audiotape the conversations and lectures in a classroom. Then, they utilize voice recognition and ML algorithms to provide generalized estimations, in the form of scores extracted from essential aspects of educator speech. In a comparison with human interpreters, they observed that automatic methods were relatively precise and that voice recognition mistakes had little effect on performance. Therefore, they state that actual instructor conversation can be captured and evaluated for automated feedback. Jensen et al. [14] also address the issue of designing a framework for automatic educator feedback, that necessitates several considerations about data harvesting processes, automatic assessment and the way feedback is displayed.

Gao et al. [11] use machine learning algorithms and computer vision algorithms to analyze video recordings of the teacher's lectures and extract features such as the speaker's posture, movement, eye contact, and facial expressions. The extracted features are then used to train a machine learning model to predict the performance of the lecturer. The approach was tested on a dataset of real classroom recordings and the results showed promising accuracy in predicting teacher performance when compared to human evaluations. Zhao & Tang [24] use video cameras and audio sensors to collect data from the classroom environment and ML algorithms to analyze the data and extract features such as teacher's speaking rate, student engagement, and teacher's body language. The extracted features are used to generate a quantitative score of the teacher's performance. The proposed system was tested in real classroom conditions and showed promising results in terms of accuracy and objectivity compared to traditional manual observation methods. In comparison to the aforementioned approaches, in our case we incorporate feedback from related stakeholders to define the biometric features used for estimating lecture quality, so that the set of features extracted provide an accurate depiction of lecture quality. Furthermore, apart from quantitative evaluation, the proposed system was evaluated by relevant stakeholders, to ensure the usefulness of the end-result to the educational process.

3 Defining a Good Lecture Style Profile

To define the profile of good lecture style, a thorough research in the existing bibliography in combination with information derived from educators, students and chief education officers was utilized. As a result of the literature review [4, 5, 17, 23] characteristics of good and bad lecturing styles were gathered. For example, good lecturing styles include features related to level of commitment [4], interaction and communication skills [8], promotion of critical thinking, teamwork and creativity [4], giving directions, helping and giving feedback, avoiding negative words [5], and body gestures [23].

To further refine the profile defined based on the related literature, interviews with stakeholders were staged. During the interviews, participants watched typical you-tube videos showing 'good' and 'bad' examples of lecturing, and they indicated specific actions regarded as indications of good and bad lecturing styles. Interviews were conducted with two chief education officers, two teachers and two students. The views of all three categories of participants are highly important as chief education officers perform the process of educator assessment, while educators and students are directly involved in the educational process. The total duration for each interview was about 30 min. After watching each video, participants rated the quality of the lectures they watched, and respond to questions related to the level of lecture quality, the specific actions observed that related to good and bad lecturing styles, and they also commented on the body language, expression, and speech characteristics of the lectures.

Interview data analysis was carried out with the use of codification qualitative techniques [6] in which words, sentences and phrases that had similar conceptual meaning and were important for the research, were arranged in groups whereas data of minor importance were taken apart. This procedure has been repeated to ensure the validity of the codification. Based on the interview findings, most of the participants expressed the view that effective teachers are proficient in using technology, exhibit positive body language (such as facial expressions, head and hand movements), maintain an engaging tone of voice, actively move around the classroom, provide constructive feedback, motivate students, led by example in terms of their attitudes and behavior (such as refraining from using their phone, or drinking in class), are well-prepared, and utilize modern teaching methodologies.

All features defined were assessed with respect to the feasibility of extracting them from a video captured using a static camera pointed at the lecturer, so that a final set of features that relate to facial expression, body activity, speech, hand movement and facial pose was defined. Furthermore, based on findings from the literature and interview responses, the values corresponding to good and bad lecturing types were defined (See Table 1). More information about the features extracted are provided in Sect. 4.

Table 1. Lecture quality metrics.

Modality	Values for Good Lecture Style	Values for Bad Lecture Style
Facial Expressions	Happiness, Surprise, Neutral	Anger, Fear, Disgust, Sad
Body Activity	Attending, Writing, Hand Raising	Absent, Telephone Call, Texting, Looking Elsewhere
Speech	Word Density (35%–55%) Speaking Speed (150–250 words per minute) Speech Intonation (40%–60%)	Word Density ($<$35%, $>$55%) Speaking Speed ($<$150, $>$250 words per minute) Speech Intonation ($<$40%, $>$60%)
Hand Movement	Moving	Stationary
Facial Pose	Left, Right, Up, Down and Forward	Far-Left, Far-Right, Far-Up, Far-Down, Backwards

4   Lecture Style Quality Score Estimation.

Following the determination of the key features, dedicated techniques were used for extracting those features from video recordings and estimating lecture quality metrics, as shown in Fig. 2, and exemplified in the following subsections.

4.1   Facial Expressions

Expression recognition is performed using a cascade classifier [2] to detect the lecturer's face, and a Convolutional Neural Network (CNN) trained using the FER2013 dataset to classify seven basics facial expressions (anger, disgust, fear, happiness, neutral, sad, surprise) [15]. According to Hou et al. [12], anger, disgust, fear and sad are considered negative emotions while happiness, surprise and neutral are considered positive emotions in relation to the teaching process. When the expressions of happiness, surprise, and neutral are detected the lecture quality score is increased, whereas the detection of anger, fear, disgust, and sad expressions leads to a quality score decrease.

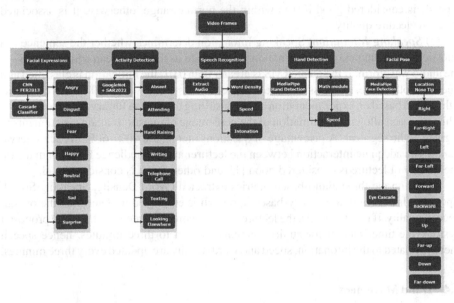

Fig. 2. Overview of lecture quality features and feature extraction methods

4.2 Activity Detection

The proposed system recognizes seven key activities associated with bad/good lecture styles. In particular the system recognizes the following actions: Absent from the camera point of view, attending, raising hand(s), writing, telephone call, texting, and looking elsewhere. The classification of the seven classes was based on a tuned GoogleNet architecture [9] used for assessing in-class student activity. The proposed system classifies the activities attending, writing and hand raising as good lecture styles while the activities absent, telephone call, texting, and looking elsewhere are classified as bad lecture styles (see Table 1).

4.3 Speech Recognition

Audio characteristics extracted from video segments are used for estimating lecture quality. The following features are extracted:

(a) Word Density: Non-silent audio intervals in a given speech segment are detected, and the percentage of non-silent against silent parts is estimated providing in that way

a metric for Word Density. According to the literature [19], the average word density of teachers is 35–55%, thus word density values between 35%–55% are associated with high lecture quality, whereas values outside the recommended range are associated with low lecture quality.

(b) Speaking Speed: Speaking speed is estimated by dividing the number of words detected in a speech segment over by the segment duration. The range of normal levels of human speech is between 150 and 250 words per minute [16], hence the speaking speed (speed) is considered good if it is within the normal range, otherwise it is associated with low lecture quality.

(c) Speaking Intonation: Speaking Intonation determines whether the sentence is a question or a statement [10]. Intonation is estimated as the root mean square (RMS) of the audio waveform. If the mean RMS is greater than 0.01, the intonation is classified as a question; otherwise, it is classified as a statement. The specific value of 0.01 was chosen as a threshold based on experimentation after consulting the librosa library documentation[1]. This approach allows the estimation of the percentage of questions against statements in a given audio segment. A percentage of questions among the 40%–60% in each interval denotes an adequate interaction between the lecturer and the audience hence in that case the quality of lecture is considered good [1], and otherwise it is considered bad.

Based on the three audio-based metrics extracted (Word Density, Speaking Speed, Speaking Intonation), a majority-based approach is employed to determine the overall speech quality. If good prevails, the lecture quality score is incremented. For the proposed system, the time interval for audio segments was set to three minutes, hence speech metrics related to the intonation, speed and word density are updated every three minutes.

4.4 Hand Movement

Hand Detection is performed using Mediapipe Hand Detection [22] and the location of detected hands is used for estimating the speed and direction of hand movements. Hand Speed is calculated as the distance between the current center and the previous center of the hand divided by the number of frames elapsed. If the hands move in a given interval, hands are classified as "moving" and are considered as a good lecture feature. Otherwise, hands are classified as "stationary", and associated as a bad lecture style. The system analyzes hand movements, incrementing the score by 1 if hand movement is detected and 0 when no movement is detected (see Table 1).

4.5 Facial Pose Estimation

Facial pose estimation is performed using Mediapipe Face Detection [20] and enables to determine if the lecturer is looking *right, left, up, down, far-left, far-right, far-up, far-down, forward and backwards*. If a face is detected in the current frame, the nose tip is also located. The position of the nose tip relative to the bounding box around the face allows the calculation of the direction that the lecturer is looking. In addition, an eyeCascade detector was used to detect eyes in a video frame. If the algorithm does not detect eyes, it assumes that the person is not looking towards the audience. If the

---

[1] Https://librosa.org/doc/latest/generated/librosa.feature.rms.html

lecture is looking right, left, up, down and forward are classified as good facial pose as in that case there is eye-contact between the lecturer and the audience, otherwise the head direction is associated with a bad lecture (see Table 1).

4.6 Merging Metrics

Overall, the proposed system utilizes five modalities (Facial Expressions, Body Activity, Speech, Hand Movement, and Facial Pose), and a positive measure for a given modality increases the total quality score by one. As a result, possible values for the quality score range between zero to five, where zero means that none of the modalities resulted in a positive score regarding lecture quality and a score of five indicates that all modalities produced a positive lecture quality score (see Fig. 3). The total score is calculated by summing the scores of each frame and dividing by the number of frames, and the total score is presented on the console providing real-time feedback to the lecturer (see Fig. 4 (left)). Figure 4 (right) shows an illustration of the lecture quality graph for a given lecture.

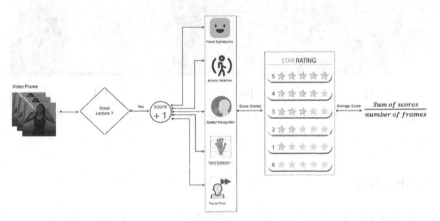

Fig. 3. Evaluation of the total quality score, based on modality-specific scores.

Indicative frames classified as good lecture or bad lecture are shown in Fig. 5. The image frame in Fig. 5(a) is considered to show a good lecture-style because it includes positive facial expressions (happiness), positive activity detection (hand raising), hand movements, and facial pose (forward) that ensures eye-contact with the audience. For that interval speech features were not among the range of acceptable values, hence the overall score was four out of five. The image frame in Fig. 5(b) is considered to show a poor lecture-style quality because no positive facial expressions were detected, a negative action (looking elsewhere) and facial pose (backward) were detected, and the speech features were not among the range of acceptable values. However, since hand movements were detected, the score was assigned a score of one out of five. The image frame in Fig. 5(c) is considered to be an example of poor lecture-style quality because a negative activity was detected (making a telephone call), while and facial pose (far-right), and the speech features were not among the range of acceptable values. However, since hand movements and a positive facial expression (neutral) was detected, the overall score was estimated to a value of two out of five.

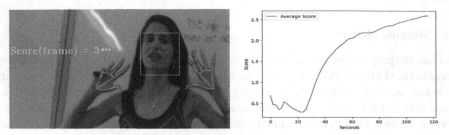

Fig. 4. Score for each frame (left) and average score (right) for the two-minute video printed on the console.

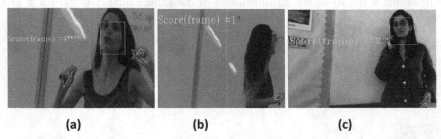

(a)　　　　　　　　　　　**(b)**　　　　　　　　　　　**(c)**

Fig. 5. Typical screenshots where good (a) or bad lecture styles (b)–(c) are detected.

5 Evaluation

The extraction of specific features was tested individually, and quantitative results indicate that all features can be extracted with reasonable accuracy. The overall application operates efficiently in cases where the camera is located at a close distance from the speaker and the microphone is close to the speaker. In cases, where the speaker is at a far distance from the camera/microphone, proper detection of the body parts and extraction of audio features cannot be achieved accurately. Hence, in its current form the proposed system applies to cases where the lecturer does not move in a class, and the camera is located at a reasonable distance from the lecturer. The use of suitable microphones attached on the lecturer is recommended.

To investigate the acceptance of the proposed methodology, a preliminary user evaluation using semi-structured interviews has been carried out with two chief education officers, two teachers and two students. Initially, participants used the application in real time, and then they answered questions regarding their impressions, about biometric features, and possible ways to improve the application. The results showed that all participants consider the system to be an innovative idea as this system can provide real-time feedback. Participants also stated that features used accurately reflect the lecture style quality. Regarding ways to improve, participants mentioned that the camera may not only focus on the teacher but also on the students so that student feedback is also considered as part of the evaluation process.

6 Conclusions

A pilot automated system for evaluating the quality of the educators' lectures, based on the definition and extraction of a set of biometric features was presented. The proposed application extracts multiple features such as facial expressions, body activity, speech, hand movement, and facial pose, which are combined to provide a lecture style quality score for each frame as well as an overall score for the whole lecture. The acceptance of the application was evaluated by chief education officers, teachers and students regarding the functionality, usefulness of the application, and possible improvements. The results showed that participants found the application novel and useful in providing automated feedback regarding lecture quality, so that the overall teaching process is benefitted. In the future, we plan to further refine the metrics considered, and their combination to produce the total quality score, while the applications will be thoroughly evaluated. Furthermore, based on the user evaluation comments, additional cameras, and cameras attached on the lecturer, will be used so that the cases that the lecturer moves in a class are considered.

Acknowledgements. This project was partially supported by EU's H2020 Research and Innovation Programme (Grant Agreement No 739578) and the Government of the Republic of Cyprus.

References

1. Almeida, P.A.: Can I ask a question? The importance of classroom questioning. Procedia Soc. Behav. Sci. **31**, 634–638 (2012)
2. Amal, V. S., Suresh, S., Deepa, G.: Real-time emotion recognition from facial expressions using convolutional neural network with Fer2013 dataset. In: Ubiquitous Intelligent Systems: Proceedings of ICUIS 2021, pp. 541–551. Springer Singapore (2022). https://doi.org/10.1007/978-981-16-3675-2_41
3. Jeff, A., et al.: (2016) Better Feedback for Better Teaching: A Practical Guide to Improving Classroom Observations. Wiley (2016)
4. Azer, S.A.: The qualities of a good teacher: how can they be acquired and sustained? J. R. Soc. Med. **98**(2), 67–69 (2005)
5. Bambaeeroo, F., Shokrpour, N.: The impact of the teachers' non-verbal communication on success in teaching. J. Adv. Med. Educ. Prof. **5**(2), 51–59 (2017). PMID: 28367460; PMCID: PMC5346168
6. Barriball, K.L., While, A.: Collecting data using a semi-structured interview: a discussion paper. J. Adv. Nurs. Inst. Subscript. **19**(2), 328–335 (1994)
7. Bhatia, M., Kaur, A.: Quantum computing inspired framework of student performance assessment in smart classroom. Trans. Emer. Telecommun. Technol. **32**(9), 1–22 (2021). PMCID: PMC5346168

8. Crosby, R.H.J.: AMEE Guide No 20: The good teacher is more than a lecturer-the the twelve roles of the teacher. Med. Teach. **22**(4), 334–347 (2000)

9. Dimitriadou, E., Lanitis, A.: Using student action recognition to enhance the efficiency of tele-education. In: VISIGRAPP (5: VISAPP) pp. 543–549 (2022)

10. Eady, S.J., Cooper, W.E.: Speech intonation and focus location in matched statements and questions. J. Acoust. Soc. Am. **80**(2), 402–415 (1986)

11. Gao, B.: Research and implementation of intelligent evaluation system of teaching quality in universities based on artificial intelligence neural network model. Math. Probl. Eng. **2022**, 1 (2022). https://doi.org/10.1155/2022/8224184

12. Hou, C., Ai, J., Lin, Y., Guan, C., Li, J., Zhu, W.: Evaluation of online teaching quality based on facial expression recognition. Future Internet **14**(6), 177 (2022)

13. Emily, J., et al.: Toward automated feedback on teacher discourse to enhance teacher learning. In: Proceedings of the 2020 CHI Conference on Human Factors in Computing Systems (2020)

14. Jensen, E., Pugh, S.L., D'Mello, S.K.: A deep transfer learning approach to modeling teacher discourse in the classroom. In: LAK21: 11th International Learning Analytics and Knowledge Conference, pp. 302–312 (2021)

15. Lasri, I., Solh, A.R., El Belkacemi, M.: Facial emotion recognition of students using convolutional neural network. In: 2019 third International Conference on Intelligent Computing in Data Sciences (ICDS), pp. 1–6. IEEE (2019)

16. Lewandowski, L., Wood, W., Miller, L.A.: Technological applications for individuals with learning disabilities and ADHD. In Computer-Assisted and Web-Based Innovations in Psychology, Special Education, and Health, pp. 61–93. Academic Press (2016)

17. Miller, P.W.: Nonverbal Communication. What Research Says to the Teacher. NEA Professional Library, PO Box 509, West Haven, CT 06516 (1988)

18. Mohammadreza, E., Safabakhsh, R.: Lecture quality assessment based on the audience reactions using machine learning and neural networks. Comput. Educ. Artific. Intell. **2**, 100022 (2021)

19. Rantala, L., Haataja, K., Vilkman, E., Körkkö, P.: Practical arrangements and methods in the field examination and speaking style analysis of professional voice users. Scandinavian J. Logoped. Phoniat. **19**(1–2), 43–54 (1994)

20. Singh, A.K., Kumbhare, V.A., Arthi, K.: Real-time human pose detection and recognition using MediaPipe. In: Reddy, V.S., Prasad, V.K., Wang, J., Reddy, K. (eds.) Soft Computing and Signal Processing. ICSCSP 2021. Advances in Intelligent Systems and Computing, vol. 1413. Springer, Singapore (2022). https://doi.org/10.1007/978-981-16-7088-6_12

21. Srivastava, M., Saurabh, P., Verma, B.: IOT for capturing information and providing assessment framework for higher educational institutions—a framework for future learning. In: Soft Computing for Problem Solving: SocProS 2018, vol. 2, pp. 249–261 (2020)

22. Veluri, R.K., Sree, S.R., Vanathi, A., Aparna, G., Vaidya, S.P.: Hand gesture mapping using MediaPipe algorithm. In: Proceedings of Third International Conference on Communication, Computing and Electronics Systems, pp. 597–614 (2022)

23. Pi, Z., Liu, W., Ling, H., Zhang, X., Li, X.: Does an instructor's facial expressions override their body gestures in video lectures? Comput. Educ. **193**, 104679 (2023)

24. Zhao, Y., Tang, W.: Modeling and analysis of college teaching quality based on Bp neural network. In: 3rd International Conference on Advancement of the Theory and Practices in Education (ICATPE 2019) (2019)

Highly Crowd Detection and Counting Based on Curriculum Learning

Lidia Fotia, Gennaro Percannella, Alessia Saggese[(✉)], and Mario Vento

Department of Information Engineering, Electrical Engineering and Applied
Mathematics (DIEM), University of Salerno, Fisciano, Italy
{lfotia,pergen,asaggese,mvento}@unisa.it

Abstract. Highly crowd counting is a rapidly growing field, driven by
the increasing demand for accurate and real-time crowd monitoring.
Within this context, in this paper we formulate the problem in terms
of point detection and we propose a novel training strategy, especially
devised for point detection networks. The baseline architecture we use
is Point to Point Network (P2PNet), that have shown impressing accuracy results in both localization and crowd counting task. In order to
be able to deal with both sparse and very dense scenarios, and to well
generalize both indoor and outdoor, we propose a brain-inspired training strategy based on curriculum learning, combined with a customized
data augmentation technique. The main idea is that the neural network
has to mimic human learning by initially taking into account the easy
samples (sparse scenes) and then moving on to the more challenging
ones (the ones with thousands of persons). The experimentation has
shown impressive results. Indeed, with respect to the baseline solution,
we obtain an improvement of 59%, 62% and 48% over the three indices
we have considered, respectively MAE, MSE and nAP. An example of
the proposed system in action is shown at the following link: https://
youtu.be/yAHe7CI60hE.

Keywords: Highly crowd counting · Point detection · Curriculum
learning

1 Introduction

In recent years, video analytic has emerged as a powerful tool for crowd estimation, enabling real-time monitoring of large crowds starting from the analysis of
the videos acquired by surveillance cameras spread over the territory. However,
accurately estimating crowd density in highly crowded environments is still a
challenging task.

First attempts have been made by approaching the problem with deep
learning-based detection algorithms, especially devoted to detect the presence
of heads or individuals [13]. Anyway, the high level of occlusion (only a part
of the head is often visible), the complex and dynamic nature of crowds, and
the limited resolution of people images (typically only a few dozen pixels are

© The Author(s), under exclusive license to Springer Nature Switzerland AG 2023
N. Tsapatsoulis et al. (Eds.): CAIP 2023, LNCS 14185, pp. 13–22, 2023.
https://doi.org/10.1007/978-3-031-44240-7_2

available for each person) cause drop in performance in highly crowded environments. Furthermore, it is worth to mention that, given the low resolution of the persons, the ground truth available is typically just a point (instead than the bounding box of the head or of the individual), thus the bounding boxes need to be generated automatically by means of properly defined heuristics. As evident, even if having the advantage of providing in output a direct way for localizing the person, the automatic ground truth generation may cause confusion during the training [16].

In order to deal with the low resolution of persons to be counted, combined with the presence of dense scenes, in recent years there has been a growing interest in video analytic based crowd estimation techniques based on density map [2,8,10], that can accurately estimate crowd density in highly crowded environments by learning a relationship between the crowd density and the image's visual features. Basically, starting from the raw image, a new image representing the density map is computed by a properly designed CNN and the estimated count is performed by summing over the predicted density map [5]. Anyway, they share a similar problem with the objects detection method, in the sense that the ground truth density map is still something automatically generated.

In order to face with this issue, but still exploiting the advantage of object detection methods able to provide as output the exact position of the persons, point based detection methods have emerged. The idea is to use directly the point labels (without any intermediate representation) to supervise the network, and to generate directly points as output [16].

Despite these advances and the increasing number of proposed papers in the literature, there are still many open challenges [7]. These include the need for large amounts of annotated data for training, acquired not in a single environment but instead in all those real situations we expect the system may work. Furthermore, there is also a need for robust algorithms that can operate in real-time, in all those environments detailed before, and both in sparse and dense contexts. For this reason, we introduce a real-time system for counting and locating people in highly crowded situations: we exploit a point based framework, whose output is the position of each person, identified by a point. We decide to use as a reference network the Point to Point Network (P2PNet) [16], which has shown impressive results, ranking in the first positions in most of the benchmarks where the method have been tested. Starting from P2PNet, we did a preliminary analysis, which has shown a drop in the performance over sparse and night scenarios. For this reason, we introduce two new features with respect to the baseline P2PNet: (i) a data augmentation strategy based on the combination of a sliding window approach with standard pixel-wise data augmentation techniques; (ii) a bio-inspired training procedure based on curriculum learning. A crowd counting method based on curriculum learning training strategy can offer several key advantages over traditional training methods, including improved generalization capabilities, faster convergence, better handling of imbalanced data, and better handling of noise. These advantages can make curriculum learning a valuable approach for developing more robust and accurate crowd counting methods for use in real-world applications.

This paper is organized as follows. In Sect. 2 the contribution and the novelty of our approach respect to the state-of-the-art is discussed. Section 3 gives a brief overview of the considered dataset. The experimental setting and performance comparison are presented in Sect. 4, before drawing some conclusions in Sect. 5.

2   Proposed Approach

In this paper we design and develop a real-time system for counting and locating people in highly crowded situations, by automatically analyzing the frames acquired by video surveillance camera.

We decide to exploit a point based framework, whose output is the position of each person, identified by a point (instead than a bounding box). In particular, within this framework, one of the best networks available in the literature is Point to Point Network (P2PNet) [16], that we decide to use as a reference network. P2PNet employs VGG16 as a backbone and adds two separate heads, namely one for points regression and one for score classification, in a multitask framework. It can be thus used for both counting and localization.

It is important to highlight that, given this formulation of the problem, we do not need to generate the density maps to be provided as input to the network, but instead the points manually defined on the images by human annotators already represent the ground truth to be used for feeding the network at training stage. This is an important and not negligible feature, since we are avoiding any potential errors in the ground truth generation due to a wrong a posteriori generation of the density map.

Even if very promising, some preliminary analysis over P2PNet have shown a drop in the performance over sparse and night scenarios. Starting from the above considerations, we introduce in this paper two main novelties with respect to the baseline P2PNet: (i) a data augmentation strategy based on the combination of a sliding window approach with standard pixel wise data augmentation techniques; (ii) a bio-inspired training procedure based on curriculum learning.

In more details, we define a data augmentation strategy in order to create additional observations based on available ones and thus increase the size of the training set [9]. The following techniques have been employed: random scaling, with scale factor in the range [0.7, 1.3]; random cropping; rotation, with angles in the range [20°, 60°]; gaussian blur, with a probability of 0.5; changes of brightness and contrast; random flipping, with probability of 0.5. Furthermore, in order to simulate night conditions, given the few images in the dataset related to this kind of scenario, we also employ a data augmentation based on the conversion of RGB image into grayscale.

Other than such standard pixel-wise techniques, we also adopt a sliding window [14] based selection of the patch. The main idea behind this choice is that most of the sample images depict scattered scenes, and the use of random patches (as done in P2PNet) leads to an imbalance of the data samples provided as input to the network, since it is not possible to control the distribution of the people inside the patches. Starting from this consideration, for each image we define a set of patches, obtained by a sliding window, with a random overlap. Given such set, we select the most crowded and the less crowded patch, and also two additional randomly chosen patches. In this way, we can ensure to provide to the network both dense and sparse scenes.

Starting from the augmented dataset, we propose to also explore a brain inspired training strategy based on curriculum learning (CL) [1]. The rationale is that humans could learn better while the learning objects are not presented randomly but sorted by a meaningful order, namely from the most simple to the most complex one. Imitating this pattern, CL firstly gives every training sample an index on behalf of its difficulty, and then train models from simple samples to hard samples. The difficulty of a sample depends on the number of persons contained in it. The main advantages deriving from the adoption of the CL training strategy can be summarized as follows [1]: first, it improves the generalization capability of the network, since the model gradually builds up its abilities and generalize better to new, unseen data. Also, it has been demonstrated that starting with easier examples and gradually increasing the difficulty, CL can help the model to converge faster and with a lower risk of overfitting. This results in faster training times and improved performance on the final task. Finally, CL guarantees a better handling of imbalanced data: crowd counting datasets, given the nature of the problem, are highly imbalanced, with both sparse and dense frames, namely from empty (no persons at all) and very crowded (with a high density of people). Typically, the higher is the number of people, the less number of images we have in the training set. CL can also help to mitigate this imbalance, by gradually introducing examples with higher crowd densities, allowing the model to better learn the patterns associated with high-density crowds.

3   Dataset

In order to validate the proposed system, we use a wide dataset composed by 16,587 images, obtained by combining the datasets available in the literature with images acquired by our team and manually labeled. From the available datasets, we discarded those images acquired with a frontal view, only focusing over images obtainable by surveillance cameras. Table 1 summarizes the datasets that we used in our experimentation, showing the characteristics for each of them. As we can see from the table, for each dataset we specified the number of images that we have finally considered, their resolution, the average count (AC) of persons inside the image, the maximum count (MaxC) and the minimum count (MinC). For training our system, we have considered (where available) the original partition of each dataset into training and test set. At the end, the number of images used for training are 13,940 (about 84% of the dataset), and the remaining 2,647 have been instead used for testing. Figure 1 shows some examples of used images belonging to the previously described datasets.

Fig. 1. Examples of images from the dataset used in our experimentation. For each image, we also report the specific dataset to which the image belongs to.

The details for each considered dataset are reported in the following: **Mall** [3] has been collected from the surveillance video of a shopping mall. It contains several lighting conditions, occlusions, and severe perspective distortion. **ShangaiTech Part B** [20] has been collected from a busy street of a metropolitan area in Shanghai. It presents scale changes and perspective distortion. **Venice** [12] has been collected from St. Mark's Square in Venice; it considers different points of view. **UCF-QNRF** [6] has been collected from Flickr, Web Search and Hajj footage. It has a wider variety of scenes; it considers different points of view, densities and lighting variations. **SmartCity** [19] has been collected from sidewalk and office entrance. It contains images of indoor and outdoor scenes, aimed to verify the model generalization ability on sparse scenes. Indeed, the number of persons in the scene varies from 1 to 10. **JHU-Crowd** [15] has been collected in several scenarios, where there are resolution issues and lighting variations due to different environmental and weather conditions. **CrowdSurveillance** [18] has been collected from online images and real world surveillance videos, covering more challenging scenarios with complicated backgrounds and varying number of people (from 2 up to 1420). **NWPU-Crowd** [17] has been composed by the largest density range of annotated objects with different lighting conditions. **Beijing-BRT** [4] has been collected from a video surveillance camera at Beijing bus station. The images contained shadows, glare, and sunshine interference, and time span was from morning till night.

Furthermore, we also include 172 additional images (*Our dataset* in the table) of situations not included in the above mentioned datasets, mainly with low density in outdoor environments (for example, large squares and university classrooms) and poor night-time visibility indoors (for example, subways and fairs). All the images are annotated with a point (with x-y coordinates), which represents the position of the heads of the people inside the image.

Table 1. Datasets available in the literature used in our experimentation. For each dataset, we report the number of images used in our experimentation, the maximum image resolution, the average count (AC) of persons, the minimum (MinC) and the maximum count (MaxC), respectively.

Dataset	Years	Images	Resolution	AC	MinC	MaxC
Mall [3]	2012	2,000	480 × 640	31	13	53
ShangaiTech Part B [20]	2016	711	768 × 1024	123	9	578
Venice [12]	2019	49	720 × 1280	66	50	120
UCF-QNRF [6]	2018	136	2013 × 2902	815	49	12865
SmartCity [19]	2018	50	1080 × 1920	7	1	10
JHU-Crowd [15]	2019	306	910 × 1430	346	0	25791
CrowdSurveillance [18]	2019	11,346	840 × 1342	35	2	1420
NWPU-Crowd [17]	2020	703	2191 × 3209	418	0	20033
Beijing-BRT [4]	2019	1,114	640 × 360	13	2	50

4   Experimental Results

The performance have been evaluated in terms of mean absolute error (MAE), mean squared error (MSE), and normalized average precision (nPA). This is a quite common choice for evaluating crowd counting systems.

In more details, the MAE and MSE take only into account the number of persons located in each image, and can be computed as follows:

$$MAE = \frac{1}{N} \cdot \sum_{i=1}^{N} \left| C_i^{pred} - C_i^{gt} \right| \tag{1}$$

$$MSE = \sqrt{\frac{1}{N} \cdot \sum_{i=1}^{N} \left| C_i^{pred} - C_i^{gt} \right|^2} \tag{2}$$

where N is the test images number, C_i^{pred} and C_i^{gt} represent respectively the prediction results (in terms of number of counted people) and the ground-truth (in terms of number of people inside the image).

In order to evaluate both the localization errors and counting performance, we also use the normalized Average Precision (nAP) [16]. It is computed as the Average Precision, that is the area under the Precision-Recall (PR) curve.

Thus, in order to determine if the $j - th$ predicted point $\hat{p}_j$ is a True Positive (TP) or a False Positive (FP), we first sort the predicted points depending on their confidence score, from high to low. Then, instead than evaluating the distance between the predicted point $\hat{p}_j$ and the ground truth point p_i, we consider (as in [16]) the density aware criterion, defined as:

$$1(p_i, \hat{p}_j) = \begin{cases} 1 & if \quad d(p_i, \hat{p}_j)/d_{kNN}(p_i) < \delta \\ 0 & otherwise \end{cases}$$

where $d(\hat{p}_j, p_i) = ||\hat{p}_j - p_i||_2$ is the Euclidean distance between $\hat{p}_j$ and p_i, and $d_{kNN}(p_i)$ is the average distance to the k nearest neighbors of ground truth point p_i. The parameter δ is the threshold used to manage the desired localization accuracy. In our tests, we used $\delta = 50\%$, as suggested in [16]. Finally, a predicted point $\hat{p}_j$ is considered as TP only if it could be associated to certain ground truth p_i (implying that $1(p_i, \hat{p}_j) = 1$), under the assumption that p_i has not been already matched before by any higher-ranked point [11,16].

The proposed system has been implemented in PyTorch, starting from the original implementation of P2PNet, and the tests have been conducted over an NVIDIA V100 GPU. The obtained results are reported in Table 2. In more details, in order to compare with state of the art and also to show the improvements of the proposed training strategies with respect to the considered baseline, in the table we report MAE, MSE and nAP for the following experiments: *P2PNet Baseline* is the original P2PNet proposed by the authors and whose weights have been made available by the authors itself [16]; *Proposed DA* only includes data augmentation and sliding window approach; finally, *Proposed CL* adds curriculum learning training strategy to the previous *Proposed DA*. We can note that the best performance is obtained by the proposed model trained using the curriculum learning technique combined with the proposed data augmentation technique (namely *Proposed CL*), achieving the best score over the three metrics. Indeed, it obtains the lowest MAE (5.68 vs 14.00) and MSE (16.05 vs 26.11) and the highest nAP (0.74 vs 0.50), resulting in a final improvement of 59%, 62% and 48% on the MAE, MSE and nAP, respectively, with respect to the baseline.

It is important to note that this is an impressive result, considering that P2PNet is among the best performing networks available in the literature for high crowd counting and localization. In order to evaluate how the proposed system performs in different real scenarios of interest and potentially understand any drop in performance in some special conditions, we further partition the test set according to the following criteria: sparse and dense; indoor and outdoor; night and day scenes. The obtained results are reported in Table 3.

The first raw of the table reports the results on the entire dataset of the proposed system. After that, three main sections are identified in the table, namely Dense vs Sparse, Indoor vs Outdoor and Day vs Night.

Starting from the analysis on the Dense vs Sparse scenarios, we can see a drop for both MAE and MSE in the dense scenario with respect to the overall results (MAE: 25.21 vs 5.68; MSE: 40.74 vs 16.05); vice-versa, we can also note a strong improvement of the sparse scenario with respect to the baseline (MAE: 1.72 vs 5.68; MSE: 6.08 vs 16.05). Anyway, we need to consider that such values

Table 2. Performance in terms of MAE, MSE and nAP achieved on the test set by the baseline P2PNet, the proposed system with data augmentation (DA) and the full proposed system with both data augmentation and curriculum learning (CL) training strategies.

Model	MAE ↓	MSE ↓	nAP ↑
P2PNet [16]	14.00	26.11	0.50
Proposed DA	6.43	16.15	0.67
Proposed CL	**5.68**	**16.05**	**0.74**

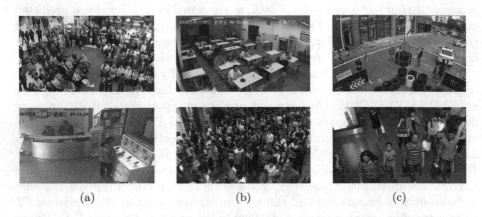

     (a)   (b)   (c)

Fig. 2. Example of images with overlay (red point) of output of the proposed system in (a) dense and sparse scenarios, (b) in indoor and outdoor scenarios, and (c) day and night scenarios. (Color figure online)

have to be considered not in absolute, but instead with respect to the average number of counted people (AC). Indeed, the AC in the dense scenes (AC = 210) is much larger than in the sparse scenes (AC = 14). Considering thus MAE and MSE with respect to AC, we can note that in both the typologies of scenario the error is about 10%. It is also important to highlight that the performance achieved on the above two scenarios by the baseline are the following: MAE: 36.21 vs 25.21; MSE: 52.10 vs 40.74 for the dense scenario and MAE: 10.20 vs 1.72; MSE: 18.73 vs 6.08 for the sparse scenario. The above reported results confirm the improvement of our method on the dense scenario, but above all on the sparse scenario, where the baseline solution shows some quite poor results. Indeed, we have to consider that the AC is 14 and that the output of that network doubles more or less such number.

    Looking at the results in Table 3, we can also note that the results are quite stable in outdoor and indoor scenario, where we have a MAE in the range 3.57–8.67 and a MSE in the range 10.76–18.35. This could be also related to the slight difference in the AC, which is 42 and 70 for indoor and outdoor scenarios, respectively. Finally, we also obtain some interesting results in Day vs Night scenario. Indeed, we can note that, having more or less the same AC (61 vs

Table 3. Performance in terms of MAE, MSE and nAP achieved on the test set by the full proposed system with both sliding window and curriculum learning (CL) training strategies and the partitions proposed system (i.e., sparse and dense scenes; indoor and outdoor; night and day) with the same training strategies. For each scenario, we report the AC, MinC and MaxC values.

Scenario	MAE ↓	MSE ↓	nAP ↑	AC	MinC	MaxC
Proposed CL	5.68	16.05	0.74	52	0	864
Dense	25.21	40.74	0.64	210	31	864
Sparse	1.72	6.08	0.74	14	0	90
Indoor	3.57	10.76	0.78	42	1	804
Outdoor	8.67	18.35	0.68	70	1	864
Day	5.54	9.14	0.69	61	3	289
Night	9.73	25.22	0.64	67	1	864

67), by night we can assist to a strong drop in the performance (MSE of 25.22 vs 16.05). Anyway, if we compare the obtained results with the one obtained in the same scenario by the baseline (MAE: 18.63; MSE: 41.93), we can say that we obtain a 65% improvement in terms of MSE and a 90% improvement in terms of MAE. The obtained results, as a whole but in particular over night and sparse scenarios, confirm that the proposed approach, including extended data augmentation and curriculum learning strategy, allows to strongly improve the baseline. Some examples of our system in action are shown in Fig. 2, where we can appreciate the high accuracy in both localization and counting.

An example of the proposed system in action is shown at the following link: https://youtu.be/yAHe7CI60hE.

5 Conclusion

In this paper, we propose a novel training strategy, especially devised for point detection networks. The baseline architecture we use in this paper is Point to Point Network (P2PNet), that have shown impressing accuracy results in both localization and crowd counting task. Starting from that, we propose a brain-inspired training strategy based on *curriculum learning*, that we combine with a customized data augmentation strategy. We evaluate the performance of our system using a dataset of highly crowded images, taken from various real-world environments, including night and day scenarios, indoor and outdoor locations, and finally sparse and very dense scenes. We obtain an impressive improvement of 59%, 62% and 48% over the three indices we have considered, namely MAE, MSE and nAP, with respect to the baseline solution. Also, we are able to strongly improve on the night and sparse scenarios, which have been demonstrated to be the ones where the baseline solution suffered the most.

References

1. Bengio, Y., Louradour, J., Collobert, R., Weston, J.: Curriculum learning. In: ICML (2009)
2. Chen, J., Wang, Z.: Multi-task semi-supervised crowd counting via global to local self-correction. Pattern Recognit. 109506 (2023)
3. Chen, K., Loy, C.C., Gong, S., Xiang, T.: Feature mining for localised crowd counting. In: BMVC, vol. 1, p. 3 (2012)
4. Ding, X., Lin, Z., He, F., Wang, Y., Huang, Y.: A deeply-recursive convolutional network for crowd counting. In: IEEE ICASSP (2018)
5. Gao, G., Gao, J., Liu, Q., Wang, Q., Wang, Y.: CNN-based density estimation and crowd counting: a survey. arXiv abs/2003.12783 (2020)
6. Idrees, H., et al.: Composition loss for counting, density map estimation and localization in dense crowds. In: ECCV, pp. 532–546 (2018)
7. Kim, T., Lee, J., Nam, J.: Comparison and analysis of SampleCNN architectures for audio classification. IEEE J. Sel. Top. Signal Process. **13**(2), 285–297 (2019)
8. Lempitsky, V., Zisserman, A.: Learning to count objects in images. In: Advances in Neural Information Processing Systems, vol. 23 (2010)
9. Lewy, D., Mańdziuk, J.: An overview of mixing augmentation methods and augmentation strategies. Artif. Intell. Rev. **56**(3), 2111–2169 (2023)
10. Li, H., Zhang, J., Kong, W., Shen, J., Shao, Y.: CSA-net: cross-modal scale-aware attention-aggregated network for RGB-T crowd counting. Expert Syst. Appl. **213**, 119038 (2023)
11. Lin, H., Ma, Z., Ji, R., Wang, Y., Hong, X.: Boosting crowd counting via multi-faceted attention. In: IEEE/CVF CVPR (2022)
12. Liu, W., Salzmann, M., Fua, P.: Context-aware crowd counting. In: IEEE/CVF CVPR (2019)
13. Liu, Y., Shi, M., Zhao, Q., Wang, X.: Point in, box out: beyond counting persons in crowds. In: Proceedings of the IEEE/CVF Conference on Computer Vision and Pattern Recognition, pp. 6469–6478 (2019)
14. da Silva, M.A.F., de Carvalho, R.L., da Silva Almeida, T.: Evaluation of a sliding window mechanism as DataAugmentation over emotion detection on speech. Acad. J. Comput. Eng. Appl. Math. **2**(1), 11–18 (2021)
15. Sindagi, V.A., Yasarla, R., Patel, V.M.: Pushing the frontiers of unconstrained crowd counting: new dataset and benchmark method. In: IEEE/CVF ICCV (2019)
16. Song, Q., et al.: Rethinking counting and localization in crowds: a purely point-based framework. In: IEEE/CVF ICCV (2021)
17. Wang, Q., Gao, J., Lin, W., Li, X.: NWPU-crowd: a large-scale benchmark for crowd counting and localization. IEEE TPAMI **43**(6), 2141–2149 (2020)
18. Yan, Z., et al.: Perspective-guided convolution networks for crowd counting. In: IEEE/CVF ICCV (2019)
19. Zhang, L., Shi, M., Chen, Q.: Crowd counting via scale-adaptive convolutional neural network. In: IEEE WACV (2018)
20. Zhang, Y., Zhou, D., Chen, S., Gao, S., Ma, Y.: Single-image crowd counting via multi-column convolutional neural network. In: IEEE CVPR (2016)

Race Bias Analysis of Bona Fide Errors in Face Anti-spoofing

Latifah Abduh(✉) and Ioannis Ivrissimtzis

Durham University, Durham DH1 3LE, UK
{latifah.a.abduh,ioannis.ivrissimtzis}@durham.ac.uk

Abstract. The study of bias in Machine Learning is receiving a lot of attention in recent years, however, few only papers deal explicitly with the problem of race bias in face anti-spoofing. In this paper, we present a systematic study of race bias in face anti-spoofing with three key features: we focus on the classifier's bona fide errors, where the most significant ethical and legal issues lie; we analyse both the scalar responses of the classifier and its final binary outcomes; the threshold determining the operating point of the classifier is treated as a variable. We apply the proposed bias analysis framework on a VQ-VAE-based face anti-spoofing algorithm. Our main conclusion is that race bias should not necessarily be attributed to different mean values of the response distributions over the various demographics. Instead, it can be better understood as the combined effect of several possible characteristics of these distributions: different means; different variances; bimodal behaviour; the existence of outliers.

Keywords: Face presentation attacks · face anti-spoofing · race bias

1 Introduction

Face recognition is the method of choice behind some of the most widely deployed biometric authentication systems, currently supporting a range of applications, from passport control at airports to mobile phone or laptop login. A key weakness of the technology, is its vulnerability to *presentation attacks*, where imposters attempt to gain wrongful access by presenting in front of the system's camera a photo, or a video, or by wearing a mask resembling a registered person. As a solution to this problem, algorithms for presentation attack detection (PAD) are developed, that is, binary classifiers trained to distinguish between the bona fide samples coming from live subjects, and those coming from imposters.

Here, we deal with the problem of race bias in face anti-spoofing algorithms. The proposed race bias analysis process has three key characteristics. First, the focus is on the bona fide error, that is, on genuine people wrongly classified as imposters. Biases in this type of error have significant ethical, legal and regulatory ramifications, and as it has recently pointed out "creates customer annoyance and inconvenience", [12]. Secondly, we do not analyse just the final binary

N. Tsapatsoulis et al. (Eds.): CAIP 2023, LNCS 14185, pp. 23–32, 2023.
https://doi.org/10.1007/978-3-031-44240-7_3

classification outcome, but also the scalar responses of the network prior to thresholding. Thirdly, we treat the value of the threshold, which determines the classifier's operating point on the ROC curve, as a variable. We do not assume it is fixed by the vendor of the biometric verification system in a black-box process.

We demonstrate the proposed bias analysis approach on a face anti-spoofing algorithm based on the Vector Quantized Variational Autoencoder (VQ-VAE) architecture, [20]. The network is trained and validated on the SiW database, and tested for bona fide racial bias on the SiW and RFW databases. Hypotheses are tested using the chi-squared test on the binary outcomes, the Mann-Whitney U test on the scalar responses, and the Hartigan's Dip for testing bimodality in the response distributions.

Our main finding is that racial bias can be attributed to several characteristics of the response distributions at the various demographics: different means; different variances; bimodality; outliers. As a secondary contribution, we also demonstrate that a database which does not specialise in face anti-spoofing, such as RFW, can nevertheless be used to analyse face anti-spoofing algorithms.

The rest of the paper is organised as follows. In Sect. 2, we review the relevant literature. In Sect. 3, we describe the experimental setup. In Sects. 4, and 5 we present the bias analysis on the SiW and RFW databases, respectively. We briefly conclude in Sect. 6.

2   Background

We briefly review the area of face anti-spoofing, and then focus on previous studies of bias in machine learning, and PAD in particular.

2.1   Face Anti-spoofing

The state-of-the-art in face anti-spoofing [5,14,25–28,30,31], is based on various forms of deep learning, such as Central Difference Convolutional Networks (CDCN) [27,28], or transformers [23]. Following some earlier approaches [4,15], the state-of-the-art may also utilise depth information [22,24,25,30], usually estimated by an independently trained neural network, while the use GAN estimated Near Infrared (NIR) information was proposed [14].

Regarding the face anti-spoofing databases we use in this paper, our training dataset is from the *SiW* database, introduced in [15]. It comprises videos of 165 subjects of four types of ethnicities: 35% of Asian and 35% Caucasian and 23% Indian, and 7% African American. The bias analysis is performed on SiW with the subject annotated for ethnicity type by us, and the already annotated RFW database [21], which is widely used in the bias analysis literature. RFW again comprises four types of ethnicities: Caucasian, Asian, Indian, and African.

2.2 Bias in Machine Learning

Because of the ethical, legal, and regulatory issues associated with the problem of bias within human populations, there is a considerable amount of research on the subject, especially in face recognition (FR). A recent comprehensive survey can be found in [17], where the significant sources of bias are categorised and discussed, and the negative effect of bias on downstream tasks is pointed out.

In one of the earliest studies of bias in FR, predating deep learning, [18] reported differences in the performance on humans of Caucasian and East Asian descent between Western and East Asia developed algorithms. In [9], several deep learning-based FR algorithms are analysed and a small amount of bias is detected in all of them.

In [10], the authors compute cluster validation measures on the clusters of the various demographics inside the whole population, aiming at measuring the algorithm's potential for bias, rather than actual bias. Their result is negative, and they argue for the need of more sophisticated clustering approaches. In [19], the aim is the detection of bias by analysing the activation ratios at the various layers of the network. Similarly to our work, their target application is the detection of race bias on a binary classification problem, gender classification in their case. Their result is positive in that they report a correlation between the measured activation ratios and bias in the final outcomes of the classifier. However, it is not clear if their method can be used to measure and assess the statistical significance of the expected bias.

In Cavazos et al. [6], similarly to our approach, most of the analysis assumes a one-sided error cost, in their case the false acceptance rate, and the operating thresholds are treated as user-defined variables. However, the analytical tools they used, mostly visual inspection of ROC curves, do not allow for a deep study of the distributions of the similarity scores, while, here, we give a more in-depth analysis of the response distributions, which is the equivalent of the similarity scores. In Pereira and Marcel [8], a fairness metric is proposed, which can be optimised over the decision thresholds, but again, there is no in-depth statistical analysis of the scores.

The literature on bias in presentation attacks is more sparse. Race bias was the key theme in the competition of face anti-spoofing algorithms on the CASIA-SURF CeFA database [13]. Bias was assessed by the performance of the algorithm under a cross-ethnicity validation scenario. Standard performance metrics, such as APCER, BPCER and ACER we reported. In [2], the standard CNN models Resnet 50 and VGG16, were compared for gender bias against the debiasing-VAE proposed in [3], and several performance metrics were reported. A recent white paper by the ID R&D company presents the results of a large-scale bias assessment experiment conducted by Bixelab, a NIST accredited independent laboratory [12]. Similarly to our approach, they focus on bona fide errors, and their aim is for the BPCER error metric to be below a prespecified threshold across all demographics. Regarding other biometric identification modalities, [7] studied gender bias in iris PAD algorithms.

3   Experimental Setup

We chose the VQ-VAE architecture because of some recently reported impressive results on various computer vision problems. For a more detailed description of the classifier, see our Arxiv preprint [1].

3.1   The VQ-VAE Classifier

The encoder consists of two convolutional layers of kernel size 4, stride step 2, padding 1; followed by a ReLU; one convolutional layer of kernel size 3, stride step 1, padding 1; followed by two residual blocks implemented as ReLU (3×3 conv, ReLU, 1×1 conv for each block). It outputs a 16×16 grid of vectors quantized on a codebook of size 512. The decoder is symmetrical to the encoder, using transposed convolutions. The model was ADAM optimised with learning rate 1e-3, for 100 epochs, with batch size 16. The weight factor β was set to 0.25.

For face detection we used the Multi-Task Cascade Convolutional Neural Network (MTCNN) [29]. The detected faces were horizontally aligned, and cropped at 64×64. As our classifier is based on anomaly detection, the training set consisted of bona fide only data, 124,000 samples. We assessed performance on a test set of 1,600 samples, 400 samples from each race, with equal split between bona fide and attack. At an operating threshold of 0.054, corresponding to the EER value at an independent validation set, we obtained an HTER of 0.169, which indicates satisfactory performance.

3.2   Overview of the Bias Analysis Process

The bias analysis process is summarised in Fig. 1. The binary outcomes of the classifiers are analysed with the chi-squared test, and the scalar responses with the Mann-Whitney U test [16].

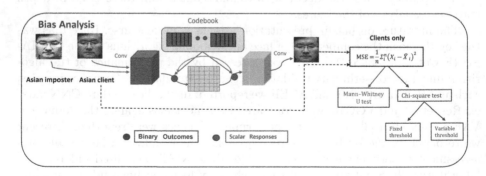

Fig. 1. The bias analysis process. The binary outcome analysis is shown in purple and the scalar response analysis in blue. (Color figure online)

4   Bias Analysis on SiW

We perform bias analysis on the bona fide samples of SiW test set in Sect. 3.

4.1   Statistical Analysis of the Binary Outcomes

First, we analyse the binary outcomes corresponding to the operating threshold 0.054, which was used in the validation of the classifier in Sect. 3. For each pair of races, we form the 2×2 contingency tables, and apply the chi-squared test, computing p-values for the hypothesis that samples from the race with the most misclassifications have higher misclassification probability. The results are summarised in Table 1. In several cases, the p-values are low, meaning that for any reasonable threshold of statistical significance, the bias hypothesis is accepted. In other cases, p-values above 0.05 mean that bias has not been detected.

Table 1. p-values of the chi-squared tests for the 0.054 threshold used in Sect. 3.

Af-As	Af-Ca	Af-In	As-Ca	As-In	Ca-In
0.1158	0.0104	0.0147	0.0000	0.0000	1.0000

Next, we treat the operating threshold as a variable. Figure 2 shows the p-values as a function of the threshold for the six pairs of races. We notice that, over the range of all thresholds, there could be several disconnected intervals corresponding to high bias (low p-values), which means that threshold optimisation for low bias should not assume a unique solution, as it is often implicitly assumed in the literature.

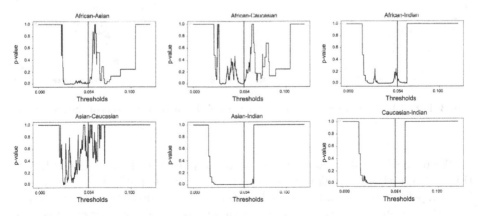

Fig. 2. For each pair of races, graphs of the p-value as a function of the threshold.

4.2   Statistical Analysis of the Scalar Responses

For an insight in the behaviour of the graphs in Fig. 2, we analyse the classifier's scalar responses on the premise that a complex behaviour of their density fun ctions, will induce complex bias behaviour. Table 2 summarises the statistics computed on the responses of each race: mean, standard deviation, and Hartigan's Dip value [11]. Figure 3 shows plots of histograms and density functions for each pair of races.

Table 2. Response means, st. dev., and Hartigan's dip values for each race in SiW.

	Af	As	Ca	In
μ	0.0418	0.0446	0.0438	0.0355
s.d.	0.0142	0.0109	0.0122	0.0096
dip	0.0299	0.0233	0.0366	0.0324

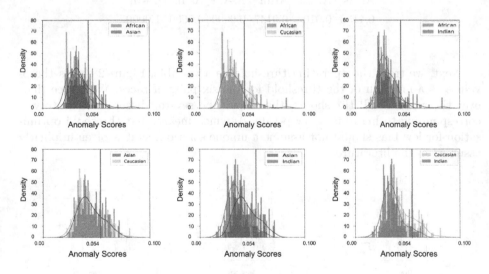

Fig. 3. For each pair of races in SiW, histograms and density functions of the responses.

We tested for statistically different mean responses with the Mann-Whitney U test, as the Shapiro-Wilk test rejected the normality hypothesis. Table 3 shows for each pair of races p-values for the hypothesis that randomly selected responses from the two populations have different values. We note that, for example, the p-value of the Asian and Indian pair is very low, and the large range of high bias thresholds in the corresponding U-shaped diagram in Fig. 2 is due to a statistically significant higher mean response on Asians compared to Indians.

Table 3. p-values of the Mann-Whitney U test on each pair of races.

Af-As	Af-Ca	Af-In	As-Ca	As-In	Ca-In
0.0001	0.0078	0.0000	0.1560	0.0000	0.0000

In contrast, the mean response difference between Asians and Caucasians is not statistically significant. Thus, the bias we can observe in the corresponding diagram in Fig. 2, which for small threshold values on the left-hand side of the diagram is statistically significant, is due to different standard deviations.

We checked for bimodality using Hartigan's Dip Test with 50 bins. For the 200 samples we have from a race, a statistical significance of 95% corresponds to a critical value of 0.037. We notice that all Dip values are below the significance threshold, and thus, all populations should be considered unimodal. In particular, that means that some very high responses on African people should be treated as outliers. We note that against all the other three races, these outliers create a second, or third region of high bias thresholds, in which regions samples from the African population are treated less favourably.

5 Bias Analysis on RFW

Here, we apply the same analysis on a test set from the RFW database, consisting of 200 images from each race. This time the race labels are part of the database, rather than being annotated by us. As RFW database is not a specialised face anti-spoofing database, we do not have imposter images and thus we do not have empirically established operating thresholds, as for example the ones corresponding to EER values. Instead, in our diagrams we indicate thresholds corresponding to bona fide error rates of: 1%, 2%, 5%, 10%, 20%.

In Fig. 4, for each race pair, we plot the p-values of the chi-squared test as a function of the threshold. We observe behaviours similar to those in Sect. 4.

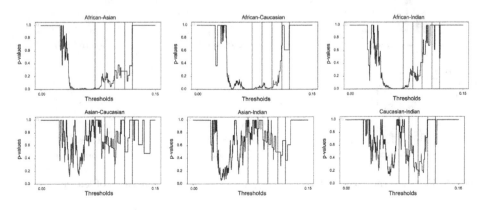

Fig. 4. For each pair of races, graphs of the p-value as a function of the threshold.

Table 4 shows the means, standard deviations and dip values for each race, and Table 5 shows the p-values of the Mann-Whitney U test for each race pair. We note in Table 4 that the Hartigan's test detects a bimodality in the responses on Indian people, having a dip value of 0.055, above the significance threshold of 0.037. This can also be verified by visual inspection of the corresponding histograms and density functions, shown in Figs. 5 for race pairs. We also note that this bimodality can be detected in the behaviour of the corresponding graphs of the p-values of the chi-squared test. Indeed, in the three graphs in Fig. 4 corresponding to Indian people, we can detect two distinct regions of higher bias, even though the second one does not reach the level of statistical significance.

Table 4. Response means, st. dev., and Hartigan's dip values for each race in SiW.

	Af	As	Ca	In
μ	0.0509	0.0579	0.0569	0.0579
s.d.	0.0175	0.0220	0.0223	0.0220
dip	0.0114	0.0225	0.0149	0.0550

Table 5. p-values of the Mann-Whitney U test on each pair of races.

Af-As	Af-Ca	Af-In	As-Ca	As-In	Ca-In
0.0004	0.0058	0.0062	0.2509	0.2743	0.4805

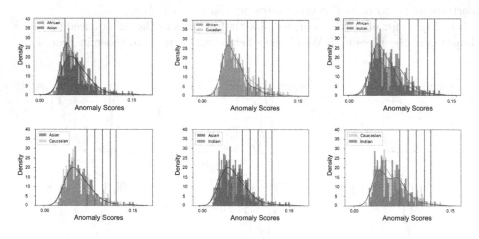

Fig. 5. For each race pair in RFW, histograms and density functions of the responses.

6   Conclusion

We conducted an empirical study of race bias in face anti-spoofing with the following characteristics: we analysed the bona fide error; the classifier's binary outcomes and scalar responses were both analysed for bias; the threshold determining the classifier's operating point was considered a variable.

Our main finding is that the behaviour of race bias depends on several characteristics of the response distributions: different means or different variances between two demographics; bimodality or existence of outliers in a certain demographic. The implication is that race bias is cannot always be attributed to different mean responses, a misconception sometimes reinforced by the fact that in statistics, colloquially, the term bias is often used to describe the component of the error corresponding to the difference in means. As a practical implication of our findings, we note that methods for automatically choosing low bias thresholds should not assume a unique solution to the problem.

In our future work, we would like to conduct a theoretical study of bias, assuming, for example, that the responses follow log-normal distributions.

References

1. Abduh, L., Ivrissimtzis, I.: Race bias analysis of bona fide errors in face anti-spoofing. arXiv:2210.05366 (2022)
2. Alshareef, N., Yuan, X., Roy, K., Atay, M.: A study of gender bias in face presentation attack and its mitigation. Future Internet **13**(9), 234 (2021)
3. Amini, A., Soleimany, A.P., Schwarting, W., Bhatia, S.N., Rus, D.: Uncovering and mitigating algorithmic bias through learned latent structure. In: Proceedings of the 2019 AAAI/ACM Conference on AI, Ethics, and Society, pp. 289–295 (2019)
4. Atoum, Y., Liu, Y., Jourabloo, A., Liu, X.: Face anti-spoofing using patch and depth-based CNNs. In: Proceedings of IJCB, pp. 319–328. IEEE (2017)
5. Cai, R., Li, H., Wang, S., Chen, C., Kot, A.C.: DRL-FAS: a novel framework based on deep reinforcement learning for face anti-spoofing. IEEE TIFS **16**, 937–951 (2020)
6. Cavazos, J.G., Phillips, P.J., Castillo, C.D., O'Toole, A.J.: Accuracy comparison across face recognition algorithms: where are we on measuring race bias? IEEE TBBIS **3**(1), 101–111 (2020)
7. Fang, M., Damer, N., Kirchbuchner, F., Kuijper, A.: Demographic bias in presentation attack detection of iris recognition systems. In: Proceedings of EUSIPCO, pp. 835–839. IEEE (2021)
8. de Freitas Pereira, T., Marcel, S.: Fairness in biometrics: a figure of merit to assess biometric verification systems. IEEE TBBIS **4**(1), 19–29 (2021)
9. Garcia, R.V., Wandzik, L., Grabner, L., Krueger, J.: The harms of demographic bias in deep face recognition research. In: Proceedings of ICB, pp. 1–6. IEEE (2019)
10. Glüge, S., Amirian, M., Flumini, D., Stadelmann, T.: How (not) to measure bias in face recognition networks. In: Schilling, F.-P., Stadelmann, T. (eds.) ANNPR 2020. LNCS (LNAI), vol. 12294, pp. 125–137. Springer, Cham (2020). https://doi.org/10.1007/978-3-030-58309-5_10
11. Hartigan, J.A., Hartigan, P.M.: The dip test of unimodality. Ann. Stat. 70–84 (1985)

12. ID R&D whitepaper: Mitigating Demographic Bias in Facial Presentation Attack Detection (2022). https://idrnd.ai/mitigating-bias-in-biometric-facial-liveness-detection

13. Liu, A., et al.: Cross-ethnicity face anti-spoofing recognition challenge: a review (2020)

14. Liu, A., et al.: Face anti-spoofing via adversarial cross-modality translation. IEEE TIFS **16**, 2759–2772 (2021)

15. Liu, Y., Jourabloo, A., Liu, X.: Learning deep models for face anti-spoofing: binary or auxiliary supervision. In: Proceedings of CVPR (2018)

16. Mann, H.B., Whitney, D.R.: On a test of whether one of two random variables is stochastically larger than the other. Ann. Math. Stat. **18**(1), 50–60 (1947)

17. Mehrabi, N., Morstatter, F., Saxena, N., Lerman, K., Galstyan, A.: A survey on bias and fairness in machine learning. ACM Comput. Surv. **54**(6), 1–35 (2021)

18. Phillips, P.J., Jiang, F., Narvekar, A., Ayyad, J., O'Toole, A.J.: An other-race effect for face recognition algorithms. ACM Trans. Appl. Percept. **8**(2), 1–11 (2011)

19. Serna, I., Peña, A., Morales, A., Fierrez, J.: Insidebias: measuring bias in deep networks and application to face gender biometrics. In: Proceedings of ICPR, pp. 3720–3727. IEEE (2021)

20. Van Den Oord, A., Vinyals, O., Kavukcuoglu, K.: Neural discrete representation learning. In: Advances in Neural Information Processing Systems, vol. 30 (2017)

21. Wang, M., Deng, W., Hu, J., Tao, X., Huang, Y.: Racial faces in the wild: reducing racial bias by information maximization adaptation network. In: Proceedings of ICCV, pp. 692–702. IEEE (2019)

22. Wang, Z., et al.: Deep spatial gradient and temporal depth learning for face anti-spoofing. In: Proceedings of CVPR, pp. 5042–5051 (2020)

23. Wang, Z., Wang, Q., Deng, W., Guo, G.: Face anti-spoofing using transformers with relation-aware mechanism. IEEE TBBIS **4**(3), 439–450 (2022)

24. Wu, H., Zeng, D., Hu, Y., Shi, H., Mei, T.: Dual spoof disentanglement generation for face anti-spoofing with depth uncertainty learning. IEEE TCSVT **32**(7), 4626–4638 (2022)

25. Yu, Z., Li, X., Shi, J., Xia, Z., Zhao, G.: Revisiting pixel-wise supervision for face anti-spoofing. IEEE TBBIS **3**(3), 285–295 (2021)

26. Yu, Z., et al.: Auto-FAS: searching lightweight networks for face anti-spoofing. In: Proceedings of ICASSP, pp. 996–1000. IEEE (2020)

27. Yu, Z., Wan, J., Qin, Y., Li, X., Li, S.Z., Zhao, G.: NAS-FAS: static-dynamic central difference network search for face anti-spoofing. IEEE TPAMI **43**(9), 3005–3023 (2020)

28. Yu, Z., et al.: Searching central difference convolutional networks for face anti-spoofing. In: Proceedings of CVPR (2020)

29. Zhang, K., Zhang, Z., Li, Z., Qiao, Y.: Joint face detection and alignment using multitask cascaded convolutional networks. IEEE Signal Process. Lett. **23**(10), 1499–1503 (2016)

30. Zhang, K.-Y., et al.: Face anti-spoofing via disentangled representation learning. In: Vedaldi, A., Bischof, H., Brox, T., Frahm, J.-M. (eds.) ECCV 2020. LNCS, vol. 12364, pp. 641–657. Springer, Cham (2020). https://doi.org/10.1007/978-3-030-58529-7_38

31. Zhang, Y., et al.: CelebA-spoof: large-scale face anti-spoofing dataset with rich annotations. In: Vedaldi, A., Bischof, H., Brox, T., Frahm, J.-M. (eds.) ECCV 2020. LNCS, vol. 12357, pp. 70–85. Springer, Cham (2020). https://doi.org/10.1007/978-3-030-58610-2_5

Fall Detection with Event-Based Data: A Case Study

Xueyi Wang[1]([✉]) [iD], Nicoletta Risi[1] [iD], Estefanía Talavera[2] [iD],
Elisabetta Chicca[1] [iD], Dimka Karastoyanova[1] [iD], and George Azzopardi[1] [iD]

[1] University of Groningen, Nijenborgh, 9742 AG Groningen, The Netherlands
{xueyi.wang,n.risi,e.chicca,d.karastoyanova,g.azzopardi}@rug.nl
[2] University of Twente, Drienerlolaan, 7522 NB Enschede, The Netherlands
e.talaveramartinez@utwente.nl

Abstract. Fall detection systems are relevant in our aging society aiming to support efforts towards reducing the impact of accidental falls. However, current solutions lack the ability to combine low-power consumption, privacy protection, low latency response, and low payload. In this work, we address this gap through a comparative analysis of the trade-off between effectiveness and energy consumption by comparing a Recurrent Spiking Neural Network (RSNN) with a Long Short-Term Memory (LSTM) and a Convolutional Neural Network (CNN). By leveraging two pre-existing RGB datasets and an event-camera simulator, we generated event data by converting intensity frames into event streams. Thus, we could harness the salient features of event-based data and analyze their benefits when combined with RSNNs and LSTMs. The compared approaches are evaluated on two data sets collected from a single subject; one from a camera attached to the neck (N-data) and the other one attached to the waist (W-data). Each data set contains 460 video samples, of which 213 are four types of fall examples, and the rest are nine types of non-fall daily activities. Compared to the CNN, which operates on the high-resolution RGB frames, the RSNN requires 200× less trainable parameters. However, the CNN outperforms the RSNN by 23.7 and 17.1% points for W- and N-data, respectively. Compared to the LSTM, which operates on event-based input, the RSNN requires 5× less trainable parameters and 2000× less MAC operations while exhibiting a 1.9 and 8.7% points decrease in accuracy for W- and N-data, respectively. Overall, our results show that the event-based data preserves enough information to detect falls. Our work paves the way to the realization of high-energy efficient fall detection systems.

Keywords: Fall detection · Wearable cameras · Event-based · Deep learning · RSNN · CNN · LSTM

1   Introduction

Elderly individuals often experience reduced control over their bodies, weaker bones, and longer recovery times in case of injuries, which increase the risk, severity, and impact of falls [1]. The act of falling poses a significant threat to the elderly population as it is considered a factor leading to a decrease in autonomy, fatalities, and harm [2]. These incidents can result in high healthcare costs and other related expenses, which can place a strain on both individuals and healthcare systems [3]. There is, therefore, a growing interest in the development of more effective, low-power, and privacy-friendly fall detection systems [4].

The aforementioned factors serve as our motivation to develop a fall detection system that can be embedded in Internet of Things (IoT) or edge computing with low energy consumption, privacy protection, and low-latency computation using minimal computational resources. In pursuit of this objective, the current study introduces a proof-of-concept to detect falls on the edge with IoT devices. This is achieved by interfacing the output of event cameras – generated via the conversion of an existing dataset with RGB video clips – with a Spiking Neural Network (SNN), which requires relatively few parameters and multiply-accumulate (MAC) operations.

Unlike traditional frame-based cameras, event-based cameras have independent pixels which respond only to changes in brightness over time [5]. The pixels operate asynchronously and report local brightness changes at the time of their occurrence. This approach has significant advantages, namely low energy consumption, high temporal resolution, low-latency event streams, and high dynamic range.

This work has two main contributions. Firstly, we provide a comparative analysis between a standard CNN operating on RGB frames along with a RSNN and a LSTM model trained on simulated event-based data. Secondly, we investigate the balance between performance and efficiency in relation to model complexity and energy consumption.

2   Related Works

In the context of fall detection, the types of sensors that have been investigated can be broadly classified into four distinct types: wearable, fixed visual, ambient sensors, and sensor fusion [6]. Wearable sensors are popular options due to their portability and ability to collect data without location limitations. Moreover, they can leverage the physiological variations of the human body. Fixed visual sensors are particularly useful as they consist of simplified hardware with good image quality and notable reliability. Different types of fixed visual sensors, including RGB cameras and RGB-D depth cameras, have been investigated in this regard [7]. The integration of wearable sensors and visual sensors has led to the emergence of wearable cameras as a promising alternative for fall detection. The fusion of various sensors can enhance the resilience of fall detection systems [6].

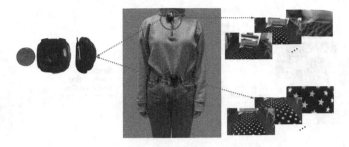

Fig. 1. Mounting of two cameras to the neck and waist of the participant. Left: front and profile photos of the camera compared to the size of a coin. Right: frame sequences collected by the wearable cameras from the two perspectives.

Over the past decade, event-based cameras have gained increasing popularity due to the advantages mentioned above. Also, event-based sensing has been employed to investigate action recognition on third-person view datasets, reflecting the increasing interest in this sensing paradigm [8]. In a recent study [9], the authors compared the performance of a CNN combined with a LSTM architecture on conventional gray-level frames with corresponding simulated event-based data with respect to human action recognition. Their results show the plausibility of using simulated event-based data to classify four different activities.

However, none of the studies mentioned above provide a fall detection solution, which is portable, low-power, and low-latency. We address these scientific challenges by investigating an event-based approach. By removing the need for cloud computing, our event-based method can provide enhanced privacy, speed, and security by processing data directly on the edge.

3   Methods

3.1   The Data Set

We introduce two new public datasets of 469 RGB video samples each, i.e., more than previous datasets [10,11], and the corresponding simulated event-based data. Two small and light-weight wearable cameras of the same type, (measuring $420 \times 420 \times 200$ mm and 25 g), were used for data collection, one attached to the neck and the other to the waist, Fig. 1. The two cameras were used to capture the events at the same time. In this respect, our dataset consists of two subsets of 469 samples each. For simplicity, the two categories will be referred to as *W-data* and *N-data*. Video recordings include 13 daily activities categorized into four types of *falls* (front falls, back falls, downside falls, and lateral falls), and nine *non-fall events* (lying, rising, sitting down, bending, stumbling, walking, standing, squatting, and sitting static). The samples were collected indoors and outdoors over two days, resulting in 213 falls and 256 non-falls per camera. The data was collected with a resolution of 1080p and a frame rate of 30 fps. Hereafter, our comparative analysis focuses on the binary classification task, i.e., on discriminating samples between *falls* and *non-falls*.

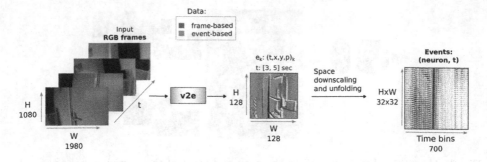

Fig. 2. Pipeline workflow with an example of a fall event. From RGB frames (1980 × 1080 pixels) to streams of events $e_k = (t, x, y, p)_k$, depicted as time surfaces, via the event-camera simulator *v2e*. The final binary representation is achieved via space downscaling and unfolding, with non-zero values (dark) of downscaled pixels (32 × 32) representing the occurrence of at least one event in the corresponding time bin.

Data Splitting: We use the same data split across the three models under investigation, CNN, LSTM, RSNN: 15% of the data is randomly selected as the test set, and the remaining data is used to generate 10 randomly selected train/validation splits with a ratio of 85:15.

From Videos to Events (*v2e*): The *v2e* simulator [12] was used to generate simulated event-based data for our experiments[1]. The tool *v2e* can produce highly realistic synthetic events from normal RGB frames. As event-camera model, we chose the Dynamic Vision Sensor (DVS)[2], with a resolution of 128 × 128 pixels. Figure 2 shows examples of original RGB frames and the corresponding event-based data for one sample of our dataset. The event data format consists of the 4-tuple $e_k = (t, x, y, p)_k$, where t_k, (x_k, y_k) and p_k refer to the time step, spatial coordinates, and polarity, respectively. An example of this data format is depicted in Fig. 2 as a time surface [5], with darker pixels indicating more recent time. Both frame- and event-based data formats are considered in our study, and processed with two pipelines; one processing the event time series (Sect. 3.2 A), and the other processing the RGB frame-based data (Sect. 3.2 B).

Event-Based Data Pre-processing: Before processing the event streams, the pixel array's spatial resolution was downscaled to 32 × 32 pixels to reduce the number of network parameters and computational resources needed for training the RSNN and LSTM. Despite the event-camera output's asynchronous nature, the models' simulation on a CPU requires defining a time binning step for the

---

[1] As a proof-of-concept study, we chose the conversion parameters for the event-camera model with no background noise, i.e., thresh = 0.2, sigma = 0.02, cutoff_hz = 0, leak_rate_hz = 0, shot_noise_rate_hz = 0.

[2] This choice was driven by ongoing research, which aims to compare current results with event-camera recordings using an embedded DVS (eDVS) [13].

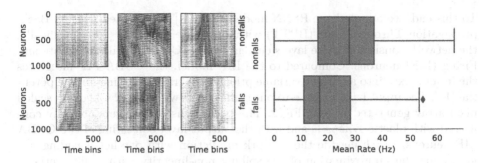

Fig. 3. (Left) Event-based data for 3 *non-fall* and 3 *fall* samples. (Right) Per-class distribution of pixels' mean firing rates across all samples in the dataset.

input event stream, which was set to $dt = 10$ms. To accommodate different video clip lengths, we extracted for each sample the time of maximum instantaneous firing rate T^*. Then, we cropped each video clip to a time window $\Delta_T = 7$sec, which was centered around the time point t^* drawn from a uniform distribution $p(t) = 1/(2\Delta)$, with $t \in [T^* - \Delta, T^* + \Delta]$ and $\Delta = 500$ms. The polarity information was discarded, and the spatial information was collapsed to a single dimension, where x and y event coordinates are mapped to a single index. This dimension corresponds to the number of input neurons $n_{\text{neurons},1}$ of the RSNN (and input nodes of the LSTM). The resulting event-based representation has dimensions: $n_{\text{neurons},1} \times (10^3 \Delta_T)/dt$, Fig. 2. Figure 3 displays three randomly selected samples for each of the two classes, *fall* and *non-fall*.

To assess whether the simulated event-based data preserves the relevant information for the problem at hand, we first quantified the performance of a standard classifier, namely a linear Support-Vector Machine (SVM), operating on "time-collapsed data", i.e., when the temporal information of the input time series is removed. In this representation, each video sample is represented by a 1-dimensional vector, where each element is the sum of all events at the corresponding location. Results are illustrated and discussed in Sect. 4.

3.2 Fall Detection Approach

A) Classifiers for the Event-Based Data. This section describes the RSNN and the LSTM models used to classify the event time series.

Events + RSNN: As the natural interface of event-based sensing is event-based processing, we assessed the performance of an RSNN for fall detection.

To this end, we adapted the RSNN model from [14] and trained it using Back-propagation Through Time (BPTT) with surrogate gradients [15]. Specifically, the network consists of three layers current-based (CUBA) Leaky Integrate and Firing (LIF) neurons. Compared to the LIF model, the CUBA LIF integrates the input spikes into a current variable prior to generating the membrane potential [16]. The input layer has one-to-one connections with the 32×32 down-scaled pixel array generated by $v2e$, Fig. 2. The two downstream layers are fully connected with plastic synapses, and with the output layer consisting of two CUBA LIF neurons, which encode the network prediction with one-hot encoding. By leveraging the approximation of the spiking non-linearity with a differentiable function, surrogate gradients were computed using PyTorch's differentiation. The network was trained by minimizing the Negative Log-Likelihood Loss (L_{nll}). For each input μ, the network predicted probability p_i of class i was computed as the softmax of the maximum membrane potential of the readout units, $U_i[t]$ for $i \in [0, 1]$, measured across the time window Δ_T. When averaged over an input batch of size N, with $M = 2$ output classes (*fall* or *nonfall*), the L_{nll} results in:

$$L_{nll} = \frac{1}{N} \sum_{\mu}^{N} \left[-\sum_{i}^{M} y_i log(p_i) \right]_{\mu},$$ (1)

where y_i is the true probability. To constrain the membrane potential fluctuations around $U_i = 0$, a regularizing term L_{reg} was formulated as follows:

$$L_{reg} = -\frac{1}{N} \sum_{\mu}^{N} \Big(\log\big(1 + \exp(U_\mu)\big) + \log\big(1 + \exp(-U_\mu)\big) \Big).$$ (2)

The total training loss is defined as $L_{tot} = L_{nll} + \alpha L_{reg}$, where $\alpha = 0.5$ was used for the surrogate gradient descent.

The RSNN hyperparameters were determined by means of a Hyper-Parameters Optimization (HPO) procedure implemented using the Neural Network Intelligence (NNI) toolkit [17]. A total of $N = 250$ experiments were performed over the ten train/validation splits to find the optimal subset of network hyperparameters with the Anneal tuner algorithm.

Events + LSTM: An LSTM network was used to process the temporal data. Specifically, we implemented a three-layer LSTM model following the RSNN structure, with the first layer comprising LSTM nodes with an input shape of (1024, 700), Fig. 2, followed by two fully connected layers. The number of hidden nodes was set equal to the number of neurons in the RSNN hidden layer.

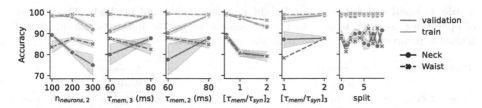

Fig. 4. Hyper-parameters Optimization. RSNN classification accuracy as a function of the model hyperparameters.

B) Classifiers for the Frame-Based Data

CNN + LSTM: We extracted 20 evenly-sampled frames from each clip within the time window $[T^* - \Delta_T/2, T^* + \Delta_T/2]$ chosen for the event-based models. This data was then fed to the pipeline comprising a ResNet50 CNN, followed by a downstream LSTM classification head.

4 Experimental Results

Baseline Classifier. We first evaluated the frame-to-event data conversion by feeding the "time-collapsed" event-based data to a linear SVM. The validation accuracy, measured over the 10 validation sets, is $81 \pm 4\%$ for the N-data and $85 \pm 5\%$ for the W-data. Given the time-based nature of the event-based data, which is inherently removed in the "time-collapsed" representation, we anticipate that our results are highly dependent on the choice of the specific time window $[T^* - \Delta, T^* + \Delta]$ used to crop the initial video. However, this preliminary analysis served only to confirm that the information content needed to address the fall-detection problem was still preserved after the frame-to-event conversion.

Hyper-Parameter Optimization. Figure 4 shows the results of the HPO experiments for the RSNN, with the classification accuracy reported as a function of the optimized hyperparameters, i.e., the membrane time constant of the hidden and output layers ($\tau_{mem,2}$, $\tau_{mem,3}$, respectively), the ratio between membrane time constant and synaptic time constant for hidden and output layers ($[\tau_{mem}/\tau_{syn}]_2$, $[\tau_{mem}/\tau_{syn}]_3$, respectively) and the number of neurons in the hidden layer ($n_{neurons,2}$). Each data point is the result of one experiment running on one randomly selected train/validation split. Note that for both W- and N-data, the architectures converge to a time constant ratio $[\tau_{mem}/\tau_{syn}]_2 = 0.5$ and $[\tau_{mem}/\tau_{syn}]_2 = 2$, respectively.

Comparative Analysis. The results of our comparative analysis are shown in Table 1, which reports all the figures of merit taken into account.

Performance: The performance analysis on the classification accuracy shows that the CNN operating on the high-resolution RGB frames reaches the best accuracy

Table 1. Results of fall detection by different data types and methods. The number of operations are with respect to the inference stage, #Par indicates the number of trainable parameters, and N_t refers to the number of time steps.

Data	Methods	Operations		# Par*	Accuracy[†]	
		MACs (N_t)	ACs (N_t)		Waist	Neck
events	LSTM	$5.7 \times 10^6 N_t$	0	0.5×10^6	0.779(±0.02)	0.897(±0.02)
events	RSNN	$2.3 \times 10^3 N_t$	$4 \times 10^5 N_t$	0.1×10^6	0.760(±0.04)	0.810(±0.03)
frames	CNN+LSTM	$8.3 \times 10^{10} + 1.6 \times 10^5 N_t{}^\diamond$	0	2.5×10^7	0.997(±0.01)	0.981(±0.01)

* With $n_{neurons,2} = 100$ for LSTM and RSNN.

◊ MACs of the pretrained Resnet50 are accounted once as the model operates on all input frames at once.

† Reported with the set of hyper-parameters obtained with HPO.

score, with 99.7% accuracy for W-data and 98.1% for N-data, and outperforms both event-based methods. This, however, comes at the cost of a larger number of trainable parameters (i.e., 2 orders of magnitude larger). By contrast, the performance gap of the RSNN model, when compared to the LSTM operating on the same input resolution, is significantly lower (2% points for W-data and 9% points for N-data).

Computational Cost: We measured the number of trainable parameters, and the number of computations required per time step in terms of accumulation (AC) and MAC operations. Given the binary nature of spiking inputs, spikes transmission in a RSNN can be approximated as ACs operations, which are less power consuming than MACs [18]. The computation of MACs and ACs for RSNN and LSTM is based on the theoretical analysis presented in [19], while the operations count for Resnet50 is calculated using THOP, a tool for operation counting, validated by previous studies [20]. Compared to the LSTM, which operates on the same type of event-based input, the RSNN requires 2000× less MACs in the inference stage.

5   Discussion and Conclusion

We propose a novel high-energy efficient methodology for fall detection. We performed a comparative analysis of this event-based approach coupled with two types of classifiers, namely RSNN and LSTM, versus a traditional CNN approach that operates on full-resolution RGB frames.

Prior to the comparative analysis, we used a linear classifier to assess whether the information content needed to detect falls is still preserved after the video-to-event conversion. In spite of the "time-collapsed" representation, the linear classifier achieved high (validation) accuracy when trained on the event count collected over the time window Δ_T. While this served as a benchmark performance for using the event-based data to detect falls, we conjecture that the performance of such a linear classifier is highly dependent on the specific choice for the time window Δ_T. Moreover, such an approach would not be ideal for learning spatio-temporal patterns, such as in fall detection, as it operates on data gathered over time windows and not on real-time streams of incoming data [14]. This is in contrast to time-based models, such as RSNNs and LSTMs, which offer promising candidate solutions to move towards online fall detection systems.

Hence, we evaluated the effectiveness of combining the event-based data stream with time-based approaches. Compared to the CNN, both event-based pipelines exhibit a drop in effectiveness. However, it is noteworthy that the CNN operates on input RGB frames of size 224×224 pixels as opposed to the 128×128 spatial resolution of the event-based pipeline, which was further downscaled to 32×32 pixels. As a result, the CNN approach comes at the cost of $200\times$ more trainable parameters than the shallow RSNN and far more MACs per step. In comparison to the LSTM approach, the number of MACs per step of the RSNN is three orders of magnitude lower based on a comparable shallow topology. This is however at the cost of a drop in accuracy. In future work, we will do a systematic analysis on the trade-off with respect to input size vs. accuracy vs. computational complexity.

In general, our research shows potential for energy-efficient pipelines for fall detection by using spike-based algorithms. Yet, based on the current experiments, in comparison to standard deep learning methods, the presented solution comes at the cost of decreased accuracy. To address this gap, in future work, we will investigate the incorporation of multiple recurrent hidden layers, explore different learning mechanisms for spike-based algorithms, and utilize Winner-Takes-All layers for real-time network predictions. To fully leverage the computational efficiency of RSNNs, future studies may focus on deploying them on specialized neuromorphic hardware that takes advantage of their event-based nature. Additionally, before deploying on an embedded system, we aim to compare our simulated event-based data with a new dataset collected using an eDVS.

We anticipate that the envisioned end-to-end event-based pipeline for fall detection can deliver novel embedded solutions for fall detection, with promising performance vs. energy efficiency trade-offs and enhanced privacy and security by processing data directly on the edge.

References

1. Elliott, S., Painter, J., Hudson, S.: Living alone and fall risk factors in community-dwelling middle age and older adults. J. Commun. Health **34**, 301–310 (2009)
2. Nooruddin, S., Islam, M.M., Sharna, F.A., Alhetari, H., Kabir, M.N.: Sensor-based fall detection systems: a review. J. Ambient Intell. Humaniz. Comput. 1–17 (2022)
3. World Health Organization. Ageing, & Life Course Unit: WHO global report on falls prevention in older age. World Health Organization (2008)
4. Igual, R., Medrano, C., Plaza, I.: Challenges, issues and trends in fall detection systems. Biomed. Eng. Online **12**(1), 66 (2013)
5. Gallego, G., et al.: Event-based vision: a survey. IEEE Trans. Pattern Anal. Mach. Intell. **44**(1), 154–180 (2020)
6. Wang, X., Ellul, J., Azzopardi, G.: Elderly fall detection systems: a literature survey. Front. Robot. AI **7**, 71 (2020)

7. Ma, X., Wang, H., Xue, B., Zhou, M., Ji, B., Li, Y.: Depth-based human fall detection via shape features and improved extreme learning machine. IEEE J. Biomed. Health Inform. **18**(6), 1915–1922 (2014)

8. Huang, C.: Event-based timestamp image encoding network for human action recognition and anticipation. In: International Joint Conference on Neural Networks, pp. 1–9. IEEE (2021)

9. Moreno-Rodríguez, F.J., Traver, V.J., Barranco, F., Dimiccoli, M., Pla, F.: Visual event-based egocentric human action recognition. In: Pinho, A.J., Georgieva, P., Teixeira, L.F., Sánchez, J.A. (eds.) IbPRIA 2022. LNCS, vol. 13256, pp. 402–414. Springer, Cham (2022). https://doi.org/10.1007/978-3-031-04881-4_32

10. Casares, M., Ozcan, K., Almagambetov, A., Velipasalar, S.: Automatic fall detection by a wearable embedded smart camera. In: International Conference on Distributed Smart Cameras, pp. 1–6 (2012)

11. Ozcan, K., Mahabalagiri, A.K., Casares, M., Velipasalar, S.: Automatic fall detection and activity classification by a wearable embedded smart camera. J. Emerg. Sel. Top. Circuits Syst. **3**(2), 125–136 (2013)

12. Hu, Y., Liu, S.C., Delbruck, T.: v2e: from video frames to realistic DVS events. In: Conference on Computer Vision and Pattern Recognition, pp. 1312–1321 (2021)

13. Conradt, J., Berner, R., Cook, M., Delbruck, T.: An embedded AER dynamic vision sensor for low-latency pole balancing. In: 2009 IEEE 12th International Conference on Computer Vision Workshops, ICCV Workshops, pp. 780–785. IEEE (2009)

14. Muller-Cleve, S.F., et al.: Braille letter reading: a benchmark for spatio-temporal pattern recognition on neuromorphic hardware. Front. Neurosci. **16**, 951164 (2022)

15. Zenke, F., Vogels, T.P.: The remarkable robustness of surrogate gradient learning for instilling complex function in spiking neural networks. Neural Comput. **33**(4), 899–925 (2021)

16. Bouanane, M.S., Cherifi, D., Chicca, E., Khacef, L.: Impact of spiking neurons leakages and network recurrences on event-based spatio-temporal pattern recognition. arXiv preprint arXiv:2211.07761 (2022)

17. Microsoft: Neural Network Intelligence (2021). https://github.com/microsoft/nni

18. Horowitz, M.: 1.1 computing's energy problem (and what we can do about it). In: 2014 IEEE International Solid-State Circuits Conference Digest of Technical Papers (ISSCC), pp. 10–14. IEEE (2014)

19. Yin, B., Corradi, F., Bohté, S.M.: Accurate and efficient time-domain classification with adaptive spiking recurrent neural networks. Nat. Mach. Intell. **3**(10), 905–913 (2021)

20. Hazarika, A., Poddar, S., Nasralla, M.M., Rahaman, H.: Area and energy efficient shift and accumulator unit for object detection in IoT applications. Alex. Eng. J. **61**(1), 795–809 (2022)

Towards Accurate and Efficient Sleep Period Detection Using Wearable Devices

Fatemeh Jokar[1]([✉]) [iD], George Azzopardi[1] [iD], and Joao Palotti[2] [iD]

[1] University of Groningen, Groningen, The Netherlands
s.f.jokar@rug.nl
[2] Earkick GmbH, Zurich, Switzerland

Abstract. Sleep monitoring has traditionally required expensive equipment and expert assessment. Wearable devices are however becoming a viable option for monitoring sleep. This study investigates methods for autonomously identifying sleep segments base on wearable device data. We employ and evaluate machine and deep learning models on the benchmark MESA dataset, with results showing that they outperform traditional methods in terms of accuracy, F1 score, and Matthews Correlation Coefficient (MCC). The most accurate model, namely Light Gradient Boosting Machine, obtained an F1 score of 0.93 and an MCC of 0.73. Additionally, sleep quality metrics were used to assess the models. Furthermore, it should be noted that the proposed approach is device-agnostic, and more accessible and cost-effective than the traditional polysomnography (PSG) methods.

Keywords: Time series analysis · Deep learning · Machine Learning · Health monitoring systems · Wearables · Sleep Segments · Heart Rate · Actigraphy

1 Introduction

Sleep is essential for maintaining good health, but a significant proportion of people - up to 30% - suffer from sleep disorders, which often go unnoticed [6,18]. While polysomnography (PSG) is the standard method for monitoring sleep in clinical settings [3], it has some limitations. For one, it is not easily accessible, as it can only be conducted in a laboratory setting. Additionally, PSG equipment is invasive and may be difficult for patients to tolerate. Wearable devices, such as actigraphy, can objectively monitor sleep non-invasively [1,22]. However, using a single sensor to detect sleep periods may not be reliable [2]. Furthermore, actigraphy has limitations, including a lack of validation studies for different consumer-grade devices, the absence of standardized methods for identifying human activities [20], and difficulty classifying wake events during sleep [13,17]. To address these limitations, our research focuses on developing an automated method for detecting sleep periods using data from wearable devices.

N. Tsapatsoulis et al. (Eds.): CAIP 2023, LNCS 14185, pp. 43–54, 2023.
https://doi.org/10.1007/978-3-031-44240-7_5

Most of the existing research in this field focuses on predicting sleep/wake patterns within a single epoch. However, our research takes a slightly different path by concentrating on identifying sleep boundaries, a concept that holds significant importance in understanding sleep architecture. Thus, the primary objective of our study is to develop an automated method that leverages data from wearable devices to effectively detect sleep periods. Given the continuous signals from heart rate and motion continuously captured over the night by a wearable device, we employed various machine learning (ML) methods to predict one or more sleep segments over the night period.

2   Related Work

Numerous algorithms were proposed to distinguish between different stages of sleep and wakefulness. These algorithms utilized participants' overnight movements as input. Several notable algorithms resulting from this research include Oakley [28], Scripps Clinic [14], Cole-Kripke [5], Sadeh [23] and Saznov [24] were developed. Recent advances in Deep Learning (DL) methods have shown promising outcomes in handling temporal medical data, particularly when applied to physiological signals [11]. However, the performance of DL is significantly dependent on both the quantity and quality of the input signal data [26]. Although the use of a large dataset as input can minimize this bias, for sleep tasks, many studies have used small patient samples.

In [7], Dong et al. extracted features from electroencephalography signals to feed into a deep neural network for detecting sleep stages. They tested window sizes ranging from 1 to 8 s to determine the most suitable window width within this range. Their work was evaluated on a dataset containing 62 healthy subjects. For sleep stage classification, Zhang et al. [32] employed an unsupervised training method using a convolutional neural network based on EEG data to classify sleep stages. The approach was tested on two datasets, one includes 25 people with sleep difficulties, in addition to another dataset with fewer subjects. The evaluation metrics included accuracy, sensitivity, specificity, kappa coefficient, and F1. Zhang et al., utilized supervised learning algorithms to classify sleep stages [30–32]. The method first extracts signals from raw electroencephalography to learn features, then classifies sleep stages based on those features. In [13], Khademi et al. worked on a dataset with 77 participants who had simultaneous PSG and actigraphy recordings while sleeping in the sleep laboratory. Khademi et al. [13] compared the results of actigraphy with PSG by assessing sleep epoch by epoch. As a result, several recent studies [12,15,16,25,27] have used the data from these devices versus PSG and actigraphy to increase sleep-tracking performance. In [17], Palotti et al. sliced the input signals into small windows of a fixed size (i.e., 10 min) and extracted features from each window to predict the binary sleep stage for the center point of the window.

Previous studies utilized supervised learning to model sleep stages, specifically neural networks to analyze EEG data for sleep stage classification [7,30–32]. Additionally, wearable devices were verified in [9], but the release of commercial products is often quicker than validation studies [4]. Due to the uncertainty surrounding the accuracy of new devices, there is a requirement for methods to be device-agnostic. Recent device-agnostic research has focused on developing handcrafted features on activity [10] and heart rate (HR) [19] to detect sleep boundaries. However, to the best of our knowledge, this problem has never been addressed with a ML approach.

3   Method

3.1   Dataset

This study utilizes data from the MESA Sleep Study[1]. The publicly available MESA Sleep Study, part of the Multi-Ethnic Study of Atherosclerosis (MESA), was conducted in six communities in the United States. MESA is by far the largest dataset that includes concurrent PSG and actigraphy data. From an initial group of 2,237 participants, 1,225 subjects were eligible for the study, while 1,000 subjects were excluded due to lack of concurrent PSG, actigraphy, and ECG data, insufficient qualified standard data, or data integrity issues. The data used in our research comes from [29], which compiled data from subjects with synchronized PSG, ECG, and actigraphy records in 30-second epochs. All participants wore an actigraphy device for one week and underwent PSG for one night at the same time.

Figure 1 shows the data from one of the participants used in the experiment, including activity and HR signals, sleep hypnogram measured by PSG, and the ground truth (GT) data. A sleep segment is defined by the onset and offset points. *Sleep onset* is the transition from awake to sleep after five or more minutes in the awake stage; and *Sleep offset* is the transition from any sleep stage to awake and maintaining the awake stage for at least five minutes. It is worth noting that we utilize the five-minute rule established by sleep experts to differentiate between nocturnal arousal and nocturnal awakenings. Nocturnal arousals are brief periods of wakefulness that occur during sleep, while nocturnal awakenings are longer periods of wakefulness [8], which we investigated in our study to enhance our understanding of sleep sessions.

3.2   Problem Modelling

We use a binary classification approach to classify each 30-second epoch as either *within* or *outside* a sleep segment. The point of interest, which is the one we must assign a label, can either be the central one, or the one at the end of the given epoch. The end-point prediction simulates a real-time task that only uses past information to make a prediction. To determine the sleep segments, we extract features from fixed-size sliding windows of 5, 10, or 20 min, which correspond to 10, 20, and 40 epochs of 30 s each. In our method, we explore three types of data preparation: centered vs. end-point, size of time window (5, 10, or 20 min), and raw vs. processed features. Two labeling approaches, centered and end-point, are

---

[1] Available at https://sleepdata.org/datasets/mesa.

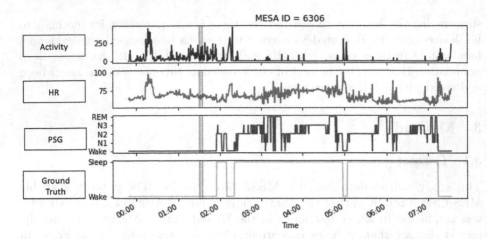

Fig. 1. Activity and HR signals captured from one of the participants over a night. Ground truth data were extracted from noisy PSG signals. The green bar indicates a sliding time window of 10 min in this example.

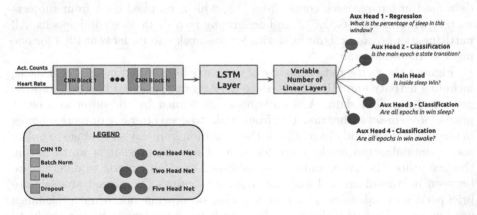

Fig. 2. The architecture of the DL model with different numbers of heads.

compared, and models are trained using either raw HR and activity counts or 137 processed features for each signal, resulting in an input of $R^{137 \times S}$ for a time window of size S. The processed features used in this study are listed in Table 1. Each of the three types of data preparation generates a distinct feature set, and in total, we experimented with 12 feature sets individually, using both ML and DL models. Table 2 summarizes the input size and the number of instances when using either the raw or processed data.

4 Models

We evaluated six ML models, namely logistic regression (LR), linear discriminant analysis (LDA), random forest (RF), extra tree classifier (ET), and light gradient

Table 1. An overview of the features extracted from the MESA dataset

Feature Name	Description
Continuous Wavelet Transform (CWT) Coefficients	It calculates a continuous wavelet transform for the Ricker wavelet. In mathematics, it is a tool that provides an over-complete representation of a signal by letting the translation and scale parameter of the wavelets vary continuously
Number of CWT Peaks	It was used to find sharp peaks among noisy data
Sum of Values	It was used to calculate the sum over the time series values
Descriptive Statistics on the Autocorrelation of the Time Series	Autocorrelation is a way of measuring and explaining the internal association between observations in a time series
Kurtosis	It was used to measure the combined weight of the distribution's tails relative to the center of the distribution
Skewness	It was used to calculate the degree of asymmetry observed in the probability distribution
Abs Energy	It calculates the absolute energy of the time series which is the sum over the squared values
Absolute Sum of Changes	It calculates the sum over the absolute value of consecutive changes
Mean, Median, Standard Deviation	It calculates the average, the number in the middle, and the standard deviation
Mean Absolute Change	It calculates the mean over the absolute differences between subsequent time series values
Mean Change	It calculates the average over time series differences
Percentage of Reoccurring Data Points to All Data Points	It was used to show the percentage of non-unique data points
Percentage of Reoccurring Values to All Values	It was used to show the percentage of values that are present in the time series more than once
Sum of Values, Variance, Variation Coefficient	It calculates the sum over the time series values and variance. And the variation coefficient returns the relative value of variation around the mean)
Evaluate Time Series	It was used to determine if they had a large standard deviation. According to a rule of thumb, the standard deviation should be a fourth of the range of the values
Variance Larger than Standard Deviation	It returns a boolean variable denoting if the variance is greater than its standard deviation
Linear Trend	It calculates a linear least-squares regression for values of the time series
Root Mean Square (RMS)	It is one of the most commonly used measures for evaluating the quality of predictions. It shows how far predictions fall from measured true values by using the Euclidean distance
Fast Fourier Transform (FFT) aggregated	It returns the spectral centroid (mean), variance, skew, and kurtosis of the absolute Fourier transform spectrum
Fast Fourier Transform (FFT) Coefficient	It calculates the Fourier coefficients of the one-dimensional discrete Fourier Transform for real input by fast
Fourier Entropy	It calculates the binned entropy of the power spectral density by using Welch's method

Table 2. The size of features, training and test sets for the raw and processed data.

	Raw Data	Processed Data
# Features	2 × window size	2 × 137
# Train Samples	17,202	17,202
# Test Samples	1,188	1,188

boosting machine (LGBM), and DL model, namely CNN-LSTM, which we chose due to its state-of-the-art performance in applications with similar characteristics. The CNN layer extracts local features, and the LSTM layer finds temporal patterns in the data. We investigated if Multitask Learning can help regularize networks in our study. Multitask Learning is a form of inductive transfer that can improve a model by introducing an inductive bias [21]. We investigate three variants of the DL model with the same internal layers but different numbers of heads, namely the *One-head*, *Two-head*, and *Five-head* nets, shown in Fig. 2. The extra heads are designed to mitigate the challenge of overfitting.

To test ML/DL model performance on unseen data, an 11-fold cross-validation was used for each of the 6 ML and 3 DL models, and for the 12 preprocessing configurations. For each of the 11 experiments, a random search was used to fine tune the hyper parameters of the models based on the respective 10 training partitions. MCC was used as the primary evaluation metric due to its advantages over F1-score for unbalanced data. The impact of the sleep segment generation methods on sleep quality metrics was assessed by evaluating the number of awakenings during the night and sleep latency. The code and datasets are publicly available[2].

5   Evaluation and Results

5.1   Baseline Study

To compare the performance of the ML and DL techniques that we investigate, we begin by employing 10 standard approaches from the existing research, whose results are shown in Fig. 3. The rescored version of the *Scripps Clinic* and *Oakley10* algorithms produced the highest MCC, with values of 0.60 and 0.59, respectively. This is consistent with the findings reported in [17].

5.2   Machine Learning and Deep Learning Models

We compared the performance of six ML with 12 different preprocessing configurations described in Sect. 3.2, as shown in Fig. 4, and found that some models were more sensitive to the preprocessing strategy than others. The LR and LDA models performed better when using processed features compared to raw signals. In contrast, LGBM and ET were less affected by the processed features

---

[2] https://github.com/joaopalotti/sleep_boundary_project.

and were most affected by the predicted epoch's position within the window. Our experiments suggest that using processed features with centered windows is more likely to produce better results, although the effect of window size on the results is difficult to determine.

We analyzed the combinatory effect of the 12 configuration strategies for DL models in Fig. 5, and found that the position of the target point (center or end-

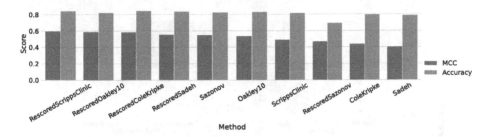

Fig. 3. Comparison of 10 baseline models in literature by MCC and accuracy.

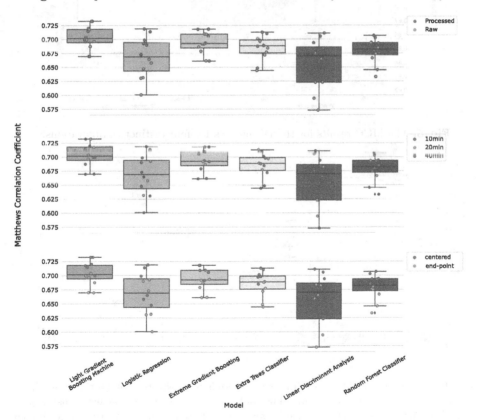

Fig. 4. The MCC results of the ML methods for 3 configurations. LGBM achieves the highest MCC score of 0.73 while using center point prediction, windows of 20 min, and processed features.

point), played an important role. Also, MCC improved with additional heads. Figure 6 presents the results of the CNN-LSTM models. The best outcome was obtained with a CNN-LSTM model trained with five heads, using processed features, with a centered window of 40 epochs, which yielded an MCC of 0.696. Table 3 summarizes the best results obtained by the baseline algorithms, and by the ML and DL models for our unbalanced dataset. Although all methods

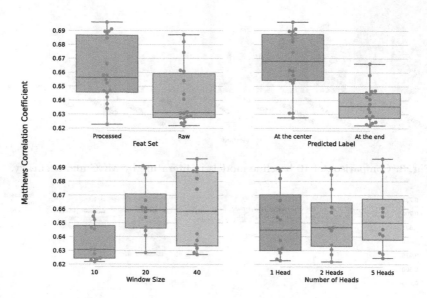

Fig. 5. The MCC results for the DL models for four distinct configurations.

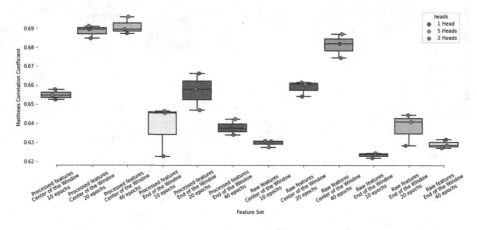

Fig. 6. Comparison of MCC results for DL models with varying configuration settings, including one, two, and five heads. The highest MCC scores were achieved using processed features with a window size larger than 20 epochs and with the target epoch positioned at the center of the window.

showed high accuracies above 0.88, the differences in $F1$ score and MCC are significant. The top 6 ML models achieved an average MCC of 0.72, while the top 3 baseline algorithms had an average MCC of 0.59. Figure 7 shows the final sleep windows for one of the participants traced by both the Rescored Oakley and Rescored Scripps Clinic algorithms with a comparison to the LGBM with the following configuration: center point, window of 20 epochs, and processed features.

6 Clinical Results

This section compares the best sleep boundary algorithm, LGBM, with traditional algorithms used in the sleep science community to calculate sleep quality metrics, such as total sleep time, sleep efficiency, and number of awakenings.

Table 3. Top scoring models for each classifier ranked by MCC.

Name	Configuration	MCC	F_1	Acc.
Rescored Scripps Clinic [14]	-	.599	.894	.898
Rescored Oakley 10 [28]	-	.598	.874	.823
Rescored Cole Kripke [5]	-	.589	.898	.845
Light Gradient Boosting Machine	Processed, Centered, 40 epochs	.732	.936	.902
Light Gradient Boosting Machine	Processed, Centered, 20 epochs	.732	.932	.898
Light Gradient Boosting Machine	Raw, Centered, 40 epochs	.719	.933	.898
Logistic Regression	Processed, Centered, 40 epochs	.718	.933	.898
Extreme Gradient Boosting	Processed, Centered, 20 epochs	.718	.929	.892
Extreme Gradient Boosting	Processed, Centered, 40 epochs	.717	.934	.898
CNN-LSTM with Five heads	Processed, Centered, 40 epochs	.696	.886	.890
CNN-LSTM with Two heads	Processed, Centered, 40 epochs	.689	.883	.888
CNN-LSTM with One head	Processed, Centered, 20 epochs	.689	.878	.882

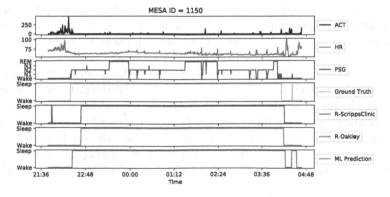

Fig. 7. An example of one participant on whom the LGBM method outperforms the Rescored Oakley and Rescored Scripps Clinic baseline methods.

As an example, Fig. 7 illustrates the comparison of top two baseline algorithms versus LGBM for one random participant. There are two awakening events in the GT signal. While both the Rescored Scripps Clinic and LGBM algorithms correctly detect the number of awakenings, the Rescored Oakely10 algorithm only identifies one of the awakenings.

Figure 8 displays the cumulative difference between the registered values of each algorithm and the GT in terms of number of awakenings. The ML model has an average error close to 0, while Rescored Oakley10 overestimates the number of awakenings per night by 1 on average. Also, in terms of sleep latency, Fig. 8 indicates that both LGBM and Rescored Oakley are the most effective approaches, with no significant differences between them. These results suggest that our proposed LGBM algorithm can serve as a valuable alternative to traditional algorithms for a better assessment of sleep quality.

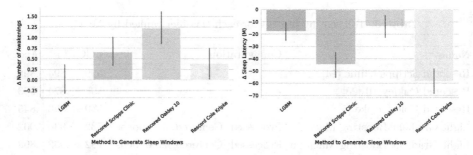

Fig. 8. Comparison of algorithms for predicting awakenings and sleep latency, with LGBM outperforming Oakley 10 for awakenings and showing similar results for sleep latency. Error bars indicate 95% confidence intervals.

7   Conclusion and Future Work

In conclusion, this study employed ML models and a combined CNN-LSTM DL model to address sleep segment classification in a time series problem. The proposed approaches demonstrated superior accuracy and MCC compared to previous methods. The LGBM model achieved the highest MCC using processed features with a window of 40 epochs, with an accuracy and $F1$ score of 0.902 and 0.936, respectively. While the study found that ML models outperformed DL models, the difference could be attributed to the size of the dataset. Limitations of the study include the exclusion of individuals with sleep disorders and the use of only nighttime data. Future research should expand on these findings by testing the models on a 24-hour dataset and exploring advanced neural network architectures, such as Transformers. Additionally, deploying the best model on commercial wearable devices would offer insights into its practical limitations.

References

1. Ancoli-Israel, S., Cole, R., Alessi, C., Chambers, M., Moorcroft, W., Pollak, C.P.: The role of actigraphy in the study of sleep and circadian rhythms. Sleep **26**(3), 342–392 (2003)
2. Baltrušaitis, T., Ahuja, C., Morency, L.P.: Multimodal machine learning: a survey and taxonomy. IEEE Trans. Pattern Anal. Mach. Intell. **41**(2), 423–443 (2018)
3. Berry, R.B., Brooks, R., Gamaldo, C.E., Harding, S.M., Marcus, C., Vaughn, B.V., et al.: The AASM manual for the scoring of sleep and associated events. Rules, Terminology and Technical Specifications, Darien, Illinois, American Academy of Sleep Medicine (2012)
4. Boudreaux, B.D., et al.: Validity of wearable activity monitors during cycling and resistance exercise. Med. Sci. Sports Exerc. **50**(3), 624–633 (2018)
5. Cole, R.J., Kripke, D.F., Gruen, W., Mullaney, D.J., Gillin, J.C.: Automatic sleep/wake identification from wrist activity. Sleep **15**(5), 461–469 (1992)
6. Czeisler, C.A.: Duration, timing and quality of sleep are each vital for health, performance and safety. Sleep Health J. National Sleep Found. **1**(1), 5–8 (2015)
7. Dong, H., Supratak, A., Pan, W., Wu, C., Matthews, P.M., Guo, Y.: Mixed neural network approach for temporal sleep stage classification. IEEE Trans. Neural Syst. Rehabil. Eng. **26**(2), 324–333 (2017)
8. Eckert, D.J., Younes, M.K.: Arousal from sleep: implications for obstructive sleep apnea pathogenesis and treatment. J. Appl. Physiol. **116**(3), 302–313 (2014)
9. Feehan, L.M., et al.: Accuracy of fitbit devices: systematic review and narrative syntheses of quantitative data. JMIR mHealth uHealth **6**(8), e10527 (2018)
10. van Hees, V.T., et al.: Estimating sleep parameters using an accelerometer without sleep diary. Sci. Rep. **8**(1), 12975 (2018)
11. Hong, S., Zhou, Y., Shang, J., Xiao, C., Sun, J.: Opportunities and challenges of deep learning methods for electrocardiogram data: a systematic review. Comput. Biol. Med. **122**, 103801 (2020)
12. Kahawage, P., Jumabhoy, R., Hamill, K., de Zambotti, M., Drummond, S.P.: Validity, potential clinical utility, and comparison of consumer and research-grade activity trackers in insomnia disorder I: in-lab validation against polysomnography. J. Sleep Res. **29**(1), e12931 (2020)
13. Khademi, A., El-Manzalawy, Y., Master, L., Buxton, O.M., Honavar, V.G.: Personalized sleep parameters estimation from actigraphy: a machine learning approach. Nat. Sci. Sleep (2019)
14. Kripke, D.F., et al.: Wrist actigraphic scoring for sleep laboratory patients: algorithm development. J. Sleep Res. **19**(4), 612–619 (2010)
15. Lee, X.K., et al.: Validation of a consumer sleep wearable device with actigraphy and polysomnography in adolescents across sleep opportunity manipulations. J. Clin. Sleep Med. **15**(9), 1337–1346 (2019)
16. Moreno-Pino, F., Porras-Segovia, A., López-Esteban, P., Artés, A., Baca-García, E.: Validation of Fitbit charge 2 and Fitbit Alta HR against polysomnography for assessing sleep in adults with obstructive sleep apnea. J. Clin. Sleep Med. **15**(11), 1645–1653 (2019)
17. Palotti, J., et al.: Benchmark on a large cohort for sleep-wake classification with machine learning techniques. NPJ Digit. Med. **2**(1), 50 (2019)
18. Partinen, M.: Epidemiology of sleep disorders. In: Handbook of Clinical Neurology (2011)

19. Perez-Pozuelo, I., et al.: Detecting sleep outside the clinic using wearable heart rate devices. Sci. Rep. **12**(1), 7956 (2022)
20. Perez-Pozuelo, I., et al.: The future of sleep health: a data-driven revolution in sleep science and medicine. NPJ Digit. Med. **3**(1), 42 (2020)
21. Ruder, S.: An overview of multi-task learning in deep neural networks. arXiv preprint arXiv:1706.05098 (2017)
22. Sadeh, A., Acebo, C.: The role of actigraphy in sleep medicine. Sleep Med. Rev. **6**(2), 113–124 (2002)
23. Sadeh, A., Sharkey, M., Carskadon, M.A.: Activity-based sleep-wake identification: an empirical test of methodological issues. Sleep **17**(3), 201–207 (1994)
24. Sazonov, E., Sazonova, N., Schuckers, S., Neuman, M., Group, C.S., et al.: Activity-based sleep-wake identification in infants. Physiol. Meas. **25**(5), 1291 (2004)
25. Schade, M.M., et al.: Sleep validity of a non-contact bedside movement and respiration-sensing device. J. Clin. Sleep Med. **15**(7), 1051–1061 (2019)
26. Sun, C., Hong, S., Wang, J., Dong, X., Han, F., Li, H.: A systematic review of deep learning methods for modeling electrocardiograms during sleep. Physiol. Meas. (2022)
27. Tal, A., Shinar, Z., Shaki, D., Codish, S., Goldbart, A.: Validation of contact-free sleep monitoring device with comparison to polysomnography. J. Clin. Sleep Med. **13**(3), 517–522 (2017)
28. Weiss, A.R., Johnson, N.L., Berger, N.A., Redline, S.: Validity of activity-based devices to estimate sleep. J. Clin. Sleep Med. **6**(4), 336–342 (2010)
29. Zhai, B., Perez-Pozuelo, I., Clifton, E.A., Palotti, J., Guan, Y.: Making sense of sleep: multimodal sleep stage classification in a large, diverse population using movement and cardiac sensing. In: Proceedings of the ACM on Interactive, Mobile, Wearable and Ubiquitous Technologies (2020)
30. Zhang, J., Wu, Y.: A new method for automatic sleep stage classification. IEEE Trans. Biomed. Circuits Syst. **11**(5), 1097–1110 (2017)
31. Zhang, J., Wu, Y.: Automatic sleep stage classification of single-channel EEG by using complex-valued convolutional neural network. Biomed. Eng./Biomedizinische Technik **63**(2), 177–190 (2018)
32. Zhang, J., Wu, Y.: Complex-valued unsupervised convolutional neural networks for sleep stage classification. Comput. Methods Programs Biomed. **164**, 181–191 (2018)

RLSTM: A Novel Residual and Recurrent Network for Pedestrian Action Classification

Soulayma Gazzeh[1,2]($\boxtimes$) (iD), Liliana Lo Presti[2] (iD), Ali Douik[1] (iD),
and Marco La Cascia[2] (iD)

[1] NOCCS Laboratory, ENISO, University of Sousse, Sousse, Tunisia
soulayma.gazzeh@eniso.u-sousse.tn
[2] Department of Engineering, University of Palermo, Palermo, Italy

Abstract. Properly training LSTMs requires long time and extensive amount of data. To improve the training of these models, this paper proposes a novel residual and recurrent neural network, Resnet-LSTM, for spatio-temporal pedestrian action recognition from image sequences. The model includes a novel layer, called MapGrad, whose goal is improving stationarity of the feature map sequences processed by the ConvLSTM. The paper demonstrates the effectiveness of the proposed model and the MapGrad layer in the spatio-temporal classification of pedestrian actions through an ablation study and comparison with state-of-the-art methods. Overall, RLSTM achieves an accuracy value of 88% and an average precision of 94% on the JAAD dataset, which is a widely used benchmark in the field. Finally, the paper empirically analyzes the effect of increasing input sequence length on standing action recognition, showing that the proposed method yields a recall of 93%.

Keywords: Pedestrian action recognition · Time series data · LSTM · Spatio-Temporal features

1 Introduction

Autonomous driving (AD) is a rapidly evolving field in computer vision whose primary focus is to ensure the safety of pedestrians, who often interact with vehicles in complex and unpredictable ways [12,13]. A crucial task for autonomous vehicles is to recognize whether or not a pedestrian is crossing the road. Preliminary steps to achieve this, involve detecting and tracking pedestrians and identifying *walking* and *standing* actions. The latter task, pedestrian action recognition (PAR), is challenging when using mobile cameras. Indeed, motion blur, the dynamic background of the street scene, variations in the pedestrians' visual appearance, and frequent occlusions complicates the action classification task. To address the problem, techniques derived from time series analysis are often employed, which allow for the processing of frame sequences to extract motion and changes in the scene over time [4–6]. However, meaningful motion patterns

© The Author(s), under exclusive license to Springer Nature Switzerland AG 2023
N. Tsapatsoulis et al. (Eds.): CAIP 2023, LNCS 14185, pp. 55–64, 2023.
https://doi.org/10.1007/978-3-031-44240-7_6

are difficult to model due to the complex interference between pedestrians' and vehicle's movements. Indeed, changes in vehicle speed and direction can lead to changes in the apparent motion of pedestrians. To model such complex temporal dependencies, Long-Short Term Model (LSTM) [7] is often used with time series due to its ability to capture both short- and long-term dependencies over time. ConvLSTM [8] has instead been used to process image sequences. In [13], LSTMs are used for action recognition despite these models are difficult to train, in the sense that training requires long time and extensive training data.

In this paper, we propose a novel end-to-end trainable deep architecture that leverages residual layers [9] and ConvLSTM for PAR. Our architecture takes advantage of a novel layer, *MapGrad*, that improves the extraction of temporal features. MapGrad builds on preprocessing techniques adopted in time series analysis and, in the context of PAR, helps improve learning of an LSTM and reduce the negative effect of camera motion on feature maps without increasing the number of model parameters. To achieve this goal, MapGrad computes the forward difference of the feature maps extracted over time from a convolutional network, thus improving the stationarity of that sequence while, at the same time, highlighting temporal feature changes.

In addition, we emphasize that the length of the input sequence (SL) should be carefully selected when designing a PAR system, as it directly impacts the real-time performance of the model and the recall of the standing action.

In summary, our contributions in this paper are:

- A novel residual and recurrent architecture (RLSTM) for PAR;
- A novel layer, MapGrad, that pre-processes feature maps before feeding a LSTM. Our ablation study shows that, in our experiments, MapGrad contributes to increase the accuracy in classification of more than 17% when processing input sequences of 7 frames;
- A study on the effect of increasing the SL on the recognition of standing pedestrians with respect to the real-time constraints of the PAR system.

The plan of the paper is as follows. Section 2 reviews works on action recognition with mobile cameras. Section 3 describes in detail the proposed architecture and the MapGrad layer. Section 4 presents experimental results on a public available benchmark and the comparison to the existing state-of-the-art techniques. Finally, Sect. 5 summarizes our main findings and describes future works.

2 Related Work

Action recognition is a widely studied field in computer vision that aims to automatically recognize human actions from image sequences. These approaches have been applied to different domains such as sports analysis [14], surveillance [15] and AD [16].

In the context of AD, the main challenges to address concern the dynamic camera motion and the complex motion patterns of pedestrians. Several deep learning (DL) architectures have been proposed for PAR using mobile cameras, including 2D/3D convolutional networks [6], recurrent networks [17], and hybrid models combining both approaches [5].

To improve pedestrian safety, several studies have investigated different approaches to detect crossing intention by considering environmental factors [18,20] and visual cues, which include analyzing the body posture [18,19] and pedestrians' motion patterns [21].

Recognizing atomic actions, such as walking and standing, is an important step towards more complex pedestrian activities recognition. For instance, the posture and motion features of pedestrians while walking or standing can provide important cues for inferring their intention to cross the road. Due to the difficulty in recognizing standing from walking, a limited number of studies [1–3] have investigated this task. This is because the visual similarity between these two actions poses a significant obstacle, especially in the presence of motion blur.

Our proposed approach differs from the previous papers as we adopt a residual and recurrent network to process a sequence of image crops of the detected pedestrians. Compared to the two-stream CNN used in [2], our approach has a simpler architecture, which is computationally more efficient. Additionally, our approach does not require pedestrian pose keypoints, as in [3], making it more robust to changes in pose and viewpoint. Finally, our use of an LSTM layer allows for the incorporation of temporal information, which is not possible in the cropbox-based AlexNet architecture employed in [1].

3   Proposed Method

Given a video acquired by the camera mounted on the vehicle, we assume that a visual tracking algorithm, for instance DeepSort [10] or Track R-CNN [11], detects and tracks pedestrians. Our goal is to classify sequences of image crops to infer the pedestrians' actions. These action sequences can be modeled as 4D tensors of size $[L \times H \times W \times C]$, with C indicating the number of channels of the L images with height H and width W.

Our model, which we refer to as Spatio-Temporal Resnet-LSTM (RLSTM), takes in input action sequences and infers if the pedestrian is walking or standing.

3.1   Spatio-Temporal RLSTM

As shown in Fig. 1, RLSTM combines both spatial and temporal information of an input sequence to achieve robust PAR. It is composed of two sub-networks.

The first sub-network is the spatial feature extraction module, and focuses on time-independent spatial features extraction, since it computes convolutional features on each image crop in the action sequence. The module employs the first two residual blocks of a pre-trained ResNet50, and two additional convolutional layers before the output is passed to the temporal feature extraction module. The second sub-network models behavioral features from the action sequences by using a ConvLSTM2D layer, and uses them to classify the input action sequence.

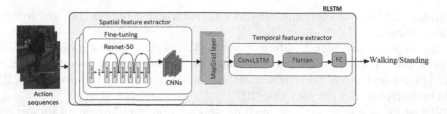

Fig. 1. Our proposed RLSTM model for PAR includes a spatial feature extraction module from the input action sequences, and a temporal feature extraction module for modeling behavioral features. Our MapGrad layer is inserted between these modules to transform the feature maps to be processed by the ConvLSTM layer.

In this module, convolutional and LSTM memory cells learn spatio-temporal patterns in the input sample.

In between the two modules, the MapGrad layer has the goal of transforming the extracted spatial features in a way that is suitable for the ConvLSTM2D layer to learn the pedestrians' behavioral patterns.

3.2 MapGrad Layer

In AD, the camera moves with the vehicle. Thus, the background of each frame changes dynamically, making it difficult to accurately model motion patterns when pedestrians are standing or walking. To address this problem, it is important both to extract suitable spatial features and, in the meantime, to take into account the temporal context in which the pedestrian action develops.

A common preprocessing in time series analysis is called *de-meaning*, which is to make the series zero-mean. Inspired by this, we implemented a layer to make zero-mean the sequences of feature maps that feed our ConvLSTM2D layer. In our formulation, the mean is computed only over the temporal dimension.

Given a spatial feature map F_t corresponding to the t-th frame, we element-wise subtract the mean feature map M_t in a temporal window to ensure that features are centered around zero, allowing subsequent analysis to focus on relative changes in pixel values. It helps normalizing the brightness levels and reducing the impact of lighting variations.

Our experimental results show that this feature map pre-processing contributes to greatly improve the learning of the ConvLSTM2D. Probably, making the feature maps zero-mean, contributes to reducing the effects of the dynamically changing background, and allows the model to focus on the spatio-temporal patterns relevant to the classification of pedestrians' action.

Aside from making the spatial feature maps zero-mean, our MapGrad layer uses temporal differentiation. This technique is adopted in time series analysis to improve the stationarity of the series [22]. It consists in computing the forward difference of the feature maps F_t extracted from consecutive image crops of the input sequence. In this way, MapGrad highlights the temporal changes between feature maps, which helps to isolate the pedestrian motion patterns.

Temporal differencing can be represented as:

$$D_t = F_t - F_{t-1} \tag{1}$$

where D_t is the difference between the feature maps, and the output of the MapGrad layer.

Implementation Details. To train our model, we use the ADAM optimizer with a binary cross-entropy loss function and a batch size of 10. To prevent overfitting, we incorporate dropout regularization with a rate of 0.5 after each convolutional layer to enhance the stability and convergence of the training process. Furthermore, we lower the initial learning rate of 10^{-3} to 10^{-6} for further optimization. During training, we employ early stopping to prevent overfitting.

4   Experimental Results

This section details the experiments conducted to demonstrate the effectiveness of our proposed model. We first describe the dataset used in the experiments, the experimental protocol and the data pre-processing. To highlight the contribution of our novel MapGrad layer and of the overall model, we conducted ablation studies. We also trained our model on sequences of varying length. Finally, we compared our best trade-off with the state-of-the-art.

4.1   Dataset

This work employs Joint Attention in Autonomous Driving (JAAD) dataset [1], which is widely used in pedestrian behavior recognition research. The dataset includes 346 short videos (5–20 s long), for a total of 82K frames. Videos are acquired at 30 frames per second, and each frame is annotated for pedestrian behaviors. Overall, the dataset contains annotations for 686 pedestrians.

The ground-truth annotations include the pedestrians' bounding boxes and behavioral tags like, for instance, actions (i.e., *standing* and *walking*) or behavioral attributes (i.e., *"cross"* and *"look"*). Only action classes are used in this study. Each pedestrian may perform multiple actions within a single video, switching from standing to walking or vice versa.

JAAD dataset suffers from imbalanced classes with 974 standing action sequences and 2524 walking. Variation in visibility on the road (Fig. 2), weather conditions, and partial or full occlusions (Fig. 3) between pedestrians or due to objects in the scene can make accurate recognition of pedestrian actions difficult.

Evaluation Metrics. To provide a comprehensive understanding of our RLSTM performance, we report several evaluation metrics such as accuracy value, F1-score, precision, recall, and average precision (AP).

The accuracy value measures the number of correctly classified samples, while the F1-score, precision, and recall metrics provide a more detailed assessment of the model's performance per class. We also report the AP metric, which measures the area under the precision-recall curve.

(a) Sunset   (b) Sunrise

Fig. 2. The figure shows two images captured at different day time. As shown, this results in changes of the visibility on the road.

Fig. 3. The figure shows images of a pedestrian taken while the vehicle is moving. The pedestrian is severely occluded, which makes harder recognizing his/her action.

Fig. 4. The figure shows a sequence of images cropped around a walking pedestrian.

Data Preparation. We implemented a data generator to facilitate data augmentation while reducing storage and computational requirements. Our data generator leverages tracking data (pedestrians' bounding boxes) and class labels (walking/standing), to generate a sequence of N image crops to feed our model. In our experiments, N was set to 7, 10 and 15.

To ensure the quality of the resulting image sequences, samples with full occlusion are filtered out. To maintain the aspect ratio of the pedestrian detection, the square crops of the pedestrian images also include a larger area surrounding the pedestrians (Fig. 4). Image crops are then rescaled to a (224×224) size. The data generator produces balanced batches of action sequences by uniformly sampling over the time dimension. Since our model includes pre-trained residual blocks, input images were normalized by subtracting the mean RGB values and scaling the pixel values in the range $[-1, 1]$.

4.2   Ablation Study

Our model includes several components and layers. Table 1 reports the ablation study conducted to evaluate the impact of each component on PAR.

Each row of the table refers to a different model and all experiments are conducted by considering a sequence length equals to 7.

ResLSTM refers to our baseline model including residual blocks from the pretrained ResNet50, Conv2D layers, and a ConvLSTM.

ResLSTM + BN + D refers to the regularized version of the previous ResLSTM model by using batch normalization (BN) and dropout layers. In particular, we adopted a BN layer after each convolutional layer to stabilize the network and improve learning. We noticed that including a BN just before the ConvLSTM2D layer was more effective in preserving temporal information, allowing the network to learn more robust features. Regularization improved the recall of the standing action.

RConv3D + BN + D refers to a regularized model including residual blocks from the pretrained ResNet50, Conv2D layers and a Conv3D layer that handles the time dimension of the feature maps. This experiment serves to highlight the contribution of the ConvLSTM to the overall accuracy of the model. As shown in the table, this model achieves similar performance to that of the regularized ResLSTM suggesting that the ConvLSTM is unable to learn the dynamics underlying to the input sequence from the extracted spatial features.

RConv3D + MapGrad refers to a model including residual blocks from the pretrained ResNet50, Conv2D layers and a Conv3D layer. In this case, no regularization technique is adopted. Instead, between the spatial feature extractor and the Conv3D layer we include our MapGrad layer. The MapGrad layer contributes to improve the accuracy value by about the 4.17% compared to the regularized RConv3D model. While the recall for the walking action increases, the one for the standing action decreases. This may indicate that the Conv3D has issues in discriminating between the (dynamic) background and the standing pedestrian. In our experiments, we noted that, when using the MapGrad layer, the impact of BN layers is very limited.

Centering Sequence of Maps refers to ResLSTM including centering the feature maps along the time dimension (i.e., making zero-mean the map sequence). As Table 1 shows, centering the map sequence improves over the ResLSTM.

RLSTM (with MapGrad) refers to our proposed model. It is similar to the ResLSTM model but includes the MapGrad layer between the spatial feature extractor and the ConvLSTM layer (Fig. 1). As shown in the table, MapGrad contributes to increase the accuracy in classification of more than 17% compared to the regularized ResLSTM model, and of about 21.1% compared to the simpler ResLSTM model. With respect to the RConv3D + MapGrad model, the increase in the accuracy value is of about 14.7%. While ConvLSTM and Conv3D were initially getting similar results, after the introduction of MapGrad in the model, the performance of ConvLSTM is much higher than Conv3D. Therefore, the preprocessing of feature map sequences to improve the stationarity of the series appears to have a positive effect on the training of the LSTM layer.

Impact of the Sequence-Length. Table 2 compares the performance achieved by our model when the SL assumes values 7, 10 and 15. As shown in the table, increasing the SL improves standing action recognition since the network receives

Table 1. Ablation studies

Models	Accuracy	F1-score	Precision	Recall		AP
				Standing	Walking	
ResLSTM (no preprocessing)	71	70.5	72.5	59	83	75
ResLSTM+BN+D	73	72.5	72.5	71	73	80
RConv3D+BN+D	72	71.5	72	73	70	74
RConv3D+MapGrad	75	75.5	75.5	69	82	83
ResLSTM + Centering Sequence of Maps	84	85	84	85	83	90
RLSTM (with MapGrad) (**ours**)	**86**	**87**	**87.5**	**90**	**85**	**92**

Table 2. Results achieved by RLSTM when varying the Sequence-Length

Model	Seq. Length (frames)	Observed ms	Accuracy	F1-score	Precision	Recall		AP
						Standing	Walking	
	7	200	86	87	87.5	90	85	92
RLSTM (Ours)	10	300	88	88.5	88	93	84	94
	15	500	90	90.5	90.5	94	87	96

more temporal context, and can capture the nuances of the standing action. The column *Observed ms* shows the length in milliseconds of the observed sequences. While the best performance is obtained when using 15 frames, the observed ms equals half a second, which may not ensure a quick and accurate decision in the context of AD. We note that 10-frame sequences are used in previous works [1,2].

4.3   Comparison with the State-of-the-Art

Table 3 reports the comparison of the results achieved by our model and works at the state-of-the-art on the JAAD dataset.

Our approach outperformed other methods such as the Two-Stream CNN approach in [2], the AlexNet model in [1], and the recurrent architecture in [3]. We note here that the methods in [2] uses multiple inputs. Similarly, the work in [3] takes in input also the pedestrian's pose keypoints. On the contrary, our method only takes in input sequences of image crops of the pedestrian. Despite the input of our model is simpler, it achieves superior results in all metrics with respect to the work in [3], and a comparable accuracy value with respect to [2]. Whilst it is known that recognizing the standing action is difficult [1], our approach achieves a 93% of recall value for this action that, at the best of our knowledge, is the highest value achieved on the JAAD dataset.

Table 3. Comparison to the state of the art models

Model	Input	AP	Accuracy	Recall	
				Standing	Walking
Rasouli et al. [1]	Cropboxs	83	-	-	-
Marginean et al. [3]	Pose keypoints	-	77	76	76
Park et al. [2]	First frame	-	88	72	91
	Flow images				
	Position information				
RLSTM (Ours)	Cropboxs	**94**	**88**	**93**	84

5   Conclusions and Future Work

In this paper, we proposed RLSTM, a spatio-temporal neural network for the classification of walking and standing actions in AD. RLSTM includes residual blocks, convolutional and ConvLSTM layers, and MapGrad, namely a novel feature map preprocessing layer. Our experiments show that the introduction of MapGrad to the model improves the learning of ConvLSTM without increasing the number of parameters of the model. On the JAAD dataset, MapGrad contributes to increase the accuracy in classification of more than 17%. Our experiments also show that increasing the SL significantly improves our model's ability to recognize standing actions in real time, achieving a recall of 93%.

In future work, we plan to explore more information, such as the velocity and ego-motion of the vehicle, to improve our model performance. Our final goal will be the recognition of the pedestrians' crossing intentions and we will study if it is possible to extend RLSTM to predict the pedestrians' intentions.

References

1. Rasouli, A., Kotseruba, I., Tsotsos, J.K.: Are they going to cross? A benchmark dataset and baseline for pedestrian crosswalk behavior. In: Proceedings of the IEEE International Conference on Computer Vision Workshops, pp. 206–213 (2017)
2. Park, S.K., Chung, J.H., Pae, D.S., Lim, M.T.: Binary dense SIFT flow based position-information added two-stream CNN for pedestrian action recognition. Appl. Sci. **12**(20), 10445 (2022)
3. Marginean, A., Brehar, R., Negru, M.: Understanding pedestrian behaviour with pose estimation and recurrent networks. In: 2019 6th International Symposium on Electrical and Electronics Engineering (ISEEE), pp. 1–6. IEEE (2019)
4. Yang, B., Zhan, W., Wang, P., Chan, C., Cai, Y., Wang, N.: Crossing or not? Context-based recognition of pedestrian crossing intention in the urban environment. IEEE Trans. Intell. Transp. Syst. **23**(6), 5338–5349 (2021)
5. Yang, D., Zhang, H., Yurtsever, E., Redmill, K.A., Özgüner, Ü.: Predicting pedestrian crossing intention with feature fusion and spatio-temporal attention. IEEE Trans. Intell. Veh. **7**(2), 221–230 (2022)

6. Chen, T., Tian, R., Ding, Z.: Visual reasoning using graph convolutional networks for predicting pedestrian crossing intention. In: Proceedings of the IEEE/CVF International Conference on Computer Vision, pp. 3103–3109 (2021)
7. Hochreiter, S., Schmidhuber, J.: Long short-term memory. Neural Comput. **9**(8), 1735–1780 (1997)
8. Shi, X., Chen, Z., Wang, H., Yeung, D. Y., Wong, W.K., Woo, W.C.: Convolutional LSTM network: a machine learning approach for precipitation nowcasting. In: Advances in Neural Information Processing Systems, vol. 28 (2015)
9. He, K., Zhang, X., Ren, S., Sun, J.: Deep residual learning for image recognition. In: Proceedings of the IEEE Conference on Computer Vision and Pattern Recognition, pp. 770–778 (2016)
10. Wojke, N., Bewley, A., Paulus, D.: Simple online and realtime tracking with a deep association metric. In: 2017 IEEE International Conference on Image Processing (ICIP), pp. 3645–3649. IEEE (2017)
11. He, T., Tian, Z., Huang, W., Shen, C., Qiao, Y., Sun, J.: Track R-CNN: multiple object tracking with track-RCNN. In: Proceedings of the IEEE/CVF Conference on Computer Vision and Pattern Recognition, pp. 10838–10847 (2020)
12. Liu, B., et al.: Spatiotemporal relationship reasoning for pedestrian intent prediction. IEEE Robot. Autom. Lett. **5**(2), 3485–3492 (2020)
13. Guo, D., Mordan, T., Alahi, A.: Pedestrian stop and go forecasting with hybrid feature fusion. In: 2022 International Conference on Robotics and Automation (ICRA), pp. 940–947. IEEE (2022)
14. Qi, M., Qin, J., Wu, Y., Yang, Y.: Imitative non-autoregressive modeling for trajectory forecasting and imputation. In: Proceedings of the IEEE/CVF Conference on Computer Vision and Pattern Recognition, pp. 12736–12745 (2020)
15. Mangalam, K., et al.: It is not the journey but the destination: endpoint conditioned trajectory prediction. In: Vedaldi, A., Bischof, H., Brox, T., Frahm, J.-M. (eds.) ECCV 2020. LNCS, vol. 12347, pp. 759–776. Springer, Cham (2020). https://doi.org/10.1007/978-3-030-58536-5_45
16. Noguchi, C., Tanizawa, T.: Ego-vehicle action recognition based on semi-supervised contrastive learning. In: Proceedings of the IEEE/CVF Winter Conference on Applications of Computer Vision, pp. 5988–5998 (2023)
17. Lian, J., Yu, F., Li, L., Zhou, Y.: Early intention prediction of pedestrians using contextual attention-based LSTM. Multimedia Tools Appl. **82**(10), 14713–14729 (2023)
18. Rasouli, A., Kotseruba, I., Tsotsos, J.K.: Pedestrian Action Anticipation using Contextual Feature Fusion in Stacked RNNs (2020)
19. Cadena, P.R.G., Yang, M., Qian, Y., Wang, C.: Pedestrian graph: pedestrian crossing prediction based on 2D pose estimation and graph convolutional networks. In: 2019 IEEE Intelligent Transportation Systems Conference (ITSC), pp. 2000–2005. IEEE (2019)
20. Moreno, E., et al.: Pedestrian crossing intention forecasting at unsignalized intersections using naturalistic trajectories. Sensors **23**(5), 2773 (2023)
21. Yang, C., Pei, Z.: Long-short term spatio-temporal aggregation for trajectory prediction. IEEE Trans. Intell. Transp. Syst. **24**(4), 4114–4126 (2023)
22. https://www.otexts.org/fpp/8/1

Biomedical Image and Pattern Analysis

Temporal Sequences of EEG Covariance Matrices for Automated Sleep Stage Scoring with Attention Mechanisms

Mathieu Seraphim[1]([✉]) [iD], Paul Dequidt[1] [iD], Alexis Lechervy[1] [iD], Florian Yger[1,2] [iD], Luc Brun[1] [iD], and Olivier Etard[3] [iD]

[1] Normandie Univ, UNICAEN, ENSICAEN, CNRS, GREYC, 14000 Caen, France
mathieu.seraphim@unicaen.fr
[2] LAMSADE, UMR CNRS 7243, Université Paris-Dauphine, PSL, Paris, France
[3] Université de Caen Normandie, INSERM, COMETE U1075, CYCERON, CHU de Caen, Normandie Univ, 14000 Caen, France

Abstract. Electroencephalographic (EEG) data is commonly used in sleep medicine. It consists of a number of cerebral electrical signals measured from various brain locations, subdivided into segments that must be manually scored to reflect their sleep stage. These past few years, multiple implementations aimed at an automation of this scoring process have been attempted, with promising results, although they are not yet accurate enough with respect to each sleep stage to see clinical use. Our approach relies on the information contained within the covariations between multiple EEG signals. This is done through temporal sequences of covariance matrices, analyzed through attention mechanisms at both the intra- and inter-epoch levels. Evaluation performed on a standard dataset using an improved methodological framework show that our approach obtains balanced results over all classes, this balancing being characterized by a better MF1 score than the State of the Art.

Keywords: Sleep analysis · EEG · Deep Learning · Attention · Symmetric Positive Definite matrices

1 Introduction

To study sleep patterns in the field of sleep medicine, the gold standard is the polysomnography (PSG) study, which usually includes electroencephalography (EEG), electrooculography (EOG), electromyography (EMG) and electrocardiography (ECG) recordings, corresponding to brain, eye, muscle and heart electrical activity, respectively. These signals are derived from the voltage existing

This work has been co-funded by the Normandy Region and the French National Research Agency (ANR) through a HAISCoDe Ph.D. grant. It was granted access to the HPC resources of IDRIS under the allocation 2022-AD010613618 made by GENCI, and to the computing resources of CRIANN (Normandy, France).

between electrodes over time, often with one being set as a reference. In this paper, the term "signal" shall refer exclusively to such a voltage.

The set of norms most often used to analyze PSG signals is the one defined by the American Academy of Sleep Medicine (AASM) [4]. This analysis is done by subdividing the signals into 30 s epochs, sometimes called "sleep epochs" in this paper. These may be manually scored (labeled) as being in one of five stages: wakefulness, rapid eye movement (REM) sleep, and three stages of non-REM sleep (N1, N2 and N3).

Table 1. Frequency bands that we use for EEG data analysis

	Delta	Theta	Alpha	Beta$_{low}$	Beta$_{high}$	Gamma
Hz	[0.5, 4[	[4, 8[	[8, 12[	[12, 22[	[22, 30[	[30, 45[

In this paper, we study the relevance of cerebral functional connectivity as a tool for the automated classification of sleep stages, through a study of covariations between EEG signals. In particular, we aim to obtain a high level of class-wise performance. For that purpose, we analyze timeseries of covariance matrices, computed for various frequency bands (Table 1). We base our analysis on an existing model architecture [14], itself based on successive Transformer encoders. After an overview of the existing State of the Art (SOA) in Sect. 2, we shall explain our method in Sect. 3. Finally, in Sect. 4, we present our results on a commonly used dataset, including a comparison with SOA methods.

2   State of the Art

Some approaches consider that a single signal contains enough information to classify sleep epochs [12,14,21]. A common strategy is to combine an EEG and an EOG signal with the same reference electrode by subtracting them [15–17]. Other approaches use a multitude of input signals, often including EOG or EMG signals to said input, in addition to EEG. Phan et al. [11] use one signal of each type (EEG, EOG and EMG) as input, whereas Jia et al. [7,8] use multiple of each, and additionally include one ECG signal. Given the same dataset, the latter approaches seem to yield better results.

A common approach in EEG preprocessing pipelines is the extraction of relevant frequency components, since sleep stages are characterized by events with specific frequential components [4]. As such, Phan et al. [11,12,14] compute time-frequency images to use as input of their model.

Manual scoring of a sleep epoch takes into consideration said epoch's context - i.e. information contained in neighboring sleep epochs. Similarly, the architectures of models used for this task often include contextual information in the classification process. Such sequence-based models can be divided into two sections: intra-epoch (extracting features from each epoch in the input sequence) and

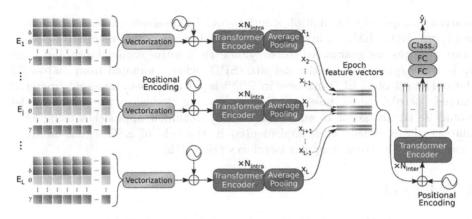

Fig. 1. Our model. $(E_1, ..., E_L)$ is the input sequence, with E_j referring to the central epoch. $\hat{y}_j$ is the output classification of the model. N_{intra} and N_{inter} refer to the number of sublayers in our intra- and inter-epoch Transformer encoders.

inter-epoch (combining said features). Convolutional neural networks (CNNs) can be used at the intra-epoch level, usually followed at the inter-epoch level by recurrent neural networks (RNNs) [12,15–17]. Phan et al. expand on both the RNN and attention mechanism approaches. In [11,12], they utilize bi-directional RNNs at both the intra-epoch and inter-epoch levels, whereas they use Transformer encoder-based attention mechanisms [18] in [14]. Similarly, Zhu et al. [21] use attention blocs inspired by said encoders at both levels, together with convolutions and other more classic layers. It has been stated that the performance of sequence-based State of the Art automatic sleep scoring models is currently near perfect, with little room for improvement [13]. While we do not dispute that claim in absolute terms, we have noticed a discrepancy in class-wise performance, particularly regarding the N1 stage (see Sect. 4.4). Therefore, our main focus is to correct for this discrepancy.

Our chosen axis of analysis concerns functional connectivity. In other words, one may study the connectivity between different brain regions through correlations detected between them, often independently of the structural (i.e. physical) connectivity between said regions [6]. In the context of sleep studies, it has been proven that sleep induces a characteristic cerebral response, describable in terms of functional connectivity [5]. Jia et al. [7,8] explicit these inter-region relationships through graph timeseries. Their intra-epoch section is a graph learning model, with each node corresponding to an electrode. These graphs are then convolved both spatially and temporally in the inter-epoch section. Note that most graph convolution methods do not assign a specific weight to each node, nor do they use the relative positioning of said nodes. For the proposed graphs, however, each node corresponds to an electrode, so ignoring node specificity in such a way might actually be a drawback.

In this paper, we perform an analysis of functional connectivity, estimated through the covariations of brain signals. For this purpose, we analyze covariance matrices computed from multiple simultaneous EEG signals, excluding other signal types (EOG, EMG...) in order to focus exclusively on brain activity. Covariance matrices are guaranteed to be symmetric positive semi-definite, but tend to be fully symmetric positive definite (SPD) when computed from real-world data. The set of all SPD matrices in $\mathbb{R}^{n \times n}$ is a Riemannian manifold (metered curved space), and we postulate that preserving this geometry in our model would be advantageous to our classification, as similar approaches using SPD matrices have already been implemented in the field of EEG signal analysis, most notably in brain-computer interfaces (BCI) [19].

3   Method

3.1   From EEG Signals to Covariance-Derived SPD Matrices

As do Zhu et al. [21], we apply a z-score normalization to our EEG signals, in order to harmonize their means and standard deviations. Moreover, according to the AASM [4], the signal components indicative of the current sleep stage have specific frequential properties. In order to allow the network to more effectively analyze them, we filter our EEG signals along the six frequency bands presented in Table 1. This is done through a fourth-order Butterworth bandpass filter.

The discrete events indicative of a sleep epoch's proper classification are around one second in length. To capture them, we elected to subdivide our recordings into one second segments. Each sleep epoch is therefore subdivided into 30 non-overlapping segments. On each segment, we compute a covariance matrix between the n electrodes. We verify that the resulting matrices are properly SPD, and add the matrix $\mathbb{I}_n \times 10^{-5}$ to those who aren't. This is done on the unfiltered and filtered signals, resulting in a total of 7 data channels.

Two main families of metrics have been defined on the set of SPD matrices. The so-called affine invariant metrics [10] are invariant to affine transformations, but have some drawbacks - for instance, it is impossible to compute an algebraic mean using such a metric, though algorithmic approximations do exist. LogEuclidean metrics [2] do not showcase the same invariance properties, but are significantly easier to work with. The LogEuclidean distance between two SPD matrices A and B is defined as:

$$\delta_{LE}^P(A, B) = \|log(P^{-1/2}AP^{-1/2}) - log(P^{-1/2}BP^{-1/2})\|_F \qquad (1)$$

This metric relies on the bijection existing between the manifold and its tangent space, the space of symmetric matrices, by way of the matrix logarithm and exponential functions. The parameter P may be interpreted as a center of projection onto said space.

Given a covariance matrix, the only mono-signal information stored is the variance of the signal along the segment. Additional signal-specific features may be added using Eq. 2, which "augments" a covariance matrix C, preserving its SPD property while adding a feature vector V (referred to as a "side vector"), weighted by a factor α (with $V_\alpha = \alpha V$):

$$M = \left(\begin{array}{c|c} C + V_\alpha V_\alpha^T & V_\alpha \\ \hline V_\alpha^T & 1 \end{array} \right) \tag{2}$$

Each epoch entering the model is thus represented by 7 channels of 30 SPD covariance matrices, and their associated side vectors. Multiple side vectors may be computed per matrix, such as its mean, maximum value, or average power spectral density (PSD) over the corresponding one second segment.

Being biological, our EEG data is marked by the specificities inherent to each recording, that are then transferred to our covariance matrices. In order to reduce said specificities, we compute every recording-wise covariance matrix G, and use them to apply a whitening operation [20] onto the relevant matrices:

$$M' = G^{-1/2} M G^{-1/2} \tag{3}$$

The idea is to operate a "transport" of the data M centered around G to be centered around $\mathbb{I}_n$ instead. We perform this shift for each recording and compute distances between centered SPD matrices using Eq. 1, with $P = \mathbb{I}_n$. If need be, both M and G are augmented with the relevant side vectors.

3.2   The Model

Our model architecture uses Transformer encoders at the intra- and inter-epoch levels, as does [14]. It takes as input a timeseries of sleep epochs, composed of a central epoch and l epochs on either side, for a total of $L = 2l+1$. These sequences are constructed with maximum overlap, with classification on the central epoch. Thus, the first and last l epochs of each recording are not classified.

Our model starts with a vectorization layer. It performs the augmentation of matrices by their weighted side vectors (Eq. 2), followed by the whitening operation. The nature of the side vectors V, and the value of their weight α, are model hyperparameters. Using n electrodes, we project our SPD matrices of $\mathbb{R}^{(n+1) \times (n+1)}$ onto their tangent set (Sect. 3.1), and vectorize the upper triangular of the resulting symmetric matrix onto $\mathbb{R}^{\frac{(n+1)(n+2)}{2}}$ [2]. These operations being bijective, all Euclidean operations on these vectors are interpretable as LogEuclidean operations on the augmented matrices.

These vectors undergo a positional encoding [18]. The channels are then concatenated and fed to a first, intra-epoch Transformer encoder, composed of a number of sequential sublayers. The fully connected layers present in each encoder sublayer allow for a mixing of the elements of each input vector, and therefore a mixing of the original channels. In order to obtain a single feature vector per sleep epoch, the output of the intra-epoch encoder layer passes through an average pooling layer. The resulting L epoch feature vectors are then fed through another positional encoding layer, followed by an inter-epoch encoder.

Only the output vector corresponding to the central sleep epoch is preserved, passing through two fully connected layers, each followed by a ReLU activation and a dropout layer. A final fully connected "classification" layer reduces the output to the desired 5 data points (one per class), and this classification is then fed to a softmax-including cross-entropy loss function.

We optimize this model using the Adam algorithm, with the function parameters β_1, β_2 and ϵ set to 0.9, 0.999 and 10^{-7} respectively. The weight decay is a hyperparameter, and so are the model's learning rate λ and the corresponding exponential decay parameter γ_λ.

Our architecture can be seen in Fig. 1. The number of sublayers and attention heads of each encoder, the size of parameter tensors for the fully connected layers and the various dropout probabilities are all hyperparameters. Our hyperparameter-obtaining strategy is described in Sect. 4.2 , and the obtained values are presented in the annex.

4   Experiments

4.1   Dataset Used

We chose to validate our model on the SS3 subset of the Montreal Archive of Sleep Studies (MASS) dataset [9], as it is heavily utilized within the SOA and contains a large number of electrodes to choose from for our analysis. Said subset is made up of 62 subjects, with a single full-night recording per subject and 20 EEG channels in common. Each EEG signal went through a notch filter at 60 Hz as well as a lowpass and highpass filter with cutoff frequencies of 0.30 Hz and 100 Hz respectively. This dataset is unbalanced, with the largest and smallest classes (N2 and N1) respectively containing 50.24% and 8.16% of its sleep epochs.

In order to capture a significant range of signals, and to limit redundancy between neighboring electrodes, we chose electrodes F3, F4, C3, C4, T3, T4, O1 and O2. This selection has a relatively homogeneous distribution with regards to the cranium, with inter-hemispheric symmetry to capture relevant variations along that axis. All of these signals are captured with a common reference electrode, located behind the left ear.

4.2   Model Validation

As is best practice, we subdivide our database into three subsets: training, validation and test. We utilize a k-fold cross-validation scheme, using the same fold-wise subset separation as Seo et al. [15] in order to facilitate comparisons. Each of the $k = 31$ folds are divided into 50, 10 and 2 recordings for each training, validation and testing set respectively. The 31 folds' testing sets add up to the 62 recordings in SS3, with no overlap. We set the parameter l of our network to 10, as is done in [14]. We rebalance each fold's training set through oversampling, with each class having as many elements as N2 has. The validation and test sets aren't rebalanced, though test sets are further restricted (Sect. 4.3).

Every hyperparameter research is ran using the Tree-structured Parzen Estimator algorithm [3], as implemented by Optuna [1]. This research is done on the same randomly selected fold. The best hyperparameters are then utilized to train the model on all folds. We use the macro-averaged F1 score (MF1) as our main performance statistic, as it reflects imbalances in class-wise classification performance, and is widely used throughout the SOA. All statistics are summarized over the 31 folds by computing their mean and standard deviation.

Table 2. Ablation study and comparison to the SOA.

	Method	Balanced statistics		Unbalanced statistics	
		MF1	Macro accuracy	General accuracy	Kappa
0	SleepTrans. [14]	73.97 ± 3.50	76.37 ± 4.35	81.25 ± 3.54	0.722 ± 0.046
1	IITNet [15]	78.48 ± 3.15	**81.88 ± 2.89**	83.90 ± 3.03	0.763 ± 0.043
2	DeepSleepNet [16]	78.14 ± 4.12	80.05 ± 3.47	84.81 ± 3.70	0.773 ± 0.052
3	GraphSleepNet [8]	75.58 ± 3.75	79.75 ± 3.41	80.97 ± 4.35	0.724 ± 0.057
4	Our method	**79.78 ± 4.56**	81.76 ± 4.61	**85.05 ± 4.97**	**0.776 ± 0.069**
5	No covariance	77.39 ± 5.82	79.76 ± 4.95	82.61 ± 6.01	0.741 ± 0.081
6	No side vectors	78.14 ± 4.10	80.56 ± 3.95	83.38 ± 4.16	0.753 ± 0.060

Table 3. F1 scores per class.

	Method	N3 F1	N2 F1	N1 F1	REM F1	Wake F1
0	[14]	74.26 ± 12.36	86.72 ± 3.28	47.60 ± 6.37	83.84 ± 6.99	77.40 ± 8.63
1	[15]	**81.97 ± 8.91**	88.15 ± 2.84	56.01 ± 6.54	85.14 ± 5.64	81.11 ± 8.49
2	[16]	80.38 ± 9.35	**89.25 ± 3.12**	53.52 ± 8.24	86.67 ± 5.34	80.86 ± 9.04
3	[8]	74.77 ± 12.12	84.84 ± 4.22	50.80 ± 8.06	85.09 ± 7.38	82.42 ± 7.43
4	Ours	78.17 ± 11.49	88.66 ± 4.59	**58.43 ± 6.41**	**86.91 ± 7.79**	**86.73 ± 6.42**

4.3 Reproducing the State of the Art

In order to compare our results to the State of the Art, we selected four approaches. hree of those are DeepSleepNet [16], often used as a benchmark, IITNet [15], whose cross-validation folds we are using, and GraphSleepNet [8], which also analyses functional connectivity. The fourth, SleepTransformer [14], shall be discussed subsequently.

All three have their code available on GitHub, and were trained on MASS SS3 in their respective papers. IITNet, GraphSleepNet and DeepSleepNet use sequences of epochs as inputs, of size equal to 10, 5 and 25 respectively. Like us (Sect. 3.2), IITNet and GraphSleepNet use each sequence to classify a single epoch, respectively the last and central epoch of the sequence. In contrast, DeepSleepNet outputs one classification per epoch in their sequences, which are constructed without overlap. Because of this, for each recording, IITNet won't classify the first 9 epochs, GraphSleepNet will ignore the first and last 2, and DeepSleepNet might ignore up to 24 epochs at the end.

All three models use a similar results aggregation strategy. For each fold, the best trained parameters are used to compute predictions on the test set. Despite originating from different models, these predictions are concatenated, and statistics are computed over this unified predictions tensor. As the number of sleep epochs per recording is not homogeneous, neither are the test sets. This strategy therefore results in an implicit weighting effect, giving more importance to sets of parameters computed on folds with larger test sets.

In order to better compare these methods to our model, we retrained these models with our metrics, folds, and results summarizing methods (Sect. 4.2). All methods were adapted to select their best fold learned parameters through their validation MF1 score. In the spirit of fairness, we rebalanced GraphSleepNet and IITNet's training sets through oversampling. DeepSleepNet already does this when pretraining its intra-epoch submodel, and its multi-label sequences can't be rebalanced in that way. We did not change any of their model architectures, and used their published hyperparameters.

The fourth SOA method presented is our reimplementation of the original SleepTransformer model. Compared to our model, this method uses a custom attention softmax layer instead of our average pooling. We also replicated their preprocessing using a recombined Fz-Cz signal from MASS SS3. It was trained with our methodology, including a hyperparameter research.

The obtained results (Tables 2 and 3) differ from those originally published, which may stem for the aforementioned methodological differences. To harmonize all test sets, we have elected to exclude the classification of the first and last 24 epochs of each recording. The training or validation sets remain, however, unchanged. This has been applied to all results presented in this paper.

4.4   Analysis of Results

Aside from lines 1, 2 and 3 of Tables 2 and 3, all presented results are preceded by a hyperparameter research.

Line 0 of Tables 2 and 3 show us the results obtained through our reimplementation of SleepTransformer. As we can see, they are the lowest of all presented methods. Due to the similarities between our approaches, one might view these as the baseline for our architecture's performance.

As stated in Sect. 3.2, we tested multiple side vector types in our hyperparameter research. The one that consistently performed the best was the vector of mean PSDs. The other chosen hyperparameters are described in the annex.

The last 3 lines of Table 2 give an overview of the obtained results. Line 4 corresponds to our results, trained on the best hyperparameters mentioned above. A surprising hyperparameter is the value of α (Sect. 3.1) of 99.53. This implies that the side vectors have a large impact on the final classification, and thus that our network favors a signal-specific input (one not obtained through covariance). To assess the relevance of covariances altogether, we removed all covariance information from our data (i.e. the non-diagonal elements of the covariance matrices), and reran our model. As seen in line 5 of Table 2, all statistics but Kappa are lower than the ones of line 4 by about 2%. This is coherent with the literature, as decent performances have been obtained on MASS without relying on covariations. We also trained our model on the original covariance matrices themselves, with no side vector augmentation (as seen in line 6). We obtain similar results to line 4 and superior results to line 5, thus implying that considering covariations adds a net benefit.

When it comes to the rest of the reran State of the Art, lines 1 through 4 of Table 2 shows that our model performs better in all measured metrics except for macro-averaged accuracy, where we are a close second. In addition, Table 3 shows that our method outperforms the others in REM, Wake and N1 sleep classification. As seen by the scores and standard deviations, though, the quality of predictions varies much per class, for both the State of the Art and us. In particular, N1 sleep epochs seem particularly hard to classify, but our method shows a two points lead over the next best one in that regard. This lead would explain our ranking in terms of MF1 score (Table 2).

All-in-all, Tables 2 and 3 show that a method based in part on covariance information provides results either equivalent or superior to the State of the Art on this problem (relative to the chosen statistics), with notable improvements to performance on the N1 stage, though it also benefits from signal-specific inputs.

5   Conclusion

We have presented our novel approach for automatic scoring of sleep stages through an analysis of the covariations between EEG signals. Motivated by the high imbalance between the classification of said stages, we established a fairer methodology for training and validating models on this problem. The results validate our hypothesis on the relevance of such covariations in this context, and by extension, that of functional connectivity.

Appendix

The hyperparameters corresponding to the best version of our model are:
Side vectors: PSD; α: 99.53; intra-epoch encoder: 5 sublayers, 15 attention heads, fully connected components of size 1024, dropout of 6.2×10^{-5}; intra-epoch encoder: 6 sublayers, 5 attention heads, fully connected components of size 256, dropout of 8.1×10^{-3}; final fully connected layers: of size 2048, dropout of 1.4×10^{-3}; learning rate (λ): 4.9×10^{-5}, γ_λ at 0.94; weight decay at 1.76×10^{-6}.

Many thanks to Huy Phan [11–14] for answering all our questions.

References

1. Akiba, T., Sano, S., Yanase, T., Ohta, T., Koyama, M.: Optuna: a next-generation hyperparameter optimization framework. In: Proceedings of the 25th ACM SIGKDD International Conference on Knowledge Discovery & Data Mining, pp. 2623–2631 (2019)

2. Arsigny, V., Fillard, P., Pennec, X., Ayache, N.: Log-euclidean metrics for fast and simple calculus on diffusion tensors. Magn. Reson. Med. **56**(2), 411–421 (2006)
3. Bergstra, J., Bardenet, R., Bengio, Y., Kégl, B.: Algorithms for hyper-parameter optimization. In: Advances in Neural Information Processing Systems, vol. 24 (2011)
4. Berry, R.B., et al.: AASM scoring manual updates for 2017 (version 2.4) (2017)
5. Bouchard, M., Lina, J.M., Gaudreault, P.O., Dubé, J., Gosselin, N., Carrier, J.: EEG connectivity across sleep cycles and age. Sleep **43**(3) (2019)
6. Eickhoff, S., Müller, V.: Functional connectivity. In: Toga, A.W. (ed.) Brain Mapping, pp. 187–201. Academic Press, Waltham (2015)
7. Jia, Z., et al.: Multi-view spatial-temporal graph convolutional networks with domain generalization for sleep stage classification. IEEE Trans. Neural Syst. Rehabil. Eng. **29**, 1977–1986 (2021)
8. Jia, Z., et al.: Graphsleepnet: adaptive spatial-temporal graph convolutional networks for sleep stage classification. In: IJCAI, pp. 1324–1330 (2020)
9. O'reilly, C., Gosselin, N., Carrier, J., Nielsen, T.: Montreal archive of sleep studies: an open-access resource for instrument benchmarking and exploratory research. J. Sleep Res. **23**(6), 628–635 (2014)
10. Pennec, X., Fillard, P., Ayache, N.: A riemannian framework for tensor computing. Int. J. Comput. Vision **66**(1), 41–66 (2006)
11. Phan, H., Chén, O.Y., Tran, M.C., Koch, P., Mertins, A., De Vos, M.: Xsleepnet: multi-view sequential model for automatic sleep staging. IEEE Trans. Pattern Anal. Mach. Intell. **44**(9), 5903–5915 (2022)
12. Phan, H., et al.: L-seqsleepnet: whole-cycle long sequence modelling for automatic sleep staging (2023)
13. Phan, H., Mikkelsen, K.: Automatic sleep staging of EEG signals: recent development, challenges, and future directions. Physiol. Meas. **43**(4), 04TR01 (2022). https://doi.org/10.1088/1361-6579/ac6049
14. Phan, H., Mikkelsen, K., Chén, O.Y., Koch, P., Mertins, A., De Vos, M.: Sleeptransformer: automatic sleep staging with interpretability and uncertainty quantification. IEEE Trans. Biomed. Eng. **69**(8), 2456–2467 (2022)
15. Seo, H., Back, S., Lee, S., Park, D., Kim, T., Lee, K.: Intra- and inter-epoch temporal context network (IITNET) using sub-epoch features for automatic sleep scoring on raw single-channel eeg. Biomed. Signal Process. Control **61**, 102037 (2020)
16. Supratak, A., Dong, H., Wu, C., Guo, Y.: Deepsleepnet: a model for automatic sleep stage scoring based on raw single-channel eeg. IEEE Trans. Neural Syst. Rehabil. Eng. **25**(11), 1998–2008 (2017)
17. Supratak, A., Guo, Y.: Tinysleepnet: an efficient deep learning model for sleep stage scoring based on raw single-channel EEG. In: 2020 42nd Annual International Conference of the IEEE Engineering in Medicine Biology Society (EMBC), pp. 641–644 (2020)
18. Vaswani, A., et al.: Attention is all you need. In: Guyon, I., et al. (eds.) Advances in Neural Information Processing Systems, vol. 30. Curran Associates, Inc. (2017)
19. Yger, F., Berar, M., Lotte, F.: Riemannian approaches in brain-computer interfaces: a review. IEEE Trans. Neural Syst. Rehabil. Eng. **25**(10), 1753–1762 (2017)
20. Yger, F., Sugiyama, M.: Supervised logeuclidean metric learning for symmetric positive definite matrices (2015)
21. Zhu, T., Luo, W., Yu, F.: Convolution-and attention-based neural network for automated sleep stage classification. Int. J. Environ. Res. Public Health **17**(11), 4152 (2020)

A Complete AI-Based System for Dietary Assessment and Personalized Insulin Adjustment in Type 1 Diabetes Self-management

Maria Panagiotou[1], Ioannis Papathanail[1], Lubnaa Abdur Rahman[1], Lorenzo Brigato[1], Natalie S. Bez[2], Maria F. Vasiloglou[1], Thomai Stathopoulou[1], Bastiaan E. de Galan[3,4,5], Ulrik Pedersen-Bjergaard[6,7], Klazine van der Horst[2], and Stavroula Mougiakakou[1(✉)]

[1] University of Bern, Bern, Switzerland
{maria.panagiotou,ioannis.papathanail,stavroula.mougiakakou}@unibe.ch
[2] Bern University of Applied Sciences, Bern, Switzerland
[3] Department of Internal Medicine, Maastricht University Medical Centre+, Maastricht, The Netherlands
[4] CARIM School for Cardiovascular Diseases, Maastricht University, Maastricht, The Netherlands
[5] Department of Internal Medicine, Radboud University Medical Centre, Nijmegen, The Netherlands
[6] Nordsjællands Hospital Hillerød, University of Copenhagen, Hillerød, Denmark
[7] Department of Clinical Medicine, University of Copenhagen, Copenhagen, Denmark

Abstract. People living with type 1 diabetes (PwT1D) face multiple challenges in self-managing their blood glucose levels, including the need for accurate carbohydrate counting, and the requirements of adjusting insulin dosage. Our paper aims to alleviate the demands of diabetes self-management by developing a complete system that employs computer vision to estimate the carbohydrate content of meals and utilizes reinforcement learning to personalize insulin dosing. Our findings demonstrate that this system results in a significantly greater percentage of time spent in the target glucose range compared to the combined standard bolus calculator treatment and carbohydrate counting. This approach could potentially improve glycaemic control for PwT1D and reduce the burden of carbohydrate and insulin dosage estimations.

Keywords: Diabetes · Computer Vision · Reinforcement Learning · Dietary Assessment · Deep Learning

1 Introduction

Diabetes is a chronic metabolic disorder caused by insulin deficiency that is either absolute (type 1 diabetes - T1D) or relative to the level of insulin resistance

---

M. Panagiotou and I. Papathanail—Authors contributed equally to this work.

N. Tsapatsoulis et al. (Eds.): CAIP 2023, LNCS 14185, pp. 77–86, 2023.
https://doi.org/10.1007/978-3-031-44240-7_8

(type 2 diabetes - T2D). Effective diabetes management is essential to prevent the risk of both glucose excursions (i.e., hypo- and hyperglycaemia) and long-term vascular complications (e.g., retinopathy, nephropathy, and cardiovascular disease events) by controlling the blood glucose (BG) concentration [4].

To manage diabetes and prevent the onset of diabetes-related complications, people with diabetes (PwD) need to monitor their BG levels carefully and maintain them within a target range, which requires estimation of the optimal insulin dose. The amount of prandial insulin dose depends, among others, on the consumed meal's carbohydrate (CHO) content [25]. However, the CHO estimation is challenging even for PwD trained in CHO counting. Previous studies [1,5] showed that using automated meal estimation systems based on Artificial Intelligence (AI) improved glycaemic control in PwD. However, no study has introduced a complete system for insulin adjustment in the case of Multiple Daily Injections (MDI) therapy using Self-Monitoring Blood Glucose (SMBG) measurements and an AI-based dietary assessment system for the translation of food images into CHO content.

Hence, our main contribution is a complete system composed of two AI-based modules: 1) goFOOD^{TM}, for estimating the food's CHO content based on captured food images, and 2) Adaptive Basal-Bolus Advisor (ABBA), for the daily, personalized adjustment of both basal and bolus insulin administration. These two modules' previous versions were published in [17,27]. This work improves the glycaemic control of PwD by utilizing a system that incorporates the food's nutrient composition and insulin without relying on the person's skills in CHO estimation.

2   Related Work

2.1   Computer Vision in Dietary Assessment

Typically, automatic dietary assessment systems consist of three stages: 1) food segmentation, 2) food recognition, and 3) food volume estimation and nutrient/ calorie calculation. Convolutional Neural Networks (CNNs) are becoming more and more popular for the first two steps of the pipeline, i.e., segmentation [20,31] and recognition [17,19,21] since they outperform classical machine learning (ML) methods [3,12,22]. A plethora of different approaches can be used for the volume estimation step. Geometry-based estimation is performed from single images if a depth sensor is available [14,20,28] or multiple images, otherwise [8,17]. Learning-based methods have also been proposed [16,18]. However, generalization issues usually make them less effective than geometry-based methods.

2.2   Reinforcement Learning in Blood Glucose Control

Over the last few years, several Reinforcement Learning (RL) approaches have been proposed for the personalized adjustment of insulin intake. Most of them rely on Continuous Glucose Monitor (CGM) data and pump therapy. For instance, Zhu et al. proposed a deep-Q learning agent to predict the basal insulin value [32] and a DDPG-based Actor-Critic (AC) model for insulin bolus control, which also supports MDI therapy [33]. In [10], authors proposed a Q-learning approach to optimize CHO ratios and the basal rate adaptively. Recent work [15] combined evolutionary, deep-Q learning, AC, and uncertainty estimation algorithms to modulate insulin sensitivity and Carbohydrate-to-Insulin Ratio (CIR) for meal boluses and reference basar rate both pump therapy and insulin pen. Pioneering work [6] proposed an AC method initialized with information transferred from insulin to glucose signals. Sun et al. [26] extended and further validated the latter algorithm, while in [27], the authors used SMBG measurements and MDI therapy instead of CGM data and pump therapy.

3 Methodology

3.1 System Outline

The proposed system presented in Fig. 1 combines a computer vision-based module for food nutrient estimation and an RL algorithm for personalised insulin adjustment, respectively named goFOOD^{TM} and ABBA. goFOOD^{TM} receives two meal images from different angles, guided by the system, as input and estimates its nutrient content. The pipeline for this module is as follows: 1) segmentation of the different food items, 2) recognition of each food item, and 3) volume estimation using two food images (and in the case of Android phones, a reference card placed near the food) and CHO calculation based on open access food composition databases. For the output of the recognition algorithm, we choose the ground truth class out of the top-3 predicted classes based on the assumption that the user could select it. The CHO estimation of goFOOD^{TM} is then used as input for the RL-based algorithm, ABBA, that suggests the insulin dosage for the PwD. The ABBA algorithm is based on an AC, model-free, self-learning algorithm that adjusts the CIR and the basal insulin values. The two modules are described in detail in the next section.

3.2 Computer Vision Module

For the segmentation module, we selected a state-of-the-art segmentation network (Mask R-CNN) [9]. Since large open-source segmentation datasets are scarce, we trained the network to perform a binary segmentation task of food items versus background. Segmented food items are then fed into a recognition network that predicts the food/drink class in three layers: coarse, middle, and fine (e.g., meat/red meat/meatball). Since the training classification dataset contains label noise, we selected a noise-robust approach to train the network and make accurate predictions. For this reason, we used the noisy label learning method DivideMix [13], which is also proven to work well with food images [21]. The selected classification network architecture is a RegNetY-16GF [23].

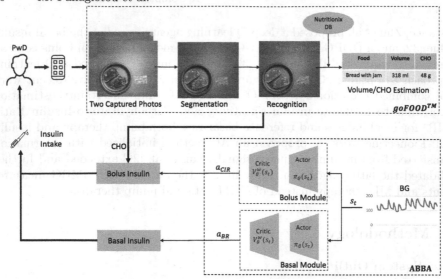

Fig. 1. Complete System Pipeline using Android Technology

The volume estimation module employs the stereo matching process whereby we use two images, with both the meal and a reference card placed in the field of view, captured at different angles (90° and 75°), same as in [17]. If equipped with an iPhone[1], users can capture a stereo pair of images without needing a reference card. The images are rectified based on key points obtained from the detected reference card and the predicted segmentation mask. Using this method, we attempt to solve the need for having the food items placed on a plate, a major limitation in previous works [5,11]. A disparity map is then produced for each food item which is re-projected to a 3D point cloud, followed by outlier removal. The food volume and, thus, the nutrient content of the meal is then calculated based on our nutrient content database, which we aggregated from Nutritionix[2] and AcquaCalc[3].

3.3 Reinforcement Learning Module

As mentioned, the proposed RL algorithm is an extension of previously published work [26,27]. The original AC basal-bolus advisor updates the CIR and basal insulin values at the end of each day, according to the daily glycaemic profile collected from the previous day. Differently, our approach aims to adjust the CIR and the basal insulin based on the BG measurement before each meal and bedtime. Another improvement of our approach consists of training only two models (i.e., one for basal and bolus) rather than four (i.e., one for basal and for each meal). Having a generalized bolus predictor enables the PwD to have more than three main meals with insulin injection.

---

[1] Models with dual camera.
[2] https://www.nutritionix.com/natural-demo.
[3] https://www.aqua-calc.com/calculate/food-volume-to-weight.

The state vector contains features computed similarly to [26]. As an extension, we add the difference between the BG levels of the previous bedtime and the current morning to the basal state. Furthermore, we add a bias parameter to the actor parameter vector θ and an additional dimension featuring a unit to the bolus state. To ensure that the final decision of the policy is safe for the PwD, we introduced a safety rule such that the basal insulin and CIR rate change does not exceed $\pm 40\%$ of the initial CIR and basal insulin and $\pm 25\%$ of the previous CIR and basal insulin. The initial values are defined from the simulator and are increased by 10% [27]. We also implemented a custom version of the reward function originally introduced in [32]. We adjusted the thresholds of the step-like reward function after empirical investigations to improve performance. We simplify the actor control policy P_e, originally defined in [26], as $P_e = P_a + \epsilon$, where $\epsilon = 0.05 \cdot ||F_k||^2 \cdot \mathcal{N}(0, 1)$ is the exploration and $P_a = s_t \cdot \theta_t$ is the control action policy. For the initialization of the policy parameter vector we calculate the transfer entropy similar in [7].

4 Experimental Setup

4.1 Food-Related Datasets

To train the segmentation network, images from publicly available and in-house food datasets were collected and segmented as food and non-food (background). For the training of the classification network, we gathered more than 175,000 web-crawled images or images from publicly available datasets belonging to 18 coarse, 34 middle, and 298 fine categories. Therefore, the classification training dataset contains natural label noise (i.e., some food labels are incorrect).

To evaluate our complete system, we employed meal images that were previously collected in a study[4] where 50 participants from the general population had to use the goFOOD^{TM}Lite app [29] under real-life conditions (e.g., varying lighting and distance from the food, blurriness, etc.) to record their meals for one day. We collected approximately 800 meal images, and the involved dietitians performed the 24-hour recall to estimate the users' nutrient intake. We refer to this collection as the Swiss Real Life 2022 dataset (*SwissReLi2022*).

To test the segmentation and recognition modules, we merged the *SwissReLi2022* and part of another dataset [2].

4.2 In Silico Environment

The DMMS.R simulator, which offers multiple in silico subject populations, including T1D, T2D, and Pre-Diabetes cohorts, was utilized to evaluate the developed algorithmic approach[5]. Specifically, we used a T1D cohort of 11 virtual adults using SMBG measurements and MDI therapy provided by the simulator. BG levels were measured using the virtual SMBG device, while long-acting and rapid-acting insulin was used to simulate insulin treatment for insulin pen users.

---

[4] "Nutritional assessment: comparison between an automated tool (goFOOD^{TM}) and conventional methods" - Number: 2020-00419.

[5] https://tegvirginia.com/software/dmms-r.

4.3 Scenario

A two-week scenario is designed for testing the complete system. We randomly selected 24 images from the *SwissReLi2022*, 6 for each meal tag (breakfast, lunch, dinner, and snack). We then generated a sequence of meals for two weeks, with four meals per day. We used the dietitian's dietary assessment based on 24h-recall as the reference. However, even though the 24-hour recall is considered the gold standard, it still can lack accuracy, as it has been shown from previous studies, where the misestimation of the dietitians was approximately 15 g of CHO [30]. The meals were announced 5 min before the injection, and the meal duration was 15 min. In addition, similar to [26,27], we simulate the inter-day variability of insulin sensitivity (SI) with a uniformly distributed variability of ±25% and the "dawn phenomenon". We used a bolus advisor (BA) [25] along with the basal rate provided by the simulator as a baseline method to compare our RL algorithm.

We tested two versions of goFOOD^{TM}. The full version outputs the amount of the CHO of the meal, and the goFOOD^{TM}Mini version outputs a label depending on the CHO size. In particular, the final estimation of goFOOD^{TM}Mini has five categorical levels: Extra Small ($CHO < 10$ g), Small (10 g $\leq CHO \leq 40$ g), Medium (40 g $< CHO < 70$ g), Large (70 g $\leq CHO \leq 100$ g), Extra Large ($CHO > 100$ g) as suggested by healthcare professionals. The algorithm does not suggest an insulin dose when the CHO is less than 10 g.

We evaluated six complete systems made of the following modules, BA or ABBA for insulin advisor and simulated PwT1D misestimations, goFOOD^{TM}Mini, or goFOOD^{TM} for the CHO estimation, as seen in Table 1. In particular, for the CHO misestimations of PwT1D, we used a mean absolute percentage error of a 35% based on a study where PwT1D were randomly selected, without documented CHO counting training [24].

5   Results

5.1 Complete System

To assess the effectiveness of the proposed system and compare it to the baseline method, we utilized four widely-used glycemic metrics commonly employed in the diabetes technology community. These metrics are as follows: percentage time in the glucose target range of 70–180 mg/dL (TIR), percentage time below 70 mg/dL (TBR), percentage time above 180 mg/dL (TAR), and units of Total Daily Insulin (TDI) Dose. Results are expressed by mean values from the 11 virtual adults.

Table 1 shows the performance of the proposed system on the 11 adult virtual cohort. We observe that ABBA achieves a higher TIR and lower TBR than BA in all the cases. Moreover, goFOOD^{TM} performs significantly better than both goFOOD^{TM}Mini and the simulated PwT1D. The TDI is also lowest when using both goFOOD^{TM} and ABBA, meaning that the PwT1D need to inject less insulin. To summarize, combining the two proposed modules offers the best BG control, high ease-of-use since the PwT1D do not need to manually estimate the CHO content of their meals.

Table 1. Performance of the proposed system on 11 adult virtual cohort. Statistical significance (t-test on two related samples) with a p-value less than 0.005 for the TIR is noted with *. (↑)/(↓) higher/lower is better.

Insulin Advisor	CHO Estimation	TIR (↑)	TAR (↓)	TBR (↓)	TDI (↓)
BA	Simulated PwT1D	71.70	**11.08**	17.35	36.45
ABBA	Simulated PwT1D	**75.66***	15.25	**9.09**	**26.05**
BA	goFOOD^{TM}Mini	72.35	17.14	10.5	35.67
ABBA	goFOOD^{TM}Mini	**79.88***	**14.5**	**5.56**	**26.03**
BA	goFOOD^{TM}	75.11	15.15	9.76	35.55
ABBA	goFOOD^{TM}	**86.30***	**11.04**	**2.67**	**25.74**

5.2   Computer Vision Module

We separately tested the segmentation network on the testing set and the classification network using the ground truth segmented items. The segmentation network achieved a mean average precision and an intersection over union of 65.15% and 82.66%, respectively. The classification network achieved a top-1/top-3 accuracy of 58.0/70.5%, 70.1/83.7%, and 78.4/88.2% outperforming the model without the noise-label approach that had an accuracy of 56.4/67.8%, 67.5/82.1%, and 75.6/86.3% for the fine, middle, and coarse categories, accordingly.

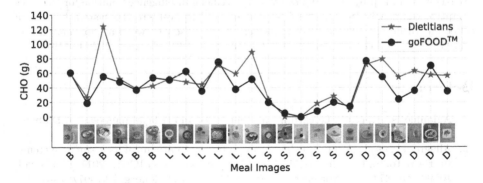

Fig. 2. CHO estimations from the dietitians and goFOOD^{TM} for the 24 meal images randomly selected from *SwissReLi2022*. Breakfast (B), Lunch (L), Snack (S), and Dinner (D) are the tags for the meal types.

In addition, we compared the complete dietary assessment pipeline, with the dietitians' estimations for the CHO content. Figure 2 shows the estimations for the 24 meals used in the scenario described in Sect. 4.1. In general, we observed that the CHO estimations of goFOOD^{TM} are very close to those of the dietitians achieving a mean absolute error of 13.96 g of CHO. There are few exceptions, e.g., the 3rd breakfast, where the segmentation module did not separate between the different bread slices, or the 6th lunch, where the recognition module did not properly recognize the different ingredients. Therefore, in these cases the system under-evaluated the volume of the food. Despite these misestimations, as seen in Table 1, the system consistently outperforms the simulated PwT1D. The ABBA algorithm, being personalized and adaptive, effectively handles these misestimations and surpasses the BA algorithm.

6   Conclusion

We present a complete AI-based system that automatically performs CHO estimation based on two meal images followed by insulin suggestion. The results are promising and show that the combination between the dietary assessment module and the automated insulin suggestion algorithm is significantly better than the baseline method. In future work, we plan to improve the system pipeline by allowing the user to manually change the predicted volume for the food items if unsatisfactory. Our framework could enhance the quality of life of PwT1D by offering personalized BG control and reduced time for CHO estimation and can potentially decrease therapy costs by reducing the amount of insulin needed. The proposed approach will be tested in a clinical trial involving adults and adolescents with T1D and adults with T2D.

Acknowledgements. This work was supported in part by the European Commission and the Swiss Confederation - State Secretariat for Education, Research and Innovation (SERI) within the project 101057730 Mobile Artificial Intelligence Solution for Diabetes Adaptive Care (MELISSA). The food images used to evaluate the system have been collected within the "Nutritional assessment: comparison between an automated tool (goFOOD^{TM}) and conventional methods" study (BASEC Number: 2020-00419).

References

1. Agianniotis, A., et al.: Gocarb in the context of an artificial pancreas. J. Diabetes Sci. Technol. **9**(3), 549–555 (2015)
2. Allegra, D., et al.: A multimedia database for automatic meal assessment systems. In: Battiato, S., Farinella, G.M., Leo, M., Gallo, G. (eds.) ICIAP 2017. LNCS, vol. 10590, pp. 471–478. Springer, Cham (2017). https://doi.org/10.1007/978-3-319-70742-6_46
3. Anthimopoulos, M.M., Gianola, L., Scarnato, L., Diem, P., Mougiakakou, S.G.: A food recognition system for diabetic patients based on an optimized bag-of-features model. IEEE J. Biomed. Health Inform. **18**(4), 1261–1271 (2014)
4. Association, A.D.: Diagnosis and classification of diabetes mellitus. Diabetes care **33**(Suppl._1), S62–S69 (2010)

5. Bally, L., et al.: Carbohydrate estimation supported by the gocarb system in individuals with type 1 diabetes: a randomized prospective pilot study. Diabetes Care **40**(2), e6–e7 (2017)
6. Daskalaki, E., Diem, P., Mougiakakou, S.G.: Personalized tuning of a reinforcement learning control algorithm for glucose regulation. In: 2013 35th Annual International Conference of the IEEE Engineering in Medicine and Biology Society (EMBC), pp. 3487–3490. IEEE (2013)
7. Daskalaki, E., Diem, P., Mougiakakou, S.G.: Model-free machine learning in biomedicine: feasibility study in type 1 diabetes. PLoS ONE **11**(7), e0158722 (2016)
8. Dehais, J., Anthimopoulos, M., Shevchik, S., Mougiakakou, S.: Two-view 3D reconstruction for food volume estimation. IEEE Trans. Multimedia **19**(5), 1090–1099 (2016)
9. He, K., Gkioxari, G., Dollár, P., Girshick, R.: Mask R-CNN. In: Proceedings of the IEEE International Conference on Computer Vision, pp. 2961–2969 (2017)
10. Jafar, A., El Fathi, A., Haidar, A.: Long-term use of the hybrid artificial pancreas by adjusting carbohydrate ratios and programmed basal rate: a reinforcement learning approach. Comput. Methods Programs Biomed. **200**, 105936 (2021)
11. Jia, W., Wu, Z., Ren, Y., Cao, S., Mao, Z.H., Sun, M.: Estimating dining plate size from an egocentric image sequence without a fiducial marker. Front. Nutr. **7**, 519444 (2021)
12. Kawano, Y., Yanai, K.: Foodcam: a real-time food recognition system on a smartphone. Multimedia Tools Appl. **74**, 5263–5287 (2015)
13. Li, J., Socher, R., Hoi, S.C.: Dividemix: learning with noisy labels as semi-supervised learning. arXiv preprint arXiv:2002.07394 (2020)
14. Lo, F.P.W., Sun, Y., Qiu, J., Lo, B.P.: Point2volume: a vision-based dietary assessment approach using view synthesis. IEEE Trans. Industr. Inf. **16**(1), 577–586 (2019)
15. Louis, M., Ugalde, I.R., Gauthier, P., Adenis, A., Tourki, Y., Huneker, E.: Safe reinforcement learning for automatic insulin delivery in type i diabetes. In: Reinforcement Learning for Real Life Workshop, NeurIPS 2022 (2022)
16. Lu, Y., Allegra, D., Anthimopoulos, M., Stanco, F., Farinella, G.M., Mougiakakou, S.: A multi-task learning approach for meal assessment. In: Proceedings of the Joint Workshop on Multimedia for Cooking and Eating Activities and Multimedia Assisted Dietary Management, pp. 46–52 (2018)
17. Lu, Y., et al.: goFOODTM: an artificial intelligence system for dietary assessment. Sensors **20**(15), 4283 (2020)
18. Meyers, A., et al.: Im2calories: towards an automated mobile vision food diary. In: Proceedings of the IEEE International Conference on Computer Vision, pp. 1233–1241 (2015)
19. Mezgec, S., Koroušić Seljak, B.: Nutrinet: a deep learning food and drink image recognition system for dietary assessment. Nutrients **9**(7), 657 (2017)
20. Papathanail, I., et al.: Evaluation of a novel artificial intelligence system to monitor and assess energy and macronutrient intake in hospitalised older patients. Nutrients **13**(12), 4539 (2021)
21. Papathanail, I., et al.: A feasibility study to assess mediterranean diet adherence using an AI-powered system. Sci. Rep. **12**(1), 17008 (2022)
22. Pouladzadeh, P., Kuhad, P., Peddi, S.V.B., Yassine, A., Shirmohammadi, S.: Food calorie measurement using deep learning neural network. In: 2016 IEEE International Instrumentation and Measurement Technology Conference Proceedings, pp. 1–6. IEEE (2016)

23. Radosavovic, I., Kosaraju, R.P., Girshick, R., He, K., Dollár, P.: Designing network design spaces. In: Proceedings of the IEEE/CVF Conference on Computer Vision and Pattern Recognition, pp. 10428–10436 (2020)
24. Rhyner, D., et al.: Carbohydrate estimation by a mobile phone-based system versus self-estimations of individuals with type 1 diabetes mellitus: a comparative study. J. Med. Internet Res. **18**(5), e101 (2016)
25. Schmidt, S., Nørgaard, K.: Bolus calculators. J. Diabetes Sci. Technol. **8**(5), 1035–1041 (2014)
26. Sun, Q., et al.: A dual mode adaptive basal-bolus advisor based on reinforcement learning. IEEE J. Biomed. Health Inform. **23**(6), 2633–2641 (2018)
27. Sun, Q., Jankovic, M.V., Mougiakakou, S.G.: Reinforcement learning-based adaptive insulin advisor for individuals with type 1 diabetes patients under multiple daily injections therapy. In: 2019 41st Annual International Conference of the IEEE Engineering in Medicine and Biology Society (EMBC), pp. 3609–3612. IEEE (2019)
28. Thames, Q., et al.: Nutrition5k: towards automatic nutritional understanding of generic food. In: Proceedings of the IEEE/CVF Conference on Computer Vision and Pattern Recognition, pp. 8903–8911 (2021)
29. Vasiloglou, M.F., et al.: The human factor in automated image-based nutrition apps: analysis of common mistakes using the gofood lite app. JMIR Mhealth Uhealth **9**(1), e24467 (2021)
30. Vasiloglou, M.F., et al.: A comparative study on carbohydrate estimation: gocarb vs. dietitians. Nutrients **10**(6), 741 (2018)
31. Wu, X., Fu, X., Liu, Y., Lim, E.P., Hoi, S.C., Sun, Q.: A large-scale benchmark for food image segmentation. In: Proceedings of the 29th ACM International Conference on Multimedia, pp. 506–515 (2021)
32. Zhu, T., Li, K., Herrero, P., Georgiou, P.: Basal glucose control in type 1 diabetes using deep reinforcement learning: an in silico validation. IEEE J. Biomed. Health Inform. **25**(4), 1223–1232 (2020)
33. Zhu, T., Li, K., Kuang, L., Herrero, P., Georgiou, P.: An insulin bolus advisor for type 1 diabetes using deep reinforcement learning. Sensors **20**(18), 5058 (2020)

COFI - Coarse-Semantic to Fine-Instance Unsupervised Mitochondria Segmentation in EM

Anusha Aswath[1][(✉)] , Ahmad Alsahaf[2] , B. Daan Westenbrink[3] ,
Ben N. G. Giepmans[2] , and George Azzopardi[1]

[1] Bernoulli Institute, University Groningen, Groningen, The Netherlands
a.aswath@rug.nl
[2] Department of Biomedical Sciences of Cells and Systems, University Medical Center Groningen, Groningen, The Netherlands
[3] Department of Cardiology, University Medical Center Groningen, Groningen, The Netherlands

Abstract. Instance segmentation is crucial for insightful analysis in the increasing use of large-scale electron microscopy (EM) to gain a better understanding of disease causes or progression. Instance segmentation is a more granular version of semantic segmentation, as it identifies and distinguishes individual object instances, whereas semantic segmentation only identifies object classes. In this study, we introduce a two-stage unsupervised approach called COFI, which stands for Coarse-Semantic to Fine-Instance segmentation, for the application of mitochondria segmentation in large-scale 2D EM images. In its first stage, it produces a rough region mask by clustering image patches and prompting a user to select the regions of interest. This is followed by a boundary delineation method based on the brain-inspired COSFIRE filter which is augmented by an inhibition component that makes it robust to image texture and noise. The effectiveness of the proposed COFI approach is evaluated on an EM dataset of the heart muscle of a mouse tissue, which consisted of four tiles of 16384×16384 pixels, containing a total of 2287 instances of mitochondria among other subcellular structures. It consistently achieved panoptic quality measures that are substantially superior to competing supervised methodologies. Besides its elevated effectiveness, the proposed COFI approach is conceptually simple and sufficiently versatile as the structure of interest is not intrinsic to the method.

Keywords: Instance segmentation · unsupervised · mitochondria

1 Introduction

Segmentation is an important step in the analysis of electron microscopy (EM) images in biology. Through segmentation, sub-cellular structures can be identified and labeled, which improves the biological understanding of the analyzed

N. Tsapatsoulis et al. (Eds.): CAIP 2023, LNCS 14185, pp. 87–97, 2023.
https://doi.org/10.1007/978-3-031-44240-7_9

samples. EM is increasingly being employed in large-scale biological initiatives, whether for volume imaging (3D EM) or large-area mapping (2D EM). In both methods, the goal to resolve nanoscale features (2–10 nm/pixel) is linked with the desire to set these findings in a larger context, which could be a large area or a 3D volume. High-throughput large-scale EM imaging is now possible due to enhanced automation that generates petabytes of image data [1,2]. Hence, there is a need for developing automatic tools for EM segmentation.

Large-scale 2D EM or nanotomy[1] provides an unbiased analysis of structures in EM images with the right cellular context [1]. We propose a new methodology for instance segmentation of mitochondria in 2D EM. Instance segmentation involves assigning each pixel to the correct class – mitochondria in this case – and identifying each component of that class as a separate instance. Figure 1 shows an example of a cropped region from an EM image with multiple mitochondria and corresponding ground truth maps of semantic, contour, and instance segmentation. Mitochondria are the primary energy providers for cell activities, thus essential for metabolism. Results of instance segmentation can be used to quantify morphological properties of mitochondria, which is not only crucial to basic research, but also informative to the clinical studies of several diseases.

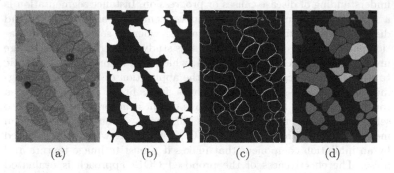

(a)   (b)   (c)   (d)

Fig. 1. Example of expected segmentation. (a) A region with apposing mitochondria, and the ground truth (b) semantic, (c) contour and (d) instance segmentation maps.

We propose a two-stage unsupervised pipeline. The first stage entails unsupervised semantic segmentation through clustering of overlapping patches using their feature embeddings encoded by a pre-trained network and prompting a user to select regions of interest among the resulting clusters. The second stage involves the COSFIRE filter approach with surround inhibition for edge delineation. It is inspired by simple cells of the mammalian visual cortex, and is robust to delineating edges and lines in the presence of texture [3].

---

[1] www.nanotomy.org.

2 Related Work

Previous methods for mitochondria segmentation have primarily used hand-crafted features [4] or those derived using supervised learning to encode images [5,6]. The success of encoder-decoder architectures such as FCN, U-Net, and DeepLabv3+ for semantic segmentation, has enabled pixel-wise classification of EM images. Relevant image regions can also be obtained using prior knowledge of an object's shape or texture through fragment matching. Due to its adaptability to noise and local variations, such methods are, however, more effective for image denoising and texture synthesis than pixel-based techniques. The work in [7] investigated a patch processing approach based on region homogeneity, utilizing CNNs as feature extractors and performing boundary refinement using watersheds. Boundary-based segmentation is a preferred technique for instance segmentation due to its ability to provide fine-grained results in combination with other techniques such as object proposals or region-based segmentation to improve performance. Instance segmentation of mitochondria was preferred with semantic region mapping and boundary prediction, in comparison with top-down approaches, as variability in their appearances, shape, and the presence of overlapping instances makes the use of object proposal networks impractical [8].

Manually marking ground truth in EM images is tedious, which makes supervised methods challenging. This may be addressed by transfer learning, which takes a supervised model that was pre-trained on a large dataset and fine-tunes it on a different dataset. Self-supervised learning has emerged as a label-free alternative to pre-training, utilizing a contrastive loss function to learn meaningful representations. It can achieve high accuracy in various downstream tasks through fine-tuning with a simple linear classification or an MLP head [9]. Pre-trained models for unlabeled EM data have become possible with the release of CEM1.5M, a large and diverse dataset that provides ample cellular context [10].

The brain-inspired COSFIRE filter approach that we use here has proven to be effective for unsupervised delineation of curvilinear structures in complex and noisy backgrounds. It achieves orientation selectivity by aggregating the collective responses of a set of difference-of-Gaussian functions that are linearly aligned in their areas of support [11]. This approach has demonstrated success in various applications, such as delineating blood vessels in retinal fundus images, roads and rivers from aerial images [12,13]. The COSFIRE model has been extended with push-pull inhibition [14] and surround suppression [3]. The push-pull inhibition is effective in suppressing high-frequency noise, while surround suppression inhibits responses in the neighbourhoods of dominant contours.

3 Method

The proposed COFI method comprises two components. First, it uses a pre-trained network to generate a rough object location map by clustering embeddings and selecting regions of interest. Then, the instance-level fine delineation is performed by the inhibition-augmented COSFIRE filter approach.

3.1   Dataset Description and Annotation

The proposed pipeline is evaluated on a nanotomy dataset of the heart muscle of a mouse tissue, which consisted of the four tiles shown in Fig. 2. Manual annotation of individual instances was a laborious task due to various factors such as high-resolution noise, image artifacts, surrounding structures with similar textures, and side-by-side mitochondria. Manual delineating all 2287 instances of mitochondria, took approximately 8 hours per tile, totaling four working days. The instance segmentation ground truth masks were obtained using the polygon tool of ImageJ [15] and were further proofread by biomedical experts.

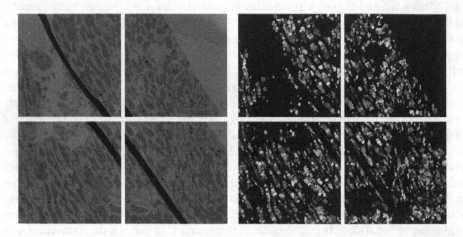

Fig. 2. EM data set used here. Left: Set of four 2D EM tiles of 16384×16384 pixels each at a resolution of $2.5\,\mathrm{nm/pixel}$. Right: Corresponding ground truth instance maps.

3.2   Coarse Semantic Segmentation

The first stage utilizes feature embeddings of image patches from networks pretrained using unsupervised contrastive learning. The contrastive loss function L compares pairs of image representations to separate representations from different images and brings together those from different views of the same image:

$$L = \frac{1}{2N} \sum_{i=1}^{N} \sum_{j=1}^{N} [y(i,j) \cdot d(f_i, f_j) + (1 - y(i,j)) \cdot \max(margin - d(f_i, f_j), 0)] \quad (1)$$

where N is the number of training samples, $y(i,j)$ is a flag indicating whether the pair of features (f_i, f_j) is from the same image $(y(i,j) = 1)$ or different images $(y(i,j) = 0)$, $d(f_i, f_j)$ is the distance between the features of images i and j (e.g., Euclidean distance), and $margin$ is a hyperparameter that controls the distance between features from different images.

We use 128×128 pixel-sized patches with 50% overlap to partition a given 2D EM image. These values are chosen as they provide a good tradeoff between information content and region homogeneity. The embeddings contain inherent distances that distinguish similar input image patches from dissimilar ones, which are then clustered using K-means into relevant regions. By using a graphical user interface, a biologist then manually selects the clusters that correspond to the regions of interest, i.e., those containing mitochondria. The output of this first component in our pipeline is a binary map that is produced by merging all patches that belong to the selected clusters[2], Fig. 3.

1. Encode input

2. Cluster patches

3. Select clusters

4. Coarse mask

Fig. 3. Coarse semantic segmentation. An encoder extracts features from input image patches followed by clustering and selection of clusters to produce the coarse mask.

3.3   Fine Instance Segmentation

Fine instance segmentation is achieved by simultaneously processing each connected component in the binary coarse semantic map. This part of our pipeline consists of the following steps: a) membrane delineation with the inhibition-augmented COSFIRE filter, b) watershed segmentation, and c) object selection.

A. Inhibition-Augmented COSFIRE Filter. A COSFIRE filter can be configured to be selective for any given pattern of interest. For this application, where the goal is to delineate boundaries, we configure a COSFIRE filter to be selective for lines. It takes input from a linearly aligned set of responses of a difference-of-Gaussians (DoG) filter. We denote by B a line-selective COSFIRE filter, which is defined as a set of 3-tuples:

$$B = \{(\sigma_i, \rho_i, \phi_i) \mid i = 1, \ldots, n\} \qquad (2)$$

where each tuple i indicates the distance ρ_i and the polar angle ϕ_i of the response of a DoG filter whose outer standard deviation is σ_i. The inner standard deviation of the DoG function is set to $0.5\sigma_i$. The COSFIRE filter's response $r_B(x, y)$ in a given (x, y) location is the geometric mean of the n DoG responses at the polar coordinates defined in B, with respect to (x, y). For a more in-depth

---

[2] Effectively, user selection of clusters can be assisted by cluster validity indices, in that the user gets automatic suggestions of which other clusters are mostly similar to the already selected ones.

explanation of the technical details and how COSFIRE filters achieve rotation-invariance, we refer the reader to [16].

COSFIRE filters can be augmented with surround suppression in the same way as originally proposed in [17]. This is needed here to accentuate the membranes while ignoring the inner cristae for the delineation of mitochondria. The surround inhibition term is computed for every (x, y) location by convolving a normalized center-off DoG function I_γ (γ denotes the standard deviation of the inner Gaussian function) with the COSFIRE response map r_B. Further to [3] the standard deviation of the outer Gaussian function is set to 4γ. Normalization of this DoG kernel consists of first applying the Heaviside step function, which maps all negative values to zero and all positive values to 1. Then all values of one are L_1-normalized such that their sum equals to 1. The final COSFIRE response map R is then achieved by the linear function:

$$R = r_B - \alpha r_{I_\gamma} \qquad (3)$$

where α denotes the inhibition strength. Figure 4 shows examples of COSFIRE response maps for different α values. The inhibition term suppresses responses to spurious strokes (i.e. cristae) in the surrounding of mitochondria walls.

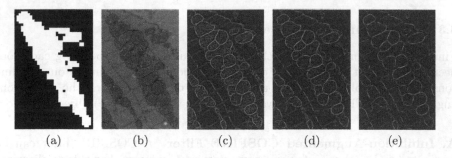

(a)   (b)   (c)   (d)   (e)

Fig. 4. Examples of boundary delineations with a COSFIRE filter. (a) A connected component from the coarse segmentation map, (b) the corresponding EM region, and COSFIRE response maps for (c) $\alpha = 0$, (d) $\alpha = 1$ and (e) $\alpha = 2$.

The response map R is transformed to a binary contour map by first thinning R with non-maximum suppression to obtain the ridges and then by applying hysteresis thresholding, which is characterized by the high t_h and low t_l threshold values. We keep t_h as a hyperparameter and set $t_l = 0.5t_h$.

B. Watershed Segmentation. First, the Euclidean distance map is computed from the thresholded COSFIRE binary map obtained above and all values below the mean distance are set to zero. The resulting thresholded distance map is used to generate the first watershed output (Fig. 5b). In the second stage, the ridges of the watershed output of the first stage are superimposed on the thresholded distance map (Fig. 5c) and used to generate the final watershed output (Fig. 5d).

C. Object Selection. First, the objects that fall outside the coarse semantic mask are removed. For the remaining components, we compute the contrast from the gray-level co-occurrence matrix (GLCM) determined from the corresponding intensity pixels of the input image and keep all objects with a contrast less than λ standard deviations from the mean.

4   Experiments and Results

We evaluate the performance of the proposed method in three different setups. The first two, which we denote by UG and US, use (U)nsupervised semantic segmentation with networks that are pre-trained on the (G)eneral ImageNet dataset [9] and on the (S)pecific CEM1.5M dataset [10] of EM images with many instances of mitochondria, respectively. For the third approach, denoted by SS, we replace the unsupervised stage with the state-of-the-art MitoNet, which is a (S)upervised ConvNet trained for (S)emantic segmentation of mitochondria. Finally, we compare the results of these three methods with the (S)supervised (I)nstance segmentation variant of MitoNet [18], denoted by SI.

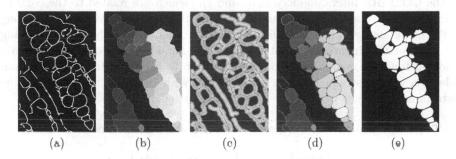

| (a) | (b) | (c) | (d) | (e) |

Fig. 5. Example of fine instance segmentation from a COSFIRE contour map. (a) COSFIRE binary map, which is used as input to the (b–d) watershed algorithm followed by (e) object selection to achieve the final instance segmentation.

Performance Measures. We measure two performance indicators, namely the global similarity measure Intersection-Over-Union (IoU) and the Panoptic Quality (PQ), which is a more detailed measure suitable for instance segmentation. IoU is the intersection between the predicted (PR) and ground truth (GT) masks divided by the union of the two masks, across all pixels in a given image. PQ unifies both segmentation and detection, making it a useful metric for cellular EM segmentation [19]. They are defined as:

$$IoU = \frac{PR \cap GT}{PR \cup GT} \tag{4}$$

$$PQ = \underbrace{\frac{\Sigma_{j \in TP} IoU(GT^j, PR^{j*})}{|TP|}}_{\text{Segmentation Quality (SQ)}} \times \underbrace{\frac{|TP|}{|TP| + \frac{1}{2}|FP| + \frac{1}{2}|FN|}}_{\text{Detection Quality (DQ)}} \tag{5}$$

where TP, FP, and FN stand for the number of true positive, false positive, and false negative objects, respectively. Following the mitochondria instance segmentation work in [8], we consider a mitochondrium as TP if it has at least 30% IoU overlap with a GT object. The FP and FN objects are the unmatched segments in PR and GT, respectively. $PR^{j,*}$ denotes the object in PR that is matched with the largest overlapping region (in IoU) with GT^j.

Experiments. Pre-trained encoders (ResNet50) of UG and US were applied to all 128×128 sized patches of the four tiles, which represented each of them with a 2048-element feature vector obtained from the last layer of the encoder. The vectors were then min-max normalized. Next, we applied truncated SVD to reduce the dimensions from 2048 to 1000, in order to enhance clustering effectiveness by eliminating noise and irrelevant features. These lower-dimensional vectors were then clustered using K-Means with $(K =)$ 10 clusters. Finally, three and four clusters, respectively, were selected for the UG and US methods by visually inspecting the clustering results.

For the second stage, we applied a grid search to fine-tune three parameters of the COSFIRE filters, namely σ, α, and t_H, which are related to the contour thickness, inhibition strength, and hysteresis thresholding, respectively, along with the parameter λ which we used in the object selection step. The fine-tuning was done on the single component shown in Fig. 4 and Fig. 5, which was randomly selected from the coarse semantic segmentation in the first stage. The random selection was constrained to pick a component with 10 to 20 mitochondria. The determined parameters are: $\sigma = 4$, $\alpha = 2$, $t_H = 0.6$, and $\lambda = 2.5$.

Table 1. Comparison of the coarse semantic segmentation outputs using IoU.

Method	Tile 1	Tile 2	Tile 3	Tile 4
UG	0.64	0.69	0.67	0.64
US	0.66	0.69	0.69	0.68
SS	0.81	0.84	0.81	0.83

Results. We report two sets of results. Table 1 presents the IoUs of the UG, US, and SS that measure the quality of the coarse semantic segmentation for each of the four tiles with respect to GT. The second set of results is illustrated in Fig. 6 shows PQ – the product of the segmentation quality (SQ) and detection quality (DQ) – that measures the quality of the final instance segmentation. The consistently high SQ of the UG, US, and SS methods is attributable to the precise delineation by the COSFIRE filter, which yields fine instance segmentation masks. The DQ metric indicates the effectiveness of detecting the right components. While our UG and US unsupervised variants achieve modest IoUs in the first stage due to under-segmentation, their final detection quality outperforms that of the supervised counterparts. Among them, the US approach achieves the best performance, which can be attributed to the fact that the underlying encoder was pre-trained on the dataset CEM1.5 of EM images.

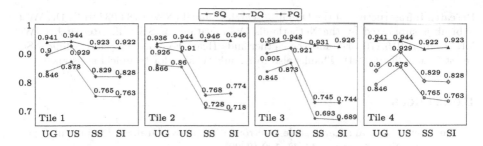

Fig. 6. Line plots of SQ, DQ, and PQ for all four tiles. The two unsupervised variants UG and US show consistent superiority over their supervised counterparts SS and SI.

5   Discussion and Conclusion

The results of the instance segmentation indicate that the proposed unsupervised variants, UG and US, of the COFI approach perform substantially better than the supervised approach despite having very coarse segmentation maps. This improvement is attributable to the COSFIRE operator, whose inhibition component makes it particularly effective in delineating the walls of apposing mitochondria in challenging backgrounds. The initial stage of the COFI method has the greatest influence on the detection quality (DQ). Any missing components from the first stage cannot be recovered by the COSFIRE filter in the second stage. It is also remarkable that for our images although the UG method uses an encoder that was pre-trained on ImageNet, it still yields very high results that come very close to the best results achieved with an encoder that was pre-trained on the more specific CEM1.5 dataset of EM images (US). To gain more insight, we augment the COSFIRE delineation operator with a supervised semantic segmentation approach (SS) based on MitoNet. The results show that the COSFIRE operator performs equally well as the supervised instance segmentation (SI) on MitoNet-based semantic maps.

The proposed COFI approach is unsupervised and versatile, in that the structure of interest (mitochondria here) is not an intrinsic component. The patch-based classification of high-resolution EM images provides the necessary redundancy to capture semantically important textured regions, which is then fine-tuned in the second stage by the COSFIRE filter. The COSFIRE filter with inhibition turned out to be very robust in delineating the mitochondria walls from the cristae within them. In future work, we will evaluate the proposed COFI approach on bigger datasets, other cellular tissues and different sub-cellular structures that are important for the study of biological processes.

Acknowlegements. This project has received funding from the Centre for Data Science and Systems Complexity at the University of Groningen (www.rug.nl/research/fse/themes/dssc/). Part of the work has been performed in the UMCG Microscopy and Imaging Center (UMIC), sponsored by ZonMW grant 91111.006 and the Netherlands Electron Microscopy Infrastructure (NEMI), NWO National Roadmap for Large-Scale

Research Infrastructure of the Dutch Research Council (NWO 184.034.014). Dr. Westenbrink is supported by the Netherlands Organisation for Scientific Research (NWO VENI, grant 016.176.147) and the Netherlands Heart Foundation Senior Clinical Scientist Grant (2019T064). Thanks also to Anouk Wolters for technical assistance.

References

1. de Boer, P., et al.: Large-scale electron microscopy database for human type 1 diabetes. Nat. Commun. **11**(1), 1–9 (2020)
2. Titze, B., Genoud, C.: Volume scanning electron microscopy for imaging biological ultrastructure. Biol. Cell **108**(11), 307–323 (2016)
3. Melotti, D., Heimbach, K., Rodríguez-Sánchez, A., Strisciuglio, N., Azzopardi, G.: A robust contour detection operator with combined push-pull inhibition and surround suppression. Inf. Sci. **524**, 229–240 (2020)
4. Lucchi, A., Li, Y., Fua, P.: Learning for structured prediction using approximate subgradient descent with working sets. In: Proceedings of the IEEE Conference on Computer Vision and Pattern Recognition, pp. 1987–1994 (2013)
5. Luo, Z., Wang, Y., Liu, S., Peng, J.: Hierarchical encoder-decoder with soft label-decomposition for mitochondria segmentation in EM images. Front. Neurosci. **15**, 687832 (2021)
6. Yuan, Z., Ma, X., Yi, J., Luo, Z., Peng, J.: HIVE-Net: centerline-aware hierarchical view-ensemble convolutional network for mitochondria segmentation in EM images. Comput. Methods Programs Biomed. **200**, 105925 (2021)
7. Oztel, I., Yolcu, G., Ersoy, I., White, T., Bunyak, F.: Mitochondria segmentation in electron microscopy volumes using deep convolutional neural network. In: 2017 IEEE International Conference on Bioinformatics and Biomedicine (BIBM), pp. 1195–1200. IEEE (2017)
8. Wei, D., et al.: MitoEM dataset: large-scale 3D mitochondria instance segmentation from EM images. In: Martel, A.L., et al. (eds.) MICCAI 2020. LNCS, vol. 12265, pp. 66–76. Springer, Cham (2020). https://doi.org/10.1007/978-3-030-59722-1_7
9. Chen, T., Kornblith, S., Swersky, K., Norouzi, M., Hinton, G.E.: Big self-supervised models are strong semi-supervised learners. Adv. Neural. Inf. Process. Syst. **33**, 22243–22255 (2020)
10. Conrad, R., Narayan, K.: CEM500K, a large-scale heterogeneous unlabeled cellular electron microscopy image dataset for deep learning. Elife **10**, e65894 (2021)
11. Azzopardi, G., Petkov, N.: A CORF computational model of a simple cell that relies on LGN input outperforms the gabor function model. Biol. Cybern. **106**, 177–189 (2012)
12. Azzopardi, G., Strisciuglio, N., Vento, M., Petkov, N.: Trainable COSFIRE filters for vessel delineation with application to retinal images. Med. Image Anal. **19**(1), 46–57 (2015)
13. Strisciuglio, N., Petkov, N.: Delineation of line patterns in images using B-COSFIRE filters. In: 2017 International Conference and Workshop on Bioinspired Intelligence (IWOBI), pp. 1–6. IEEE (2017)
14. Strisciuglio, N., Azzopardi, G., Petkov, N.: Robust inhibition-augmented operator for delineation of curvilinear structures. IEEE Trans. Image Process. **28**(12), 5852–5866 (2019)
15. Schneider, C.A., Rasband, W.S., Eliceiri, K.W.: NIH image to ImageJ: 25 years of image analysis. Nat. Methods **9**(7), 671–675 (2012)

16. Azzopardi, G., Rodríguez-Sánchez, A., Piater, J., Petkov, N.: A push-pull CORF model of a simple cell with antiphase inhibition improves snr and contour detection. PLoS ONE **9**(7), e98424 (2014)
17. Grigorescu, C., Petkov, N., Westenberg, M.: Contour detection based on nonclassical receptive field inhibition. IEEE Trans. Image Process. **12**(7), 729–739 (2003)
18. Conrad, R., Narayan, K.: Instance segmentation of mitochondria in electron microscopy images with a generalist deep learning model trained on a diverse dataset. Cell Syst. **14**(1), 58–71 (2023)
19. Kirillov, A., He, K., Girshick, R., Rother, C., Dollár, P.: Panoptic segmentation. In: Proceedings of the IEEE/CVF Conference on Computer Vision and Pattern Recognition, pp. 9404–9413 (2019)

Empirical Study of Attention-Based Models for Automatic Classification of Gastrointestinal Endoscopy Images

Ricardo Espantaleón-Pérez[1] , Isabel Jiménez-Velasco[1] ,
Rafael Muñoz-Salinas[1,2] , and Manuel J. Marín-Jiménez[1,2(✉)]

[1] Department of Computing and Numerical Analysis, University of Córdoba,
Córdoba, Spain
mjmarin@uco.es
[2] Maimonides Institute for Biomedical Research of Córdoba (IMIBIC),
Córdoba, Spain

Abstract. Automatic and accurate analysis of medical images is a subject of great importance in our current society. In particular, this work focuses on gastrointestinal endoscopy images, as the study of these images helps to detect possible health conditions in those regions. Published works on this topic mainly used traditional classification methods (e.g., Support Vector Machines) or more modern techniques, such as Convolutional Neural Networks. However, little attention has been paid to more recent approaches such as Transformers or, in general, Attention-based Deep Neural Networks. This work aims to evaluate the performance of state-of-the-art attention-based models on the problem of classification of gastrointestinal endoscopy images. The experimental results on the challenging Hyper-Kvasir dataset indicate that attention-based models achieve performance equal to or better than that obtained by previous models, needing fewer parameters. In addition, a new state of the art on Hyper-Kvasir (i.e., 0.636 F1-Macro) is obtained by the fusion of two MobileViT models with only 20M parameters. The source code will be published here: https://github.com/richardesp/Attention-based-models-for-Hyper-Kvasir/.

Keywords: Attention · Transformers · Endoscopy · Medical Image

1 Introduction

The analysis of gastrointestinal endoscopy images is of great importance for the accurate diagnosis and treatment of a wide range of gastrointestinal disorders. Endoscopy images provide clinicians with direct visual access to the inner surfaces of the gastrointestinal tract, enabling them to identify abnormalities

Supported by projects TED2021-129151B-I00/AEI/10.13039/ 501100011033/European Union NextGenerationEU/PRTR and PID2019-103871GB-I00 of the Spanish Ministry of Economy, Industry and Competitiveness.

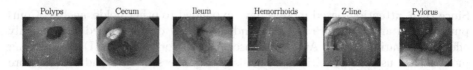

Fig. 1. Hyper-Kvasir dataset of annotated endoscopy images. Sample images belonging to six out of the 23 available classes.

such as ulcers, polyps, and tumors. The timely and accurate diagnosis of these abnormalities is crucial for effectively treating and preventing complications. The development of computer vision systems able to support the diagnosis of medical doctors is currently an important line of research [15].

In recent years, several approaches have addressed the problem of automatic classification of gastrointestinal endoscopy images. There are several works focused on the classification and segmentation of cancerous artifacts in the digestive tract, including polyps based on the quality of the present mucosa [3,4,14]. In turn, these types of models can serve as decision support for the timely detection of various gastric cancers [12]. These works use models mostly based on Convolutional Neural Networks with different levels of complexity, such as ResNet [3], DenseNet [3,16], MobileNet [9,19] or EfficientNet [10]. Despite these attempts, the problem of automatic classification of endoscopy images is far from solved.

From the computer vision viewpoint, in recent years, attention mechanisms have shown that image classification accuracy can be improved in several tasks [7], as they allow the models to focus on the most relevant parts of the image. In this work, we are interested in, on the one hand, investigating if models incorporating attention mechanisms are able to improve the classification performance on endoscopy images. And on the other hand, if it is possible to find a compact model, in terms of parameters, offering a good trade-off between accuracy and computational cost.

For this purpose, we have selected four families of state-of-the-art attention-based models (MobileViT, CoAtNet, CMT and DaViT) and the largest public dataset of endoscopy images, i.e., Hyper-Kvasir [3]. Then, the main contribution of this paper is an extensive evaluation of four types of attention-based models, with different levels of complexity, on the largest public annotated dataset of gastrointestinal endoscopy images, Hyper-Kvasir. The results of this study include a new state of the art on the classification task using a moderated number of model parameters (i.e., 20M using MobileViT models).

The rest of this paper is organized as follows. Section 2 presents the attention-based models evaluated in this study. Then, the dataset selected to perform the experiments is described in Sect. 3. The experimental results are presented in Sect. 4. And finally, the paper concludes in Sect. 5 including future research lines.

2   Attention-Based Models

Attention-based models initially emerged in the field of Natural Language Processing and were popularized by the success of models such as Transformer [17].

Since then, attention-based models have expanded to other fields, such as Computer Vision and Signal Processing, and have been demonstrated to be highly effective in various tasks. Attention-based models for vision are Deep Learning models that use the attention mechanism to process images and videos more effectively. Unlike traditional neural networks that process the entire image uniformly (treating all parts of the input sequence equally), attention-based models focus on specific parts of the image that are most relevant to the task at hand, focusing on a few specific aspects at a time and ignoring the rest. They do this by assigning different weights to each part of the image according to its importance to that task. This allows larger, more complicated tasks to be reduced to smaller, more manageable areas of attention to understand and process them sequentially. In this section, we will present the attention-based models for vision that have been selected for our experimental study.

2.1 MobileViT Family

MobileVit [13] is a family of computer vision models based on the Transformer (ViT) architecture [7] and characterized by their computational efficiency and their ability to process large-scale images. These models use attention blocks to process images as patches instead of traditional convolution. MobileVit models have been optimized for implementation on mobile devices, making them lighter and more efficient in terms of computational resources and memory consumption. Different versions of this architecture have been designed to suit different performance and size requirements. These models have been demonstrated to be very effective in various computer vision tasks, such as object detection and image classification. For the proposed study, two versions of the MobileViT architecture are used: the XS version of MobileViT, which has 2M of parameters, and a larger version with 18M of parameters.

2.2 CoAtNet

CoAtNet (Convolutional Attention Network) [5] is a deep neural network model that combines convolutions with attention mechanisms to take advantage of both in extracting features from images of different data sizes. The architecture uses cascaded attention blocks combined with convolutional layers to capture contextual and spatial features of images efficiently. Specifically, the architecture comprises parallel contextual attention blocks (CABs) and convolutional blocks. CAB blocks are responsible for extracting meaningful features from images using attention. One of the outstanding features of CoAtNet is its adaptive resizing mechanism, which automatically adjusts the input size to match the size required by the attention layers. This allows the model to process data of any input size without additional preprocessing.

2.3 CMT

CMT (CNNs meet Transformers) [11] is a deep neural network model applied to vision. It is a hybrid architecture incorporating transformer attention blocks into a standard convolutional network. The attention blocks are inserted into different layers of the CNN, allowing the model to capture both local and global features of the images. Attention is applied in parallel across channels, rows and columns, allowing the model to capture spatial and channel relationships at various scales. The idea behind CMT is to take advantage of the ability of convolutions to capture local patterns and the ability of transformer attention blocks to model long-distance relationships and nonlinear interactions between different features. In addition, CMT introduces an attention modulation technique to adapt attention based on local image features. This allows the model to adjust attention to specific regions of the image that are more relevant to the task at hand.

2.4 DaViT

DaViT (Dual Attention Vision Transformers) [6] is a deep learning model based on Vision Transformers(ViT) that uses two types of attention to improve performance in computer vision tasks: spatial attention and channel attention. Spatial attention refers to the model's ability to focus on specific regions of the image, which allows the model to pay more attention to important image features and ignore irrelevant features. Channel attention refers to the model's ability to focus on specific features in different layers of the neural network, which allows the model to learn to distinguish different types of features in the image. Compared to the ViT model, DaViT uses a dual-path structure in its architecture, allowing the model to capture global and local information from the image.

3 Dataset and Metrics

This section presents both the dataset used for performing our experimental study and the metrics used to compare the selected models (Sect. 2).

3.1 Hyper-Kvasir Dataset

The Hyper-Kvasir dataset [3] is currently the largest public dataset of colonoscopies in computer vision. It contains a total of 10,662 labeled images representing 23 different classes. Some example images are shown in Fig. 1. The classes are structured according to the Gastrointestinal (GI) tract's location and the pathological finding type.

The dataset contains images from four high-level categories: (*i*) **Anatomical landmarks**, which are used during the endoscopy process to obtain references and confirm that all critical areas have been examined, existing in both the upper and lower GI tracts; (*ii*) **Mucosal quality**, where complete visualization of the mucosa is crucial for detecting pathological findings, with the Boston Bowel Preparation Scale (BBPS) used as a classification measure in the colon; (*iii*) **Pathological findings**, which are anomalies that can affect all parts of the gastrointestinal tract depending on the pathology being treated and are often inferred from the intestinal mucosa walls; and, (*iv*) **Therapeutic interventions**, where intervention is required when a lesion or pathological finding is discovered, such as lifting and resecting a polyp, dilation of a stenosis, or injection of a bleeding ulcer.

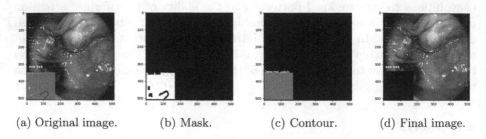

(a) Original image.   (b) Mask.   (c) Contour.   (d) Final image.

Fig. 2. Green patch removal. Process of removing the green patch broken down into the different steps carried out.

Data Preprocessing. We have observed the presence of green patches in the images for certain critical classes. These patches appear in the same location in the image but vary in position along the y-axis and size. In some cases, these green patches can occupy a significant portion of the image (around 32% of the total area). In our opinion, the presence of these patches may bias the training and resulting model. We have developed a method to remove them automatically. In particular, contour detection algorithms [2] have been used to subsequently perform the most precise polygonal adjustment possible to avoid removing too much information from the original image.

The process involves the following main steps (see Fig. 2): (*i*) *Detection and thresholding of the green pixels* by defining the color interval that includes the 'green' hue and masking the values meeting the color condition; and (*ii*) *Contour detection algorithm*, which is a process performed to facilitate the detection of the contour of the rectangular region on the original image. Finally, a bitwise logical operation is applied to the mask to remove the defined rectangular region.

3.2   Performance Metrics

Due to the class imbalance present in the dataset, the model's performance will be evaluated using micro and macro F1-scores. These performance metrics are preferred over accuracy [14] and other metrics, providing a more accurate conclusion about the model's performance. The equations of the metrics are shown below:

$$F1 = 2 \cdot \frac{\text{precision} \cdot \text{recall}}{\text{precision} + \text{recall}} \qquad F1_{\text{macro}} = \frac{1}{N} \sum_{i=1}^{N} F1_i \qquad (1)$$

$$F1_{\text{micro}} = \frac{2 \cdot \sum_{i=1}^{N} \text{TP}_i}{2 \cdot \sum_{i=1}^{N} \text{TP}_i + \sum_{i=1}^{N} \text{FP}_i + \sum_{i=1}^{N} \text{FN}_i} \qquad (2)$$

where TP, FP and FN indicate the True Positives, False Positives and False Negatives, respectively, and N the number of classes.

A 2-fold evaluation will be carried out using 50% of the stratified data, using the splits proposed by the Hyper-Kvasir article [3], and the models will be evaluated using F1 metrics.

It is worth mentioning that, in this case, improving the macro variant over the micro variant is considered more relevant since the classes related to cancerous artifacts in colonoscopies have a very limited number of samples. Therefore, it is convenient to weigh and average the classes equitably to improve the classifier.

Table 1. Training details. A summary of the model architectures, batch sizes, optimizers, learning rates, and weight decay values used in the experiments.

Model	Batch Size	Optimizer	Learning Rate	Weight Decay
MobileViT	64	AdamW	0.0001	0.00001
CoAtNet	16	AdamW	0.0001	0.00001
CMT	32	AdamW	0.001	0.0001
DaViT	16	AdamW	0.001	0.00001
MobileViT Large	16	Adam	0.0001	0.001

4 Experiments and Results

The experiments have been designed to directly compare with the original Hyper-Kvasir article without applying any additional pre-processing [3], considering only the removal of green patches to favor the generalization of the model.

To determine the improvements compared to the previous state of the art, the training has been carried out using the original splits and keeping the green patches, in order to conclude whether attention-based models and hybrid architectures improve compared to the previous ones.

4.1 Implementation Details

The purpose of these experiments is to determine whether current attention-based architectures are interesting compared to the previous state-of-the-art ones and whether there are significant improvements to be made by opting for these models for this type of problem. For this analysis, as discussed in Sect. 3, the green patches have been removed in order to draw conclusions about possible biases in the model. In turn, training has been conducted both with and without the green patches, using the splits proposed by the Hyper-Kvasir article [3], to determine whether these models outperform the previous state-of-the-art ones.

All models are pre-trained on the ImageNet dataset because they outperform the previous state-of-the-art ones when pre-trained on sufficiently large datasets [7]. However, we do not freeze any weights. In our early experiments, models without pre-training were also tested, but the results were lower than the ones obtained with pre-trained models. The images have been rescaled to a resolution of 224 × 224. In our study, we applied several data augmentation techniques, including random image rotation up to a maximum of 40°, random width and height shifts with a maximum range of 20% of the image size, random shearing of up to 20% to mimic perspective or viewing angle, and a random zoom factor of up to 20% to simulate different distances between the object and the camera. Additionally, we allowed horizontal flipping of images, effectively doubling the amount of available training data and helping models learn symmetries. We have used third-party libraries for the attention-based models, available online[1]. All input and output layers have been adapted to the respective format required by each of the models.

Table 2. Architecture comparison. Results comparing the pre-processed dataset removing green patches and using the default dataset with green patches. The results are obtained using data augmentation and class weighting.

Model	Parameters	FLOPs	Non-green patches		Green patches	
			F1-Macro	F1-Micro	F1-Macro	F1-Micro
MobileViT	2M	1.6×10^{10}	*0.618*	*0.890*	*0.630*	0.892
MobileViT Large	18M	11.2×10^{10}	0.604	**0.892**	**0.634**	**0.900**
CMT	9M	2.6×10^{10}	0.579	0.873	0.605	0.854
CoAtNet	23M	8.3×10^{10}	**0.619**	0.889	0.626	*0.895*
DaViT	87M	31.1×10^{10}	0.598	0.876	0.609	0.878

In order to improve the macro variant, given the class imbalance, we apply class weighting using the method *compute class weight* indicated by the Sckit Learn library [1].

As a preliminary starting point, a Bayesian hyperparameter optimization has been performed with the purpose of optimizing resources regarding grid-based search methods [18]. The possible values of the learning rate and weight decay are in the set $\{0.00001, 0.0001, 0.001, 0.01\}$. The set of values for the batch size is as follows $\{16, 32, 64, 128, 256\}$. Adam, AdamW, and AdaDelta have been used as optimizers. All hyperparameters used for each architecture are provided in Table 1 to facilitate the training of the models for the proposed problem.

4.2 Comparison of Architectures

After the previously performed hyperparameter optimization, the training of the models presented in Sect. 2 will be carried out using the preprocessed dataset indicated in Sect. 3.

---

[1] Base models: https://github.com/leondgarse/keras_cv_attention_models.

As previously commented, given the data imbalance, it has been considered appropriate to prioritize macro metrics through weighting in those classes with fewer samples. Therefore, in certain cases, micro metrics worsen slightly in exchange for very favorable improvements in macro F1 compared to the results obtained in previous articles [3,14]. The obtained results are summarized in Table 2. We observe that the MobileViT architectures offer the best average results, followed by CoAtNet.

4.3   Influence of the Green Patches

As previously mentioned, the original dataset presents green patches on specific images (see Fig. 2). The results proposed by the Hyper-Kvasir article [3] used the default dataset without any preprocessing of the green patches. Therefore, we decided to train the models both with and without the green patches, using the same hyperparameters and architectures, to compare their influence on the model results. Note that if we wanted to obtain a classification model able to deal with endoscopy images from a third-party dataset, we could not assume the existence of these green landmarks. The obtained results are included in Table 2.

Table 3. State of the art. Our best models (w/o removing green patches) are compared to other published models. The best directly comparable results (same splits and image resolution; top five rows) are marked in bold.

Model	Split	Resolution	Parameters	F1-Macro	F1-Micro
MobileViT Large (ours)	2-fold	224 × 224	18M	0.634	0.900
Late fusion (ours)*	2-fold	224 × 224	20M	**0.636**	0.905
DenseNet-161 [3]	2-fold	224 × 224	28M	0.619	0.907
ResNet-152 [3]	2-fold	224 × 224	60M	0.606	0.906
ResNet-152 & DenseNet-161 [3]	2-fold	224 × 224	88M	0.617	**0.910**
Teacher-Student(EfficientNetB6) [10]	2-fold	336 × 336	43.3M	-	0.886
DenseNet-161 [16]	2-fold	512 × 512	28M	0.635	-
MobileNet-V2 [19]	5-fold	512 × 512	3.4M	0.651	-
ResNet-50x1/BiT-M[8]	5-fold	640 × 512	-	-	0.918
MobileNet-V2 [9]	5-fold	Unknown	3.4M	0.641	-

(*): Averaged MobileViT Large & MobileViT with α=0.6

We observe that, in general, the results obtained using images without the green patches are lower than the ones obtained with the unmodified images. This suggests that those green regions contain information used by the models (see Fig. 3). This fact may imply that, in those cases, the actual features of the digestive tract are not properly exploited.

Note that we have also experimented with a training set combining the original images and the ones where the green patches were removed. As a reference, for the MobileViT-Large the obtained performance values are 0.625 and 0.889, for F1-macro and F1-micro, respectively.

4.4 Comparison to the State of the Art

Inspired by [3], we perform a late fusion of the two best models obtained in our previous experiments. Late fusion involves averaging the predictions of the last softmax layer between models, setting a weighting parameter α that determines the weight to assign to each model, in this case, to the first model indicated. The final results are included in Table 3. All model comparisons have been made with those that used the original 23 classes without any grouping, in order to have a common starting point despite the differences in experimental conditions that certain articles present (i.e., different splits and image resolution).

Fig. 3. Extraction of attention on trained models (a) with and (b) without green patches. Example of bias in the presence of the green patch at classification time. Brighter areas indicate higher attention. (Color figure online)

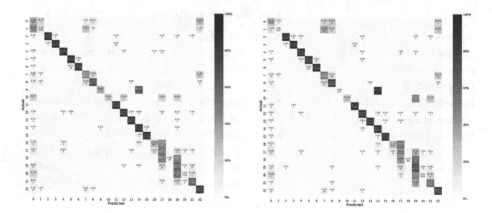

Fig. 4. Confusion matrices on Hyper-Kvasir. Obtained from our best model on the corresponding test splits. Zoom in for details. (View in digital format).

We observe improvement by performing the ensemble of models compared to their results individually. Our best fusion model, obtained through the ensemble of MobileViT architectures, has a total of 20M parameters (2M+18M), achieving an F1-macro value of 0.636. As a reference, the ensemble model described in [3] has 88M parameters, achieving 0.617 F1-macro performance.

In the resulting confusion matrices (see Fig. 4) on the original splits in tests proposed by the Hyper-Kvasir article [3], it is possible to observe the same classification problem that existed in previously proposed models, where the classes representing the different degrees of 'ulcerative colitis' pose a difficulty in classifying these instances.

For the sake of completeness, we have included in Table 3 other methods existing in the literature that present classification results on Hyper-Kvasir. However, their experimental setup is not directly comparable to ours. For example, a higher F1-macro value is reported by the recent work of [19], where the image resolution is twice ours and the number of training samples is larger (5-fold cross-validation) than ours. Using the same 2-fold split we use, the work in [16] presents the results obtained using a DenseNet-161 (28M parameters) at a resolution of 512×512 pix. This higher resolution model achieves a similar F1-Macro compared to our lower resolution MobileViT with only 18M parameters. These results support the benefit of using attention-based models for this task.

5   Conclusions and Future Work

This work presents an empirical study of attention-based models for classifying gastrointestinal endoscopy images. The selected models were evaluated on the challenging Hyper-Kvasir dataset [3], achieving state-of-the-art results on the classification task. The results show that the lightweight models from the MobileViT family offer very favorable results considering their reduced number of parameters, and compared to previous non-attention-based models. In addition, a late fusion approach on two selected models shows a boost in the classification performance.

This work has also studied the influence on the classification accuracy of some existing green landmarks in the images of the Hyper-Kvasir dataset. The experimental results suggest that the presence of those image artifacts may compromise the generalization capability of the trained models on this dataset, for direct use on other endoscopy datasets.

As future work, we plan to study in-depth the image regions attended by the different models and validate their possible medical relevance in collaboration with medical doctors. In addition, we may consider performing pre-training with the rest of the unlabeled Hyper-Kvasir dataset using unsupervised learning techniques (e.g., AutoEncoders or clustering).

References

1. Compute class weight in sklearn utils. https://scikit-learn.org/stable/modules/generated/sklearn.utils.class_weight.compute_class_weight.html
2. Structural analysis and shape descriptors. https://docs.opencv.org/3.4/d3/dc0/group__imgproc__shape.html#ga17ed9f5d79ae97bd4c7cf18403e1689a
3. Borgli, H., Thambawita, V., Smedsrud, P.H., Hicks, S., et al.: Hyperkvasir, a comprehensive multi-class image and video dataset for gastrointestinal endoscopy. Sci. Data **7**(1), 283 (2020)

4. Chen, P.J., Lin, M.C., Lai, M.J., Lin, J.C., et al.: Accurate classification of diminutive colorectal polyps using computer-aided analysis. Gastroenterology **154**(3), 568–575 (2018)
5. Dai, Z., Liu, H., Le, Q.V., Tan, M.: Coatnet: marrying convolution and attention for all data sizes. In: NEURIPS, vol. 34 (2021)
6. Ding, M., Xiao, B., Codella, N., Luo, P., et al.: DaViT: dual attention vision transformers. In: Avidan, S., Brostow, G., Cissé, M., Farinella, G.M., Hassner, T. (eds.) ECCV 2022. LNCS, vol. 13684, pp. 74–92. Springer, Cham (2022). https://doi.org/10.1007/978-3-031-20053-3_5
7. Dosovitskiy, A., Beyer, L., Kolesnikov, A., Weissenborn, D., et al.: An image is worth 16x16 words: transformers for image recognition at scale. In: ICLR (2021)
8. Galdran, A., Carneiro, G., Ballester, M.A.G.: A hierarchical multi-task approach to gastrointestinal image analysis. In: ICPR Workshops and Challenges (2021)
9. Galdran, A., Carneiro, G., González Ballester, M.A.: Balanced-MixUp for highly imbalanced medical image classification. In: de Bruijne, M., et al. (eds.) MICCAI 2021. LNCS, vol. 12905, pp. 323–333. Springer, Cham (2021). https://doi.org/10.1007/978-3-030-87240-3_31
10. Gjestang, H.L., Hicks, S.A., Thambawita, V., Halvorsen, P., Riegler, M.A.: A self-learning teacher-student framework for gastrointestinal image classification. In: 2021 IEEE 34th International Symposium on CBMS (2021)
11. Guo, J., Han, K., Wu, H., Tang, Y., et al.: CMT: Convolutional neural networks meet vision transformers. In: IEEE/CVF CVPR (2022)
12. Hirasawa, T., Aoyama, K., Tanimoto, T., Ishihara, S., et al.: Application of artificial intelligence using a convolutional neural network for detecting gastric cancer in endoscopic images. Gastric Cancer **21**, 653–660 (2018)
13. Mehta, S., Rastegari, M.: MobileViT: light-weight, general-purpose, and mobile-friendly vision transformer. In: ICLR (2022)
14. Pogorelov, K., Randel, K.R., Griwodz, C., Eskeland, S.L., et al.: Kvasir: a multi-class image dataset for computer aided gastrointestinal disease detection. In: Proceedings of ACM on Multimedia Systems Conference, pp. 164–169 (2017)
15. Shen, D., Wu, G., Suk, H.I.: Deep learning in medical image analysis. Ann. Rev. Biomed. Eng. **19**, 221–248 (2017)
16. Thambawita, V., Strümke, I., Hicks, S.A., Halvorsen, P., et al.: Impact of image resolution on deep learning performance in endoscopy image classification: an experimental study using a large dataset of endoscopic images. Diagnostics **11**(12), 2183 (2021)
17. Vaswani, A., Shazeer, N., Parmar, N., Uszkoreit, J., et al.: Attention is all you need. In: NeurIPS, vol. 30 (2017)
18. Wu, J., Chen, X.Y., Zhang, H., Xiong, L.D., et al.: Hyperparameter optimization for machine learning models based on Bayesian optimization. J. Electron. Sci. Technol. **17**(1), 26–40 (2019)
19. Yue, G., Wei, P., Liu, Y., Luo, Y., et al.: Automated endoscopic image classification via deep neural network with class imbalance loss. IEEE Trans. Instrum. Meas. **72**, 1–11 (2023)

Classification of Breast Micro-calcifications as Benign or Malignant Using Subtraction of Temporally Sequential Digital Mammograms and Machine Learning

Kosmia Loizidou[1]([✉]), Galateia Skouroumouni[2], Gabriella Savvidou[3], Anastasia Constantinidou[4], Christos Nikolaou[4], and Costas Pitris[1]

[1] KIOS Research and Innovation Center of Excellence,
University of Cyprus, Nicosia, Cyprus
cloizi01@ucy.ac.cy
[2] Radiology Department, German Oncology Center, Limassol, Cyprus
[3] Medical School University of Cyprus and the Bank of Cyprus Oncology Centre,
Nicosia, Cyprus
[4] Radiology Department, Limassol General Hospital, Limassol, Cyprus

Abstract. Cancer ranks as the second leading cause of mortality worldwide with breast cancer accounting for approximately 20% of all new cancer cases reported globally. Mammography is the most effective screening tool for the early diagnosis of breast cancer. However, the current practice of evaluating mammograms by two radiologists, and a third in case of disagreement, highlights the challenges faced even by experts in identifying potential abnormalities. To address these challenges, Computer-Aided Diagnosis (CAD) systems are being developed to assist radiologists in breast cancer diagnosis. This study proposes a classification approach for biopsy-confirmed benign and malignant Micro-Calcifications (MCs), using subtraction of temporally sequential digital mammograms combined with feature-based machine learning. The algorithm's performance was evaluated on a dataset retrospectively collected for this work, including 128 images from 32 patients, with precisely annotated MC locations and biopsy confirmations. Several features were extracted and a combination of feature selection algorithms was employed to identify the most critical subset of features. Ten classifiers were evaluated using leave-one-patient-out and k-fold cross-validation (k = 4 and 8). An Artificial Neural Network (ANN) achieved the highest performance, with 90.63% sensitivity, and 85.39% accuracy. These findings demonstrate the potential of the proposed algorithm to be translated into clinical practice as a second-reading tool for the classification of breast MCs as biopsy-confirmed benign or malignant.

Keywords: breast cancer · Computer-Aided Diagnosis (CAD) · digital mammography · temporal subtraction · machine learning

N. Tsapatsoulis et al. (Eds.): CAIP 2023, LNCS 14185, pp. 109–118, 2023.
https://doi.org/10.1007/978-3-031-44240-7_11

1   Introduction

Cancer, is the second leading cause of global mortality. According to the American Cancer Society (ACS), in the United States alone approximately 3,200,000 new cancer cases and 904,000 deaths are expected by 2040 [4]. Among these cases, breast cancer accounts for approximately 20% and ~30% of all female cancers [2]. Mammography, the key screening tool for breast cancer diagnosis, dropped the mortality of the disease by about 42%, and significantly improved patient prognosis [11]. Current protocols require evaluation by two radiologists, and the involvement of a third expert, in case of a disagreement. However, when it comes to dense breast tissue, mammograms exhibit increased intensity and variations that closely resemble certain abnormalities. Due to this similarity, the sensitivity of mammography is reduced by approximately 30%, resulting in an elevated risk of breast cancer [12].

Micro-Calcifications (MCs) inside a mammogram are considered suspicious signs that warrant further assessment. They appear as bright spots due to the higher X-ray attenuation coefficient of calcium, compared to surrounding normal breast tissue [15]. Radiological classification of breast MCs as benign or suspicious relies on crucial parameters such as shape, texture, and distribution. Although the majority of MCs are benign and do not need intervention, Micro-Calcification Clusters (MCCs) are considered precursors to cancer [13]. In the case of a suspicious finding, a biopsy will confirm whether it is malignant. Accurate classification of benign and malignant MCs remains a challenge due to their small size, wide morphological variations, and the high intensity of the background. Computer-Aided Diagnosis (CAD) systems aim to assist radiologists in the detection and classification of breast MCs by exploiting advanced algorithms and machine learning techniques [11].

The classification of biopsy-confirmed benign vs. malignant MCs has gained significant attention in the literature, leading to the development of various algorithms [11]. However, the vast majority of these studies utilize only the most recent mammographic view of a patient, neglecting the importance to compare prior images of the same patient. These comparisons are routinely conducted by clinicians to identify newly developed abnormalities, or regions displaying rapid changes between the screenings and are often considered suspicious [16]. Temporal analysis is proposed in the literature for the comparison of sequential mammograms, and it has been applied for the detection and classification of breast MCs [11]. However, studies based on temporal analysis offer no advantage over utilizing only the most recent mammographic view, when the abnormality is entirely new, with no traces in prior examinations.

In this work, an algorithm that combines subtraction of temporally sequential mammograms with feature-based machine learning for the classification of breast MCs as biopsy-confirmed benign or malignant is proposed. Temporal subtraction, previously introduced by this research group, has shown significant advantages in the detection and radiological classification of breast MCs [9], and masses [10]. A new dataset was collected specifically for this study. Pre-processing was first applied, and then, image registration along with tem-

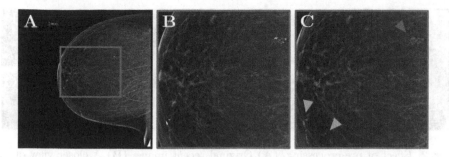

Fig. 1. Dataset example. **(A)** Recent Mammogram. **(B)** A closer view of the area outlined by the red square in **(A)**, showing MCs and a Micro-Calcification Cluster (MCC). **(C)** The region in **B** with precise annotation of MC and MCC locations, as annotated by two expert radiologists. The green arrows in **C** indicate benign MCs, while the red arrow indicates the suspicious MCC.

poral subtraction took place. Following, the detection and segmentation were performed and subsequently, various features were extracted and ranked using five feature selection algorithms. The suspicious MCs were classified as biopsy-confirmed benign or malignant using the most successful methodology.

2   Materials and Methods

2.1   Data Collection and Description

A dataset containing 32 pairs of full-field digital mammograms (from women 38 to 83 years) with both benign and suspicious MCs in their most recent mammographic images, was retrospectively collected from local hospitals. Inclusion in the study necessitated the availability of a normal, or benign prior mammographic view, with an average interval of 2 years.

For every participant, two mammographic views, the Cranio-Caudal (CC, view from above) and Medio-Lateral Oblique (MLO, angled view) were collected. Two sequential screening rounds were included for every participant, resulting in a database with a total of 128 images ($2 \times 2 \times 32$). An expert radiologist selected the eligible patients, and along with a second radiologist, assessed the mammograms to mark the MCs as radiological benign or suspicious. Suspicious cases were subsequently confirmed as malignant through biopsies, followed by histopathological analysis. Among the 32 women who underwent biopsies, 21 had biopsy-confirmed benign MCs, 5 had biopsy-confirmed malignant MCs, and 6 were diagnosed with Ductal Carcinoma In Situ (DCIS), which is recognized as the earliest form of breast cancer. For the purposes of this study, the biopsy-confirmed malignant cases and the cases diagnosed with DCIS were considered as 1-class associated with malignancies. This is the first dataset that includes temporally sequential digital mammograms, along with precise annotations of each individual MC (Fig. 1).

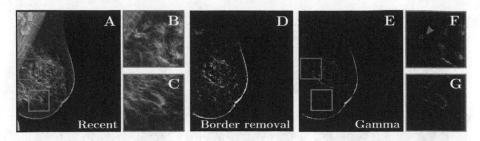

Fig. 2. Effect of pre-processing. (**A**) Original recent image. (**B**) A closer view of the area outlined by the red square in **A** showing an area with MCs. (**C**) A closer view of the area outlined by the green square in **A**, showing an area without MCs. (**D**) Image after border removal. (**E**) Final processed image after gamma correction. (**F**) A closer view of the area outlined by the red square in **E**, showing the same area as **B**, after pre-processing. (**G**) A closer view of the area outlined by the green square in **E**, showing the same area as **C**, after pre-processing.

2.2   MCs Detection and Segmentation

Normalization, border removal, and gamma correction were applied consecutively to both recent and prior mammographic views, to eliminate unnecessary information. Border removal was employed to effectively eliminate high-intensity regions connected to the border, including the pectoral muscle in the MLO views [6]. Subsequently, gamma correction was implemented to enhance the contrast of the images by suppressing low-intensity regions, producing a new filtered image with high-intensity areas and thus, possible breast abnormalities [8]. Figure 2 presents an example of the pre-processing steps applied.

Recent and prior mammographic views were then registered to account for variations in breast compression, changes in breast shape, and potential human error during screening. Various image registration techniques were developed specifically for mammograms [11]. Demons registration [14] was selected in this case, as it effectively tracked the MCs changes over time, without introducing any errors. After the registration, temporal subtraction was performed by subtracting the prior-registered mammogram, from the recent one. An example of temporal subtraction is presented in Fig. 3. To evaluate the effectiveness of the subtraction, a comparison was conducted between the Contrast Ratio (CR) of the subtracted image and the CR of the most recent mammogram, without any pre-processing.

The subtracted image underwent further processing using a range filter, to further enhance the abnormalities and remove any unnecessary areas [1]. Segmentation of Regions of Interest (ROIs) followed, using a three-step procedure: thresholding, application of morphological operations, and elimination of the periphery pixels. Initially, the images were converted into binary through thresholding, enabling the elimination of low-intensity regions. The threshold value was chosen to optimize the global classification rate. Subsequently, the binary image underwent morphological processing, using erosion and closing. Erosion was employed with a radius of 1 pixel, which is smaller than the typical radius of

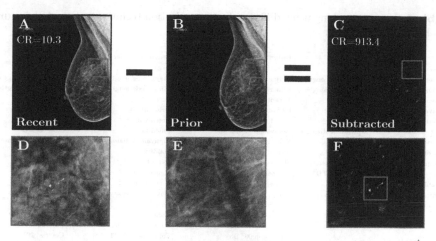

Fig. 3. Example of temporal subtraction. **(A)** Most recent mammogram. **(B)** Prior mammogram. **(C)** Subtracted image created after subtracting the registered version of **B** from **A**. **(D–F)** A closer view of the areas outlined by the red squares in **A–C**. The rectangles enclose suspicious MCs, which were not subtracted.

an MC, while closing was applied with a radius of 10 pixels, to identify the constituents of MCCs. In the final step, high-intensity regions that could potentially lead to areas falsely identified as MCs were eliminated. These regions correspond to the skin of the breast, which can not contain MCs but may not be entirely removed during the registration and subtraction process due to misalignment. For the training of the algorithms, the ground truth provided by the radiologists was used.

2.3   Feature Extraction and Selection

In total 96 features were extracted from each suspicious MC, taking into consideration the characteristics that are routinely assessed by clinicians to determine the suspicion level of an MC. These features were divided into four categories: shape, intensity, First-Order Statistics (FOS), and Gray-Level Co-Occurrence Matrix (GLCM) features. They included: area, circularity, compactness, convex area, eccentricity, equivalent diameter, Euler number, extent, filled area, major and minor axis length, orientation, perimeter, solidity, shape ratio, average, minimum, and maximum intensity, entropy, kurtosis, skewness, smoothness, standard deviation, variance, contract, correlation, energy, and homogeneity. Each GLCM feature was extracted at four different angles ($0°$, $45°$, $90°$, and $135°$) and the mean and standard deviation (STD) were calculated, resulting in 24 values for each offset D. To determine the most suitable offset, three values were tested ($D_1 = 5$, $D_2 = 15$, and $D_3 = 25$). Consequently, a total of 72 GLCM features were extracted.

Table 1. Feature ranking using different feature selection techniques. Selected features are highlighted in bold.

t-test	MRMR	Feature Importance Random Forest	Feature Importance Extra Trees	SelectKBest
Area	**Area**	**Area**	**Area**	**Area**
Major axis length	**Major axis length**	**Major axis length**	**Major axis length**	**Major axis length**
Minor axis length	**Minor axis length**	**Minor axis length**	**Minor axis length**	**Minor axis length**
Eccentricity	**Eccentricity**	**Eccentricity**	**Eccentricity**	**Eccentricity**
Convex area	**Convex area**	**Convex area**	Orientation	**Convex area**
Filled area	Euler number	**Filled area**	**Convex area**	**Filled area**
Euler number	**Equivalent diameter**	**Equivalent diameter**	**Filled area**	Euler number
Equivalent diameter	**Solidity**	**Solidity**	**Equivalent diameter**	**Equivalent diameter**
Solidity	**Extent**	**Extent**	**Solidity**	**Solidity**
Extent	Minimum intensity	Maximum intensity	**Extent**	**Extent**
Perimeter	Contrast STD D3	Skewness	Perimeter	Perimeter
Circularity	**Circularity**	Kurtosis	Average intensity	Skewness
Compactness	**Compactness**	STD	Maximum intensity	Contrast 90° D1
Shape ratio	**Shape ratio**	Correlation 0° D1	Skewness	Contrast 135° D1
		Correlation 45° D1	Kurtosis	Contrast mean D1
		Correlation 45° D2	Correlation 45° D2	Contrast 0° D2
		Correlation 90° D3	Correlation 90° D3	Contrast 90° D2
		Circularity	**Circularity**	Contrast 135° D2
		Compactness	**Compactness**	Contrast mean D2
		Shape ratio	**Shape ratio**	Contrast 45° D3

Feature selection was necessary to eliminate unnecessary features and improve the classification performance. A comparison was conducted between five methods: t-test, Maximum Relevance-Minimum Redundancy (MRMR), feature importance, using both random forest and extra trees, and, SelectKBest. As seen in Table 1, each feature selection algorithm produced different feature rankings, since they rely on unique principles. Thus, to identify the most significant features, the results from all methods were combined by applying a majority rule (i.e. keep the high-ranked features from all the methods), and a new feature vector was created (features in bold in Table 1). With this approach, the classification accuracy was increased, compared to using a single feature selection technique.

As is often the case in real-life scenarios, this dataset was imbalanced, with unequal numbers of benign and malignant MCs (229 benign vs. 32 malignant). To address this issue, Synthetic Minority Oversampling Technique (SMOTE) was employed, and new instances of the minority class were generated in the training set [3]. Feature pre-processing was also applied using least squares (l2) normalization, to scale all the samples and adjust the range of their values.

2.4 Training and Comparison of Classifier Designs

Nine classifiers were evaluated for the classification task, including Linear Discriminant Analysis (LDA), k-Nearest Neighbor (k-NN), Support Vector Machine (SVM), Naive Bayes (NB), Multi-Layer Perceptron (MLP), AdaBoost (ADA), Bagging (BAG), Gradient Boosting (GB), and Voting, using Python (v. 3.7.7), and Scikit-learn (v. 0.23.1). Different Artificial Neural Network (ANN) configurations were also evaluated using Keras (v. 2.3.1). Eleven patients were associated with biopsy-confirmed malignancies, thus, their correct identification was

Table 2. Comparison of the classification results in suspicious MCs as biopsy-confirmed benign or malignant using LOPO CV

Classifier	Sensitivity [%]	Specificity [%]	Accuracy [%]	AUC
LDA	75.00	66.38	67.42	0.71
k-NN	78.13	69.36	70.41	0.74
SVM	93.75	64.26	67.79	0.79
NB	81.25	60.43	62.92	0.71
MLP	90.63	68.09	70.79	0.79
ADA	50.00	76.60	73.41	0.63
BAG	43.75	82.98	78.28	0.63
GB	46.88	80.85	76.78	0.64
Voting	87.50	61.70	64.79	0.76
ANN	**90.63**	**84.68**	**85.39**	**0.88**

crucial since they need immediate attention. Conversely, 21 women underwent an unnecessary biopsy, as it turned out later, and their suspicious abnormalities were eventually benign. However, it is more important to accurately identify patients associated with malignancies, thus the classification was shifted towards the malignant cases.

Regarding the validation approach, Leave-One-Patient-Out (LOPO) Cross-Validation (CV) was used during training, along with k-fold CV (k = 4 and 8). This approach was critical, in order to ensure that the algorithm was working only with unknown patients, thus, to avoid bias from adding images of the same patient in both the test and training sets. Similarly, in k-fold CV the folds were created per patient, rather than randomly dividing the MCs. The suspicious MCs were classified as biopsy-confirmed benign or malignant. The performance was evaluated by computing sensitivity, specificity, accuracy, and the Area Under the receiver operating characteristic Curve (AUC).

3   Experimental Results

An average reduction of 65% in image intensity was achieved using image registration and subtraction, a result of removing structures that have remained unchanged between screenings. The average CR of the subtracted images was ~50 times higher compared to the recent mammographic view. The processing time for these operations was an average of ~15 min per image pair (Intel® Core™ i7 2 GHz; Intel Corp., Santa Clara, CA, USA).

Feature selection identified the most important features for the classification task (features in bold in Table 1) and those features were added into the classifiers that were optimized using LOPO CV. The highest classification performance was achieved using an ANN in a LOPO CV scheme, with 90.63% sensitivity, 84.68% specificity, 85.39% accuracy, and 0.88 AUC (Table 2). For

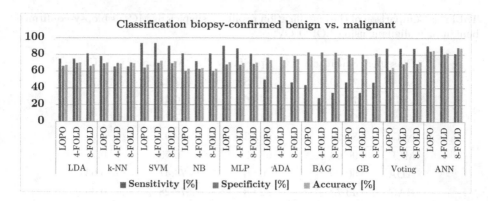

Fig. 4. Classification results of the MCs as biopsy-confirmed benign or malignant using various classifiers and CV methods.

the LDA, the linear discriminant criterion was used, without prior probabilities. As for the k-NN, the number of k nearest neighbors was set to 11, and the nearest tie-breaking algorithm was selected. SVM was implemented using a polynomial kernel. NB was implemented using the normal distribution. For the Ensemble Voting, polynomial SVM, NB, and MLP were combined in a hard voting scheme. The selected ANN architecture consisted of 1 hidden layer (96) with 5,714 trainable parameters. ReLU activation function was employed in the input and hidden layers, and softmax activation function in the output layer. Adam optimizer was selected, and batch normalization, dropout regularization, and Gaussian noise regularization were incorporated to enhance the network's robustness. The batch size was set to 128, the learning rate was 0.0001, and the network was trained for 100 epochs. In addition, k-fold CV (k = 4 and 8) was employed to validate the robustness of the method (Fig. 4).

4   Discussion

An ANN reached 90.63% accuracy using LOPO CV, with an average of 0.6 false positives per image for the classification of the MCs as biopsy-confirmed benign or malignant. Although some misclassifications occurred, the clinical impact would have been minimal if the algorithm was actually implemented. Out of 32 malignant MCs, 3 were misclassified as benign, in 2 patients. However, these 2 patients had other malignancies, thus their care would not have been compromised. To evaluate the robustness of the method, k-fold CV was implemented, in addition to LOPO CV. In this case, the performance experienced a slight drop since fewer patients were included in each training round, compared to the 32 patients in the LOPO CV scheme. This drop exemplifies the need for additional training data, while also demonstrating the algorithm's potential to accurately classify new data.

Given that this is the first application of temporal subtraction for this task, direct comparison with other state-of-the-art techniques is challenging. However,

Table 3. Comparison of algorithms for the classification of MCs as benign or malignant using sequential mammograms and feature-based machine learning

Reference	Dataset	Classifier	Validation method	Results ACC [%]	Results AUC
Hadjiiski et al. (2002) [7]	65 pairs	LDA	leave-one-out (per patient)	–	0.87 temporal 0.81 single
Filev et al. (2008) [5]	261 pairs	LDA	leave-one-out (per patient)	–	0.81 temporal 0.72 single
Proposed	**32 pairs**	**ANN**	**LOPO CV (per patient)**	**85.39**	**0.88 temporal**

the findings of this work are more accurate than those reported in the literature for the classification of benign vs. malignant MCs using sequential mammograms (Table 3), in terms of the AUC. Unlike temporal analysis utilized in the literature, the subtraction of temporally sequential mammograms proposed in this work can effectively track and classify newly developed abnormalities, or regions that changed significantly between the screenings.

Despite the promising results, a larger patient population is required to prove the advantages of combining temporal subtraction with feature-based machine learning. Ideally, the algorithm should also be verified on an independent external dataset. Unfortunately, publicly available databases cannot be utilized for the purposes of this project, since they neither contain sequential mammograms nor include images annotated at the level of individual MCs as in this study.

5   Conclusion

In this study, an algorithm for the classification of biopsy-confirmed benign and malignant breast MCs using a combination of subtraction of temporally sequential digital mammograms, and feature-based machine learning was introduced. Ninety six features were extracted and ranked using a majority rule, with five different feature selection techniques. The most significant features were subsequently fed to the classifiers. The highest classification performance was achieved using an ANN with 85.39% accuracy and 0.88 AUC. Encouraged by the promising findings, the proposed methodology will be further tested on larger datasets. Deep learning algorithms will also be evaluated if large volumes of annotated data that are needed for proper training of such complex algorithms are collected. Furthermore, the algorithm can be applied to other kind of breast abnormalities in mammograms. The algorithm also has the potential to be translated into clinical practice as a breast cancer classification tool, to assist radiologists in the double reading of mammograms, especially in the Population Screening Program of Cyprus and in less-developed countries.

Acknowledgment. The publication of this paper is supported by the European Union's Horizon 2020 research and innovation programme under grant agreement No 739551 (KIOS CoE) and the Government of the Republic of Cyprus through the Cyprus Deputy Ministry of Research, Innovation and Digital Policy.

References

1. Bailey, D.G., Hodgson, R.M.: Range filters: local intensity subrange filters and their properties. Image Vis. Comput. **3**(3), 99–110 (1985)
2. Beura, S.: Development of features and feature reduction techniques for mammogram classification. Ph.D. thesis, Department of Computer Science and Engineering National Institute of Technology Rourkela (2016)
3. Chawla, N.V., et al.: Smote: synthetic minority over-sampling technique. J. Artif. Intell. Res. **16**, 321–357 (2002)
4. Ferlay, J., et al.: Global cancer observatory: cancer tomorrow. International Agency for Research on Cancer, Lyon (2022). https://gco.iarc.fr/tomorrow. Accessed 24 Oct 2022
5. Filev, P., et al.: Automated regional registration and characterization of corresponding microcalcification clusters on temporal pairs of mammograms for interval change analysis. Med. Phys. **35**(12), 5340–5350 (2008)
6. Gonzalez, W., Eddins: Digital Image Processing Using MATLAB, 2nd edn. Gatesmark Publishing (2010)
7. Hadjiiski, L.M., et al.: Computer-aided characterization of malignant and benign microcalcification clusters based on the analysis of temporal change of mammographic features. In: Medical Imaging 2002: Image Processing, vol. 4684, pp. 749–753. International Society for Optics and Photonics (2002)
8. Huang, S.C., et al.: Efficient contrast enhancement using adaptive gamma correction with weighting distribution. IEEE Trans. Image Process. **22**(3), 1032–1041 (2013)
9. Loizidou, K., Skouroumouni, G., Pitris, C., Nikolaou, C.: Digital subtraction of temporally sequential mammograms for improved detection and classification of microcalcifications. Eur. Radiol. Exp. **5**(1), 1–12 (2021). https://doi.org/10.1186/s41747-021-00238-w
10. Loizidou, K., et al.: Automatic breast mass segmentation and classification using subtraction of temporally sequential digital mammograms. IEEE J. Transl. Eng. Health Med. **10**, 1–11 (2022)
11. Loizidou, K., et al.: Computer-aided breast cancer detection and classification in mammography: a comprehensive review. Comput. Biol. Med. 106554 (2023)
12. Medicine, Y.: Dense breasts - fact sheets - Yale medicine (2022). https://www.yalemedicine.org. Accessed 24 Oct 2022
13. Oliver, A., et al.: A review of automatic mass detection and segmentation in mammographic images. Med. Image Anal. **14**(2), 87–110 (2010)
14. Pennec, X., Cachier, P., Ayache, N.: Understanding the "Demon's algorithm": 3D non-rigid registration by gradient descent. In: Taylor, C., Colchester, A. (eds.) MICCAI 1999. LNCS, vol. 1679, pp. 597–605. Springer, Heidelberg (1999). https://doi.org/10.1007/10704282_64
15. Rangayyan, R.M., et al.: A review of computer-aided diagnosis of breast cancer: toward the detection of subtle signs. J. Franklin Inst. **344**(3–4), 312–348 (2007)
16. Timp, S., et al.: Computer-aided diagnosis with temporal analysis to improve radiologists' interpretation of mammographic mass lesions. IEEE Trans. Inf Technol. Biomed. **14**(3), 803–808 (2010)

Fourier Descriptor Loss and Polar Coordinate Transformation for Pericardium Segmentation

Lu Liu[1]([envelope])[iD], Christoph Brune[1][iD], and Raymond Veldhuis[1,2][iD]

[1] University of Twente, 7511 AE Enschede, The Netherlands
{l.liu-2,c.brune,r.n.j.veldhuis}@utwente.nl
[2] Norwegian University of Science and Technology, Gjøvik, Norway

Abstract. Epicardial adipose tissue (EAT) located inside the pericardium is a marker for increased risk of many cardiovascular diseases. Automatic segmentation methods for pericardium or EAT are necessary to support the otherwise extremely time-consuming manual delineation in CT scans. Powerful deep learning-based methods have been applied to such segmentation tasks. However, existing methods primarily rely on region-based or distribution-based loss functions, such as Dice loss or cross-entropy loss. Unfortunately, these approaches overlook the informative anatomical priors, such as the shape of the pericardium. In light of this, our work introduces an innovative approach by proposing and comparing a shape-based loss that leverages anatomical priors derived from Fourier descriptors. By incorporating the anatomical prior, we aim to enhance the accuracy and effectiveness of pericardium or EAT segmentation. The Fourier descriptor loss can be used individually or as a regularizer with region-based losses such as the Dice loss for higher accuracy and faster convergence. As a regularizer, the proposed loss obtains the highest mean intersection of union (96.76%), Dice similarity coefficient (98.20%), and sensitivity (98.55%) outperforming the Dice and cross-entropy loss. We show the effect of the Fourier descriptor loss with fewer and weighted descriptors. The results show the efficiency and flexibility of the Fourier descriptor loss and its potential for segmenting shapes.

Keywords: Fourier descriptors · segmentation neural networks · pericardium segmentation · shape-based loss functions

1 Introduction

Epicardial adipose tissue (EAT) is the fat inside the pericardium, and recent findings indicate its positive correlation with the risk of coronary artery disease, cardiovascular disease, etc. [1]. However, due to technical limitations and anatomy complexity, the manual segmentation of EAT or pericardium in medical images is time-consuming. Nowadays, deep neural networks have shown great performance in many medical image segmentation applications. Most efficient deep

N. Tsapatsoulis et al. (Eds.): CAIP 2023, LNCS 14185, pp. 119–129, 2023.
https://doi.org/10.1007/978-3-031-44240-7_12

learning-based methods for pericardium or EAT segmentation [2] are trained with loss functions such as the Dice loss [3] and the cross-entropy loss [4]. Some researchers have explored utilizing the shape information in segmentation networks to improve or guide deep neural networks for better accuracy [5,6]. A recent review paper on anatomy-aided deep learning for medical image segmentation [7] indicates many ways to use shape information. For pericardium segmentation, the pericardium shape could be an informative input. To involve that in segmentation networks, it is needed to find a way to model or represent the shape information. The Fourier series and Fourier transform are powerful tools for shape representation in many computer vision applications. By applying them, shape information could be represented by the Fourier descriptors (FDs) in the frequency domain for further analysis. Especially, with the Fourier series, a few descriptors are enough to represent the shape of the pericardium. Thus, in this paper, we propose a method that uses the shape information represented by the FDs in the loss function as well as pre-processing with polar coordinate transformation to improve segmentation performance.

1.1   Related Work

Loss Functions. The most widely used losses for segmentation are distribution-based losses and region-based losses [5,6]. Distribution-based losses guide the training process by minimizing the dissimilarity between the ground truth distribution and the predicted distributions, e.g. the cross-entropy loss [4] and its variations. Region-based losses guide the training process by minimizing the false predictions or maximizing the overlap regions between the predicted segmentation and the ground truth region, e.g. the Dice loss [3]. Besides these two types of losses, boundary-based losses have shown interesting effects on medical image segmentation. These losses usually work as a regularization term with a distribution-based or region-based loss [6]. The idea of boundary-based losses is to reduce the distance between two segmented regions, e.g. the boundary loss [8] and the Hausdorff distance loss [9]. However, these losses need to be trained with a region-based loss such as Dice loss to maintain the training stability. There is more study on minimizing distance or using distance map loss penalty [10]. The boundary-based losses incorporate the boundary information due to their theoretical concept, while boundary information is not identical to shape information. Recently, Kervadec et al. [11] introduced loss functions based on a few global shape descriptors such as the volume of segmentation, the location of the centroid, the average distance to the centroid, and the length of the contour. Their experiments show that simple shape descriptors are effective for segmentation. Although their shape descriptor loss did not outperform the cross-entropy loss, it shows the potential.

Fourier Series and Fourier Transformation for Shape Representation. The Fourier descriptor is widely used to encode shape features and has been applied to image/shape retrieval [12,13]. It is a contour-based shape descriptor obtained by representing a closed contour using the Fourier Series. In signal processing, the Fourier series creates new descriptors to represent the frequency domain knowledge. Some works applied 2D Fourier transform for the frequency domain analysis of images. Usually, the 2D Fourier transform is used in 2D images to generate hand-crafted features for further processing. The frequency features could be used for image classification, image registration [14], and the Fourier domain training framework [15]. Fourier space losses proposed by Fuoli et al. [16] improve the accuracy in high-frequency content for image super-resolution by working directly in the frequency domain. Experiments showed that by combining spatial domain and frequency domain losses, the image quality is improved. A more integrated way is to apply a frequency domain representation within the neural network. Han et al. [17] introduced a Fourier convolutional neural network for image classification. They designed the Fourier convolutional layers that apply the 2D Fourier transform with small random kernel sizes to study the frequency domain knowledge. To sum up, the frequency domain knowledge for image analysis and shape analysis is of great significance and has shown its ability in many applications.

1.2   Contribution

To leverage shape information, we introduce a novel Fourier descriptor loss (FD loss) that utilizes Fourier descriptors in relation to the Euclidean distance between boundary points and a point within the boundary. And we validate it on the pericardium segmentation. To improve the segmentation performance and simplify FD loss calculation, we apply pre-processing steps including selecting the region of interest and a polar coordinate transformation. The experimental results show that the pre processing leads to better segmentation for all the tested losses. As an alternative to the commonly-used Dice loss, we investigate how the FD loss works individually and as a regularizer in combination with Dice loss. When working individually, FD loss does not outperform the Dice loss or cross-entropy loss, but it shows visually competitive results. When working as a regularizer with the Dice loss, the compound loss shows improved segmentation accuracy and higher convergence speed. In addition, as the FDs represent the frequency domain knowledge, we show the effect of FD loss with fewer FDs and the effect of FD loss with the weighted frequency content of a contour for improving its smoothness.

2   Methodology

Let $I : \Omega \subset \mathbb{R}^2 \to \mathbb{R}$ denotes a training image with spatial domain Ω, and $g : \Omega \to \{0, 1\}$ denotes a binary ground truth of the image. Similarly, $s : \Omega \to \{0, 1\}$ is a binary predicted segmentation of the image. The FD loss is formulated based on the distance between sample points on the boundary and the centroid of the segmentation. Thus, with the spatial domain Ω, δG denotes a representation of the boundary of the ground truth region G and δS

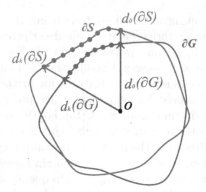

Fig. 1. Visualizing the computation of distances between boundary sample points and the centroid for Fourier descriptor loss calculation.

denotes the boundary of the segmentation region defined by the network output. Figure 1 shows how to compute the distance between the sample points on the boundary and the centroid. We denote the ground truth map as $g(x, y)$ where x, y are the Cartesian coordinates of pixels. And we denote the map $\tilde{g}(r, \theta)$ in polar coordinates with the centroid origin $O(x_c, y_c)$ as shown in Fig. 1, where $r(x, y) = \sqrt{(y - y_c)^2 + (x - x_c)^2}$, and $\theta(x, y) = angle(y - y_c, x - x_c)$. Thus, we have $g(x, y)$ and $\tilde{g}(r, \theta) = 1$ if inside the boundary while $g(x, y)$ and $\tilde{g}(r, \theta) = 0$ if outside the boundary. Similarly, we have $s(x, y)$ and $\tilde{s}(r, \theta) = 1$ if inside the boundary while $s(x, y)$ and $\tilde{s}(r, \theta) = 0$ if outside the boundary. We define the shape signature of the target by the distance between the sample points on the boundary and the centroid. Assume we have K sample points on the boundary. Thus, the distance between the kth sample point on the boundary of the ground truth and the centroid is defined as: $d_k(\delta G) = \int_0^r \tilde{g}(\rho, k\frac{2\pi}{K})d\rho$. For calculation, we approximate it as $d_k(\delta G) = \sum_{r=0} \tilde{g}(r, k\frac{2\pi}{K})$. Similarly, for the kth sample points on the output segmentation: $d_k(\delta S) = \sum_{r=0} \tilde{s}(r, k\frac{2\pi}{K})$. Applying this to all sample points, we obtain sequences of distance measurements $D(\delta G) = d_0(\delta G), d_1(\delta G), ..., d_{K-1}(\delta G)$, and $D(\delta S) = d_0(\delta S), d_1(\delta S), ..., d_{K-1}(\delta S)$. With K sample points, the FDs are defined as the discrete Fourier series of the sequence of distance measurements:

$$c_n = \sum_{k=0}^{K-1} d_k e^{-jnk\frac{2\pi}{N}} \tag{1}$$

Thus, we obtain N complex FDs from $D(\delta G)$ and $D(\delta S)$. In practice, we usually make $N = K$ for the FD calculation. The FD loss is defined as the L1 norm of the dissimilarity between the FDs of ground truth and predicted segmentation.

$$\mathcal{L}_{FD} = \sum_{n=0}^{N-1} |c_n^G - c_n^S| \tag{2}$$

Due to the limitation of this type of FD, we exclude non-convex shapes with strong curvatures. One advantage of the Fourier series is that we can always reconstruct the original shapes with the inverse Fourier transform and miss very little information about the original shapes. In addition, we could remove some FDs to capture only the significant features. When training with the FD loss function, images are transformed into polar coordinates with a fixed origin of the reference labels. Before applying the polar coordinate transformation, we extract a region of interest (ROI) in a circular shape from the original 2D image based on the reference labels. Then, as shown in Fig. 2, polar coordinates transformation applies to the circular ROI. For better visibility, we enlarge the polar-coordinate-transformed images to the same size as the original images. With the polar-coordinate-transformed images, the distance between the sample points on the boundary and the centroid can be calculated by measuring the number of pixels inside the boundary along the horizontal axis.

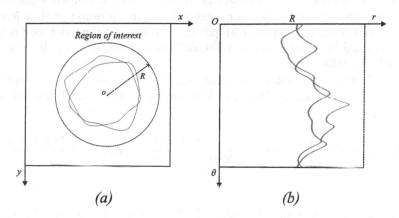

(a)   (b)

Fig. 2. Demonstration of pre-processing steps, including FD loss calculation and polar coordinate transformation. Figure (a) shows the original image in Cartesian coordinates, while Figure (b) displays the pre-processed image used for training, validation, and testing, enabling FD loss computation

3 Experiments

Our experimental objective is threefold: (a) To demonstrate the impact of FD loss both as an individual loss and as a regularizer. (b) To assess the effectiveness of the pre-processing steps employed. (c) To investigate the influence of the number and weights of Fourier descriptors on the performance. All of our experiments focus on pericardium segmentation in low-dose CT scans.

3.1 Data

Chest computed tomography (CT) scanning from the Risk Or Benefit IN Screening for CArdiovascular Diseases (ROBINSCA) dataset [18] is used for experiments in this work. It is performed using a second-generation dual-source computed tomography system. This is a multi-center dataset with CT screening performed at the Gelre Hospital, the Bronovo Hospital, and the University Medical Center Groningen. The labels of the region inside the pericardium are annotated by an experienced radiologist using the open-source medical imaging processing software 3D Slicer [19]. As 2D boundary information is used in the loss calculation, we process 3D images as a stack of independent 2D images, which are fed into the network. All the images are resized to 256 × 256 pixels for further processing. For our experiments, 154 CT scans (11000 slices) were annotated for further training (9000 slices), validation (1000 slices), and testing (1000 slices).

3.2 Implementation Details

We employed the U-net++ with backbone VGG16 by Zhou et al. [20] as the deep learning architecture in our experiments. U-net++ is a nested U-net architecture for medical image segmentation that is widely used in related segmentation tasks. To train our model, we employed the Adam optimizer with a learning rate of 0.001 and early stopping with patience of 30. And the batch size is 8. For implementation, we used Keras and TensorFlow and ran the experiments on an NVIDIA RTX 6000 GPU.

For evaluation, we employed the common Mean Intersection of Union (MIU), Dice Similarity Coefficient (DSC), and Sensitivity (SEN), which are defined as follows,

$$MIU = \frac{1}{N}\frac{P(Y \bigcap \hat{Y})}{P(Y \bigcup \hat{Y})}, DSC = \frac{1}{N}\frac{2 \cdot P(Y \bigcap \hat{Y})}{P(Y) + P(\hat{Y})}, SEN = \frac{1}{N}\frac{P(Y \bigcap \hat{Y})}{P(Y)}$$

where N indicates the number of slices, Y denotes the ground truth, $\hat{Y}$ denotes the predictions, and $P(\cdot)$ denotes the number of pixels.

3.3 Results

Quantitative Evaluation. To show the effect of the FD loss, we compared it to two commonly used loss functions, the Dice loss and the cross-entropy loss, with both original data and pre-processed data. Table 1 lists the results of the corresponding experiments. Overall, with pre-processing, all the losses show improved performance. The FD loss individually can not outperform the Dice loss or cross-entropy loss, but its performance is competitive and convincing visually as shown in Fig. 3. Boundary-based losses are often used as a regularizer with distributed-based losses or region-based losses [5], so as the FD loss. We tested the compound loss with both the Dice loss and the FD loss. As the value range of the FD loss is larger than that of the Dice loss, a weight of 0.01 is applied to the FD loss. With the compound loss, we obtained results of MIU: 96.79%, DSC: 98.20%, and SEN: 98.55%, which outperforms both Dice loss and cross-entropy loss. In addition, the convergence speed of the compound loss (converge at the 13th epoch) is much higher than the Dice loss (converge at the 30th epoch). With Fig. 3, we visualize the pericardium segmentation results of various loss functions in a CT slice. We can see that the manual labeling is not perfect with noise and mislabelled pixels on the pericardium boundary. In the example manual label, there are some pixels mislabelled as the region inside the pericardium around the right boundary. In the segmentation results of the Dice loss in Fig. 3(c), some pixels in that region still are mislabelled. With the FD loss, both Fig. 3(d) and Fig. 3(e) have better segmentation results in that region.

Table 1. Performance of losses with U-net++ backbone VGG16.

Pre-processing	Loss	MIU (%)	DSC (%)	SEN (%)
No	Cross-entropy loss	92.21	95.95	95.42
	Dice loss	92.20	95.94	96.38
	FD loss	90.21	94.85	94.09
Yes	Cross-entropy loss	96.58	97.61	98.28
	Dice loss	96.52	98.12	98.24
	FD loss	95.56	96.68	97.71
	FD	Dice loss	**96.76**	**98.20**	**98.55**

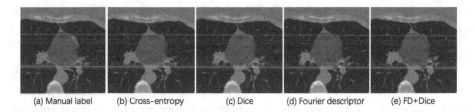

(a) Manual label   (b) Cross-entropy   (c) Dice   (d) Fourier descriptor   (e) FD+Dice

Fig. 3. The figure illustrates the visualization of different segmentation results within the pericardium region: (a) Manual label, (b) Cross-entropy loss, (c) Dice loss, (d) FD loss, and (e) Compound loss (FD + Dice).

Effect with Fewer Fourier Descriptors in the Fourier Descriptor Loss. The key to the FD loss is the shape descriptors. By default, we utilize the same number of descriptors as sample points on the contour, which is, in our case, 256. For loss calculation, we use the absolute values of the FDs. Due to the symmetric relation of the FDs, by default, every shape is represented by 128 real number FDs. As FDs represent the shape information in the frequency domain, we could control the shape information in the loss function by controlling descriptors. By removing high-frequency descriptors, the shape information in small scales which could be the noise is neglected. In addition, the computation cost is reduced. In Table 2, we show the experiment results of the FD loss with 128, 64, 32, 16, and

8 descriptors. The results indicate that more descriptors do not lead to better segmentation. With our data, 64 descriptors result in the best performance. We also tested the compound loss of the 64 descriptor loss and the dice loss, which lead to 96.69% in MIU, 98,15% in DCS, and 98.56% in SEN.

Table 2. Performance of FD loss with fewer FDs.

#descriptors	MIU (%)	DSC (%)	SEN (%)
128	95.56	96.68	97.71
64	95.94	97.50	98.02
32	95.62	97.26	97.90
16	95.12	96.98	97.48
8	94.94	97.03	97.63

Weighing Fourier Descriptors in the Fourier Descriptor Loss. As the FDs represent shape information in the frequency domain, by weighing the descriptors we could weigh the shape representations of the corresponding frequency. There may be some shape representations that are more important for segmentation. As the low-frequency descriptors represent the global shape, we apply higher weights to them to get the global shape better considered. We applied Sigmoid-based weights to the FDs c_n. The Sigmoid function is define as $\sigma(x) = \frac{1}{1+e^{-x}}$. Assume we have N FDs, with a selected range of $[a, b]$, for the nth FD, the corresponding weight is $\sigma(a - \frac{a-b}{N} * n)$. Thus, the loss becomes

$$\mathcal{L}_{FD}^{\sigma} = \sum_{n=0}^{N-1} \sigma(a - \frac{a-b}{N} * n)|c_n^G - c_n^S| \tag{3}$$

With a positive a and a negative b, we apply higher weights to low-frequency descriptors while lower weights to high-frequency descriptors. As shown in Table 3, with $[a, b] = [4, -4]$, we obtained better results (MIU: 96.18% [+0.62%], DSC: 97.40% [+0.72%], SEN: 98.21% [+0.5%]).

Table 3. Performance of FD loss with Sigmoid-weighted Fourier descriptors.

$[a, b]$	MIU(%)	DSC(%)	SEN (%)
$[3, -5]$	96.12	97.27	98.21
$[4, -4]$	96.18	97.40	98.21
$[5, -3]$	95.07	96.96	97.46
$[6, -2]$	95.76	97.37	97.91
$[7, -1]$	95.80	97.48	97.98

4 Conclusions and Future Work

We have presented a method of FD loss and polar coordinate transformation for pericardium segmentation. The pre-processing with polar coordinate transformation overall leads to better segmentation for all losses. A recent work by Alblas et al. [21] for artery vessel wall segmentation also showed better results with polar coordinate transformation. Compared to other boundary-based losses such as the boundary loss [8] and Hausdroff distance loss [9] which need to be trained with a region-based loss, the FD loss can be trained individually. Although, when working individually, FD loss can not outperform region-based losses like the Dice loss and cross-entropy loss. It has shown the potential to improve both the performance and convergence speed when working as a regularizer of the Dice loss. Due to the physical meaning and invertibility of FDs, our loss has more interpretability. As we worked with medical images, the labels of the pericardium were annotated manually. There are unavoidable noise and mislabeled pixels around the boundary in the manual labels. Compared to the manual labels, the predicted segmentation is smoother with less noise along the boundary.

A main limitation of the method is that it can not apply to non-convex shapes with strong curvatures. The centroid must locate inside the shape for further polar coordinate transformation. The cause of the limitation is the application of the Fourier series to the shape signature along the boundary. There may be alternative ways to avoid this limitation by using a 2D Fourier transform. In this work, we focus on 2D CT slices as the manual labels were annotated in 2D manners.

For future work, it is possible to explore a similar approach in 3D cylinder coordinates since many medical images are 3D images. Although the Fourier transforms only apply to 1D or 2D signals, a recent work by Wiesner et al. [22] shows a similar transform in 3D for encoding the cell shape. All in all, we have shown the potential of FD loss and polar coordinate transformation in pericardium segmentation with shape/boundary-based formulation, but the generalization of this method is an open field for further research.

Acknowledgment. This work is supported by ZonMw under project B3CARE (project number 104006003). This project has received funding from the EU Horizon 2020 research and innovation program under the Marie Sklodowska-Curie grant agreement No 777826. CB acknowledges support from the Dutch 4TU HTSF program Precision Medicine.

References

1. Dey, D., Nakazato, R., Li, D., Berman, D.: Epicardial and thoracic fat-noninvasive measurement and clinical implications. Cardiovasc. Diagn. Ther. **2**, 85 (2012)
2. He, X., et al.: Automatic segmentation and quantification of epicardial adipose tissue from coronary computed tomography angiography. Phys. Med. Biol. **65**, 095012 (2020)

3. Milletari, F., Navab, N., Ahmadi, S.: V-net: fully convolutional neural networks for volumetric medical image segmentation. In: 2016 Fourth International Conference On 3D Vision (3DV), pp. 565–571 (2016)

4. Ronneberger, O., Fischer, P., Brox, T.: U-net: convolutional networks for biomedical image segmentation. In: Navab, N., Hornegger, J., Wells, W.M., Frangi, A.F. (eds.) MICCAI 2015, Part III. LNCS, vol. 9351, pp. 234–241. Springer, Cham (2015). https://doi.org/10.1007/978-3-319-24574-4_28

5. Ma, J., et al.: Loss odyssey in medical image segmentation. Med. Image Anal. **71**, 102035 (2021)

6. El Jurdi, R., Petitjean, C., Honeine, P., Cheplygina, V., Abdallah, F.: High-level prior-based loss functions for medical image segmentation: A survey. Comput. Vision Image Underst. **210**, 103248 (2021)

7. Liu, L., Wolterink, J., Brune, C., Veldhuis, R.: Anatomy-aided deep learning for medical image segmentation: a review. Phys. Med. Biol. **66**, 11TR01 (2021)

8. Kervadec, H., Bouchtiba, J., Desrosiers, C., Granger, E., Dolz, J., Ayed, I.: Boundary loss for highly unbalanced segmentation. In: International Conference On Medical Imaging With Deep Learning, pp. 285–296 (2019)

9. Karimi, D., Salcudean, S.: Reducing the Hausdorff distance in medical image segmentation with convolutional neural networks. IEEE Trans. Med. Imaging **39**, 499–513 (2019)

10. Caliva, F., Iriondo, C., Martinez, A., Majumdar, S., Pedoia, V.: Distance map loss penalty term for semantic segmentation. ArXiv Preprint ArXiv:1908.03679 (2019)

11. Kervadec, H., Bahig, H., Letourneau-Guillon, L., Dolz, J., Ayed, I.: Beyond pixelwise supervision for segmentation: a few global shape descriptors might be surprisingly good! In: Medical Imaging With Deep Learning, pp. 354–368 (2021)

12. Zhang, D., Lu, G.: Study and evaluation of different Fourier methods for image retrieval. Image Vision Comput. **23**, 33–49 (2005)

13. Kunttu, I., Lepisto, L., Rauhamaa, J., Visa, A.: Multiscale Fourier descriptor for shape-based image retrieval. In: 2004 Proceedings of the 17th International Conference on Pattern Recognition, ICPR 2004, vol. 2, pp. 765–768 (2004)

14. Abche, A., Yaacoub, F., Maalouf, A., Karam, E.: Image registration based on neural network and Fourier transform. In: 2006 International Conference of the IEEE Engineering in Medicine and Biology Society, pp. 4803–4806 (2006)

15. Lin, J., Ma, L., Yao, Y.: A Fourier domain training framework for convolutional neural networks based on the Fourier domain pyramid pooling method and Fourier domain exponential linear unit. IEEE Access **7**, 116612–116631 (2019)

16. Fuoli, D., Van Gool, L., Timofte, R.: Fourier space losses for efficient perceptual image super-resolution. In: Proceedings of the IEEE/CVF International Conference on Computer Vision, pp. 2360–2369 (2021)

17. Han, Y., Hong, B.: Deep learning based on Fourier convolutional neural network incorporating random kernels. Electronics **10**, 2004 (2021)

18. Vonder, M., et al.: Coronary artery calcium imaging in the ROBINSCA trial: rationale, design, and technical background. Acad. Radiol. **25**, 118–128 (2018)

19. Fedorov, A., et al.: 3D Slicer as an image computing platform for the quantitative imaging network. Magn. Reson. Imaging **30**, 1323–1341 (2012)

20. Zhou, Z., Rahman Siddiquee, M.M., Tajbakhsh, N., Liang, J.: UNet++: a nested U-net architecture for medical image segmentation. In: Stoyanov, D., et al. (eds.) DLMIA/ML-CDS -2018. LNCS, vol. 11045, pp. 3–11. Springer, Cham (2018). https://doi.org/10.1007/978-3-030-00889-5_1

21. Alblas, D., Brune, C., Wolterink, J.: Deep-learning-based carotid artery vessel wall segmentation in black-blood MRI using anatomical priors. In: Medical Imaging 2022: Image Processing, vol. 12032, pp. 237–244 (2022)

22. Wiesner, D., Nečasová, T., Svoboda, D.: On generative modeling of cell shape using 3D GANs. In: Ricci, E., Rota Bulò, S., Snoek, C., Lanz, O., Messelodi, S., Sebe, N. (eds.) ICIAP 2019, Part II. LNCS, vol. 11752, pp. 672–682. Springer, Cham (2019). https://doi.org/10.1007/978-3-030-30645-8_61

Stroke Risk Stratification Using Transfer Learning on Carotid Ultrasound Images

Georgia D. Liapi[1]($\boxtimes$) (iD), Christos Markides[2] (iD), Christos P. Loizou[1] (iD),
Maura Griffin[3], Andrew Nicolaides[4] (iD), and Efthyvoulos Kyriacou[1] (iD)

[1] Department of Electrical Engineering, Computer Engineering and Informatics,
Cyprus University of Technology, 3036 Limassol, Cyprus
gd.liapi@edu.cut.ac.cy

[2] Department of Electrical Engineering, Computer Engineering and Informatics,
Frederick University, 1036 Nicosia, Cyprus

[3] Vascular Noninvasive Diagnostic Centre, London, UK

[4] Vascular Screening and Diagnostic Center, Nicosia, Cyprus

Abstract. Transfer learning (TL) reuses knowledge from real-world objects to perform faster and accurate image classification tasks in related content. Multiple studies have shown evaluated deep learning (DL) models in atherosclerotic plaque classification (Asymptomatic, AS, or Symptomatic, SY), using carotid ultrasound (CUS) images, with only a few studies examining TL in this task. In this study, we use TL to classify plaques in CUS longitudinal images, upon image standardization. Overall, 189 images were included (189 patients; 95 SY and 94 AS), which we distributed into training, validation and final evaluation, following the 90–10% data split rule. Our image standardization steps included: image resolution normalization, intensity normalization, and speckle noise removal, followed by cropping of the examples to the plaque region of interest (ROI) and resizing to uniform dimensions. The Xception (Chollet, 2017) and the MobileNet (Howard et al., 2017) were evaluated in this study, by freezing their backbone architecture (pre-trained on ImageNet) and adding new dense layers, which we trained to classify AS and SY cases. The classification accuracy (CA) of Xception and MobileNet was found at 85% and 75%, respectively. Xception yielded an 81.8% and 88.9% precision for the AS and SY cases, respectively. We also extracted saliency maps (AS or SY), from the best model's classification layer, during evaluation, to acquire an intuition for plaque areas that play important role in model decision. In the future, we plan to repeat this work with a larger standardized dataset, to also fine-tune layers in model backbones and improve model classification performance.

Keywords: Transfer Learning · Carotid Plaque · Carotid Ultrasound · Stroke Risk Stratification · Saliency Maps

N. Tsapatsoulis et al. (Eds.): CAIP 2023, LNCS 14185, pp. 130–139, 2023.
https://doi.org/10.1007/978-3-031-44240-7_13

1 Introduction

1.1 Artificial Intelligence-Based Stroke Risk Assessment

Ischemic stroke risk stratification from carotid atherosclerosis can be based on carotid plaque detection and characteristics, as well as patient clinical data [1]. Carotid B-mode ultrasound imaging is the most common imaging modality for experts to analyze carotid plaque features. In previous studies, CUS atherosclerotic plaque components were identified and classified in AS and SY patients, which enabled a better understanding of their role in disease prognosis, while they were also used to develop computational models for stroke risk assessment [2–7]. During the past ten years, there was an increase in the scientific approaches attempting to automate the process of carotid plaque classification, using CUS images and Machine Learning (ML) or DL models, trained either from scratch or used with TL.

Deep Learning-Based Stroke Risk Assessment. In [8], Lekadir et al. developed a custom convolutional neural network (CNN), which they trained to differentiate between lipid, fibrous and calcified plaque examples, reaching a 75 ± 16% mean ± standard deviation (m ± std) pixel level plaque CA. Shen et al. [9], developed a multi-task learning model, hosting two associated tasks, one to classify plaques in CUS images into four types (intimal thickening, weak echo, hybrid echo, strong echo) using a custom DL model (4 dense blocks similar to DenseNet-161), and one performing regression of characteristics derived from patient reports, to improve the plaque CA. They reached a 79.82 ± 0.38% CA, over all types.

Later on, Guang et al. [10] designed a DL-system for automatic plaque characterization into stable or vulnerable, in contrast-enhanced CUS videos, including interdependent processes for marker symbol removal, blending of B-mode video frames (VFs) with contrast-enhanced CUS VFs, and plaque region of interest (ROI) detection and classification. To extract ROI features from all VFs per video, they employed Xception [11] (with TL), while they fused all extracted features from each video and fed them into a classifier to decide the plaque type, reporting sensitivity (SE) and specificity (SP) at 79.2% and 84.4%, respectively. Additionally, Ma et al. [12] proposed a DL multilevel strip pooling, building on the visual geometry group backbone architecture, to classify plaque (arbitrarily sized) in CUS images, into echo-reach, echo-intermediate and echolucent. They reached a 92.1% and 95.6% SE and SP, respectively.

Also, Skandha et al. [13], developed a computational system for carotid plaque classification in CUS images (AS or SY), consisted of different DL and TL models, trained with predefined augmented dataset versions and they showed that their best DL model outperformed their best TL model, yielding 95.66 ± 1.55% and 83.33 ± 3.35% CA, respectively. In an additional study [14], the same group used TL again, for plaque classification in CUS images, but they trained the models with images from 2 different medical centers (individually or by combining examples). Their results showed that TL outperformed DL (94.55% versus 93.55% CA, respectively; average from the 2 datasets). The same group also published a study [15], where they investigated the potential of merging DL and ML models, for stroke risk stratification, trained with CUS plaque images from 2 different datasets and concluded that a CNN-ML combination (CNN-decision tree model) yielded the highest CA (99.50 ± 1.47%), on mixed image dataset. Finally, to alleviate the problem of arbitrarily sized carotid plaques in CUS images, Ma et al. [16] developed a DL model, trained with transverse and longitudinal views, from bilateral CUS images, for stroke risk stratification, which occupied 2 types of subnetworks, one for feature extraction and one for feature downsampling, with the latter one hosting different object-specific pooling strategies for feature downsampling. They achieved a 97.3% CA.

Transfer Learning-Based Stroke Risk Assessment. Apart from the previously mentioned studies [13–15], where TL-based carotid plaque classification experiments were included, there have been only a few studies solely investigating the contribution of TL in stroke risk stratification, using CUS plaque images (see Table 1). In 2019, Panayides et al. [17] applied TL using the backbones of popular CNNs (pre-trained on ImageNet), as CUS plaque ROI image feature extractors (for AS and SY cases), feeding the resulting features into a logistic regression model for classification and achieved 78% precision (PR), for ResNet and MobileNet. In 2021, Sanagala et al. [18] (see also Table 1), evaluated 10 CNN models for stroke risk assessment, using them with TL and augmented versions of the same CUS plaque dataset (AS and SY cases). They used the backbone of each model (trained on ImageNet) as feature extractor and a new set of dense layers, from which the last one was used for CUS plaque classification. From the 10 TL models they tested, MobileNet yielded the highest carotid plaque CA at 96.1 ± 3. The rest of the TL-based carotid plaque classification studies, given in Table 1, have been described in the previous Section.

Table 1. Summary of the studies examining TL for atherosclerotic plaque classification in CUS images (only the best TL model from each study is reported in this table).

Year	Study	N images AS/SY	CNN Model	PPR RN/IN/D	ML Type	TL Type	k-fold CV	Input Size	CA m ± std%	PR %
2019	[17]	1121 108/1013	ResNet50 MobileNet	✓/✓/×	LG	FE + ML	-	NG	NG	78[a] 78[a]
2020	[13]	346 196/150	VGG16	✓/✓/×	-	FE + NDLs	✓	256^2	83.3 ± 3.4[b]	85
2021	[14]	346 196/150 160 110/50	VGG19	×/✓/×	-	FE + NDLs	✓	256^2	94.6[c]	-
2021	[18]	346 196/150	MobileNet	✓/✓/×	-	FE + NDLs	✓	128^2	96.1 ± 3[b]	-
2022	[15]	346 196/150	VGG19	✓/✓/×	-	FE + NDLs	✓	256^2	96.6 ± 1.1[d]	-
2023	This study	189 94/95	Xception	✓/✓/✓	-	FE + NDLs	-	W: 256 H: 128	85[d]	85.5

AS: Asymptomatic, CA: Classification Accuracy, CV: Cross Validation, D: Despeckled, FE: Feature extractor, H: Height, IN: Intensity-normalized, LG: Logistic Regression, ML: Machine Learning, N: Number, NDLs: New Dense Layers, NG: Not given, PPR: Pre-processing, PR: Precision, RN: Resolution-normalized, SY: Symptomatic, TL: Transfer Learning, W: Width.
[a]Weighted average of SY and AS resulted precision, [b]With Data Augmentation, [c]Over the mean of all datasets, [d]Mixed dataset.

Although there have been noticeable TL-based carotid plaque CA results in previous studies, the intervention in the plaque CUS image primary size, to support each model's input dimensions, has not been fully reported. Resizing of the CUS images changes the content to an extent, especially when the final dimensions do not closely resemble the primary plaque ROI dimensions. Also, in many of these studies, where high CAs have been reached, there has been extensive data augmentation on the images, some of which includes skewness, that might not represent actual variations met in real carotid plaque examples. Moreover, in studies where multiple CUS image datasets have been used, image resolution normalization has not been applied, but statistical analysis has been followed.

To solve the above-mentioned inconsistencies, in this study we propose a stroke risk assessment approach, established on TL-based plaque classification (AS versus SY) in CUS images (from different medical centers), where the examples are first subjected to standardization, with the model input size decided based on the actual average plaque ROI dimensions.

2 Materials and Methods

All the methodology steps, followed in this study, are shown in Fig. 1 and explained in the following sections.

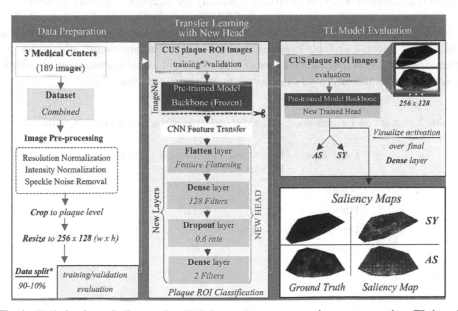

Fig. 1. Holistic view of all steps for CUS image dataset preparation, preprocessing, TL-based carotid plaque classification and extraction of saliency maps per category, as followed in this study. AS: Asymptomatic, CNN: Convolutional Neural Network, CUS: Carotid Ultrasound, ROI: Region of Interest, SY: Symptomatic. *With data shuffling and class balance.

2.1 Carotid Ultrasound Images and Patient Data

In this study, we included 189 CUS longitudinal images (189 patients; 94 AS and 95 SY), which came from 3 medical centers (in Cyprus, Greece, and United Kingdom). In all patient cases, the carotid stenosis degree was higher than 50%. Each image was accompanied by a plaque-specific ROI annotation, manually selected by an experienced ultrasonographer and vascular surgeon.

2.2 Image Preprocessing

All CUS images were resolution-normalized to 20 pixels/millimeter (with bicubic interpolation) as in [18] and intensity-normalized as in [24], while speckle noise removal was applied with a hybrid-median filter (over the entire image, with a 5×5 window and 2 iterations) using the software in [19]. Then, each image was cropped to the plaque bounding box area and resized to 256×128 pixel size, while the carotid background surrounding the plaque was removed. It is important to mention that the actual m ± std deviation for CUS plaque width and height, in the resolution-normalized samples, prior to the final resizing, was 208 ± 102 and 69 ± 31 pixels, respectively.

2.3 Transfer Learning Models

In this study, we evaluated two deep CNNs, namely the Xception [20] and the MobileNet [21] (primarily trained on ImageNet), in CUS plaque classification based on TL. We removed the existing final classification layer, attached to the backbone of each model and inserted new layers (see Table 2 and Fig. 1) to tailor their weights towards atherosclerotic plaque classification. The final number of filters (128), in the first dense layer we added, was selected empirically, after trials with less and more neurons.

Table 2. Set of new DL network layers, added at the top of the selected models, in this study.

Layer Type	Number of Neurons	Activation Function	Rate
Flatten	–	–	–
Dense	128	ReLu	–
Dropout	–	–	0.6
Dense	2	Softmax	–

2.4 Model Training Process

Both the Xception and MobileNet were used through Keras/TensorFlow (Python). We split the data with the 90–10% rule approximately (155 images for training; 77 AS and 78 SY, 14 for validation; 7 AS and 7 SY, and 20 for testing; 10 AS and 10 SY) and shuffled them. We trained the added layers given in Table 2, with 'early stopping', with 18 and 16 patience (for Xception and MobileNet, respectively), monitoring the validation loss. The final epochs were 47 and 36 for Xception and MobileNet, respectively. The batch size was set to 31 for both models. We also used minor (on the fly) augmentation (4 degrees rotation range and horizontal flip).

2.5 Model Carotid Plaque Classification Performance

To assess model CUS plaque classification performance, we calculated the following metrics, based on true positives (TP) and negatives (TN), and false positives (FP) and negatives (FN): CA (TP+TN/(TP+TN+FP+FN)), PR (TP/(TP+FP)), Recall (TP/(TP+FN)), and F1-score ((2 × PR × Recall)/(PR+Recall)), as explained in [22].

2.6 Saliency Maps Per Carotid Plaque Category

In order to derive a primary intuition of the carotid plaque areas that the best model in this study paid more attention to and better understand the plaque subareas (pixel populations) that mostly contributed to sample classification, we visualized the SMs (AS or SY, according to the given example) in our evaluated images. The SMs (vanilla saliency) were extracted from the last dense layer of the best model (trained on the CUS plaque ROIs) following the process introduced in [23] and developed in [24], where the 'softmax' function must be replaced by linear activation. Saliency was computed as the gradient of the output category with respect to the input example. In essence, the results are model attention heatmaps.

3 Results

As explained above, for this study we 'freezed' the backbone layers in Xception and MobileNet and trained two new dense layers (see Table 3) for CUS plaque classification. An initial attempt to continue with 'unfreezing' the last convolutional block per model and update the corresponding weights, led to early overfitting, due to the limited amount of the available training images.

The CUS plaque classification performance per model, in this study, is given in Table 3. More specifically, Xception outperformed MobileNet, reaching 82% and 89% PR, for the ASs and SYs, respectively, and an 85% CA. Overall, both models exhibited higher PR when distinguishing the SY cases.

As explained in Sect. 2.6, we also generated the SMs, for all the AS and SY CUS plaque images, evaluated with Xception. Three SMs per carotid plaque category, are shown in Fig. 2 (in grayscale). Noticeably, Xception seems to have partially relied on AS and SY plaque areas (ground truth), where pixel intensity exhibits great (abrupt) differences. These SMs were extracted to provide a primary view on the plaque ROI components that play important role in plaque classification.

Table 3. Transfer learning model CUS plaque classification performances, as found in this study.

Model	Class	N samples	Precision	Recall	F1-Score	CA
Xception	AS	10	**0.82**	**0.90**	**0.86**	**0.85**
	SY	10	**0.89**	**0.80**	**0.84**	
MobileNet	AS	10	0.73	0.80	0.76	0.75
	SY	10	0.78	0.70	0.73	

AS: Asymptomatic, CA: Accuracy, N: Number, SY: Symptomatic. Best results are given in bold.

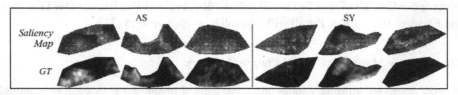

Fig. 2. Saliency maps for AS and SY Xception-classified (last dense layer) CUS plaque images, as extracted in this study. AS: Asymptomatic, GT: Ground Truth, SY: Symptomatic.

4   Discussion

In this study, we applied TL on standardized CUS plaque images, for stroke risk stratification. We evaluated Xception and the MobileNet (pre-trained on ImageNet), using their backbones as feature extractors and merging them with a new set of dense layers, which we trained for CUS plaque classification.

Data standardization is a crucial step when ML, DL or statistical analysis is involved. We have noticed that several DL-based CUS plaque classification studies do not use or do not report appropriate data standardization strategies. For example, when CUS images from different medical centers and machines are used, a uniform image resolution should be considered. In [14], different image datasets, with different image resolutions were used. In contrast, in [17], all images were resolution- and intensity-normalized, prior to utilization in TL, for feature extraction.

A similar notion exists for image intensity normalization, for CUS plaque images from different medical centers. All studies given in Table 1 have applied a similar image intensity normalization method, as introduced and developed in [25].

Regarding speckle noise removal, to the best of our knowledge, there has not been a previous TL-based CUS plaque image classification study applying despeckling, prior to model training, although it has been found that speckle noise removal (using a hybrid-median filter) is a process that not only improves the visual perception by experts, but also gives better texture and video quality metrics [26].

Also, compared to previous relevant studies [13–15] and [18], here we concluded on the model input size based on the average plaque ROI dimensions as resulted after image resolution normalization (as reported in Sect. 2.2). This prevents large changes in the carotid plaque major and minor axes, prior to model training.

Furthermore, it is important to mention that the data augmentation strategies followed in cases of limited amount of data, especially when medical images are involved, should be justified. More specifically, there have been studies ([13–15] and [18]) using aggressive data augmentation in CUS plaque images without appropriate reporting (such as shearing of axes; missing the corresponding kernel values). Simple transformations, such as image flipping (horizontal or vertical), or rotation (to a logical range of degrees) are not expected to alter the primary label for a given image sample. More complex approaches, such as shearing (skewness) on the x- or y-axis of a given image might cause large modifications in a primary image content, and thus point to a different represented label; especially, in the context of carotid atherosclerosis, where AS and SY plaques often include components with common image features. In this study, we applied minor data augmentation (a 4 degree rotation range and horizontal flip; on the fly) and reached an 85% CUS plaque CA.

The main effort of this study is to develop a system to be used for stroke risk stratification, starting from image standardization. To the best of our knowledge, this study is the first to evaluate TL-established stroke risk stratification with CUS plaque images, based on preceding image resolution normalization, intensity normalization and speckle noise removal. Additionally, in this study we extracted the SMs for all the AS and SY cases, included in our evaluation data, to acquire a primary visual understanding of the carotid plaque components that mostly contribute to case classification. Based on these SMs, in future studies, we will develop an explainable DL model to further analyze and characterize these specific areas with regard to their synthesis, such as calcification of plaque, lipid core lipid, fibrous or calcified area, as verified and discussed in [27] and [28].

Finally, as in the current study the CUS plaque ROIs were manually selected by an experienced vascular surgeon (a time-consuming task), the TL-based stroke risk stratification methodology we presented here will be repeated, such that the primary carotid plaque ROIs will be generated automatically by the model we have recently proposed and evaluated in [29].

Conclusion. Overall, this study showed that the application of proper image preprocessing combined with TL-based CUS plaque image classification, returns reliable CAs and PRs for both the AS and SY cases. In the future, we will update the current results, with a larger dataset, where we plan to also update weights in the last convolutional block layers, per model, under a k-fold cross validation protocol.

Limitations. In this study, we had a limited amount of data available, with regards to the needs of a TL-based model training process, although they came from 3 different medical centers and allowed a primary good carotid plaque CA. The lack of data also did not encouraged the utilization of a k-fold cross validation model training process or the updating of weights in the last convolutional layers in Xception. We also applied resizing to our samples, to some extent.

Acknowledgment. This study is part of the two-year 'AtheroRisk' Project (Call: "Restart 2016–2020", Proposal: EXCELLENCE/0421/0292), funded by the Cyprus Research and Innovation Foundation.

References

1. Paraskevas, K.I., Nicolaides, A.N., Kakkos, S.K.: Asymptomatic Carotid Stenosis and Risk of Stroke (ACSRS) study: what have we learned from it? Ann. Transl. Med. **8**(19), 1271 (2020)
2. Kyriacou, E.C., Petroudi, S., Pattichis, C.S., Pattichis, M.S., et al.: Prediction of high-risk asymptomatic carotid plaques based on ultrasonic image features. IEEE Trans. Inf. Technol. Biomed. **16**(5), 966–973 (2012)
3. Kakkos, S.K., Griffin, M.B., Nicolaides, A.N., Kyriacou, E., et al.: The size of juxtaluminal hypoechoic area in ultrasound images of asymptomatic carotid plaques predicts the occurrence of stroke. J. Vasc. Surg. **57**(3), 609–618 (2013)
4. Loizou, C.P., Pantziaris, M., Theofilou, M., Kasparis, T., Kyriakou, E.: Texture analysis in ultrasound images of carotid plaque components of asymptomatic and symptomatic subjects. In: Papadopoulos, H., Andreou, A.S., Iliadis, L., Maglogiannis, I. (eds.) AIAI 2013. IFIPAICT, vol. 412, pp. 282–291. Springer, Berlin, Heidelberg (2013). https://doi.org/10.1007/978-3-642-41142-7_29
5. Doonan, R.J., Gorgui, J., Veinot, J.P., Lai, C., et al.: Plaque echodensity and textural features are associated with histologic carotid plaque instability. J. Vasc. Surg. **64**(3), 671–677 (2016)
6. Roy-Cardinal, M.H., Destrempes, F., Soulez, G., Cloutier, G.: Assessment of carotid artery plaque components with machine learning classification using homodyned-k parametric maps and elastograms. IEEE Trans. Ultrason. Ferroelectr. Freq. Control **66**(3), 493–504 (2019)
7. Constantinou, K.P., Constantinou, I.P., Pattichis, C.S., Pattichis M.S.: Medical image analysis using AM-FM models and methods. IEEE Rev. Biomed. Eng. **14**, 270–289 (2021)
8. Lekadir, K., Galimzianova, A., Betriu, À., Del Mar Vila, M., et al.: A convolutional neural network for automatic characterization of plaque composition in carotid ultrasound. IEEE J. Biomed. Health Inform. **21**(1), 48–55 (2017)
9. Shen, H., Zhang, W., Wang, H., Ding, G., Xie, J.: NDDR-LCS: a multi-task learning method for classification of carotid plaques. In: 2020 IEEE International Conference on Image Processing (ICIP), Abu Dhabi, United Arab Emirates, pp. 2461–2465. IEEE (2020)
10. Guang, Y., He, W., Ning, B., Zhang, H., et al.: Deep learning-based carotid plaque vulnerability classification with multicentre contrast-enhanced ultrasound video: a comparative diagnostic study. BMJ Open **11**(8), e047528 (2021)
11. Chollet, F.: Xception: Deep Learning with Depthwise Separable Convolutions. arXiv, (2017). http://arxiv.org/abs/1610.02357
12. Ma, W., Cheng, X., Xu, X., Wang, F., et al.: Multilevel strip pooling-based convolutional neural network for the classification of carotid plaque echogenicity. Comput. Math. Methods Med. **2021**, 1–13 (2021)
13. Skandha, S.S., Gupta, S.K., Saba, L., Koppula, V.K., et al.: 3-D optimized classification and characterization artificial intelligence paradigm for cardiovascular/stroke risk stratification using carotid ultrasound-based delineated plaque: AtheromaticTM 2.0. Comput. Biol. Med. **125**, 103958 (2020)
14. Saba, L., Sanagala, S.S., Gupta, S.K., Koppula, V.K., et al.: A multicenter study on carotid ultrasound plaque tissue characterization and classification using six deep artificial intelligence models: a stroke application. IEEE Trans. Instrum. Meas. **70**, 1–12 (2021)
15. Skandha, S.S., Nicolaides, A., Gupta, S.K., Koppula, V.K., et al.: A hybrid deep learning paradigm for carotid plaque tissue characterization and its validation in multicenter cohorts using a supercomputer framework. Comput. Biol. Med. **141**, 105131 (2022)
16. Ma, W., Xia, Y., Wu, X., Yue, Z., et al.: Object-specific four-path network for stroke risk stratification of carotid arteries in ultrasound images. Comput. Math. Methods Med. **2022**, 1–17 (2022)

17. Panayides, A., Kyriacou, E., Nicolaides, A., Pattichis, C.S.: Stroke risk stratification using transfer learning. In: 41st IEEE Engineering in Medicine and Biology Conference (EMBC). Berlin, Germany (2019)
18. Sanagala, S.S., Nicolaides, A., Gupta, S.K., Koppula, V.K., et al.: Ten fast transfer learning models for carotid ultrasound plaque tissue characterization in augmentation framework embedded with heatmaps for stroke risk stratification. Diagnostics 11(11), 2109 (2021)
19. Kakkos, S.K., Nicolaides, A.N., Kyriacou, E., Pattichis, C. S., et al.: Effect of zooming on texture features of ultrasonic images. Cardiovasc Ultrasound 4(8) (2006)
20. Loizou, C.P., Pattichis, C.S.: Despeckle filtering algorithms and software for ultrasound imaging. Synth. Lect. Algorithms Softw. Eng. 1(1), 1–166 (2008)
21. Howard, A.G., Zhu, M., Chen, B., Kalenichenko, D., et al.: MobileNets: Efficient Convolutional Neural Networks for Mobile Vision Applications. arXiv (2017). http://arxiv.org/abs/1704.04861
22. Hicks, S.A., Strümke, I., Thambawita, V., Hammou, M., et al.: On evaluation metrics for medical applications of artificial intelligence. Sci Rep. 12(1), 5979 (2022)
23. Simonyan K., Vedaldi A. and Zisserman A.: Deep inside convolutional networks: Visualising image classification models and saliency maps. arXiv (2014). https://doi.org/10.48550/arXiv.1312.6034
24. Raghavendra, K., et al.: Keras-Vis. GitHub. https://github.com/raghakot/keras-vis
25. Elatrozy, T., Nicolaides, A., Tegos, T., Zarka, A.Z., et al.: The effect of B-mode ultrasonic image standardization of the echodensity of symptomatic and asymptomatic carotid bifurcation plaque. Int. Angiol. 7(3), 179–186 (1998)
26. Loizou, C.P., Kasparis, T., Christodoulides, P., Theofanous, C., et al.: Despeckle filtering in ultrasound video of the common carotid artery. In: 12th IEEE International Conference on Bioinformatics & Bioengineering (BIBE), pp. 721–726. IEEE, Larnaca, Cyprus (2012)
27. Reilly, L.M., Lusby, R.J., Hughes, L., Ferrell, L.D., et al.: Carotid plaque histology using real-time ultrasonography. Clinical and therapeutic implications. Am. J. Surg. 146(2), 188–193 (1983)
28. El-Barghouty, N.M., Levine, T., Ladva, S., Flanagan, A., Nicolaides, A.: Histological verification of computerised carotid plaque characterisation. Eur. J. Vasc. Endovasc. Surg. 11(4), 414–416 (1996)
29. Liapi, G.D., Gemenaris, M., Loizou, C.P., Kyriacou, E., et al.: Automated segmentation and classification of the atherosclerotic carotid plaque in ultrasound videos. In: 24th International Conference on Digital Signal Processing (DSP), pp. 1–4. IEEE, Rhodes, Greece (2023)

A Comparative Study of Explainable AI models in the Assessment of Multiple Sclerosis

Andria Nicolaou[1]($\boxtimes$) (iD), Nicoletta Prentzas[1] (iD), Christos P. Loizou[2](iD),
Marios Pantzaris[3] (iD), Antonis Kakas[1] (iD), and Constantinos S. Pattichis[1] (iD)

[1] Department of Computer Science, University of Cyprus, Nicosia, Cyprus
{nicolaou.andria,prentzas.nicoletta,antonis,pattichi}@ucy.ac.cy
[2] Department of Electrical Engineering, Computer Engineering and Informatics,
Cyprus University of Technology, Limassol, Cyprus
christos.loizou@cut.ac.cy
[3] Cyprus Institute of Neurology and Genetics, Nicosia, Cyprus
pantzari@cing.ac.cy

Abstract. Multiple Sclerosis (MS) is characterized by complex and heterogeneous nature and as a result, there's currently no cure. Medications can help control the progression and ease the symptoms of MS. The scientific interest in the field of explainable artificial intelligence (AI) comes to the surface and aims to assist computer-aided diagnostic systems to be established in medical use by providing understandable and transparent information to the experts. The objective of this study was to present different learning methods of explainable AI models in the assessment of MS disease based on clinical data and brain magnetic resonance imaging (MRI) lesion texture features and compare them by focusing on the main findings. The learning methods used machine learning and argumentation theory to differentiate subjects with relapsing-remitting MS (RRMS) from progressive MS (PMS) subjects and provide explanations. The results showed that the different learning methods achieved a high accuracy of 99% and gave similar explanations as they extracted the same set of rules. It is hoped that the proposed methodology could lead to personalized treatment in the management of MS disease.

Keywords: Multiple Sclerosis · Brain MRI · Lesions · Texture Features · Clinical Data · Machine Learning · Rule Extraction · Argumentation · Explainable AI

1 Introduction

Multiple Sclerosis (MS) is a complex autoimmune disease affecting the central nervous system and is the leading cause of non-traumatic neurological disability in young adults [1]. Both environmental and genetic factors are believed to contribute to MS susceptibility. Environmental influences such as smoking, childhood obesity, infectious mononucleosis, and low serum vitamin D are consistently associated with increased MS risk [1, 2]. While it may be possible to assess an individual's MS susceptibility based on genetic data and risk factor exposure, the practicality of routinely predicting MS development faces theoretical and practical challenges [1].

N. Tsapatsoulis et al. (Eds.): CAIP 2023, LNCS 14185, pp. 140–148, 2023.
https://doi.org/10.1007/978-3-031-44240-7_14

MS is traditionally seen as having two distinct stages. In the initial stage, there is inflammation that leads to relapsing-remitting disease (RRMS). In the later stage, there is neurodegeneration that results in a progressive form of the disease (PMS). This progression can be defined as either secondary progressive MS or primary progressive MS, depending on the symptoms and the disability [2]. The hallmark of MS is the appearance of white matter (WM) lesions that can be seen using Magnetic Resonance Imaging (MRI) to diagnose the progression of the disease [2].

Recent advancements in artificial intelligence (AI) have led to its widespread use, demonstrating exceptional performance in numerous tasks through complex machine learning (ML) systems. However, the increased complexity has made these systems function like "black boxes," raising concerns about their operation and decision-making processes [3]. This lack of transparency has hindered their adoption in healthcare. Consequently, explainable AI has gained significant attention, focusing on developing methods that can explain and interpret ML models [3].

The objective of this study was to present the learning method of two different explainable AI models focused on the assessment of MS disease progression and compare them by discussing their findings. Both learning methods are based on ML and argumentation theory.

2 Materials

A dataset of 87 MS subjects (34 males, and 53 females) was examined at different time points. MRI images of 66 RRMS and 21 PMS were obtained using different MRI scanners and different sequences (T1w, T2w, and FLAIR). The expert neurologist (co-author, M. Pantzaris) manually segmented the brain MS lesions in a blinded manner where the segmented areas were intensity normalized between the grayscale values of 0 and 255. Clinical data were also investigated including demographic, and neurological measurements, such as functional system (FS) scores defining 0: 'Normal', 1: 'Signs Only', 2: 'Mild', 3: 'Moderate', 4: 'Severe', and 5: 'Loss' [4].

Texture features were extracted from all the segmented MS lesions and were estimated by averaging the corresponding values for all lesions of each patient. The following selected group features were extracted [5]: first-order statistics (FOS), spatial grey level dependence matrix (SGLDM), neighborhood grey tone difference matrix (NGTDM), and Fourier power spectrum (FPS). Min-max normalization was performed between the values 0.0 and 1.0, where a fixed number of 3 bins that has the same number of observations to each bin (quantile strategy) was defined. The bins were encoded using the ordinal method, where 0 refers to 'Low', 1 refers to 'Medium' and 2 refers to 'High'. In addition, feature selection was applied by computing the analysis of variance (ANOVA) test. The 5 features with the highest F-value, from both clinical data and texture features, were selected (see Table 1).

Data were collected from 87 subjects coming from two groups: 66 RRMS (G1) and 21 PMS (G2) (see Table 2). As shown in Table 2, data were oversampled using the synthetic minority over-sampling technique (SMOTE) which creates new samples for the minority group of the model (G2) with the same statistical properties [6]. Splitting using 80% for the training and 20% for the evaluation set and the target class as a stratified parameter was applied.

Table 1. Selected clinical data and brain MRI lesion texture features.

Clinical data
cerebellarFS, slowtongueFS, facialFS, sensoryFS, dysarthriaFS
Brain MRI lesion texture features
contrastNGTDM, varianceFOS, variancesumsquaresSGLDM, sumvarianceSGLDM, angularsumFPS

FS: Functional Systems, NGTDM: Neighbourhood Grey Tone Difference Matrix, FOS: First-Order Statistics, SGLDM: Spatial Grey Level Dependence Matrix, FPS: Fourier Power Spectrum.

Table 2. Data distribution of the models.

Data sets	Subjects	RRMS (G1)	PMS (G2)
Initial	87	66	21
Over-sample minority	132	66	66
Training	106	53	53
Evaluation	26	13	13

RRMS: Relapsing-Remitting MS, PMS: Progressive MS.

3 Methods

3.1 Learning Method A

The first learning method utilized ML and argumentation theory. The ML algorithms random forest (RF), and gradient boosting (GB) were used. During model training, the grid search method was applied to find the optimal combination of hyper-parameters of each model [7], based on a stratified 10-fold cross-validation. Rules were extracted on training using the TE2rules algorithm [8] that converts a tree ensemble (TE) to a rule list (RL). Then, rule selection was performed selecting the models with high training accuracy and a minimum sample of rules. Argumentation-based reasoning was applied using Gorgias' theory [9], which involves constructing arguments using a basic argument scheme, connecting a set of premises to the claim of the argument. The extracted rules were modified as object-level arguments that can support contradictory claims, leading to arguments attacking one another. Moreover, the use of priority on object-level arguments can express a local preference between arguments and establish relative strength, tightening the attack relation between them. The performance of the learning method was based on the average evaluation set performance for 10 runs.

3.2 Learning Method B: ArgEML

The second learning method called ArgEML [10] is an argumentation framework for explainable machine learning, based on a novel approach that integrates sub-symbolic methods with logical methods of argumentation to provide explainable solutions to learning problems [11]. In the framework of ArgEML argumentation is used both as a target language for ML and the explanations of the ML predictions. The learning algorithm generates argumentation theories in the context of Gorgias argumentation framework [9], by processing a set of data and optionally a list of decision rules that represent some knowledge of the data (hybrid mode of operation). The ArgEML approach views the notion of prediction from a different perspective than that of a traditional ML model, by means of relaxing the requirement of accuracy by distinguishing two notions of *definite prediction* (single conclusion that can be either correct or wrong) and *ambiguity* (multiple conflicting conclusions) recognition. In this perspective, if we cannot uniquely or definitely predict, but can focus the prediction on a set of alternatives and can give justifications for the alternatives, then we consider that we still have a valuable output of learning. For these difficult cases, an argumentation theory will generate a *dilemma*. Dilemmas include multiple conflicting conclusions with explanations for each particular conclusion. A dilemma can be considered neither a correct nor a wrong prediction. For that reason, dilemmas are included in a new *learning assessment* (5) metric for evaluating the performance of a theory. More information on the framework and methodology can be found in [12]. The ArgEML system: α-version[1] is a Java implementation of the methodology that we can use to learn and evaluate Gorgias' argumentation theories.

3.3 Evaluation Metrics

The performance of the two learning methods was based on the evaluation set (see Table 2). The following evaluation metrics were used:

$$Accuracy = \frac{TP + TN}{TP + FP + TN + FN} \ (1), Precision = \frac{TP}{TP + FP} \ (2),$$

$$Recall = \frac{TP}{TP + FN} \ (3), F1 \ score = \frac{2 \ x \ Precision \ x \ Recall}{Precision + Recall} (4)$$

where TP and TN denote the number of true positive and true negative instances that are correctly identified, and FP and FN indicate the number of false positive and false negative instances that are incorrectly classified, respectively.

The Learning Assessment (LA) metric, introduced in [12] for the evaluation of the argumentation theories generated by ArgEML, is a generalization of the standard classification accuracy metric, that gives a holistic evaluation of an argumentation theory that balances definite errors and dilemmas:

$$\begin{aligned} &Learning \ assessment(LA) \\ &= \frac{definite \ correct \ predictions(TP + TN) + dilemmas * wa}{total \ number \ of \ predictions(TP + FP + TN + FN)} \end{aligned} \quad (5)$$

where *wa* corresponds to a weight factor for ambiguity, defined as 1/(number of labels in target class).

---

[1] https://github.com/nicolepr/argeml

4   Results

4.1   Learning Method A

Tables 3 and 4 illustrate the RL generated from the selected RF and GB models, respectively. It is shown that two rules consisting of only one feature can describe the target group G1 (see Table 3). In addition, some features are strong enough to differentiate the subjects into two different groups (G1 vs G2) as both RF and GB models extracted the same feature rules (e.g., *cerebellarFS*, *sensoryFS*). It's worth mentioning that the contrast from the NGTDM group is the only texture feature observed in the RL.

4.2   Learning Method B: ArgEML

In this work, we used the ArgEML system in hybrid mode to learn an argumentation theory from the dataset described in Sect. 2. Following the process of "Learning method A", we utilized 10 subsets of train/test sets, to train a RF model and extract decision rules using the inTrees algorithm [13]. We used the rules extracted from the best-performing models on the train and test sets with an Accuracy of 100% to run the ArgEML system, one time for each set of train/test/rules, and decide/learn the best-performing argumentation theory. ArgEML in hybrid mode processes the decision-rules given as input and generates an initial theory that contains a compact set of arguments (~rules) that cover the training data. Table 5 illustrates the compact set of rules extracted from a selected best-performing RF model and chosen by ArgEML for initialing the argumentation theory.

4.3   Evaluation of the Learning Methods

According to Tables 3, 4, and 5, it is observed that the different learning methods gave similar rules. These rules consisted of the clinical data and more specifically, the cerebellar and the sensory function systems' measures. Furthermore, it is highlighted that the brain MRI lesion texture features can be found in the rules with a length greater than 2 (see Tables 3 and 4). It's worth mentioning that the ArgEML learning method gave rules with a length equal to 1, meaning that the theory can differentiate the subjects of MS (G1 vs G2) with only one feature (see Table 5).

Table 6 summarizes the performance of the learning methods using the evaluation set based on a stratified 10-fold cross-validation (see Table 2). It is obvious that the use of the argumentation theory in both learning methods reached a high accuracy of 99% which makes the explainable AI models predict and provide explanations with high fidelity.

Table 3. Rules extracted from a selected RF model in learning method A.

Rules	Group
IF *cerebellarFS* = Normal **OR** SignsOnly **OR** Mild	**G1**
IF *sensoryFS* = Normal **OR** SignsOnly **OR** Mild	**G1**
IF (*cerebellarFS* = Moderate **OR** Severe **OR** Loss) **AND** (*sensoryFS* = Moderate **OR** Severe **OR** Loss)	**G2**
IF (*contrastNGTDM* = Medium **OR** High) **AND** (*dysarthriaFS* = SignsOnly **OR** Mild **OR** Moderate **OR** Severe **OR** Loss) **AND** (*sensoryFS* = Normal **OR** SignsOnly **OR** Mild)	**G2**

FS: Functional Systems, NGTDM: Neighborhood Grey Tone Difference Matrix, G1, G2: Subjects with RRMS and PMS, respectively.

Table 4. Rules extracted from a selected GB model in learning method A.

Rules	Group
IF *sensoryFS* = Normal **OR** SignsOnly **OR** Mild	**G1**
IF *cerebellarFS* = Normal **OR** SignsOnly **OR** Mild	**G1**
IF (*cerebellarFS* = Moderate **OR** Severe **OR** Loss) **AND** (*sensoryFS* = Moderate **OR** Severe **OR** Loss) **AND** *slowtongueFS* = SignsOnly	**G1**
IF (*cerebellarFS* = Moderate **OR** Severe **OR** Loss) **AND** (*sensoryFS* = Moderate **OR** Severe **OR** Loss)	**G2**
IF (*contrastNGTDM* = Medium **OR** High) **AND** (*facialFS* = Mild **OR** Moderate **OR** Severe **OR** Loss) **AND** (*sensoryFS* = Normal **OR** SignsOnly **OR** Mild)	**G2**

FS: Functional Systems, NGTDM: Neighborhood Grey Tone Difference Matrix, G1, G2: Subjects with RRMS and PMS, respectively.

Table 5. Rules extracted from a selected RF model and ArgEML(theory initialization) in learning method B.

Rules	Group
IF *sensoryFS* = Normal **OR** SignsOnly **OR** Mild	**G1**
IF *cerebellarFS* = Normal **OR** SignsOnly **OR** Mild	**G1**
IF *slowtongueFS* = Normal	**G1**
IF *sensoryFS* = Moderate **OR** Severe **OR** Loss	**G2**
IF *slowtongueFS* = SignsOnly **OR** Mild **OR** Moderate **OR** Severe **OR** Loss	**G2**

FS: Functional Systems, G1, G2: Subjects with RRMS and PMS, respectively.

Table 6. Evaluation of the two learning methods.

Learning method	Accuracy	Precision	Recall	F1 score
A: RF + ARG	99%	99%	99%	99%
A: GB + ARG	99%	99%	100%	99%
B: ArgEML	99%	99%[a]	99%[a]	99%

RF: Random Forest, GB: Gradient Boosting, ARG: Argumentation theory.
[a]Dilemmas were considered both as FP and FN.

5   Discussion

The objective of this study was to compare two learning methods of explainable AI models in the assessment of MS disease based on clinical data and brain MRI lesion texture features. Both learning methods used ML and argumentation theory to differentiate subjects with RRMS from PMS subjects, providing explanations with a high accuracy of 99%. The main findings showed that:

1) Different learning methods can give the same explanation as long as they extracted the same rules.
2) Cerebellar and sensory function systems' rules were strong enough to identify and explain the type of MS disease. The contrast from the NGTDM group was the only brain MRI lesion texture feature found in the rules.

A previous study from our group [14] performed rule extraction from brain MRI lesion texture features using decision trees to assess MS disease progression. The main findings showed that simple rules including only one texture feature group (e.g. FPS) without the combination of other feature groups can achieve high accuracy greater than 70%. Another recent study from our group [15] implemented an explainable AI model with embedded rules in the assessment of brain MRI lesions in MS disease based on Amplitude Modulation – Frequency Modulation (AM-FM) multi-scale feature sets. Different ML models were used to classify the MS subjects with a low disability and subjects with a high disability. Argumentation-based reasoning was performed using the extracted rules from models with a high accuracy of 98%. It was demonstrated that the proposed model could differentiate the MS subjects by providing understandable information for the progression of the disease.

Other MS studies investigated explainability using local interpretable model-agnostic explanations (LIME) and Shapley additive explanations (SHAP). More specifically, Basu et al. [16] developed multivariate ML models to predict MS disease activity using extreme GB and applied SHAP methods to identify the predictive covariates for early identification of MS. A large-scale study was used including demographic, neurological, and laboratory measures, as well as MRI assessment. The models achieved a balanced accuracy of 80%. The findings showed that the number of treatment weeks, the new combined unique active lesion count, the new T1 hypointense lesion count, and the age-related MS severity score were the top predictive covariates. In addition, Olatunji et al. [17] used different ML models and interpreted them utilizing SHAP and LIME methods for early screening of MS. The input data of the models included clinical features, such as demographic and other laboratory measures. The results indicated that Extra Trees outperformed the rest of the models with an accuracy of 95%. The greatest impact on the model's prediction was shown by age, systolic blood pressure, and alkaline phosphatase.

6   Concluding Remarks

In a medical diagnosis system, clarity and transparency are crucial factors for gaining the trust of medical experts. Since the underlying causes of MS are still not that clear, it is essential to develop an explainable AI model in the assessment of MS disease. This study presented two different learning methods of explainable AI models which used ML and argumentation theory to identify the progression of the disease and explain its causes. By comparing the two learning methods, it's concluded that they can give the same explanation as selected features are strong enough to assess the disability and differentiate the MS subjects. Further work needs to be carried out using more subjects.

References

1. Hone, L., Giovannoni, G., Dobson, R., Jacobs, B.M.: Predicting multiple sclerosis: challenges and opportunities. Front. Neurol. **12**, 1–8 (2022)
2. Dobson, R., Giovannoni, G.: Multiple sclerosis-a review. Eur. J. Neurol. **26**, 27–40 (2019)
3. Linardatos, P., Papastefanopoulos, V., Kotsiantis, S.: Explainable AI: a review of machine learning interpretability methods. Entropy **23**, 1–45 (2021)
4. Kurtzke, J.F.: Rating neurologic impairment in multiple sclerosis: an expanded disability status scale (EDSS). Neurology **33**(11), 1444–1452 (1983)
5. Loizou, C.P., Petroudi, S., Seimenis, I., Pantziaris, M., Pattichis, C.S.: Quantitative texture analysis of brain white matter lesions derived from T2-weighted MR images in MS patients with clinically isolated syndrome. J. Neuroradiol. **42**(2), 99–114 (2015)
6. Chawla, N.V., Bowyer, K.W., Hall, L.O., Kegelmeyer, W.P.: SMOTE: Synthetic minority over-sampling technique. J. Artif. Intell. Res. **16**, 321–357 (2002)
7. Pedregosa, F., Varoquaux, G., Gramfort, A., Michel, V.: Scikit-learn: Machine learning in Python. J. Mach. Learn. Res. **12**, 108–122 (2013)
8. Lal, G.R., Chen, X., Mithal, V.: TE2Rules: extracting rule lists from tree ensembles, pp. 1–17 (2022)
9. Kakas, A.C., Moraitis, P., Spanoudakis, N.I.: GORGIAS: applying argumentation. Argument Comput. **10**, 55–81 (2019)
10. Prentzas, N., Gavrielidou, A., Neophytou, M., Kakas, A.: Argumentation-based Explainable Machine Learning (ArgEML): a real-life use case on gynecological cancer. In: CEUR Workshop Proceedings, vol. 3208 (2022)
11. Prentzas, N., Nicolaides, A., Kyriacou, E., Kakas, A., Pattichis, C.: Integrating machine learning with symbolic reasoning to build an explainable ai model for stroke prediction. In: Proceedings - 2019 IEEE 19th International Conference on Bioinformatics and Bioengineering, BIBE 2019, pp. 817–821. Institute of Electrical and Electronics Engineers Inc. (2019)
12. Prentzas, N., Pattichis, C., Kakas, A.: Explainable machine learning via argumentation. In: Communications in Computer and Information Science. Springer (2023)
13. Deng, H.: Interpreting tree ensembles with inTrees. Int. J. Data Sci. Anal. **7**(4), 277–287 (2018). https://doi.org/10.1007/s41060-018-0144-8

14. Nicolaou, A., Loizou, C.P., Pantzaris, M., Kakas, A., Pattichis, C.S.: Rule extraction in the assessment of brain mri lesions in multiple sclerosis: preliminary findings. In: Tsapatsoulis, N., Panayides, A., Theocharides, T., Lanitis, A., Pattichis, C., Vento, M. (eds.) CAIP 2021. LNCS, vol. 13052, pp. 277–286. Springer, Cham (2021). https://doi.org/10.1007/978-3-030-89128-2_27

15. Nicolaou, A., et al.: An explainable artificial intelligence model in the assessment of brain MRI lesions in multiple sclerosis using amplitude modulation – frequency modulation multi-scale feature sets. In: 24th International Conference on Digital Signal Processing (DSP), pp. 1–4. Rhodes, Greece (2023)

16. Basu, S., Munafo, A., Ben-Amor, A.F., Roy, S., Girard, P., Terranova, N.: Predicting disease activity in patients with multiple sclerosis: an explainable machine-learning approach in the Mavenclad trials. CPT Pharm. Syst. Pharmacol. 11, 843–853 (2022)

17. Olatunji, S.O., Alsheikh, N., Alnajrani, L., Alanazy, A., Almusairii, M., et al.: Comprehensible machine-learning-based models for the pre-emptive diagnosis of multiple sclerosis using clinical data: a retrospective study in the Eastern province of Saudi Arabia. Int. J. Environ. Res. Public Health 20 (2023)

General Vision - AI Applications

Biometric Recognition of African Clawed Frogs

Fabian L. Prins[1], Dario Tomanin[2], Julia Kamenz[2], and George Azzopardi[1(✉)]

[1] Bernoulli Institute for Mathematics, Computer Science and Artificial Intelligence, University of Groningen, Groningen, The Netherlands
`g.azzopardi@rug.nl`
[2] Molecular Systems Biology, Groningen Biomolecular Sciences and Biotechnology Institute, University of Groningen, Groningen, The Netherlands

Abstract. The African clawed frog (*Xenopus laevis*) is a commonly used model organism for cell biological, developmental, and biomedical research. For health monitoring and experimental quality control purposes, it is desirable to identify individual frogs regularly throughout their life. Current methods for identification are often invasive and associated with significant investment costs. Identification based on images of the biometric pattern on a frog's back has been implemented in some laboratories, but so far has been performed manually and therefore is time-consuming and limited to small group sizes. This work proposes a novel pipeline for data acquisition, pre-processing, and training of a classification model based on pattern recognition. The pipeline is structured around laboratory frog colonies and smartphone usage. In order to achieve a lightweight system in our evaluation we consider a MobileNet ConvNet pre-trained on ImageNet. Two feature sets are evaluated on a new data set of 1,647 image samples collected from 160 frogs: RGB images, and 3-channel contour maps (i.e. CORF3D). The results indicate that the CORF3D feature set is favoured over RGB. CORF3D achieved the best performance of 99.94% average accuracy, while RGB had the best performance of 98.79%. Analysis of misclassifications shows that bad predictions are often caused by bad lens focus, light reflections, and positional inconsistency in pattern extraction, which can be addressed during data acquisition. The proposed methodology is, therefore, an effective solution for the recognition of *Xenopus laevis*.

Keywords: Frog recognition · Biometric analysis · Convolutional neural networks · Contour maps · CORF3D

1 Introduction

Since the beginning of the 20th century, the African clawed frog (*Xenopus laevis*) has been functioning as a powerful model system for cell biological and developmental research questions as well as a human disease model [1]. The animals are fully aquatic and their well-being benefits from being housed in larger groups

N. Tsapatsoulis et al. (Eds.): CAIP 2023, LNCS 14185, pp. 151–161, 2023.
https://doi.org/10.1007/978-3-031-44240-7_15

instead of individual tanks. The group housing setup constitutes a challenge for recording the experimental and health history of the individual frogs. Currently, a variety of marking methods are practised, such as record cards, Visible Implant Elastomer (VIE), photography, toe clipping, microchips, tattooing, and branding [2]. These methods can, however, be invasive with negative health consequences for the animal, expensive, and cumbersome. Ideally, a frog should be able to be identified quickly and easily. Since the African clawed frogs have unique skin patterns, visual recognition seems to be the obvious non-invasive method of choice. Needless to say, the task of manually comparing database images with the frog of interest is laborious and grows more complex with increasing numbers of frogs in single tanks.

In this paper, we present a complete pipeline including data acquisition, data pre-processing, and image classification for a colony of African clawed frogs. The resulting method will enable researchers to take a picture of the frog of interest with their smartphone and receive the frog's unique identification as a result.

The rest of the paper is organised as follows. Section 2 covers the background and related work. Section 3 describes our dataset and recognition methodology. Section 4 presents the experiments and their results. Section 5 discusses the experimental results, followed by the conclusions in Sect. 6.

2   Background and Related Work

At the University of Groningen, a colony of 160 female *Xenopus laevis* is housed in support of research into the biochemical regulation of cell division [3]. For this purpose, individual animals are hormone-stimulated about every three to six months. Hormone stimulation induces oocyte maturation and ovulation. The resulting laid eggs are then used for biochemical studies, while the animal is undergoing a rest period. Egg quality can differ significantly between different individuals and strongly impact experimental results [4]. However, it is unclear whether genetic or environmental factors are the main determinants of egg quality. Insights into the different determinants is largely limited by a lack of easy-to-implement methods to identify individual animals and link the ID to experimental and health histories. Invasive labeling methods (e.g. microchips, toe nail clipping) are discouraged as they are often associated with negative health impacts. The proposed solution is to automatically identify the frogs by the coloured pattern on their backs, which is assumed to be a unique biometric feature for each animal.

A study on localisation and identification of African clawed frogs was conducted in [5]. Their data set consists of top-down images of individual frogs in an open, white container filled with water. A total of 60 frogs were photographed, one photo per frog with varied lighting conditions and distances to the container. Their novel extraction process was highly successful in terms of stability. It consists of greyscaling, thresholding, morphological closing, calculating the frog's barycentre and orientation by maximising the head-tail distance, extraction, resizing and normalising. The square extraction area was used for five feature sets: raw pixels, Gabor filters, granulometry, Histogram of Oriented Gradients (HoG), and Scale Invariant Feature Transform (SIFT). To investigate the robustness for each feature set, five additional data sets were created through data augmentation: rotation, affine transform, scale, blur, and Gaussian noise. The experiment consisted of comparing the accuracy of all five feature sets on a nearest neighbour classifier based on L1-norm distance for each data set. The raw pixel data scored the best on the majority of the augmented data sets.

Recently, the CORF3D feature set was introduced as part of the automatic recognition of Holstein cattle from their coat pattern based on RGB and infrared images [6]. The CORF3D feature set is a stack of three contour maps generated by the inhibition-augmented CORF operator using different strengths of the inhibition term for each layer. The inhibition term determines the extent of suppression in regions with high-frequency noise. The CORF operator has been found to be very effective in various applications [7–11]. In [12], it was also demonstrated that a ConvNet classification model trained with CORF contour maps is more robust to high-frequency noise than one that is trained with RGB images. [6] demonstrated that ConvNets fed with CORF3D feature maps outperform those that use the original RGB channels. Further analysis showed that a fusion of both RGB and CORF3D features can achieve the most superior performance on a Holstein cow recognition problem in a farm with 383 cows.

3 Methodology

The proposed methodology for the problem at hand is inspired by the work in [6]. It includes (1) data acquisition, (2) a pre-processing step that extracts the frog from the background, aligns it in a vertical orientation, and crops a square region from the back of the frog, (3) feature extraction, and (4) classification.

3.1 Data Acquisition

The University of Groningen is housing a colony of 160 female *Xenopus laevis* in accordance with national animal welfare laws and reviewed by the Animal Ethics Committee of the Royal Netherlands Academy of Arts and Sciences (KNAW) under a project license granted by the Central Committee Animal Experimentation (CCD) of the Dutch government and approved by the University of Groningen (IvD), with project license number AVD 10500202114408. The colony is divided into groups of ten to twenty individuals in aquatic tanks. The dataset consists of 1,647 images for 160 classes (i.e. frogs), with an average of 10.3 images per class. Below we elaborate on the photography setup and measures for robustness.

Photography Setup. Frogs were photographed individually in an uncovered transparent container filled with water placed on a white surface. *Xenopus laevis* rapidly change their pigment intensity – but not their individual pattern – if housed on different surfaces. The frogs at the University of Groningen are

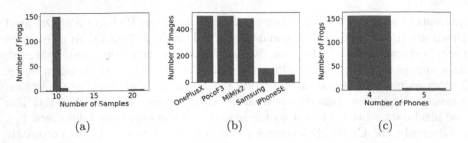

Fig. 1. (a) Distribution of samples per frog with the majority of frogs having ten photos each, and four outliers with 20 or more photos. (b) The number of photos taken per phone, and (c) the number of different phones used per frog.

normally housed in tanks with dark blue surface and therefore show a darker pigmentation. However, when housed in transparent boxes on a yellow surface, their pigment lightens significantly. To account for these changes in pigmentation, frogs were housed in transparent boxes on a yellow surface for approximately 24 h and pictures were taken throughout this time period. Each container was marked with a visible number to later associate the pictures to the individual frog; i.e. for ground truth labelling. Picture acquisition was performed by using at least four different smartphones per frog. A tripod was placed next to the container such that a smartphone can be placed straight above the centre of the container. By photographing the frogs one-by-one, the chance of frogs overlapping, turbulence in the water, and the additional complexity of localising multiple frogs in pre-processing is avoided. During experimental procedures and for health assessments, the frogs were commonly isolated, hence, this imaging setup is highly compatible with the general workflow of the researchers. The angle and distance from the mounted camera to the containers were kept fixed.

Robustness Measures. With the aim of making the model more robust, photos were taken at different times of day, on different days, and with the cameras of different smartphones. These factors influence the position of the frog in the tank and characteristics such as the picture's contrast and sharpness. The sample distributions are illustrated in Fig. 1. In total, five smartphones were used: Xiaomi Mi Mix 2, Xiaomi POCO F3, OnePlus X, iPhone SE, and Samsung Galaxy S7. The first three smartphones were used three times per frog. The iPhone SE and Samsung Galaxy S7 were used only once per frog, where the former is used only for the first three tanks, and the latter for all other tanks, due to a technicality with transferring the photos. The cameras of the smartphones that we used have different resolutions. In landscape orientation, the resolutions are: OnePlus X: 4160×3120 px, iPhone SE and Samsung Galaxy S7: 4032×3024 px, and Xiaomi Mi Mix 2 and Xiaomi POCO F3: 4000×3000 px. The distribution of images taken per smartphone is illustrated in Fig. 1a. Due to miscommunication, four frogs from tank 3 were also later mistakenly placed in tank 10. As a result, these four frogs were photographed twice as much, and by five different phones instead of four. This is demonstrated in Fig. 1a and Fig. 1c. The filenames have been updated such that the filenames for the four tank 10 frogs are now their corresponding tank 3 frogs. The dataset is made publicly available[1].

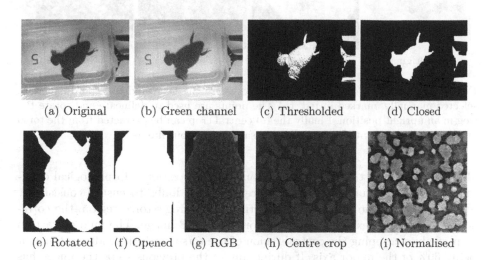

(a) Original   (b) Green channel   (c) Thresholded   (d) Closed

(e) Rotated   (f) Opened   (g) RGB   (h) Centre crop   (i) Normalised

Fig. 2. Example of pattern extraction from a given (a) RGB image, (b) downscaled green channel, (c) binarisation, (d) morphological closing, (e) extraction of the largest component and rotation, (f) limb removal with morphological opening, (g) the corresponding region extracted from the RGB image, (h) central square crop, (h) normalised with histogram equalisation on colour intensity.

3.2 Pattern Extraction

Pattern extraction can be done in two ways; unsupervised or semi-supervised. The former refers to a fully automatic extraction that relies on thresholding and morphological operations. The latter expects the user to indicate the tip of the frog's head and the tip of its tail.

Unsupervised. Figure 2 illustrates the automated pattern extraction which begins by taking the green channel from a given RGB image and downsizing it to 20% relative size to reduce grainy details and speed up the process. The green channel is the most appropriate for detecting the frogs due to their green and yellow tint. The green channel is then thresholded by setting to 1 all pixels in the range [20, 80] and 0 otherwise. Morphological closing with a disk structuring element of size 20 px is then used to fill in any black holes. The largest region is identified as the frog and is rotated vertically based on its major axis. By comparing the areas of the top and bottom halves of the extracted component

---

[1] https://doi.org/10.34894/PYPNU6.

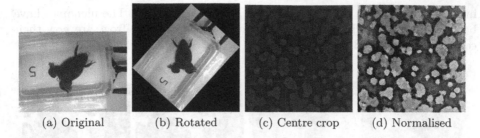

(a) Original   (b) Rotated   (c) Centre crop   (d) Normalised

Fig. 3. Example of a given (a) RGB image where the head and tail coordinates are selected manually, marked in red. (b) The points are used to delineate and rotate the frog in an upright position. Finally the (c) central crop can be extracted from the torso and (d) normalised with histogram equalisation on colour intensity.

allows us to ensure that the frog is in an upright position. Morphological opening with a disk structuring of 75 px removes the limbs to ensure consistency in the final extraction area. After identifying the frog's torso region, the corresponding region is extracted from the original RGB image. The final extraction step involves cropping the central region of the torso, with the width and height being 60% of the minor axis. If during any of the previous steps the image has become completely black, or if 10% of the pixels in the final crop are black, the extraction is considered to have failed and the sample is discarded. When this happens, in practice, the system would ask the user to take another photo. In this work, we remove any photographs from the dataset that fail this extraction step.

Semi-supervised. As shown in Fig. 3, this approach requires the user to indicate two key points; the tips of the head and tail. These points are used to delineate and rotate the frog based on the given coordinates. The rest of the pipeline to obtain a centre crop from the torso is the same as used for the above approach.

3.3   Contour Delineation

Next, we normalise, resize and delineate the contours of the extracted patterns as described below.

Normalisation. The square RGB crop is converted to the HSV colour model. Subsequently, the intensity channel is normalised by histogram equalisation, which ensures the full range of colour intensity is used. The normalised HSV image is then converted back to RGB.

Scaling. The images are resized to 224 × 224 px such that every extracted pattern has the same resolution. The mentioned dimensions are chosen to meet the requirements of the MobileNet classification model that we use.

CORF Contour Maps. The CORF3D feature set is extracted by following the steps outlined in [6]. The feature descriptors use the CORF operator with push-pull inhibition, which produces better signal-to-noise ratios compared to other contour detection methods [13]. Four hyper-parameters are available in push-pull CORF: σ, β, α, and the high threshold t_H used for hysteresis thresholding[2]. As indicated in [6], we create the three contour maps that form the CORF3D descriptor by applying the CORF operator with different values of α ($\alpha \in \{0, 1.8, 3.6\}$, and setting $\beta = 4$ and $t_H = 0.005$. In our experiments we evaluate with different values of σ. Figure 4 illustrates the three CORF contour maps for a given pattern.

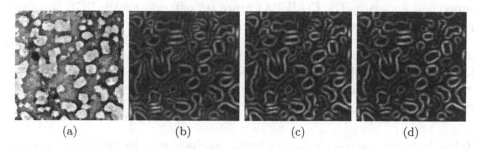

| (a) | (b) | (c) | (d) |

Fig. 4. (a) Extracted pattern in greyscale, and its CORF contour maps with $\sigma = 5.0$ and inhibition factors (b) $\alpha = 0$, (c) $\alpha = 1.8$, and (d) $\alpha = 3.6$.

4   Experiments

4.1   Data Set

The data set consists of 160 classes (i.e. frogs) and 1,647 samples (i.e. photos), for an average of 10.3 samples per class. However, as the distribution in Fig. 1 shows, four frogs with 20 to 21 photos give the distribution a positive skew. Out of the 160 classes, 151 (94.4%) have exactly 10 samples. In total, two feature sets are constructed, namely RGB and CORF3D. The RGB feature set consists of the red, green, and blue channels. The CORF3D feature map consists of three contour maps of different inhibition factors ($\alpha \in \{0.0, 1.8, 3.6\}$). Furthermore, six different standard deviations are evaluated ($\sigma \in \{2.5, 3.0, 3.5, 4.0, 4.5, 5.0\}$).

4.2   Experimental Setup

In order to achieve a lightweight solution, we have opted for the MobileNetv1 classification model [14], which has been pre-trained on the ImageNet dataset and has a forward pass with a computational cost of 0.569GFlops. The model is evaluated with 5-fold cross-validation with both the RGB and the CORF3D

---

[2] The low threshold is set to $0.5t_H$.

feature sets, generated by the unsupervised and semi-supervised approaches. Due to 25 failed frog extractions, the unsupervised approach is evaluated with $(1{,}647 - 25 =)$ 1,622 samples. Both approaches have 1 RGB and 6 CORF3D with different σ feature sets. This experimental design results in (7 feature sets × 2 pattern extraction methods =) 14 experiments.

4.3 Results

Table 1 reports the average accuracy, standard deviation, and number of misclassifications for the 14 experiments. The accuracy ranges from 95.07% to 97.60% for the unsupervised frog extraction method and 98.73% to 99.94% for the semi-supervised approach. The CORF3D feature set outperforms the RGB counterpart for all experiments except semi-supervised CORF3D with $\sigma \in [3.0, 3.5]$, yielding the best average accuracy rate of 99.94%. The last column of Table 1 shows the total number of misclassifications over all five folds. Higher σ (i.e. finer edges are less likely to appear) appear to positively affect the model's performance. This is especially apparent in the semi-supervised results, while the correlation is weaker for the unsupervised results.

Table 1. Average accuracy across the 5-fold cross-validation for the two frog extraction methods and the two feature sets. The last column shows the total number of misclassifications across all five folds.

Frog extraction	Features	Accuracy (%)	Misclass. (#)
		Out of 1,622 samples	
Unsupervised	RGB	95.07 ± 1.22	80
	CORF3D$_{\sigma=2.5}$	95.93 ± 0.76	66
	CORF3D$_{\sigma=3.0}$	96.67 ± 1.02	54
	CORF3D$_{\sigma=3.5}$	97.29 ± 0.63	44
	CORF3D$_{\sigma=4.0}$	97.60 ± 0.94	39
	CORF3D$_{\sigma=4.5}$	97.53 ± 0.96	40
	CORF3D$_{\sigma=5.0}$	97.23 ± 0.34	45
		Out of 1,647 samples	
Semi-supervised	RGB	98.79 ± 0.69	20
	CORF3D$_{\sigma=2.5}$	99.21 ± 0.31	13
	CORF3D$_{\sigma=3.0}$	98.72 ± 1.65	21
	CORF3D$_{\sigma=3.5}$	98.73 ± 1.84	21
	CORF3D$_{\sigma=4.0}$	99.70 ± 0.27	5
	CORF3D$_{\sigma=4.5}$	99.51 ± 0.68	8
	CORF3D$_{\sigma=5.0}$	99.94 ± 0.12	1

5   Discussion

As the results demonstrate, the pipeline that relies on the semi-supervised app-roach of frog extraction outperforms the unsupervised one for both RGB and CORF3D feature sets with a maximum accuracy rate of 99.94%. Such a result means that for every 10,000 images with a colony of 160 frogs six images get misclassified. This improvement in performance is attributable to the assisted localisation by user input, yielding better input for the classification model. Nev-ertheless, the results achieved by the unsupervised approaches are also notable. The difference in performance is due to the imperfect automatic localisation and orientation of the frog, which seems to be caused by light reflections on the water surface, difference in crop area, and blurriness in the images. This study does not consider steps in pre-processing to correct these issues. The difference in crop area is caused by imperfect head/tail coordinates from data acquisition, and bent backs of the frog, as the extraction area assumes the line between head and tail to be straight. Alternative methods must be considered to ensure the same area is extracted for all images per frog. Light reflections may be elimi-nated by modifying the camera setup. Blurriness can be prevented by paying closer attention to the camera's focus before taking the picture. We speculate that a practical way to improve the performance of the unsupervised approach is to take multiple pictures (e.g. 3) of the same frog from different angles and the most popular determined label will be assigned to the query frog.

Future work may also consider including data augmentation to create syn-thetic training samples with the mentioned practical challenges in photography (e.g. out of focus, blurriness, among others). Moreover, the current data acqui-sition methodology, which was required to train our system, is labour-intensive, as it requires the frogs to be placed in individual housing containers for up to 24 h. This is deemed necessary to be able to take photos of individual frogs over a period to account for changes in pigmentation intensity due to changes in the housing environment. It would also be worth investigating data augmentation techniques to mimic changes in light reflections, lens focus, and frog position, to ease the burden on the data collectors. In [5], the authors demonstrated that RGB feature sets work well when blur augmentation is applied.

In order to address turnover in the colony of frogs in a lab, one may consider learning a similarity function, with Siamese networks [15] for instance. With such an approach, in principle, adding and removing frogs from a colony would not require relearning the classification model. Adding new frogs would only require to have a few reference images.

6   Conclusion

In this work, we leverage the skin pattern of the African clawed frogs as a biometric feature to develop a frog recognition method. By means of experi-mentation, we demonstrated that the proposed non-invasive approach offers an effective solution for the problem at hand. We offer two variants of our solution, one that is completely automatic (unsupervised) and the other that requires the user to indicate the tips of the head and tail of the photographed frog (semi-supervised). The results show a tradeoff between user effort and accuracy. Although the unsupervised approach achieves high accuracy rates of up to 97.16%, the semi-supervised approach only requires two user clicks and improves the results significantly, reaching an accuracy rate of 99.94%.

In particular, the CORF3D feature set substantially outperforms the RGB feature set in both unsupervised and semi-supervised approaches, which demonstrates its effectiveness in this application. We limit our evaluation to the MobileNet classification model as our overarching aim is to have a lightweight system, which can operate on a smartphone without having to involve a cloud infrastructure, thus yielding low latency and high resilience.

References

1. De Robertis, E.M., Gurdon, J.B.: A brief history of xenopus in biology. Cold Spring Harb. Protoc. **2021** (2021)
2. Reed, B.: Guidance on the housing and care of the African clawed frog. Xenopus laevis (2005)
3. Kamenz, J., Gelens, L., Ferrell, J.E., Jr.: Bistable, biphasic regulation of PP2A-B55 accounts for the dynamics of mitotic substrate phosphorylation. Curr. Biol. **31**, 794–808.e6 (2020)
4. Murray, A.W.: Cell cycle extracts. Methods Cell Biol. **36**, 581–605 (1991)
5. Tek, F.B., Cannavo, F., Nunnari, G., Kale, İ: Robust localization and identification of African clawed frogs in digital images. Ecol. Inform. **23**, 3–12 (2014). Special Issue on Multimedia in Ecology and Environment
6. Bhole, A., Udmale, S.S., Falzon, O., Azzopardi, G.: CORF3D contour maps with application to Holstein cattle recognition from RGB and thermal images. Expert Syst. Appl. **192**, 116354 (2022)
7. Azzopardi, G., Strisciuglio, N., Vento, M., Petkov, N.: Trainable COSFIRE filters for vessel delineation with application to retinal images. Med. Image Anal. **19**(1), 46–57 (2015)
8. Strisciuglio, N., Azzopardi, G., Vento, M., Petkov, N.: Multiscale blood vessel delineation using B-COSFIRE filters. In: Azzopardi, G., Petkov, N. (eds.) CAIP 2015. LNCS, vol. 9257, pp. 300–312. Springer, Cham (2015). https://doi.org/10.1007/978-3-319-23117-4_26
9. Strisciuglio, N., Azzopardi, G., Petkov, N.: Robust inhibition-augmented operator for delineation of curvilinear structures. IEEE Trans. Image Process. **28**(12), 5852–5866 (2019)
10. Strisciuglio, N., Azzopardi, G., Petkov, N.: Detection of curved lines with B-COSFIRE filters: a case study on crack delineation. In: Felsberg, M., Heyden, A., Krüger, N. (eds.) CAIP 2017. LNCS, vol. 10424, pp. 108–120. Springer, Cham (2017). https://doi.org/10.1007/978-3-319-64689-3_9
11. Melotti, D., Heimbach, K., Rodríguez-Sánchez, A., Strisciuglio, N., Azzopardi, G.: A robust contour detection operator with combined push-pull inhibition and surround suppression. Inf. Sci. **524**, 229–240 (2020)

12. Bennabhaktula, G.S., Antonisse, J., Azzopardi, G.: On improving generalization of CNN-based image classification with delineation maps using the CORF push-pull inhibition operator. In: Tsapatsoulis, N., Panayides, A., Theocharides, T., Lanitis, A., Pattichis, C., Vento, M. (eds.) CAIP 2021. LNCS, vol. 13052, pp. 434–444. Springer, Cham (2021). https://doi.org/10.1007/978-3-030-89128-2_42

13. Azzopardi, G., Rogriguez-Sanchez, A., Piater, J., Petkov, N.: A push-pull CORF model of a simple cell with antiphase inhibition improves snr and contour detection. PloS One **9**, e98424 (2014)

14. Howard, A.G., et al.: MobileNets: efficient convolutional neural networks for mobile vision applications. arXiv preprint arXiv:1704.04861 (2017)

15. Koch, G., Zemel, R., Salakhutdinov, R., et al.: Siamese neural networks for one-shot image recognition. In: ICML Deep Learning Workshop, Lille, vol. 2 (2015)

Teacher-Student Synergetic Knowledge Distillation for Detecting Alcohol Consumption in NIR Iris Images

Sanskar Singh[✉], Ravil Patel, Vandit Tyagi, and Avantika Singh[iD]

IIIT Naya Raipur, Raipur, Chhattisgarh, India
{sanskar21102,ravil21102,vandit21102,avantika}@iiitnr.edu.in

Abstract. Detection of alcohol consumption is critical for ensuring fitness for duty (FFD) at workplace. It ensures employee safety and productivity by reducing accidents and injuries while improving work efficacy. In this paper, we propose a framework based on teacher-student collaborative knowledge distillation for detecting alcohol consumption in NIR (Near-Infrared) iris images. Specifically, this research focuses on analyzing the impact of alcohol consumption on iris and pupil movements. We provide interesting experimental analysis and related discussions that demonstrates suitability of NIR camera based captured iris images for detecting alcohol consumption. Furthermore, this research can be seen as a progressive measure towards integrating alcohol detection in iris based biometric authentication systems.

Keywords: Alcohol detection · Fitness for duty · Knowledge distillation · Periocular NIR iris images · Vision Transformer

1 Introduction

Nowadays, abuse of intoxication in the workplace is rising proportionately. Working under the consumption of such substances can lead to a rise in work-related injuries, especially for laborers and heavy-machinery operators. According to a study by Pidd et al. [17], 11% of workplace accidents and injuries are caused by the consumption of alcohol. Companies incur approximately $2 billion per year in costs related to alcohol-related absenteeism. To overcome hassle, government of nations such as the UK and Australia have imposed duty of care legislation [12]. Under this legislation, employers are required to have an unambiguous policy that outlines acceptable conduct and misconduct. To ensure this fitness for duty(FFD) [18] is required in work area. To ascertain this few organisations have installed saliva and breath [8,11] analyzer for detecting alcohol consumption in the workplace. However, there are a few potential drawbacks of breath and saliva-based alcohol testing in the workplace which includes low accuracy, sensitivity and vulnerability to external influences such as mouthwash or food.

All authors have contributed equally.

© The Author(s), under exclusive license to Springer Nature Switzerland AG 2023
N. Tsapatsoulis et al. (Eds.): CAIP 2023, LNCS 14185, pp. 162–171, 2023.
https://doi.org/10.1007/978-3-031-44240-7_16

Furthermore, these type of systems in the workplace may increase the risk of COVID-19 transmission due to hygiene and close contact concerns. Henceforth it is crucial to design new mechanisms that are capable of accurate and resilient detection of the effects of alcohol on employees, ensuring their fitness for duty.

It has been proved in literature that alcohol consumption can cause dilated pupils [3]. This motivated us to propose a framework that detects alcohol consumption by analyzing Non-Infrared (NIR) iris images. NIR iris imaging does not involve any physical contact with the user, unlike other alcohol detection techniques based on physiological fluids like breath or saliva. In the case of infectious diseases like COVID-19, iris imaging technique instead of physiological fluids thus lowers the likelihood of disease transmission. Furthermore, it is also quick and efficient that can deliver outcomes in real-time, making it appropriate for applications like law enforcement and for ensuring FFD at workplace.

2   Related Works

This section gives a brief summary of earlier research conducted in pertinent literature, exploring the effects of alcohol intake on changes in the iris and its impact on an individual's ability to perform their duties effectively. Amodio et al. [2] assessed the possibility of creating a system to detect drunk driving by analyzing changes in a person's pupillary light reflex (PLR) over time. The method involves using circular hough transform to obtain the pupil diameter profile, followed by implementing a polynomial-kernel support vector machine (SVM) to categorize the subject using the 8 features extracted from the profile.

In another work, Causa et al. [5] used a stream of NIR iris video frames to estimate behavioural curves The study concentrated on applying a Criss-Cross Network (CCNet) to mask the iris and pupil segmentation, enabling the creation of characteristics based on the differences between the radii of the pupil and iris. The features produced were used to categorize the subject using a Multi-Layer-Perceptron (MLP) algorithm with an accuracy rate of 75.8%. In another notable work Arora et al. [3] studied the effects of alcohol on an iris recognition system and infer that one in five subjects under alcohol consumption may evade identification by iris recognition. Very recently, authors [20] have proposed a framework based on capsule network for detecting alcohol consumption.

3   Research Methodology

Here, in this section we will discuss the dataset used in our experimentation along with the feature extraction framework. Our proposed framework is based on teacher-student learning paradigm that relies on a distillation token [21] to ensure student network learning from the teacher network through a multi-head attention. An overview of the entire framework is presented in Fig. 1.

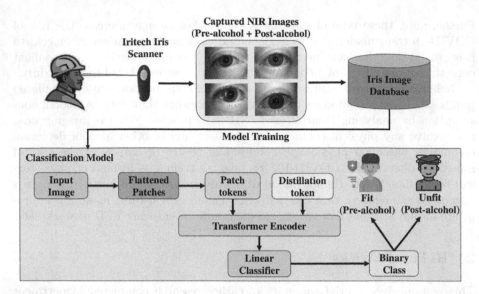

Fig. 1. Comprehensive description of the presented framework which determines fitness for duty on the basis of NIR iris images

Table 1. Statistical Description of the IAL-I Database

Session	Condition	Capture Time (min)	Images
S0	Pre-Alcohol	0	600
S1	Post-Alcohol	15	600
S2	Post-Alcohol	30	600
S3	Post-Alcohol	45	600
S4	Post-Alcohol	60	600

3.1   Dataset Description

In this study we have used IAL-I database [19]. This database consists of NIR iris images captured for total 30 subjects (24 males, 6 females) aged between 25 and 50. IAL-I dataset consists of nearly 20 similar periocular NIR iris images from each subject per session and there are total of 5 sessions. Table 1 illustrates the distribution of data. For more details kindly refer [19].

3.2   Feature Extractor

Vision Transformers (ViT) [10] can be seen as a de facto standard in the past few years for image classification tasks. Recently, aggregation of convnets and transformers integrated with self-attention mechanism have illustrated superfluous results in various domains like image classification [7], image segmentation [22] and natural language processing [14]. On continuation to this, Touvron et al. [21]

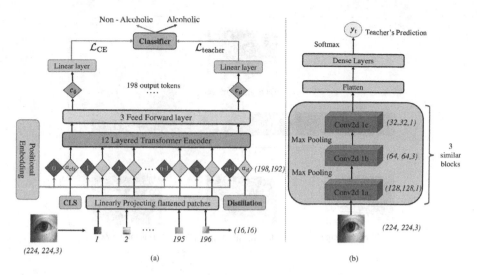

Fig. 2. (a) Generation of patch embeddings and conceptual overview of Transformer based Student model wherein CLS refers to classification token (b) Outlining Convnet based Teacher model architecture

presented a data efficient image transformer (DeiT) which suppresses the dependency of transformer on huge data. Taking inspiration from DeiT, we propose a novel architecture as depicted in Fig. 2 for detecting alcohol consumption in NIR iris images. The proposed framework comprises of mainly two parts (i) transformer based student network and (ii) convnet based teacher network. The following subsections will discuss aforementioned parts in detail.

Dataset Augmentation. In literature, classification task is mostly performed on datasets like ImageNet [9], CIFAR-100 [13], NUS-WIDE [6]. All these datasets consists of huge number of images per class. In contrary to this iris databases have limited number of images particularly in concern to post alcohol consumption images as evident form Table 1. Thus, to generate supplementary images for training our network we have used various image augmentation methods as suggested in [20]. Since, the dataset IAL-I [20] used in our study is collected in a controlled environment, nominal data augmentation methods can work well. Figure 3 depicts sample iris image with corresponding augmented images. It should be noted that image augmentation is carried out for training dataset only.

Convnet Based Teacher Network: This network takes an input iris image $I \in R^{H \times W \times C}$, where H, W and C represents image height, width and channel respectively. Assuming an image classification model f, the output of f is a label $y_t \in \{0...t\}$ where t is the number of classes. This network consists of 9 convolutional layers, with 3 layers in each block as depicted in Fig. 2. Each block

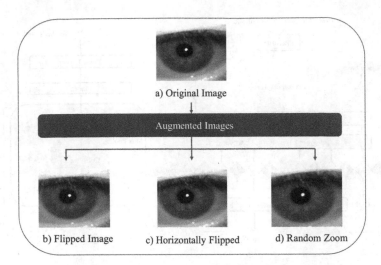

a) Original Image

Augmented Images

b) Flipped Image   c) Horizontally Flipped   d) Random Zoom

Fig. 3. Sample iris image with corresponding augmented images

is summarized as:

$$Input \xrightarrow{1\times1\,Conv} RM \rightarrow ReLU \rightarrow IFM \xrightarrow[MP]{3\times3\,Conv,} RM \rightarrow ReLU \rightarrow IFM$$
$$\xrightarrow[MP]{1\times1\,Conv} RM \rightarrow ReLU \rightarrow FM \tag{1}$$

Here in Eq. 1, RM,IFM, FM and MP stands for response map, intermediate feature map, feature map and max pooling respectively. The presented architecture was inspired from Regnet based model [15].

Transformer Based Student Network: This network takes input in the form of patches. The fixed size input iris image $I \in R^{H \times W \times C}$, (where H, W and C represents image height, width and channel respectively) is decomposed into 196 patches of size 16×16. These patches are linearly projected into 196 tokens as depicted in Fig. 2(a). Each token has a shape of $(1, D)$ where D is 192 for our case. Two additional tokens, namely the classification token (CLS) and the distillation token of same shape as $(1, 192)$, are added to the patch tokens. During training, the CLS token is a vector that can be trained and contains class embeddings. The distillation token is similar to the CLS token in that it is also trainable, but it is randomly initialized and located in a fixed last position. The main objective of the distillation token is to allow our proposed architecture to learn from the output of the teacher network while remaining equivalent to the class embedding [21]. All 198 tokens, including the CLS (a_{cls}) and distillation token (a_d), are assigned positional embeddings to incorporate spatial information. Further, these tokens are given as an input to a 12 layered transformer encoder with three Multi-Self Attention (MSA) heads as depicted in Fig. 2(a). The sequence of tokens input to the encoder is as follows:

$$\mathbf{a} = [a_{cls}, \mathbf{J}a_1, \mathbf{J}a_2, ..., \mathbf{J}a_n, a_d] + E \tag{2}$$

where n is 196, $\mathbf{J}$ depicts the patch embeddings of periocular NIR images and E refers to the positional encoding that maintains the images' spatial structure.

The encoder block employs self-attention (SA) to capture the correlations among the input tokens, utilizing three types of embeddings: Query (Q), Key (K), and Value (V). To apprehend this association, the Queries, Q, are multiplied by the transpose of Keys, K^T, to generate a vector output. This vector is then divided by the square root of the dimension D to prevent the gradient from vanishing. The final matrix undergoes a Softmax activation layer multiplied by the Values V to attain the resulting Head (H), also represented as $attention(Q, K, V)$.

$$H = attention(Q, K, V) = Softmax\left(\frac{Q \times K^T}{\sqrt{D}}\right) \times V \tag{3}$$

In the present work, the Scaled Dot-Product Attention mechanism is employed three times to attain a total of three attention heads ($H = 3$). After the self-attention operation is performed, the outputs from all attention heads are concatenated, and then they are passed through a feed-forward (FF) neural network, which includes learnable weights ($W_{learnable}$), as represented in the Eq. 4.

$$MSA = concat(SA_1, SA_2, SA_3) \times W_{learnable} \tag{4}$$

The resultant vector is then layer normalized and passed on to the final component of the encoder which is Multi-Layer Perceptron (MLP) blocks. These blocks comprise of fully coupled FF-dense layers with GeLU non-linearity. At the end of the encoder, the retrieved output tokens are again to be fed through 3 additional FF layers to obtain a context vector Z. Z comprises of 198 output tokens similar to that fed at the beginning of the encoder. The final context vector Z can be seen in Eq. 5.

$$\mathbf{Z} = [c_0, \mathbf{c}_1, \mathbf{c}_2, ..., \mathbf{c}_N, c_d] \tag{5}$$

After collecting the context vector Z, just the CLS token, c_0, and distillation token, c_d, are required for classification, which is then passed to 2 separate linear layers. c_0 and c_d tokens each have specific objective functions to learn, named student loss ($\mathcal{L}_{CE}$) and distillation loss ($\mathcal{L}_{teacher}$), to be discussed in the subsequent section. The average prediction after implication of a softmax activation function on both linear layers is used to determine whether or not the subject is fit.

Network Training Strategy: This subsection explores the various strategies utilized for training the teacher-student synergetic model. The input image is pre-processed to a shape of $(224, 224, 3)$ for feeding to both the teacher and student models. Adam optimizer is used for training with a batch size of 128. Adam is an adaptive optimization algorithm used in training machine learning models that combines the benefits of adaptive learning rates and momentum for efficient convergence. The performance of the model is evaluated using cross-entropy loss ($\mathcal{L}_{\mathrm{CE}}$). A learning rate scheduler is employed with an initial learning rate of 0.001 to obtain the local minima.

At first, we train the convnet-based teacher model to obtain the final teacher predictions, y_t. These predictions are then treated as the true label while training the distillation token in the student model. Further on, the transformer-based student model is trained where the CLS token has a separate loss given as $\mathcal{L}_{\mathrm{CE}}(\psi(Z_s), y)$. Here, ψ represents the softmax function applied over logits of the student Z_s utilizing c_0 token. Similarly, the c_d token is trained by considering the teacher's prediction as true label. The objective funtion of c_d can be depicted as $\mathcal{L}_{\mathrm{CE}}(\psi(Z_s), y_t)$. Herein, we also introduce a distillation of 0.5 on teacher model prediction. A distillation of 0.5 implies that during training, the c_d token is trained on a combination of soft targets (y_t) from the teacher model and hard targets, which is ground truth labels (y), with each target type accounting for half of the training examples. The complete process mentioned aims to replicate the teacher's predicted labels to reduce the cross-entropy loss between the highest value of the softmax function of the teacher's labels and the softmax function of the student. The final cross-entropy loss can be formulated as follows:

$$\mathcal{L}^{\mathrm{hardDistill}} = \frac{1}{2}\mathcal{L}_{\mathrm{CE}}(\psi(Z_s), y) + \frac{1}{2}\mathcal{L}_{\mathrm{CE}}(\psi(Z_s), y_t) \tag{6}$$

4   Experimental Analysis

In this section at first, we discuss the training testing protocol and then the experimental setup and result analysis. In our experimentation, we have randomly chosen 24 subjects (70%) for training and remaining 6 for testing (30%). This also enables fair comparison with the state-of-the-art approach [20] working on the same dataset. For training our feature extractor we have used five trials of random selection of training-testing dataset. The subsequent section will discuss our experimental setup and results.

4.1   Experimental Setup

The proposed feature extractor based on teacher-student collaborative distillation knowledge is implemented in Python 3.10 using Pytorch [16] and

Table 2. Calculated Evaluation Metrics for binary classification

	Precision	Recall	F1 score
Pre Alcohol	0.97	0.99	0.98
Post Alcohol	0.99	0.97	0.98

OpenCV [4] libraries. For training and evaluating the proposed framework, a PC having Intel(R) Xeon(R) CPU @ 2.00 GHz processor with 32 GB RAM and NVIDIA GPU P100 accelarator has been used.

4.2   Experimental Results

To validate the effectiveness of the proposed framework we have conducted two sets of experimentation. In first set of experimentation our goal is to identify whether the input iris image is captured in pre-alcohol session or post alcohol session. This set of experimentation can be regarded as a binary class classification. In the second set of experimentation our goal is to study the effect of alcohol on iris after alcohol consumption at different time intervals 15, 30, 45, and 60 min respectively. This set of experimentation can be regarded as a 5 class classification problem. For analyzing the performance we have employed commonly used classification task measures such as precision, recall and F1 score.

– **Binary Class Classification:** It can be inferred from Table 1 that in comparison of post-alcohol images (2400) we have very few instances of pre-alcohol images (600) in IAL-I dataset. In order to compensate this we have used randomly selected 800 images from CASIA-V4 [1] dataset for training our network. It should be noted that testing results are reported for IAL-I dataset only. Table 2 illustrates the binary class classification results in terms of precision, recall and F1 score.
– **Five Class Classification:** Under this experimentation we are trying to study the behavioral changes of the eye's CNS after alcohol consumption at 0, 15, 30, 45, and 60 min, respectively. Upon testing the model, our model showed an accuracy of 96.86% for 0th minute, 90.76% for 15th minute, 92.57% for 30th minute, 93.38% for 45th minute and 91.06% for 60th minute. The overall accuracy observed during testing phase came out to be 92.94%. Inferring from the obtained results for behaviour analysis, we can assert that the affect of consuming alcohol is most prominent at 45 min. Table 3 illustrates the five class classification results in terms of precision, recall and F1 score.

Comparative Analysis: To validate the effectiveness of the proposed framework we have compared our results with state-of-the-art approach [5,20]. To the best of our knowledge, [5,20] are the only work that has been conducted on IAL-I dataset used in our study. Table 4 provides a detailed comparison between the proposed approach and state-of-the art method. Essentially, the suggested approach achieves higher levels of accuracy in inference when compared to previous system that have been documented in the literature.

Table 3. Calculated Evaluation Metrics for five class classification

Session	Precision	Recall	F1 score
Session 0 (0 min)	0.95	0.96	0.96
Session 1 (15 min)	0.91	0.93	0.92
Session 2 (30 min)	0.93	0.93	0.93
Session 3 (45 min)	0.94	0.94	0.94
Session 4 (60 min)	0.93	0.90	0.91

Table 4. Comparison of the proposed method with the state-of-the-art approaches

Algorithm	Accuracy
Multi-Layer-Perceptron (MLP) [5]	75.8%
Fused Capsule Network [20]	92.3%
Our Proposed Framework	**98.46%**

5   Conclusion and Future Works

In this work we propose a framework that utilizes teacher-student learning paradigm for detecting alcohol consumption in NIR iris images. While we demonstrated the effectiveness of using transfer learning archetype in case encountered with small datasets (pre-alcohol iris images in our case). Furthermore, we provide detail experimental analysis to establish relation between alcohol consumption and the time elapsed after taking alcohol. Through various experiments, it can be inferred that the proposed framework outperforms the baseline state-of-the-art approach. The present work determines the fitness for duty (FFD) only on the basis of analyzing NIR iris images under the influence of alcohol, in future we would like to study the effect of drugs, lack of sleep on iris. Furthermore, we would like to deploy our proposed approach on an edge device for real-time inference.

References

1. Casia iris image database version 4.0. https://biometrics.idealtest.org/
2. Amodio, A., Ermidoro, M., Maggi, D., Formentin, S., Savaresi, S.M.: Automatic detection of driver impairment based on pupillary light reflex. IEEE Trans. Intell. Transp. Syst. **20**(8), 3038–3048 (2019). https://doi.org/10.1109/TITS.2018. 2871262
3. Arora, S.S., Vatsa, M., Singh, R., Jain, A.: Iris recognition under alcohol influence: a preliminary study. In: 2012 5th IAPR International Conference on Biometrics (ICB), pp. 336–341 (2012). https://doi.org/10.1109/ICB.2012.6199829
4. Bradski, G.: The OpenCV library. Dr. Dobb's J. Softw. Tools **25**, 120–123 (2000)
5. Causa, L., Tapia, J.E., Lopez-Droguett, E., Valenzuela, A., Benalcazar, D., Busch, C.: Behavioural curves analysis using near-infrared-iris image sequences (2022)

6. Chua, T.S., Tang, J., Hong, R., Li, H., Luo, Z., Zheng, Y.T.: NUS-WIDE: a real-world web image database from national university of Singapore. In: Proceedings of ACM Conference on Image and Video Retrieval (CIVR 2009), Santorini, Greece (2009)
7. Dai, Y., Gao, Y., Liu, F.: TransMed: transformers advance multi-modal medical image classification. Diagnostics **11**(8) (2021). https://doi.org/10.3390/diagnostics11081384, https://www.mdpi.com/2075-4418/11/8/1384
8. Delgado, M.K., et al.: Accuracy of consumer-marketed smartphone-paired alcohol breath testing devices: a laboratory validation study. Alcohol.: Clin. Exp. Res. **45**(5), 1091–1099 (2021)
9. Deng, J., Dong, W., Socher, R., Li, L.J., Li, K., Fei-Fei, L.: ImageNet: a large-scale hierarchical image database. In: 2009 IEEE Conference on Computer Vision and Pattern Recognition, pp. 248–255. IEEE (2009)
10. Dosovitskiy, A., et al.: An image is worth 16×16 words: transformers for image recognition at scale (2021)
11. Gug, I.T., Tertis, M., Hosu, O., Cristea, C.: Salivary biomarkers detection: analytical and immunological methods overview. TrAC, Trends Anal. Chem. **113**, 301–316 (2019)
12. Health, Q.: Fitness for duty: alcohol and other drugs (2020)
13. Krizhevsky, A., Nair, V., Hinton, G.: CIFAR-100 (Canadian institute for advanced research). https://www.cs.toronto.edu/~kriz/cifar.html
14. Le, N.Q.K., Ho, Q.T., Nguyen, T.T.D., Ou, Y.Y.: A transformer architecture based on BERT and 2D convolutional neural network to identify DNA enhancers from sequence information. Brief. Bioinform. **22**(5) (02 2021). https://doi.org/10.1093/bib/bbab005
15. Mahbub, M.K., Biswas, M., Miah, A.M., Shahabaz, A., Kaiser, M.S.: COVID-19 detection using chest X-ray images with a RegNet structured deep learning model. In: Mahmud, M., Kaiser, M.S., Kasabov, N., Iftekharuddin, K., Zhong, N. (eds.) AII 2021. CCIS, vol. 1435, pp. 358–370. Springer, Cham (2021). https://doi.org/10.1007/978-3-030-82269-9_28
16. Paszke, A.e.a.: PyTorch: an imperative style, high performance deep learning library. In: Wallach, H., Larochelle, H., Beygelzimer, A., d' Alché-Buc, F., Fox, E., Garnett, R. (eds.) Advances in Neural Information Processing Systems, vol. 32, pp. 8024–8035. Curran Associates, Inc. (2019). https://papers.neurips.cc/paper/9015-pytorch-an-imperative-style-high-performance-deep-learning-library.pdf
17. Pidd, K., Roche, A.M., Cameron, J., Lee, N.K., Jenner, L., Duraisingam, V.: Workplace alcohol harm reduction intervention in Australia: cluster non-randomised controlled trial. Drug Alcohol Rev. **37**, 502–513 (2018)
18. Reich, J., Kelly, M.: Empirical findings of fitness-for-duty evaluations. MedEdPublish **7**, 258 (2018). https://doi.org/10.15694/mep.2018.0000258.1
19. Tapia, J.: NIR iris images under alcohol effect (2022). https://doi.org/10.21227/dzrd-p479, https://dx.doi.org/10.21227/dzrd-p479
20. Tapia, J., Droguett, E.L., Busch, C.: Alcohol consumption detection from periocular NIR images using capsule network. In: 2022 26th International Conference on Pattern Recognition (ICPR), pp. 959–966 (2022). https://doi.org/10.1109/ICPR56361.2022.9956573
21. Touvron, H., Cord, M., Douze, M., Massa, F., Sablayrolles, A., Jégou, H.: Training data-efficient image transformers & distillation through attention (2021)
22. Yuan, F., Zhang, Z., Fang, Z.: An effective cnn and transformer complementary network for medical image segmentation. Pattern Recognit. **136**, 109228 (2023). https://doi.org/10.1016/j.patcog.2022.109228, https://www.sciencedirect.com/science/article/pii/S0031320322007075

Performance Assessment of Fine-Tuned Barrier Recognition Models in Varying Conditions

Marios Thoma[1,2]($\boxtimes$) (iD), Harris Partaourides[1] (iD), Ieswaria Sreedharan[1] (iD), Zenonas Theodosiou[1,3] (iD), Loizos Michael[1,2], and Andreas Lanitis[1,4] (iD)

[1] CYENS Center of Excellence, Nicosia, Cyprus
{m.thoma,h.partaourides,z.theodosiou}@cyens.org.cy
[2] Open University of Cyprus, Nicosia, Cyprus
loizos@ouc.ac.cy
[3] Department of Communication and Internet Studies,
Cyprus University of Technology, Limassol, Cyprus
[4] Department of Multimedia and Graphic Arts, Cyprus University of Technology,
Limassol, Cyprus
andreas.lanitis@cut.ac.cy

Abstract. Walking has been widely promoted by various medical institutions as a major contributor to physical activity that keeps people healthy. However, pedestrian safety remains a critical concern due to barriers present on sidewalks, such as bins, poles, and trees. Although pedestrians are generally cautious, these barriers can pose a significant risk to vulnerable groups, such as the visually impaired and elderly. To address this issue, accurate and robust computer vision models can be used to detect barriers on pedestrian pathways in real-time. In this study, we assess the performance of fine-tuned egocentric barrier recognition models under various conditions, such as lighting variations, angles of view, video frame rates and levels of obstruction. In this context, we collected a dataset of different barriers, and fine-tuned two representative image recognition models, assessing their performances on a set of videos taken from a predefined route. Our findings provide guidelines for retaining model performance for applications using barrier recognition models in varying environmental conditions.

Keywords: Pedestrian Safety · Egocentric Dataset · Barrier Recognition · Deep Learning

1 Introduction

Walking is a popular form of physical exercise, known for its positive impact on health. Being an aerobic and bone-strengthening activity, it can reduce the risk of chronic diseases and promote an active lifestyle [13]. Despite the widespread promotion of the benefits of walking by governments and health organizations,

N. Tsapatsoulis et al. (Eds.): CAIP 2023, LNCS 14185, pp. 172–181, 2023.
https://doi.org/10.1007/978-3-031-44240-7_17

pedestrian safety continues to be a major concern, since road accidents encompass a significant safety risk. The well-being of road users is influenced by numerous factors, such as speeding and rule violations by drivers, pedestrian negligence, and poor road conditions. Such conditions can be particularly hazardous for vulnerable groups like the elderly and disabled [6].

Poor road conditions, including inadequate lighting, unfavorable weather conditions, and poorly-maintained road surfaces, are recognized to be some of the major factors contributing to road accidents in Cyprus [1]. Several researchers have studied and analyzed the behavior of pedestrians when faced with obstacles in their path. For example, in a study conducted by Ding et al. [2], the impact of different obstacle placements on pedestrian evacuation was examined. The results showed that the presence of obstacles in pedestrian pathways resulted in a significant delay before pedestrians could maneuver past the obstacles.

Recent advancements in computer vision and mobile computing have paved the way for various applications aimed at enhancing the safety and well-being of pedestrians. Egocentric Vision is a novel approach that utilizes data collected through wearable cameras or smartphones to enable real-time recognition of obstacles hindering safe walking within urban areas. To develop effective systems and applications for smartphones, it is crucial to understand how machine learning models perform under different conditions [18]. This study focuses on the creation of deep learning models capable of automatically recognizing various barriers in real-world environments. Specifically, we utilized algorithms based on Convolutional Neural Networks and Vision Transformers to develop recognition models for nine distinct barrier types commonly found on the sidewalks of the city of Nicosia, Cyprus. Our evaluation focused on assessing the models' performance in detecting barriers under different lighting conditions, viewing angles, video frame rates, levels of obstruction in front of the barriers, and scenarios involving multiple barriers in the pedestrian's field of view, thereby simulating their use in the wild.

The remainder of the paper proceeds with Sect. 2 providing an overview of the state-of-the-art research in the field of barrier recognition. Section 3 details the entire process of the training of the recognition models that were utilized in this study. In Sect. 4, the experimental procedure for evaluating the performances of these models is illustrated, and the insights obtained from the evaluation are discussed. Finally, Sect. 5 summarizes our work, highlights its contributions, and suggests avenues for future enhancements.

2   Literature Survey

Egocentric vision is a perceptual method that involves the use of wearable cameras attached to a person to capture egocentric images or videos [12]. Notably, there has been a recent surge in egocentric video data collection worldwide, culminating in the Ego4D project [5], which compiled large amounts of day-to-day activity footage captured through wearable devices from a first-person perspective. Another such dataset was created using a camera mounted on a student to record activities such as attending lectures, driving, and eating [10].

Various technologies have been developed to improve pedestrian safety. One such technology is an obstacle detection model called ObstacleWatch, designed by Wang et al. [21], which uses acoustic signals emitted by smartphone speakers to determine the distance between the user and an obstacle. However, this approach proved to be inefficient due to the noise present in public spaces. Another application called LookUp was proposed by Jain et al. [8], which uses shoe-mounted inertial sensors to detect transitions from pedestrian walkways onto the road to alert texting pedestrians, achieved a detection rate of 90%. Liu et al. [11] developed a solution named InfraSee, which utilizes infrared sensors mounted on smartphones to detect hazardous situations and alerts the user.

WalkSafe, developed by Wang et al. [20], is a smartphone-based application that uses the smartphone's back camera to detect oncoming vehicles and alerts the user during active phone calls. The application uses decision trees to classify images and achieved an efficiency rate of 77%. A similar application, called Inspector, developed by Tang et al. [15], alerts users when they are approaching the edge of pedestrian areas. The model uses simple keypoint detection and k-means clustering for feature extraction and uses Normal Bayes and K-nearest neighbors models to classify images with an accuracy rate of 92%–99%.

TerraFirma, an application proposed by Jain et al. [9], takes a different approach, choosing to identify the material composition of pedestrian walkways, instead of obstacles on the walkways themselves, in order to warn pedestrians when they transition from walkways to the street. Support Vector Machine classifiers were used to identify various ground surface types with an accuracy rate of 90%. Another application, AutoADAS, proposed by Wei et al. [22], uses smartphone cameras to detect objects in the environment and measure their distance from the user, warning them in case a potential collision is predicted. The application utilizes the user's behavior profile collected from sensors on mobile devices, making it more personalized to the user. Similarly, Foerster et al. [4] developed SpareEye, an Android application that detects changes in the background of a mobile camera's video stream and notifies the user when the distance between objects is reduced in each frame.

Hasan et al. [7] presented a comprehensive review of existing pedestrian safety models, highlighting the limitations and potential areas for further improvement. One of the issues highlighted was that, although various egocentric datasets are available, relatively few datasets focusing on pedestrian barrier detection exist. One of the few such datasets available is that created by Theodosiou et al. [16], and is comprised of images of barriers captured from a pedestrian's perspective. The dataset was utilized to fine-tune a VGG16 model, achieving a training accuracy of 65% and validation accuracy of 55%. Subsequently, the fine-tuned VGG16 model was embedded in a smartphone application that aided pedestrians in capturing images of barriers they encountered and report their geographic location to the authorities, in order to enhance pedestrian safety [19]. Additionally, Theodosiou et al. [17] trained an object detection model using the aforementioned pedestrian-based image dataset and tested it using the Faster Region-Based CNN and Single Shot MultiBox Detector with InceptionV2, ResNet50,

Bench	Bin	Bus Stop	Large Bin	Light	Parking Prevention Barrier	Tourist Info Sign	Traffic Sign	Tree

Fig. 1. Image examples of each of the nine barrier types.

and MobileNetV2 for feature extraction. The model achieved an average precision of 88.4% and 75.6% for the Faster R-CNN and SSD models, respectively, demonstrating its efficacy in detecting barriers on sidewalks.

The use of deep learning is now the dominant approach for analyzing egocentric data. Different architectures, including convolutional neural networks, have been used with great success in egocentric and mobile applications. The limitations of smartphone devices led to the development of the MobileNetV2 algorithm designed exclusively for this purpose by investing in building models with small size and low inference time. MobileNetV2 is one of the best CNN models suitable and efficient in smartphones for image classification. The remarkable difference in MobileNetV2 is based on its inverted residual structure [14]. The low dimensional features are expanded and the resulting features undergo dimensionality reduction using a depth-wise convolution. However, demand for more efficient algorithms has led to the Vision Transformer (ViT) architecture [3] competing with the hitherto prevailing CNN architecture. The ViT architecture, which is based on the self-attention mechanism, have recently been used successfully in computer vision tasks such as image classification and object recognition.

In this work, we exploit the power of two state-of-the-art algorithms from the CNN and ViT architectures, namely the MobileNetV2 and ViT-B/16 algorithms, to build robust machine learning models to identify multiple obstacles that endanger citizens while walking in urban environments. Aiming to create applications capable of detecting obstacles under different real-world conditions, we test model performance under different lighting conditions, camera angles, camera frame rates, as well as the appearance of additional occlusions and the presence of more than one obstacle in the point of view of pedestrians.

3   Methodology

In this section, we describe the methodology used to conduct our assessment on the performance of machine learning algorithms in recognizing barriers under different conditions. Our study was conducted in three phases: data collection, model training and model assessment.

Table 1. Size of the evaluation set (in number of frames) per barrier type and lighting condition (Route 1/Route 2).

Barrier	Daylight	Cloudy	Night	Sunrise	Sunset	Angles
Bench	164/222	262/220	324/489	333/57	270/305	646/697
Bin	159/182	199/285	255/148	311/158	275/225	195/320
Bus Stop	84/141	135/296	161/232	–/–	–/–	–/–
Large Bin	256/340	241/37	200/210	236/120	151/122	342/242
Light	62/164	259/188	-/152	517/244	293/448	571/1604
Parking Prevention Barrier	1410/702	1001/308	1158/1224	1585/512	343/265	363/653
Tourist Information Sign	92/259	628/75	145/705	168/213	166/189	163/540
Traffic Sign	28/176	103/283	516/58	88/181	–/222	833/1137
Tree	85/9	37/80	31/203	86/–	–/–	316/–

3.1 Data Collection

We carefully designed our data collection process to ensure a comprehensive and diverse dataset while evaluating the performance of obstacle recognition in the city center of Nicosia under various conditions. To achieve this, we first determined a predefined route that incorporates a broad spectrum of barriers commonly encountered by pedestrians in their day-to-day activities.

Two distinct approaches were employed to collect data. Firstly, we obtained training and validation data by capturing obstacle-oriented videos. Each video was designed to highlight a single obstacle, allowing us to capture the diversity of barriers in a well-controlled manner. To facilitate the data collection process, we employed a simple and low-cost setup, comprising of a mobile phone camera. This also ensured consistent video quality under varying lighting conditions.

We identified a total of nine barriers along the predefined pedestrian route, namely: bench, bin, bus stop, large bin, light, parking prevention barrier, tourist information sign, traffic sign, and tree. Figure 1 depicts an example of each of the nine barriers. We collected two videos of each barrier, and subsequently we created an image dataset from the collected videos by extracting 600 frames per barrier at regular intervals throughout the videos ($9 \times 600 = 5400$ frames in total). We used a 70%-30% split to generate the final training and validation sets, respectively.

The second collection approach entails egocentric videos of a pedestrian walking the predefined urban route under normal walking conditions, in both directions (these will be referred to as *Route 1* and *Route 2*). This approach allowed us to capture variations in barriers and environment that a pedestrian could encounter during their daily commute. We also collected videos under different lighting conditions—daylight, cloudy, night, sunrise, and sunset—to evaluate the models' performances. Similarly, we also included videos taken from diverse angles relative to the barriers as an additional condition in our evaluation experiments. Daylight, cloudy, and night videos were collected at a standard frame rate of 30 frames per second (FPS). In contrast, videos taken during sunrise, sunset,

Table 2. Performance of the two fine-tuned models under different lighting conditions (Route 1 %/Route 2 %).

Model	Daylight	Cloudy	Night
MobileNetV2	38.3/58.6	44.2/45.3	33.1/20.0
ViT-B/16	53.5/58.7	76.1/73.8	63.3/60.0

Table 3. Model performance when using different frame rates - daylight videos were captured at 30 FPS, while sunrise, sunset and angle variation videos at 60 FPS (Route 1 %/ Route 2 %).

Model	Daylight	Sunrise	Sunset	Angles
MobileNetV2	38.3/58.6	45.3/72.4	81.7/74.7	73.5/80.8
ViT-B/16	53.5/58.7	68.0/80.7	85.1/70.9	71.7/82.3

and at various angles were recorded at an increased frame rate of 60 FPS. For the evaluation videos, we manually annotated each frame with barrier information and bounding box details. The bounding box annotation allowed for precise identification and localization of the immediate barrier within the frame, from a pedestrian's viewpoint. Unlike the initial data collection approach where a specific number of frames per barrier type was extracted, in this second approach we extracted all frames from the captured videos, resulting in varying numbers of frames per barrier type, due to differences in video takes and routes. Frames that did not contain any barriers were omitted. Table 1 shows the size of the resulting evaluation set for each of the considered conditions.

3.2   Model Training

In our study, we aim to investigate the performance of recognition models under various conditions. To achieve this, we trained a representative example from each of two widely used model architectures, namely Convolutional Neural Networks (CNNs) and Transformers, using pre-trained models on the ImageNet dataset. By fine-tuning these pre-trained models on our training and validation data, we were able to significantly reduce the training time while improving the models' performances. During the training process, we also closely monitored the models' validation performances to ensure that they were not over-fitting to the training data. Interestingly, we observed near-perfect validation performance for both models, which further highlights the effectiveness of image classification in computer vision research, especially for datasets with non-ambiguous classes.

However, it is important to evaluate how well the models perform in real-world scenarios. To this end, the following section presents a series of experiments we performed to assess the models' performances in diverse environmental conditions, which is crucial for their practical use.

4   Experimental Results

Our study consists of four experiments aimed at evaluating the performance of two representative models. In the first experiment, we analyze the obstacle classification performance of both models under different lighting conditions. Specifically, we evaluate their performances in three lighting conditions: daylight, cloudy, and night. These conditions represent the barriers encountered along the predefined route. The results of this analysis are summarized in Table 2. It is worth noting that the ViT-B/16 model consistently outperformed the MobileNetV2 model across all three lighting conditions. This outcome was expected due to the higher model capacity and complexity of ViT-B/16 compared to MobileNetV2.

Table 4. Model performance when using Bounding Boxes (vs. whole frames, that may contain multiple barrier types at once) (Route 1 %/Route 2 %).

Model	Daylight	Cloudy	Night	Sunrise	Sunset	Angles
MobileNetV2	38.3/58.6	44.2/45.3	33.1/20.0	45.3/72.4	81.7/74.7	73.5/80.8
MobileNetV2 (BB)	85.4/88.8	52.8/53.9	39.1/28.4	49.6/75.9	88.7/81.7	75.1/79.7
ViT-B/16	53.5/58.7	76.1/73.8	63.3/60.0	68.0/80.7	85.1/70.9	71.7/82.3
ViT-B/16 (BB)	82.0/90.8	76.1/73.8	63.3/60.0	68.4/79.4	89.9/85.3	72.9/84.7

Fig. 2. Example of a barrier image with superimposed obstructions in the form of human silhouettes, at various sizes (the silhouette cutouts originated from a freely available dataset [23]).

In the second experiment, our goal is to assess the impact of frame rate on the inference performance of the models. Specifically, we evaluate the performance of both models at two video frame rates, 30 FPS and 60 FPS. In this experiment, we compare the performance of the models on daylight videos with two additional lighting variations, sunrise and sunset, and angle variations during daylight. This analysis allows us to understand how different frame rates, which capture temporal information, affect the models' ability to accurately classify barriers during inference. The results of this experiment are summarized in Table 3. We observe a significant improvement in the performance of both models when the increased 60 FPS rate is used.

The third experiment focuses on measuring the performance of both models in an ideal scenario where only a single barrier type is present in each frame. To accomplish this, we utilize the Bounding Box (BB) annotations of the videos. The performances of both models are presented in Table 4. We observe a substantial improvement in the performance of both models when utilizing bounding box information.

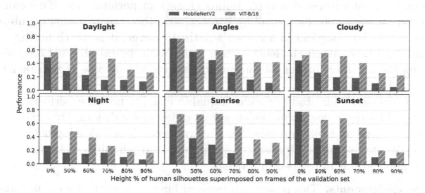

Fig. 3. Model performance when digital obstructions are superimposed on the validation set (a 0% height percentage implies no obstructions).

For the fourth experiment, we assess the models' performances when faced with digital obstructions in the camera view, specifically people at various degrees of proximity. This experiment aims to test the models' ability to handle unexpected obstructions, that may hinder their performance in real-world settings. We assessed the trained models' performances under varying levels of obstruction by digitally superimposing human silhouettes in front of the evaluation frames. We introduced five levels of obstruction, that were calculated based on the percentage of the silhouettes' height in comparison to the height of the frame. The degrees of obstruction ranged from 50% to 90%, with 10% incremental steps, as shown in Fig. 2. The results of this experiment are illustrated in Fig. 3. We observe a decrease in the performance of both models when increasing the obstruction size.

5 Conclusion

In this paper, we conducted a comprehensive analysis of fine-tuned barrier recognition models in different conditions. Through experimentation, we gained valuable insights into the models' performances under varying lighting conditions, frame rates, bounding box accuracy, and the presence of digital obstructions.

Our results consistently demonstrated that the ViT-B/16 model outperformed the MobileNetV2 model across all tested conditions. This performance advantage can be attributed to the ViT-B/16 model's higher capacity and complexity, which allows for more effective handling of challenging scenarios. However, it should be noted that utilizing the ViT-B/16 model comes with increased computational resource requirements that might exceed the capabilities of some commodity devices. Furthermore, we observed a significant improvement in the performance of both models when higher video frame rates were used. This finding underscores the importance of capturing clear, low motion-blur egocentric images to achieve accurate recognition. The inclusion of bounding box information proved to be a crucial factor in enhancing the models' recognition accuracy. By focusing on the immediate barrier through the utilization of bounding box annotations, we witnessed notable improvements in performance. This can be achieved on the application level by constraining the camera's area of interest to the immediate barriers in a carrier's path. However, it is worth noting that the models encountered challenges when faced with digital obstructions, highlighting the need for further advancements in handling unexpected obstacles in real-world scenarios.

In conclusion, our study provides valuable insights into the performance of fine-tuned barrier recognition models across different conditions. By considering our conclusions and recommendations, future research and development efforts can be directed towards improving the efficiency and reliability of barrier recognition applications in real-world settings.

Acknowledgements. This project has received funding from the European Union's Horizon 2020 research and innovation programme under grant agreement No 739578 complemented by the Government of the Republic of Cyprus through the Directorate General for European Programmes, Coordination and Development.

References

1. Angın, M., Ali, S.I.A.: Analysis of factors affecting road traffic accidents in North Cyprus. Eng. Technol. Appl. Sci. Res. **11**(6), 7938–7943 (2021)
2. Ding, Z., Shen, Z., Guo, N., Zhu, K., Long, J.: Evacuation through area with obstacle that can be stepped over: experimental study. J. Stat. Mech: Theory Exp. **2020**(2), 023404 (2020)
3. Dosovitskiy, A., et al.: An image is worth 16×16 words: transformers for image recognition at scale. In: International Conference on Learning Representations (ICLR 2021) (2021)
4. Foerster, K.T., Gross, A., Hail, N., Uitto, J., Wattenhofer, R.: SpareEye: enhancing the safety of inattentionally blind smartphone users. In: Proceedings of the 13th International Conference on Mobile and Ubiquitous Multimedia, MUM 2014, pp. 68–72. ACM (2014)
5. Grauman, K., et al.: Ego4D: around the world in 3,000 hours of egocentric video. In: Proceedings of the IEEE/CVF Conference on Computer Vision and Pattern Recognition, pp. 18973–18990 (2022)
6. Haghighi, M., Nadrian, H., Sadeghi-Bazargani, H., Hdr, D.B., Bakhtari Aghdam, F.: Challenges related to pedestrian safety: a qualitative study identifying Iranian residents' perspectives. Int. J. Inj. Contr. Saf. Promot. **27**(3), 327–335 (2020)
7. Hasan, R., Hasan, R.: Pedestrian safety using the internet of things and sensors: issues, challenges, and open problems. Futur. Gener. Comput. Syst. **134**, 187–203 (2022)

8. Jain, S., Borgiattino, C., Ren, Y., Gruteser, M., Chen, Y., Chiasserini, C.F.: LookUp: enabling pedestrian safety services via shoe sensing. In: Proceedings of the 13th Annual International Conference on Mobile Systems, Applications, and Services, MobiSys 2015, pp. 257–271. ACM (2015)
9. Jain, S., Gruteser, M.: Recognizing textures with mobile cameras for pedestrian safety applications. IEEE Trans. Mob. Comput. **18**(8), 1911–1923 (2019)
10. Lee, Y.J., Ghosh, J., Grauman, K.: Discovering important people and objects for egocentric video summarization. In: 2012 IEEE Conference on Computer Vision and Pattern Recognition, pp. 1346–1353 (2012)
11. Liu, X., Cao, J., Wen, J., Tang, S.: InfraSee: an unobtrusive alertness system for pedestrian mobile phone users. IEEE Trans. Mob. Comput. **16**(2), 394–407 (2017)
12. Mann, S., Kitani, K.M., Lee, Y.J., Ryoo, M.S., Fathi, A.: An introduction to the 3rd workshop on egocentric (first-person) vision. In: 2014 IEEE Conference on Computer Vision and Pattern Recognition Workshops, pp. 827–832 (2014)
13. Piercy, K.L., et al.: The physical activity guidelines for Americans. JAMA **320**(19), 2020–2028 (2018)
14. Sandler, M., Howard, A., Zhu, M., Zhmoginov, A., Chen, L.C.: MobileNetV2: inverted residuals and linear bottlenecks. In: Proceedings of the IEEE Conference on Computer Vision and Pattern Recognition, pp. 4510–4520 (2018)
15. Tang, M., Nguyen, C.T., Wang, X., Lu, S.: An efficient walking safety service for distracted mobile users. In: 2016 IEEE 13th International Conference on Mobile Ad Hoc and Sensor Systems (MASS), pp. 84–91 (2016)
16. Theodosiou, Z., Partaourides, H., Atun, T., Panayi, S., Lanitis, A.: A first-person database for detecting barriers for pedestrians. In: VISIGRAPP 2020 - Proceedings of the 15th International Joint Conference on Computer Vision, Imaging and Computer Graphics Theory and Applications, vol. 5, pp. 660–666 (2020)
17. Theodosiou, Z., Partaourides, H., Panayi, S., Kitsis, A., Lanitis, A.: Detection and recognition of barriers in egocentric images for safe urban sidewalks. In: Bouatouch, K., et al. (eds.) VISIGRAPP 2020. CCIS, vol. 1474, pp. 530–543. Springer, Cham (2022). https://doi.org/10.1007/978-3-030-94893-1_25
18. Theodosiou, Z., Thoma, M., Partaourides, H., Lanitis, A.: A systematic approach for developing a robust artwork recognition framework using smartphone cameras. Algorithms **15**(9), 305 (2022)
19. Thoma, M., Theodosiou, Z., Partaourides, H., Tylliros, C., Antoniades, D., Lanitis, A.: A smartphone application designed to detect obstacles for pedestrians' safety. In: Paiva, S., Lopes, S.I., Zitouni, R., Gupta, N., Lopes, S.F., Yonezawa, T. (eds.) SmartCity360° 2020. LNICST, vol. 372, pp. 358–371. Springer, Cham (2021). https://doi.org/10.1007/978-3-030-76063-2_25
20. Wang, T., Cardone, G., Corradi, A., Torresani, L., Campbell, A.T.: WalkSafe: a pedestrian safety app for mobile phone users who walk and talk while crossing roads. In: Proceedings of the Twelfth Workshop on Mobile Computing Systems & Applications, HotMobile 2012, pp. 1–6. ACM (2012)
21. Wang, Z., Tan, S., Zhang, L., Yang, J.: ObstacleWatch: acoustic-based obstacle collision detection for pedestrian using smartphone. Proc. ACM Interact. Mob. Wearable Ubiquit. Technol. **2**(4), 1–22 (2018)
22. Wei, Z., Lo, S.W., Liang, Y., Li, T., Shen, J., Deng, R.H.: Automatic accident detection and alarm system. In: Proceedings of the 23rd ACM International Conference on Multimedia, MM 2015, pp. 781–784. ACM (2015)
23. XOIO-AIR: Cutout people - Greenscreen volume 1 (2012). https://xoio-air.de/2012/greenscreen_people_01/

Keyrtual: A Lightweight Virtual Musical Keyboard Based on RGB-D and Sensors Fusion

Danilo Avola⬤, Luigi Cinque⬤, Marco Raoul Marini(✉)⬤, Andrea Princic⬤, and Valerio Venanzi⬤

Department of Computer Science, Sapienza, University of Rome,
Via Salaria 113, 00185 Rome, Italy
{avola,cinque,marini}@di.uniroma1.it,
{princic.1837592,venanzi.1852473}@studenti.uniroma1.it
https://visionlab.di.uniroma1.it

Abstract. The digital world is becoming more and more part of our everyday life. Research groups and industries have been working for years to find innovative and natural interaction ways to improve users' satisfaction with the approach to the technology. In particular, Human-Computer Interaction (HCI) made a great evolutionary leap with accurate sensors and high-computational devices. Moreover, the miniaturization of circuits made modern systems portable and affordable. Also, advanced algorithmic approaches, e.g., Machine and Deep Learning (ML and DL), strongly support achieving noticeable results at the price of potentially long training times and considerable resource requirements. In this context, we propose a novel system for playing a virtual musical keyboard exploiting an RGB and a dual-Infrared (IR) sensor. It is designed for musicians and enthusiasts for multi-purposes, e.g., training or music production. After a calibration phase, the software can be executed in real-time with responsive feedback. The main focuses of the proposal are the portability and the low-computational resources requirement. Quantitative and qualitative results highlight the system's overall effectiveness, proving that the proposed pipeline could be promising.

Keywords: Computer Vision · Human-Computer Interaction · Hand tracking · Hand gesture · Virtual musical instrument

1 Introduction

In recent years, technological improvements in hardware and algorithmic solutions provided new frontiers in Human-Computer Interaction (HCI). The evolution of technology introduced advanced solutions for different application areas, e.g., Virtual Reality (VR) in rehabilitation [4], multimodal interaction for intelligent environments [2], or gaze recognition for remote controls [24]. Also, principles related to Augmented Reality (AR) and Extended/Mixed Reality (XR/MR)

N. Tsapatsoulis et al. (Eds.): CAIP 2023, LNCS 14185, pp. 182–191, 2023.
https://doi.org/10.1007/978-3-031-44240-7_18

are inspirational approaches for providing novel interaction paradigms [3]. In this context, Machine Learning (ML) and Deep Learning (DL) played a crucial role in the efficiency and accuracy of detectors, trackers, and classifiers. Nowadays, ML-based approaches in HCI [19] are less interesting than the DL-based ones [18]. Moreover, recent methodologies provide promising results even with few samples in the involved dataset [1]. However, these solutions usually require consistent resources and often also long training times to be really effective. This fact is particularly evident in complex tasks, e.g., hand tracking and gesture recognition. Based on this scenario, we propose a novel pipeline, that combines simple and already-known algorithms, to perform hand tracking and gesture recognition applied to a virtual musical instrument. The idea aims to provide a real-time feedback system with a low computational cost and using only two input sensors, an RGB and a dual-Infrared (IR) camera. It is meant to work with portable devices and without a training phase. The document is structured as follows: In Sect. 2, an overview of the hand tracking and gesture recognition focused on virtual instruments is provided; in Sect. 3, the proposal is described; then, the conducted experiments and the collected results are shown in Sect. 4; and the final thoughts are provided in Sect. 5.

2 Related Work

For over 20 years, there have been efforts to develop systems that correctly recognize and detect the human body and its movement [11]. In particular, numerous researchers have dealt with the problem of hand recognition and gesture detection, tasks with countless applications [13].

2.1 Non-wearable Hand-Based Interaction

A "wearable" interaction system exploits invasive devices, e.g., gloves, usually attached to one or both hands [14], supporting accurate tracking but limiting the comfort for the user. Based on these assumptions, other solutions can substitute them in hand tracking tasks: the non-wearable systems [5]. A common method is to use an RGB-D sensor to retrieve accurate depth information directly from the hardware [15,25]. Unlike RGB-D, RGB sensors can only infer three-dimensional data, usually with the addition of computational cost [16]; these approaches, often, compensates for the lack of depth information by training a neural network to perform hand tracking and gesture recognition. In [20], for example, the authors used a Generative Adversarial Network (GAN) to generate fake hand images that fed a Convolutional Neural Network (CNN), namely RegNet, for detecting the hand position in the 3D space. Some other works combine Neural Networks (NNs) and RGB-D sensors to get the most relevant information from both streams [21], thus highlighting improved results and inspiring our proposal.

2.2 Natural Virtual Interfaces for Music

Based on the specific task, gesture recognizers are trained differently: gestures for playing the piano differ from those of American Sign Language (ASL), which are the reference hard task in hand gesture recognition. This fact implies that few research groups developed solutions specifically designed for playing virtual instruments. In [15], for example, the authors merged RGB-D information with finger pose/tap detection to create a completely virtual piano. In a similar work [23], another research group developed a system that exploits the combination of RGB-D data with information take from a MIDI keyboard alongside a dataset to detect the correct fingering of piano notes. It was proposed for teaching piano, and the results shown in the experimental section proved the method's effectiveness. In [9], the authors developed a simple virtual instrument using both an Oculus Rift and a Leap Motion. The instrument is similar to a piano: there are several buttons that, when touched, reproduce notes. The hands are simulated inside the 3D environment. When a hand is close enough to a button, it triggers the touch action. In [7], instead, the authors combined an Oculus Rift with the Razer Hydra to perform gesture detection and play a virtual instrument in the 3D environment. In [15], the authors proposed a combination of a depth sensor with Random Forest (RF) regression to detect and mimic the keyboard fingering on a virtual keyboard. There are also other solutions in which an actual MIDI keyboard is used, and it is combined with a stream of RGB information [23]. To the best of our knowledge, any work in literature similar to ours, either makes use of AI, MIDI keyboards, or both.

3   Proposed Method

The system aims to allow playing in real-time on a virtual keyboard that is just drawn or printed on a piece of paper. It just requires three components: a low-end computer, an RGB camera, and a depth sensor. The two devices look at the scene from the top-view, one of them slightly rotated from the orthogonal position (see Sect. 4). In Fig. 1, an overview of our architecture is shown. The pipeline faces the following issues: keyboard detection, hands detection/tracking, and key-pressed action recognition. Keyboard and hand detection are treated in the preliminary phase, exploiting well-known computer vision techniques. Hand tracking and key-presses recognition are mainly analyzed in the real-time phase, where state-of-the-art algorithms are involved.

3.1   Preliminary Phase

The preliminary phase is made of two modules: the setup and the keyboard detection phase. However, in this section, we also included the method for sensors fusion, which is exploited in both the preliminary and the real-time phase.

Setup: In the setup, only the RGB input is exploited. The first operation consists of background subtraction. Thus, a frame of the background is captured (Fig. 2a). Then, a frame with the keyboard over the background is taken (Fig. 2b). The last step provides a background subtraction, comparing the first frame with the second one according to the Mixture of Gaussian version 2 (MOG2) [6]; the result is shown in Fig. 2c.

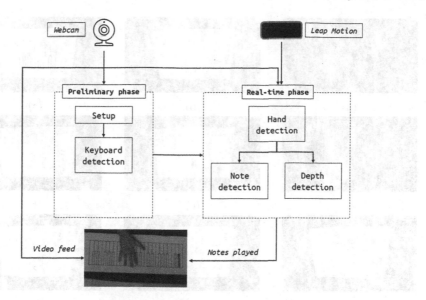

Fig. 1. Architecture of the proposed system. The webcam corresponds to the RGB input, while the Leap Motion is the depth sensor.

Keyboard Detector: The result of the setup module is given as input to the proposed keyboard detector. First, an adaptive thresholding operation is performed: it strongly highlights the drowned keyboard from the background of the paper, avoiding issues in case of low contrast between them. It is based on standard binary thresholding [26] with a threshold value of 127. Then, the Canny edge detection algorithm [8] is used to find the edges of the keyboard (Fig. 2d). The result feeds a probabilistic Hough Transform procedure [22] to find all the lines of the keyboard (Fig. 2e). Then, we apply K-means clustering [12] with $k = 3$ to fit the lines based on their rotation angles: one cluster is for horizontal lines, and the other two are for vertical lines. Two groups of vertical lines are needed due to their different rotation angles (arising from the viewpoint) for the left and the right side of the keyboard, assuming that the latter is almost centered in the frame. Given the horizontal lines, these are classified according to their y coordinate to find the top of the keyboard, where the black keys are located. Meanwhile, the vertical lines are exploited to find which belongs to the white keys and which to the black ones. Thus, a cleanup of all the lines is performed, since Hough Transform could count multiple lines on the same one: the lines that are closer than a threshold of 5 pixels (px) are merged into the same element. This threshold has been empirically calculated on an input image of width 1920 px × 1080 px of height. For white keys, we check all the lines above the starting point of black keys; vice versa for the black keys.

Sensors Fusion: The x, y coordinates of each fingertip can be retrieved from the input RGB images to recognize the pressed keys. In particular, we assume

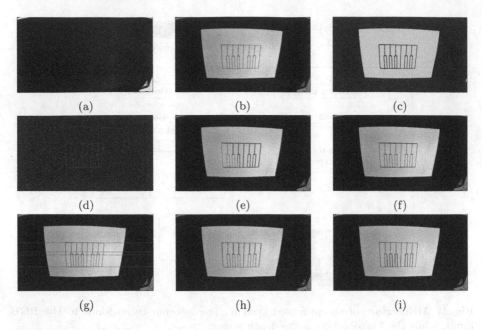

Fig. 2. Preliminary phase pipeline. (a) First frame; (b) Second frame; (c) Background highlight; (d) Canny edge detection; (e) Hough transformation; (f) Horizontal lines detection; (g) Borders highlight; (h) White tiles highlight; (i) Black tiles highlight.

that a finger is playing a note when it touches the keyboard. Considering the semi-orthogonal position of the camera from the keyboard, the closeness of the fingertip from the paper could be retrieved with depth information, the z coordinate. We firstly used MediaPipe [17] only, a library specifically designed for body and hand tracking based on a pre-trained and modified version of the Convolutional Neural Network (R-CNN). It was one of the best candidates for our purpose due to the low computational cost for predicting the hand coordinates; in addition, it could also infer the distance axis. However, empirical tests have shown that MediaPipe correctly recognized horizontal (x) and vertical (y) translations, but it is very inaccurate about the distance (z). Thus, we introduced a sided device for retrieving more accurate depth information. Among all available options, the Leap Motion sensor seemed an optimal solution due to its dual-IR camera sensor, which requires low-computational resources for obtaining high-precision tracking, especially regarding distance data. Then, the RGB and depth streams from a webcam and the Leap Motion, respectively, were simultaneously captured. With MediaPipe on the RGB data, x, y coordinates are taken, while the depth information z comes from the LeapMotion SKD on the dual-IR stream. However, both libraries are exploited for retrieving hand and finger information, thus allowing their mappings.

3.2   Real-Time Phase

The real-time phase is executed after the preliminary one. It is invoked when the setup is performed and the system is ready to make the user play the keyboard. The pseudo-code of the procedure is shown in Algorithm 1.

Touch Detection: The sound should be triggered when the finger is close enough to the keyboard. Thus, we empirically calculated that whenever a fingertip is 3 cm below the center of the palm, we assume that the player wants to press a key with the related finger. The software also considers if the finger is inside the keyboard area to ignore false positives.

Note Detection: Each time a touch detection occurs, the system gets the position of the fingertip and the key under it. Then, the mapping between each key and each Musical Instrument Digital Interface (MIDI) protocol ID is executed to play the correct frequency note (see Section **Playing Notes**). For simplification, let us consider white keys only. Assuming all indices start at 0 and supposing the note that a user plays is the i-th on the keyboard from left, we define an array that contains each note's offset in an octave with respect to its MIDI ID:

$$\text{offsets} - [0, 2, 4, 5, 7, 9, 11]. \tag{1}$$

Then, let us assume that F is the MIDI ID of the lowest note on the keyboard (e.g., if the lowest note is $C4$ according to American Standard Pitch Notation, then $F = 60$). The formula to find a note's MIDI ID is:

$$(\lfloor \frac{i}{7} \rfloor \cdot 12) + \text{offsets}[i \mod 7] + F, \tag{2}$$

where $\lfloor \frac{i}{7} \rfloor$ is the number of octaves passed, $\lfloor \frac{i}{7} \rfloor \cdot 12$ is the octave offset, and offsets$[i \mod 7]$ is the key offset, within the octave. For the black keys, the procedure is the same, but the offsets are:

$$\text{offsets} = [1, 3, 5, 8, 10], \tag{3}$$

and the final formalization becomes:

$$(\lfloor \frac{i}{5} \rfloor \cdot 12) + \text{offsets}[i \mod 5] + F. \tag{4}$$

Playing Notes: For each frame t, given N as the set of notes that are currently playing (i.e., notes that the user started playing at frame $t - k$, for some $k > 0$) and N_t as the set of notes that the user plays at frame t, the Algorithm 2 describes how the system manages which note's sound should be reproduced: where $N \setminus N_t$ contains the notes that were previously playing, and that the user is not playing anymore, at frame t; while $N_t \setminus N$ contains the notes that were not previously playing, and that the user has started playing at frame t.

Algorithm 1

---

for each frame **do**
    do *hand detection*
    do *depth detection*
    for each fingertip f **do**
        if (f is touching) $\wedge$ (f is inside the keyboard) **then**
            let n be the note that f is playing
            play note n
        end if
    end for
end for

Algorithm 2

Require: N, N_t
    for each note $n \in N \setminus N_t$ **do**
        stop playing note n
    end for
    for each note $n \in N_t \setminus N$ **do**
        start playing note n
    end for

---

4   Experimental Environment

4.1   Experimental Setup

We exploited a keyboard hand drawn on a sheet of paper. We used a laptop with an Intel Core i3-8140U CPU, 8 GB of DDR4 RAM, and no dedicated GPU, for testing the performance on a low-end device. The webcam (Logitech C920) and the Leap Motion were connected via USB3 ports. The Leap Motion was orthogonally placed above the keyboard, while the webcam was above the monitor, pointing down on the keyboard, at an angle slightly below 90° (about 75°). The software was developed in Python exploiting OpenCV, MediaPipe, and LeapMotion Python SDK.

4.2   Experiments Execution

We executed the preliminary phase with the webcam only, for avoiding inter- ferences with the Leap Motion during the calibration. In the real-time phase, we collected each (when and which) pressed key to get quantitative informa- tion about the performance of the system. Unfortunately, there is no standard protocol for testing systems like the proposed one; thus, we defined our own methodology, based on similar state-of-the-art frameworks. For each frame, an operator observes the actions of the user and manually registers when a touching action starts, as well as when it stops; this information is our ground truth. The ground truth is compared to what the program detects. In this way, we were able to calculate evaluation metrics. Then, we also collected questionnaires for retrieving qualitative results asking the participants to fill them out at the end of the run. In particular, we exploited the Usability Metric for User Experience (UMUX) questionnaire [10], which is one of the best solutions to this aim.

4.3   Results

Quantitative Results: In Table 1, the results of the executed experiments are shown. We executed 5 tests, counting for each frame the ones corresponding to a correctly played note when the fingers touch the keyboard. We also grouped the scores by different fingers because the Leap Motion is often more reliable with only some of them, specifically the thumb and the index. As noticeable, the accuracy is always close to the ground truth; however, the precision behaves very differently. It seems to be related to depth data of fingertips coordinate location: even with the Leap Motion, the movement of the fingers is very short, and the hardware is not fully capable of detecting such tiny translations.

Table 1. Experimental results. The scores are averages among the 5 runs.

	Accuracy	Precision	Recall
All fingers	95.8%	53.6%	98.4%
Only index and thumb	90.6%	56.4%	99.8%
Only index	84.4%	60.6%	100%

Qualitative Results: We also retrieved results about the perceived usability of our program. We asked 12 participants to play the keyboard with our system for 5 min and to fill out the UMUX questionnaire at the end. Among the participants that tested the system, there were people with different musical background knowledge: 6 professional piano players and 6 non-musicians were involved. The overall average is 79.86%, the minimum is 70.83%, the maximum is 87.5%, and the standard deviation is 5.6. These results highlight the effectiveness of the proposal in terms of usability, even if some collected scores underline some room for improvements, mainly in delay management.

5   Conclusions

In this work, a non-wearable hand-based interaction system for playing a virtual piano has been proposed. It exploits a combination of well-known computer vision algorithms and state-of-the-art DL-based techniques, paying particular attention to computational power. In fact, the software is specifically designed for low-end hardware, involving only two input devices, an RGB and a depth sensor. The pipeline of the proposed method is made of two steps: a calibration and a running phase. The experiments highlight that the system can manage real-time data flow, providing enough fast and accurate feedback to make the experience enjoyable for the user. The collected results prove it with a high accuracy value and a consistent UMUX score. However, there is room for improvement in terms of precision: the depth information should be more granular and the response latency of the system should be decreased. These elements will be deeply investigated in future versions of the system.

Acknoledgements. This work was supported by "Smart unmannEd AeRial vehiCles for Human likE monitoRing (SEARCHER)" project of the Italian Ministry of Defence (CIG: Z84333EA0D), "A Brain Computer Interface (BCI) based System for Transferring Human Emotions inside Unmanned Aerial Vehicles (UAVs)" Sapienza Research Projects (Protocol number: RM1221816C1CF63B), and the MICS (Made in Italy - Circular and Sustainable) Extended Partnership and received funding from Next-Generation EU (Italian PNRR - M4 C2, Invest 1.3 - D.D. 1551.11-10-2022, PE00000004). CUP MICS B53C22004130001. The research leading to these results has received funding from Project "Ecosistema dell'innovazione - Rome Technopole" financed by EU in Next Generation EU plan through MUR Decree n. 1051 23.06.2022 - CUP H33C22000420001.

References

1. Antonelli, S., et al.: Few-shot object detection: a survey. ACM Comput. Surv. **54**(11s), 1–37 (2022)
2. Avola, D., Cinque, L., Bimbo, A.D., Marini, M.R.: MIFTel: a multimodal interactive framework based on temporal logic rules. Multim. Tools Appl. **79**(19–20), 13533–13558 (2020)
3. Avola, D., et al.: Medicinal boxes recognition on a deep transfer learning augmented reality mobile application. In: Sclaroff, S., Distante, C., Leo, M., Farinella, G.M., Tombari, F. (eds.) ICIAP 2022, Part I. LNCS, vol. 13231, pp. 489–499. Springer, Cham (2022). https://doi.org/10.1007/978-3-031-06427-2_41
4. Avola, D., Cinque, L., Foresti, G.L., Marini, M.R.: An interactive and low-cost full body rehabilitation framework based on 3D immersive serious games. J. Biomed. Inform. **89**, 81–100 (2019)
5. Beddiar, D.R., Nini, B., Sabokrou, M., Hadid, A.: Vision-based human activity recognition: a survey. Multimed. Tools Appl. **79**(41), 30509–30555 (2020)
6. Benraya, I., Benblidia, N.: Comparison of background subtraction methods. In: International Conference on Applied Smart Systems (ICASS), pp. 1–5 (2018)
7. Cabral, M., et al.: Crosscale: a 3D virtual musical instrument interface. In: IEEE Symposium on 3D User Interfaces (3DUI), pp. 199–200 (2015)
8. Canny, J.: A computational approach to edge detection. IEEE Trans. Pattern Anal. Mach. Intell. **PAMI-8**(6), 679–698 (1986)
9. Fillwalk, J.: ChromaChord: a virtual musical instrument. In: IEEE Symposium on 3D User Interfaces (3DUI), pp. 201–202 (2015)
10. Finstad, K.: The usability metric for user experience. Interact. Comput. **22**(5), 323–327 (2010)
11. Foxlin, E., Harrington, M.: WearTrack: a self-referenced head and hand tracker for wearable computers and portable VR. In: Digest of Papers. Fourth International Symposium on Wearable Computers, pp. 155–162 (2000)

12. Hartigan, J.A., Wong, M.A.: Algorithm as 136: a k-means clustering algorithm. J. Roy. Stat. Soc. Ser. C (Appl. Stat.) **28**(1), 100–108 (1979)
13. Huang, L., Zhang, B., Guo, Z., Xiao, Y., Cao, Z., Yuan, J.: Survey on depth and RGB image-based 3D hand shape and pose estimation. Virtual Reality Intell. Hardw. **3**(3), 207–234 (2021)
14. Lee, B.G., Lee, S.M.: Smart wearable hand device for sign language interpretation system with sensors fusion. IEEE Sens. J. **18**(3), 1224–1232 (2018)
15. Liang, H., et al.: Barehanded music: real-time hand interaction for virtual piano. In: Proceedings of the 20th ACM SIGGRAPH Symposium on Interactive 3D Graphics and Games, pp. 87–94 (2016)
16. Liu, Y., Jiang, J., Sun, J.: Hand pose estimation from RGB images based on deep learning: a survey. In: IEEE 7th International Conference on Virtual Reality (ICVR), pp. 82–89 (2021)
17. Lugaresi, C., et al.: MediaPipe: a framework for building perception pipelines. CoRR abs/1906.08172 (2019)
18. Lv, Z., Poiesi, F., Dong, Q., Lloret, J., Song, H.: Deep learning for intelligent human-computer interaction. Appl. Sci. **12**(22), 11457 (2022)
19. Moustakis, V., Lehto, M., Salvendy, G.: Survey of expert opinion: which machine learning method may be used for which task? Int. J. Hum.-Comput. Interact. **8**(3), 221–236 (1996)
20. Mueller, F., et al.: GANerated hands for real-time 3D hand tracking from monocular RGB (2017)
21. Mueller, F., Mehta, D., Sotnychenko, O., Sridhar, S., Casas, D., Theobalt, C.: Real-time hand tracking under occlusion from an egocentric RGB-D sensor. In: Proceedings of the IEEE International Conference on Computer Vision (ICCV) (2017)
22. Mukhopadhyay, P., Chaudhuri, B.B.: A survey of hough transform. Pattern Recogn. **48**(3), 993–1010 (2015)
23. Oka, A., Hashimoto, M.: Marker-less piano fingering recognition using sequential depth images. In: The 19th Korea-Japan Joint Workshop on Frontiers of Computer Vision, pp. 1–4 (2013)
24. Riegler, A., Aksoy, B., Riener, A., Holzmann, C.: Gaze-based interaction with windshield displays for automated driving: impact of dwell time and feedback design on task performance and subjective workload. In: 12th International Conference on Automotive User Interfaces and Interactive Vehicular Applications, pp. 151–160 (2020)
25. Sanchez-Riera, J., Srinivasan, K., Hua, K.L., Cheng, W.H., Hossain, M.A., Alhamid, M.F.: Robust RGB-D hand tracking using deep learning priors. IEEE Trans. Circuits Syst. Video Technol. **28**(9), 2289–2301 (2018)
26. Xu, X., Xu, S., Jin, L., Song, E.: Characteristic analysis of Otsu threshold and its applications. Pattern Recogn. Lett. **32**(7), 956–961 (2011)

Classification of Honey Pollens with ImageNet Neural Networks

Fernando López-García[1][(⊠)], José Miguel Valiente-González[1],
Isabel Escriche-Roberto[2], Marisol Juan-Borrás[2], Mario Visquert-Fas[2],
Vicente Atienza-Vanacloig[1], and Manuel Agustí-Melchor[1]

[1] Instituto de Automática e Informática Industrial, Universitat Politècnica de València, Valencia, Spain
flopez@disca.upv.es
[2] Instituto de Ingeniería de Alimentos para el Desarrollo, Universitat Polèctinca de València, Valencia, Spain

Abstract. The classification of honey pollen grains is performed in order to classify honey according to its botanical origin, which is of great importance in terms of marketing. This visual work is currently done by human specialists counting and classifying the pollen grains in microscopic images. This is a hard, time-consuming, and subject to observer variability task. Thus, automated methods are required to overcome the limitations of the conventional procedure. This paper deals with the automatic classification of honey pollens using five representative Neural Networks coming from the ImageNet Challenge: VGG16, VGG19, ResNet50, InceptionV3 and Xception. The ground truth is composed of 9983 samples of 16 different types of pollens corresponding to citrus and rosemary pollens and its companions. The best result was obtained with the InceptionV3 network, achieving an accuracy of 98.15%, that outperforms the results obtained in previous works.

Keywords: Pollen Classification · ImageNet Challenge · Deep Learning · Convolutional Neural Networks

1 Introduction

Pollen identification is an important task in several areas, but we focus on the botanical certification of honey. This is performed via visual microscopic examination of the pollen present in honey; a process called melissopalynology. However, manual examination of the images is hard, time-consuming and subject to inter and intra observer variability. Thus, automated methods for pollen identification are required to overcome the limitations of the conventional procedure [1].

Automated pollen classification started in the later decades of the 20th century. But it has been in the 21st century where more progress has been made in this field, helped by the powerful increase in computational capacities. Previous approaches are summarized in [2] and [3]. They can be divided into image-based and non-image based methods

© The Author(s), under exclusive license to Springer Nature Switzerland AG 2023
N. Tsapatsoulis et al. (Eds.): CAIP 2023, LNCS 14185, pp. 192–200, 2023.
https://doi.org/10.1007/978-3-031-44240-7_19

[4]. Non-image based methods use alternative characteristics, for example fluorescence, Fourier-Transform infrared, and Raman spectroscopy. Image-based methods typically involve defining and extracting discriminant features from pollen images, followed by sorting via statistical or machine learning classifiers. These image-based methods fall into three different categories based on the type of used features [4]: visual/geometrical discriminant features (e.g., shape, symmetry, diameter, etc.); texture-based discriminant features (e.g., grey-level co-occurrence matrices, entropy features etc.); and a combination of the two approaches.

However, a new approach has emerged to deal with image-based pollen classification. This is Deep Learning, a method that has shown great effectiveness in other areas. This new approach uses a model that determines and extracts the features itself, rather than being defined by human specialists.

Works applying this new approach outperform the traditional methods. Most of these works are summarized in [4] where also a table is provided comparing traditional and Deep Learning approaches. Concerning the Deep Learning methods, we have several works like [5] which achieved a 94% of training accuracy on a dataset of 30 pollen types. Their results are based on the training set and no information is given about how the model behaves with unseen images. The same occurs with [6] and [7]. In the first case they achieved 100% of accuracy on 10 very different pollen grains using transfer learning with the VGG16 network. In the second case they reported 99.8% of accuracy on 5 different types of pollen. In |3| researchers improved classification of pollen grain images of the POLEN23E dataset (30 pollen types) by three different applications of Deep Learning convolutional neural networks achieving a 97% of accuracy. In a recent work [4] they obtain very good results, 98% of accuracy, on the most complete dataset until today, 19,000 samples with 46 different types. They used different techniques of image pre-processing and data augmentation to feed a pre-trained convolutional neural network, retrained by transfer learning to extract features from one of its deepest layers. Moreover, these automatically extracted features are used to perform classification with a linear discriminant classifier. The behaviour of the model is good, giving a 98% of accuracy in unseen sets of images. Also, in [8], they perform an approach similar in part to our approach and use pre-existing convolutional neural networks to classify up to 73 different types of pollens with 2523 samples. They achieve the best accuracy results with the DenseNet-201 (95.7%) and ResNet50 (94.0%) networks. Finally, in a recent work [9], they use several ImageNet Networks (InceptionV3, Xception, ResNet) in an ensemble manner to classify the Cretan Pollen Dataset v1, which is a publicly available dataset comprising images of 4034 pollen grains of 20 plant species. They achieved and accuracy of 97,5%.

In this paper we use five pre-existing networks that were developed in the context of the ImageNet Challenge to perform honey pollen classification, specifically on the citrus and rosemary pollens and its companions. And we achieve better accuracy results than the mentioned previous works. The ImageNet Challenge has taken place in recent years and was designed to obtain the best possible results on a database of 1.2 million images corresponding to 1000 different classes. The challenge is oriented to the use of deep learning and there have been several networks that have been presented in these years.

We have chosen five of the most representative: VGG16, VGG19, Inception, Xception and ResNet50.

2 Materials and Methods

2.1 Ground Truth

The ground truth was own made from microscope images and is composed of 9983 samples taken by our laboratory specialists that also labelled them. These samples correspond to 16 different types of pollens with several samples per type between 70 and 3279, see Table 1. All were samples of Orange Blossom, Rosemary and their companions (Bottom, Bubble, European Olea N.C., Cistus sp. NC, Starch, Brassicaceae, Citrus sp., Echium sp., Legumineuses, Onobrychis sp., Prunus dulcis, Quercus sp., Rosmarinus officinalis, Thymus sp., Taraxacum type, Umbellifers). See Fig. 1.

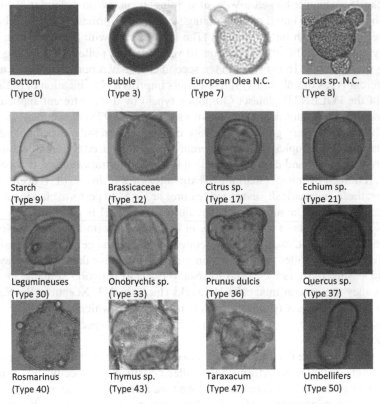

Bottom (Type 0)	Bubble (Type 3)	European Olea N.C. (Type 7)	Cistus sp. N.C. (Type 8)
Starch (Type 9)	Brassicaceae (Type 12)	Citrus sp. (Type 17)	Echium sp. (Type 21)
Legumineuses (Type 30)	Onobrychis sp. (Type 33)	Prunus dulcis (Type 36)	Quercus sp. (Type 37)
Rosmarinus (Type 40)	Thymus sp. (Type 43)	Taraxacum (Type 47)	Umbellifers (Type 50)

Fig. 1. Examples of the 16 types of studied Pollens.

It is remarkable that the samples are just like the samples that specialist use manually in melissopalynology to determine the botanical origin of the honey. They were not pre-processed and isolated, contrary to what happens in other works [9].

Table 1. Number of samples per type and percentage regards the total number.

Type	Number	Percentage	Type	Number	Percentage
Type 0	772	7.73%	Type 30	112	1.12%
Type 3	117	1.17%	Type 33	306	3.07%
Type 7	722	7.23%	Type 36	179	1.79%
Type 8	197	1.97%	Type 37	1029	10.31%
Type 9	233	2.33%	Type 40	837	8,38%
Type 12	3279	32.85%	Type 43	599	6.00%
Type 17	341	3.42%	Type 47	70	0.70%
Type 21	372	3.73%	Type 50	818	8.19%

2.2 ImageNet Networks

We used up to five pre-existing networks coming from the ImageNet Challenge: ResNet50, Xception, VGG19, VGG16, InceptionV3.

ResNet50 is a variant of ResNet model which has 48 Convolution layers along with 1 MaxPool and 1 Average Pool layer [10]. The ResNet50 architecture contains the following elements: First, an input image of 224×224 target size. Behind, a convolution layer (size 64) with a stride of size 2, then a max pooling with also a stride size of 2. Subsequently, 3 convolution layers repeated 3 times (sizes 64, 64, 256 respectively). After this we could see 3 convolution layers repeated 4 times (sizes 128, 128, 512 respectively). Then other 3 convolution layers repeated 6 times (sizes 256, 256, 1024 respectively). After those 3 more convolution layers repeated 3 times again (sizes 512, 512, 2048 respectively). Finally, there are an average pool, then a fully connected layer and at the end a SoftMax function. ResNet50 introduces a new neural network layer, the residual block, whose aim is to address the degradation problem observed while training the networks [8]. It gives us a total of 50-layer Deep Convolutional Network.

We used the InceptionV3 network that comes from Google's Inception Convolutional Neural Network (as a third edition) [11]. It was introduced during the ImageNet Recognition Challenge. It was committed on allowing deeper networks while also keeping the number of parameters from growing too large. The InceptionV3 architecture contains the following elements: First, an input image of 299×299 target size. Behind, a convolution layer (size 32) with a stride of size 2, a convolution layer (size 32) and a convolution layer (size 64). Then a MaxPool layer with a stride of size 2. After that, a convolution layer (size 64) with a stride of size 2, a convolution layer (size 80) and a convolution layer (size 192). Then, the architecture has three inception modules placed. The first module carries out convolution on an input using filters (sizes $1 \times 1, 3 \times 3$, and 3×3) followed by MaxPool (same for the others modules). The outputs are concatenated and go through to the following inception module. In the second module, a grid reduction technique is applied whose purpose is to diminish the number of parameters to become the model computationally less expensive. The process uses $1 \times n$ and $n \times 1$ convolutions instead of $n \times n$ convolutions. Last inception module takes after the second, it allows expanded the filter bank outputs to promote high dimensional representations. Finally, we would observe other MaxPool layer with a stride of size 2. Then a fully connected layer and at the end a SoftMax function.

We have also used the Xception network which is another deep convolutional neural network architecture that involves depth wise Separable Convolutions [12]. It was developed by Google researchers. It proposes an advanced deep convolutional neural network architecture based on Inception network, where Inception modules have been replaced with deeper separable convolutions. The Xception architecture contains the following elements: First, an input image of 299 × 299 target size following by operations of batch normalization and ReLU. After this, the architecture has three blocks in sequence carrying out convolution, batch normalization, ReLU, and MaxPool operations.

VGG16 and VGG19 are convolutional neural networks models proposed by K. Simonyan and A. Zisserman from the University of Oxford in [13], which have 16 and 19 layers respectively. A crucial thing about VGG16 and VGG19 is that instead of having many hyper-parameters they focused on using convolution layers of 3 × 3 filter with a stride 1 and always used the same padding and a MaxPool layer of 2 × 2 filter of stride 2. It follows this sequence of convolution and MaxPool layers consistently overall the architecture. In the end it has 2 Fully Connected layers followed by a SoftMax for output.

3 Experimental Work

All those networks were used with four different image datasets built randomly from the ground truth in a 4-fold manner, each one with images for training (80% of each pollen type), validation (10% of each pollen type) and test (10% of each pollen type). Among the parameters to be highlighted we should mention the number of epochs (30) and the learning rate (0.005). We performed Transfer Learning and Fine Tuning and trained all layers because the images of pollens are quite different to those images used in the ImageNet Challenge (dogs, cats, cars, houses, etc.) but used as the initial coefficients of the networks those coefficients obtained for the pre-existing networks on ImageNet. The different networks use different sizes of image, and the pollen samples also have different image sizes. The size of the pollen images was adjusted to the size of the image of each network. We also used Data Augmentation (rotation, shift, flip) to expand the datasets in the training process. The results can be seen on Table 2.

The best accuracy result was achieved by the InceptionV3 with an average of 98.15%. The rest of deep learning neural networks achieved also very good results. The ResNet50, Xception, VGG19 and VGG16 resulted in an average of 97.41%, 97.70%, 97.26% and 97.63%, respectively. The difference between networks is only in one point and as we can observe, the VGG16 network achieves a very good result with a difference with regards to InveptionV3 network of only 0.52 points and yet it is much simpler.

In the following figure we can see the Loss Vs Accuracy of the dataset1 for the corresponding InceptionV3 ImageNet Network. We can appreciate that there is no overfitting in the training process since the curves of train accuracy and validation accuracy do not separate more than 15%. This also happens in the rest of the networks and datasets (Fig. 2).

Table 2. Accuracy results of the ImageNet Networks.

	Dataset1	Dataset2	Dataset3	Dataset4	Average
VGG16	97.33%	97.23%	98.12%	97.83%	97.63%
VGG19	96.84%	97.43%	97.83%	96.94%	97.26%
ResNet50	98.02%	97.23%	96.64%	97.73%	97.41%
Xception	97.63%	97.53%	98.32%	97.33%	97.70%
InceptionV3	97.92%	98.32%	98.42%	97.92%	**98.15%**

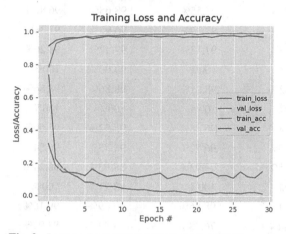

Fig. 2. Loss vs Accuracy for the InceptionV3 Network.

3.1 Results per Types and Multiclass Metrics

In this section we have computed the results of accuracy per types of pollens and networks, and we have computed several multi-class metrics in order to compare the goodness of the classification. The metrics we have used are the Precision, Recall, and F1-Score. The latter is the harmonic mean of Precision and Recall. In these cases, a value near to 1 means a good classification while a value near to 0 means a bad classification. We also have computed the multi-class version of Matthews Correlation Coefficient (MCC), which is a metric with possible values between $+1$ and -1. A coefficient of $+$1 represents a perfect prediction, 0 no better than random prediction and -1 indicates total disagreement between prediction and observation.

We have computed these metrics and results per types for the 4-fold scheme we have followed in the experiments, that is, we have results for the dataset1, dataset2, dataset3 and dataset4. In Table 3 we show the results of the average of them. We can observe that the results of metrics are correlated with the accuracy obtained in each network, being the best the InceptionV3 network. With regards to the results of accuracy per type, in general, the best results are obtained by the InceptionV3 network. It should be noted that type 30 obtains low results in all networks and that it is the Xception that gives the best result for this type. This happens with other types and other networks, which are better in some cases than InceptionV3, but in average InceptionV3 responds better.

Table 3. Accuracy results per types and networks, total accuracy and multiclass metrics.

	VGG16	VGG19	ResNet50	InceptionV3	Xception
type 0	99.68%	99.68%	99.37%	99.68%	100%
type 36	92.54%	92.55%	92.96%	98.75%	96.25%
type 50	97.63%	96.23%	98.80%	97.96%	95.66%
type 21	95.44%	95.55%	98.65%	96.82%	99.34%
type 37	98.12%	98.30%	96.93%	97.38%	97.38%
type 40	99.12%	97.13%	97.17%	98.26%	97.73%
type 9	100%	100%	99.00%	100%	99.00%
type 8	97.83%	98.81%	98.86%	98.86%	100%
type 47	100%	100%	100%	100%	96.88%
type 7	96.98%	96.28%	95.52%	97.60%	98.26%
type 43	95.93%	96.72%	98.75%	96.84%	95.54%
type 33	92.75%	93.93%	88.93%	96.24%	96.85%
type 3	100%	100%	98.21%	100%	100%
type 12	98.71%	98.86%	99.09%	99.16%	98.71%
type 30	84.44%	76.78%	78.44%	83.92%	88.02%
type 17	93.47%	89.27%	92.72%	94.99%	91.54%
Accuracy	0.9763	0.9726	0.9741	0.9815	0.9770
Precision	0.9750	0.9725	0.9750	0.9800	0.9775
Recall	0.9750	0.9725	0.9750	0.9800	0.9775
F1-score	0.9750	0.9725	0.9750	0.9800	0.9775
MCC	0.9669	0.9678	0.9641	0.9736	0.9701

4   Conclusions and Discussion

We have studied the use of Convolutional Neural Networks to perform the classification of honey pollens, specifically the rosemary and citrus pollens and its companions, in total, 16 types or classes of pollens. We have used a ground truth of 9983 samples corresponding to these types of pollens.

We have used five pre-existing Networks coming from the ImageNet Challenge: VGG16, VGG19, ResNet50, Xception and InceptionV3. We trained all layers starting from the original coefficients of ImageNet. We followed a 4-fold scheme for training and classification and the best result of accuracy was achieved by the network InceptionV3

(98.15%), but the rest of networks obtained also good results. In fact, the VGG16 network which is significantly simpler that InceptionV3 is only 0.52 percentage points from the result of the InceptionV3. The result of InceptionV3 outperforms the results obtained in previous works [9].

We also studied the accuracy results per type of pollen and network. The best average result was achieved by InceptionV3 network, but in some types other networks performed better. Finally, we computed several multi-class metrics: Precision, Recall, F1-Score and MCC (Matthews Correlation Coefficient). We observed that the results of metrics were correlated with the accuracy achieved in each network, and the best was once again the InceptionV3 network.

Future work would include more types of pollens and more networks and also the development of an own network, simpler than those used in this work.

Acknowledgment. This work is part of the project PID2019-106800RB-I00 (2019) of the Ministry of Science and Innovation (MCIN), State Research Agency MCIN/AEI/https://doi.org/10.13039/501100011033/. It is also part of the AGROALNEXT/2022/043 project, financed by the Generalitat Valenciana, the Next Generation European Union and the Recovery, Transformation and Resilience Plan of the Government of Spain.

References

1. Stillmana, E., Flenley, J.R.: The needs and prospects for automation in palynology. Quatern. Sci. Rev. **15**, 1–5 (1996)
2. Holt, K.A., Bennett, K.D.: Principles and methods for automated palynology. New Phytol. **203**(3), 735–742 (2014)
3. Sevillano, V., Aznarte, J.L.: Improving classification of pollen grain images of the POLEN23E dataset through three different applications of deep learning convolutional neural networks. PLOS ONE **13**(9) (2018)
4. Sevillano, V., Holt, K., Aznarte, J.L.: Precise automatic classification of 46 different pollen types with convolutional neural networks. PLoS ONE **15**(6) (2020)
5. Daood, A., Ribeiro, E., Bush, M.: Pollen grain recognition using deep learning. In: Bebis, G., et al. (eds.) ISVC 2016. LNCS, vol. 10072, pp. 321–330. Springer, Cham (2016). https://doi.org/10.1007/978-3-319-50835-1_30
6. Daood, A., Ribeiro, E., Bush, M.: Sequential recognition of pollen grain Z-stacks by combining CNN and RNN. In: The Thirty-First International Flairs Conference (2018)
7. Khanzhina, N., Putin, E., Filchenkov, A., Zamyatina, E.: Pollen grain recognition using convolutional neural network. In: 2018 proceedings of European Symposium on Artificial Neural Networks, Computational Intelligence and Machine Learning (ESANN 2018), Bruges (Belgium), pp. 25–27 (2018)
8. Astolfi, G., et al.: POLLEN73S: an image dataset for pollen grains classification. Eco. Inform. **60**, 101156 (2020)
9. Tsiknakis, N., et al.: Pollen grain classification based on ensemble transfer learning on the cretan pollen dataset. Plants **11**(7) (2022)
10. Feng, V.: An Overview of ResNet and its Variants (2017). https://towardsdatascience.com/an-overview-of-resnet-and-its-variants-5281e2f56035
11. Szegedy, C., Vanhoucke, V., Ioffe, S., Shlens, J., Wojna, Z.: Rethinking the Inception Architecture for Computer Vision (2015). https://arxiv.org/abs/1512.00567

12. Chollet, F.: Xception: Deep Learning with Depthwise Separable Convolutions (2016). https://arxiv.org/abs/1610.02357
13. Simonyan, K., Zisserman, A.: University of Oxford: Very Deep Convolutional Networks for Large-Scale Image Recognition (2014). https://arxiv.org/abs/1409.1556

Defocus Blur Synthesis and Deblurring via Interpolation and Extrapolation in Latent Space

Ioana Mazilu, Shunxin Wang$^{(\boxtimes)}$, Sven Dummer, Raymond Veldhuis, Christoph Brune, and Nicola Strisciuglio

University of Twente, Enschede, Netherlands
s.wang-2@utwente.nl

Abstract. Though modern microscopes have an autofocusing system to ensure optimal focus, out-of-focus images can still occur when cells within the medium are not all in the same focal plane, affecting the image quality for medical diagnosis and analysis of diseases. We propose a method that can deblur images as well as synthesize defocus blur. We train autoencoders with implicit and explicit regularization techniques to enforce linearity relations among the representations of different blur levels in the latent space. This allows for the exploration of different blur levels of an object by linearly interpolating/extrapolating the latent representations of images taken at different focal planes. Compared to existing works, we use a simple architecture to synthesize images with flexible blur levels, leveraging the linear latent space. Our regularized autoencoders can effectively mimic blur and deblur, increasing data variety as a data augmentation technique and improving the quality of microscopic images, which would be beneficial for further processing and analysis. The code is available at https://github.com/nis-research/linear-latent-blur.

Keywords: Microscope images · Deblurring · Defocus blur synthesis · Regularized autoencoders

1 Introduction

Computer vision models have become increasingly popular in biomedical image processing, particularly with the advancement of deep learning techniques, leading to improved performance for tasks like cell segmentation and disease classification [8,12,15]. However, image quality greatly impacts the performance of computer vision models. In the biomedical field, low-quality microscopy images can compromise image analysis and diagnosis.

For instance, high-resolution cell images can be obtained using a confocal microscope. An autofocus component helps find the optimal focal plane for capturing a cell slide [4]. However, this task is often complicated by out-of-focus

---

I. Mazilu and S. Wang—Contributed equally to this work.

N. Tsapatsoulis et al. (Eds.): CAIP 2023, LNCS 14185, pp. 201–211, 2023.
https://doi.org/10.1007/978-3-031-44240-7_20

light, as not all cells are on the same focal plane and have thick structures. Thus, some cell images show less sharp regions due to out-of-focus areas, complicating the automated biomedical analysis [2].

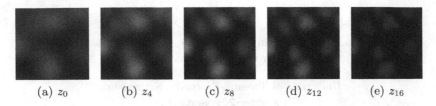

(a) z_0 (b) z_4 (c) z_8 (d) z_{12} (e) z_{16}

Fig. 1. A nuclei-labeled cell slide captured at five focal lengths. A z-stack level (ranging from z_0 to z_{16}) indicates the level of blur. We enforce linearity in the latent space among image representations of different blur levels of one slide.

Several deep-learning deblurring solutions have emerged in recent years to tackle this problem. They can be categorized into two groups: blur kernel estimation followed by deblurring [13] and kernel-free approaches [6,11,16,17]. Quan et al. [13] proposed a non-blind deblurring network based on a scale-recurrent attention module. In [16] and [1], the authors used multiscale U-net architectures for deblurring and image super-resolution tasks. These methods rely on local or global residual connections, which are useful for recovering information that may be lost through downsampling, as well as for optimizing the training process [10]. The authors of [5] proposed a defocus map estimation model. The defocus map can be used to compute the pixel-wise blur level for blur enhancement and blur kernel estimation for deblurring. Jiang et al. [3] tackled multicause blur and proposed methods to recover sharp images from either motion or defocus blur. Zhang et al. [17] reported state-of-the-art results for deblurring microscopic images using a CycleGAN-based model, which learns a reversible mapping between sharp and out-of-focus images. However, these methods entail high computational costs from the nature of the complex architectures and lack the flexibility of removing blur from images with defocus levels different from those seen during training.

In this paper, we propose a generative model that uses an autoencoder for both blur synthesis and deblurring. The unknown relation between latent representations of blur levels obtained with a vanilla autoencoder does not allow traversals of the latent space to generate images with lower or higher blur levels. We thus design training constraints that enforce a certain structure in the latent space, such as a linearity relation. We use a regular autoencoder as the baseline model and apply implicit and explicit regularization to enforce linearity among the image representations of a cell slide captured at different focal planes, such as those shown in Fig. 1. The autoencoders are trained to synthesize defocus blur. Leveraging the enforced linearity, we can synthesize a blurry image by linearly interpolating the latent representations of two images of the same cell slide with different levels of blur. Further, the linear relation among blur levels enables

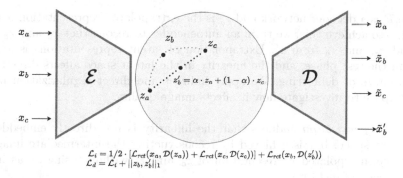

$$\mathcal{L}_i = 1/2 \cdot [\mathcal{L}_{rct}(x_a, \mathcal{D}(z_a)) + \mathcal{L}_{rct}(x_c, \mathcal{D}(z_c))] + \mathcal{L}_{rct}(x_b, \mathcal{D}(z_b'))$$
$$\mathcal{L}_d = \mathcal{L}_i + ||z_b, z_b'||_1$$

Fig. 2. Given a triplet of inputs $\{x_a, x_b, x_c\}$, we generate their corresponding reconstructions $\tilde{x}_a$, $\tilde{x}_b$, $\tilde{x}_c$ and a synthetic blurry image $\tilde{x}_b'$ based on the linearly interpolated representation z_b'. $\mathcal{E}$ and $\mathcal{D}$ are an encoder and a decoder network.

synthesizing a sharper image by extrapolating representations of blurry images from the same cell slide.

Our contributions are: 1) A model with a simple network architecture that serves as a versatile solution for both defocus blur synthesis and deblurring. 2) Adaptability to different blur levels enabling the recovery of in-focus images, even when the blur level of the reference images is unknown.

2 Proposed Method

2.1 Imposing Linearity onto Latent Space

We hypothesize that a linear relation among latent representations of images with different blur levels taken from one cell slide allows us to generate images with flexible levels of blur. As shown in Fig. 2, given a triplet of images $\{x_a, x_b, x_c\}$ captured at different focal lengths from the same cell slide, with an increasing blur level, we impose that their image representations follow the linear relationship in the latent space as:

$$z_b' = \alpha \cdot z_a + (1 - \alpha) \cdot z_c, \tag{1}$$

where $z_i = \mathcal{E}(x_i)$ is the representation of the image x_i computed with an encoder network $\mathcal{E}$, z_b' is the latent representation interpolated from z_a and z_c and corresponds to image x_b, and α is the interpolation parameter to control the level of blur. As α increases from 0 to 1, the level of blur decreases.

With the enforced linearity, we can synthesize the less blurry image $\tilde{x}_a'$, associated with x_u, by extrapolating the latent representation z_a' from the latent representations z_b and z_c of two images x_b and x_c (x_b has a lower level of blur than that of x_c), as shown below:

$$\tilde{x}_a' = \mathcal{D}(z_a') = \mathcal{D}(\frac{1}{\alpha} \cdot z_b - \frac{1 - \alpha}{\alpha} \cdot z_c), \tag{2}$$

where $\mathcal{D}$ is a decoder network and z'_a is the extrapolated representation from z_b and z_c. To achieve this, we train an autoencoder to reconstruct x_a and x_c from z_a and z_c, and x_b from z'_b. Extrapolation of latent representations is applied only in the test phase, and the linearity in the latent space affects directly the performance of deblurring. We apply indirect and direct regularization in the latent space to investigate how it affects image quality.

Indirect regularization induces that the linearity is not directly embedded in the latent space, but is achieved by reconstructing the intermediate image x_b using the interpolated representation of z_a and z_c without using x_b as input. The objective function is:

$$\mathcal{L}_i = \frac{1}{2} \cdot [\mathcal{L}_{rct}(x_a, \mathcal{D}(z_a)) + \mathcal{L}_{rct}(x_c, \mathcal{D}(z_c))] + \mathcal{L}_{rct}(x_b, \mathcal{D}(z'_b)), \qquad (3)$$

where the first term is the sum of the L_1 reconstruction losses of x_a and x_b using their corresponding learned latent representations and the second term is the L_1 reconstruction loss of the x_b decoding from the interpolated representation z'_b.

Direct regularization adds a constraint that minimizes directly the L_1 distance between the interpolated latent representation z'_b and the associated representation z_b of image x_b, thus the objective function is:

$$\mathcal{L}_d = \mathcal{L}_i + ||z_b - z'_b||_1. \qquad (4)$$

The indirect regularization may result in a latent space where interpolated latent representations are decoded into images visually similar to the real data, without forcing the non-interpolated latent codes to be linearly dependent [14]. The direct regularization explicitly ensures linearity in the latent space.

2.2   Evaluation Metrics

The goal of this study is to model a latent space with a linear constraint, such that we can exploit interpolation and extrapolation to reconstruct images with flexible levels of blur. We evaluate the geometric properties of the latent space and image quality for blur synthesis and deblurring.

Linearity in Latent Space. We quantify the degree of linear dependence among image representations based on two geometric properties. First, given three consecutive latent representations in terms of blur level, we measure their linearity based on the cosine similarity between the distance vectors obtained from each pair of neighbouring representations z_n and z_{n+1}.
We call this the Linear Dependence Score (LDS):

$$\text{LDS} = \frac{1}{N-2} \sum_{n=1}^{N-2} \frac{(z_{n-1} - z_n) \cdot (z_n - z_{n+1})}{||z_{n-1} - z_n||_2 \cdot ||z_n - z_{n+1}||_2}, \qquad (5)$$

where N is the number of blur levels in the dataset, and z_n is the latent representation of an image at blur level n. LDS ranges from -1 to 1, with higher values indicating a higher degree of compliance with the expected geometric property.

Second, since we traverse the latent space of a cell slide in fixed steps of $\frac{N}{\alpha}$, we assess whether the distance between neighbouring latent representations is equal between a pair of interpolated and a pair of non-interpolated image representations. To measure this property, we propose a metric called Average Pairwise Distance (APD):

$$\text{APD} = \frac{1}{N-1} \sum_{n=0}^{N-2} \frac{|d(z_n, z_{n+1}) - d(z'_n, z'_{n+1})|}{|d(z_0, z_{N-1})|}, \tag{6}$$

where z_n and z_{n+1} are latent representations of two consecutive images in terms of blur level. The score is normalized by the distance between the representations of the lowest and highest blur levels. APD ranges from 0 to 1 and a lower value indicates that the latent space approaches the desired structure. Moreover, visual inspection of the latent space is done by mapping the latent representations to a 2D space via PCA.

Image Quality. We evaluate image quality using a commonly used metric, Peak Signal-to-Noise-Ratio (PSNR),

$$\text{PSNR}_I^R = 20 \cdot \log_{10} \frac{\max(I)}{\sqrt{\frac{1}{mn} \sum_{i=0}^{m-1} \sum_{j=0}^{n-1} (I(i,j) - R(i,j))^2}}. \tag{7}$$

This measures the similarity between the images I and R. For instance, $\text{PSNR}_{grd}^{extru}$ compares the deblurred image using an extrapolated latent representation to the corresponding ground truth sharp image. PSNR_{grd}^b compares the reconstructed blurry image with the ground truth blurry image.

3   Experiments and Results

3.1   Dataset

We use the BBBC006v1 collection obtained from the Broad Bioimage Benchmark Collection [7], which contains 384 cell slides stained with two markers to label the nuclei and structure of cells respectively. The sets of nuclei and cell structure images are noted as w1 and w2 sets. Each cell slide is captured at 34 focal lengths. In total, there are $384 \times 2 \times 34$ images. We only use the images captured above the optimal focal plane (z-stack $= 16$) with even z-stack levels for both training and testing (z-stack ≤ 16). We split it into training, validation, and testing sets, in a 7:1:2 ratio. All z-stack levels corresponding to one cell slide are assigned to the same set. We use triplets of one slide captured at different focal lengths as input for the models. For the training phase, we use the triplets: (z_a, z_b, z_c) where $2b = a + c$ and a, b and c are even z-stack levels in the dataset. We only use even z-stack levels since changes between two consecutive blur levels (an even and an odd z-stack level) do not exhibit significant variation in the data.

3.2   Architecture and Training

As the baseline model, we design an autoencoder with a simple architecture but can achieve image reconstruction marginally well. It has five convolutional layers in the encoder and six transposed convolutional layers in the decoder. Each convolutional layer consists of a two-strided convolution with a kernel size of 3×3, followed by batch normalization and Leaky ReLU activation. In the decoder, the structure is symmetrical, with transposed convolution replacing convolution operations. The last layer is a convolutional layer with kernel size 3×3, followed by a Sigmoid activation. The encoder layers have 64, 128, 256, 512, and 1024 filters. The models are trained for 40 epochs, with batch size 40. We use Adam optimizer with learning rate 10^{-4}. We generate 10 crops of size 128×128 from each image (4 corner crops, 1 center crop, and their corresponding horizontally-flipped versions). Using the same architecture, the regularized models are trained with the proposed regularizations. We train models separately on the w1 and w2 sets, due to the difference in their data distributions.

3.3   Results

Linearity in the Latent Space. We show the 2D projections of latent representations of a set of images (from the same cell slide but captured at different focal lengths) in Fig. 3. The direct regularization forces the representations to be more clustered and arranged along a line. With indirect regularization, the distribution in the latent space of the representation of images with an increasing blur level is almost the same as that of the baseline model. We report the results on the linearity of the learned latent representations in Table 1, for the models trained on w1 and w2 sets, respectively. Direct regularization leads to substantial changes in the structure of the latent space. With direct regularization, interpolated or extrapolated latent representations lie closer in the latent space to their associated representations generated by the encoder. This means that images decoded from interpolated representations can be more similar to the images reconstructed from the latent representations of the real images, compared to those obtained with the other two models.

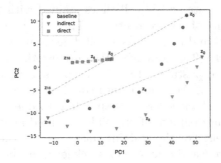

Fig. 3. 2D latent representations of a cell slide.

Table 1. Quantitative results of the linear dependence. The arrows indicate whether a lower or a higher score is desirable.

Data	Model	Baseline	Indirect	Direct
w1 set	LDS ↑	0.59	0.62	**0.76**
	APD ↓	0.036	0.028	**0.014**
w2 set	LDS ↑	0.52	0.47	**0.75**
	APD ↓	0.037	0.048	**0.031**

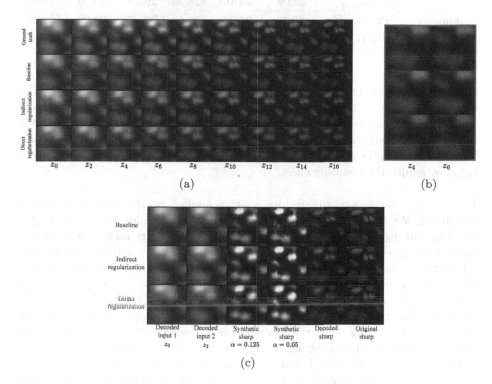

Fig. 4. (a) Synthesized blur for a nuclei-labeled slide using the baseline, indirectly and directly regularized models. Each row contains images with the blur level transitioning from z-stack 0 (left) to z-stack 16 (right), (b) Zoom-in view of the area within the frame in (a) highlights the blending effect by the baseline, (c) Example of image deblurring using 3 models. Synthetic sharp images are obtained through linear extrapolation between representations of two slides with z-stack levels 0 and 2, using different values for α.

Blur Synthesis. In Table 2, we report the comparison of the quality of images reconstructed using interpolated representations, against reconstructed images using the representations associated with ground truth blurry images ($\mathrm{PSNR}_b^{interp_b}$) and ground truth blurry images ($\mathrm{PSNR}_{grd}^{interp_b}$). We show the synthesized blurry images in Fig. 4a. With the baseline model, reconstructions from

Table 2. Results of the baseline model, and the directly- and indirectly-regularized models, on the w1 and w2 sets. Blur synthesis and deblurring are evaluated. The arrows indicate whether a lower or a higher score is better. The best scores are highlighted.

Experiment	Metric	Model					
		Baseline	Indirect	Direct	Baseline	Indirect	Direct
		w1 set			w2 set		
Blur synthesis	$PSNR_b^{interp_b}$ ↑	**31.97**	31.77	31.60	32.35	32.48	**33.05**
	$PSNR_{grd}^{interp_b}$ ↑	29.09	**31.03**	28.30	**29.78**	29.46	29.02
Deblurring	$PSNR_d^{extr_d}$ ↑	**23.89**	23.02	23.52	**22.47**	22.22	22.03
	$PSNR_{grd}^{extr_d}$ ↑	22.55	**22.60**	21.98	24.00	23.49	**24.46**

linear traversals of the latent space between two points result in visually similar images compared with the ground truth blurry images. However, the reconstructed images show a blending effect between the two source images, rather than a reliable estimation of defocus blur effect, as shown in Fig. 4b. The visual quality of the synthetic blur improves with the addition of regularization, which helps to reduce the blending effect.

Deblurring. We report the results of the quality of the deblurred images in Table 2. We show examples of deblurred images of a slide in w1 set by the baseline and regularized models in Fig. 4c. Using two blurry images, we can generate a sharper image. For the w1 set, the indirectly regularized autoencoder outperforms the baseline model when we compare the deblurred images with the reconstructed sharp images (see $PSNR_d^{extr_d}$). For the w2 set, direct regularization performs the best. We observe that there is a trade-off between the desired geometric property and the image quality when applying direct regularization. With a better regularized latent space, the reconstructed image fidelity decreases slightly, while allowing to reconstruct and generate new images with different levels of blur using linear interpolation and extrapolation of the latent representations, respectively. To account for the clustering induced by the direct regularization, we also generate synthetic sharp images with an adjusted value for α ($\alpha = 0.05$). We notice that this set of images shows slightly more sharpness compared to those using $\alpha = 0.125$. This indicates that the levels of blur are indeed encoded along the linear direction in the latent space.

With our regularized model, even when the sharp image is generated from two images with high levels of blur, a considerable level of detail is recovered. Figure 5 shows how the blur level of input images affects the deblurring process. We fix one image at z-stack 0 and vary the other one from z-stack 2 to z-stack 14. These results are in line with those from a similar study [9], where the level of detail recovered in the deblurred images decreases with an increase in the focal plane at which slides are captured.

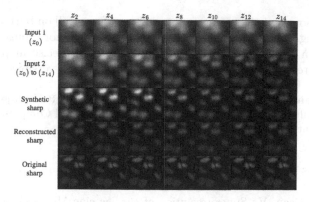

Fig. 5. Effect of the blur level in the input images on the synthetic sharp image, when the optimal interpolation parameter α is known, using the indirectly-regularized model.

4   Discussion and Future Work

Our results suggest the feasibility of blur synthesis and deblurring through linear interpolation and extrapolation in the latent space. Imposing linearity onto the latent space enables us to control the level of blur in an image by interpolating or extrapolating representations. With a simple architecture, we achieve a versatile solution for blur synthesis and deblurring, while other works are usually limited to one application.

The linear latent space enables the recovery of in-focus images, even when the blur level of the two reference images is unknown. One can dynamically adjust the value of α until reaching the optimal point. Besides, given a single blurry image as input, we can generate a second blurry image on top of it with a blur kernel, to obtain a deblurred in-focus image.

From the curvilinear trajectory demonstrated in the 2D projections of the latent representations, we conjecture that there may be two directions in the latent space, one corresponding to blur levels and the other corresponding to image content. We suggest future work on disentanglement representation learning, i.e. the representations of blur levels and image content are disentangled. This may allow for more precise reconstructions of deblurred images.

5   Conclusions

In this paper, we investigated the feasibility of models for both defocus blur synthesis and deblurring, based on linear interpolation and extrapolation in latent space. We enforce linearity among the representations of images of the same cell slide with different levels of blur, by indirect and direct regularization in the latent space. Therefore, linearly interpolating or extrapolating the representations of two differently blurred images (from the same cell slide) results in a meaningful representation that maps to an image with another level of blur.

Our results show that the regularized models perform well on both blur synthesis and deblurring. The direct regularization results in a more linear latent space compared to a regular autoencoder, enabling a more precise mapping between extrapolated representations and their non-extrapolated versions.

Acknowledgement. This work was supported by the SEARCH project, UT Theme Call 2020, Faculty of Electrical Engineering, Mathematics and Computer Science, University of Twente.

References

1. Basty, N., Grau, V.: Super resolution of cardiac cine MRI sequences using deep learning. In: Stoyanov, D., et al. (eds.) RAMBO/BIA/TIA -2018. LNCS, vol. 11040, pp. 23–31. Springer, Cham (2018). https://doi.org/10.1007/978-3-030-00946-5_3
2. Colin, L., et al.: Imaging the living plant cell: from probes to quantification. Plant Cell **34**(1), 247–272 (2021)
3. Jiang, C., et al.: Blind deblurring for microscopic pathology images using deep learning networks. CoRR abs/2011.11879 (2020)
4. Kumar, N., Gupta, R., Gupta, S.: Whole slide imaging (WSI) in pathology: current perspectives and future directions. JDI **33**, 1034–1040 (2020)
5. Lee, J., Lee, S., Cho, S., Lee, S.: Deep defocus map estimation using domain adaptation. In: CVPR 2019, pp. 12214–12222 (2019)
6. Liang, P., Jiang, J., Liu, X., Ma, J.: BambNet: a blur-aware multi-branch network for defocus deblurring (2021)
7. Ljosa, V., Sokolnicki, K., Carpenter, A.: Annotated high-throughput microscopy image sets for validation. Nat. Methods **9**, 637 (2012)
8. Lugagne, J.B., Lin, H., Dunlop, M.J.: DeLTA: automated cell segmentation, tracking, and lineage reconstruction using deep learning. PLoS Comput. Biol. **16**, 1–18 (2020)
9. Luo, Y., Huang, L., Rivenson, Y., Ozcan, A.: Single-shot autofocusing of microscopy images using deep learning. ACS Photonics **8**(2), 625–638 (2021)
10. Mao, X., Shen, C., Yang, Y.: Image denoising using very deep fully convolutional encoder-decoder networks with symmetric skip connections. CoRR abs/1603.09056 (2016)
11. Nimisha, T.M., Singh, A.K., Rajagopalan, A.N.: Blur-invariant deep learning for blind-deblurring. In: ICCV 2017, pp. 4762–4770 (2017)
12. Pandey, V., Brune, C., Strisciuglio, N.: Self-supervised learning through colorization for microscopy images. In: Image Analysis and Processing - ICIAP 2022, pp. 621–632 (2022)
13. Quan, Y., Wu, Z., Ji, H.: Gaussian kernel mixture network for single image defocus deblurring. CoRR abs/2111.00454 (2021)
14. Sainburg, T., Thielk, M., Theilman, B., Migliori, B., Gentner, T.: Generative adversarial interpolative autoencoding: adversarial training on latent space interpolations encourage convex latent distributions. CoRR abs/1807.06650 (2018)
15. Varela-Santos, S., Melin, P.: A new modular neural network approach with fuzzy response integration for lung disease classification based on multiple objective feature optimization in chest X-ray images. Expert Syst. Appl. **168**, 114361 (2021)

16. Wang, J., Han, B.: Defocus deblur microscopy via feature interactive coarse-to-fine network (2022)
17. Zhang, C., et al.: Correction of out-of-focus microscopic images by deep learning. CSBJ **20**, 1957–1966 (2022)

Unsupervised State Representation Learning in Partially Observable Atari Games

Li Meng[1]([✉]) [iD], Morten Goodwin[2,4] [iD], Anis Yazidi[3] [iD], and Paal Engelstad[1] [iD]

[1] University of Oslo, Oslo, Norway
{li.meng,paal.engelstad}@its.uio.no
[2] Centre for Artificial Intelligence Research, University of Agder,
Kristiansand, Norway
morten.goodwin@uia.no
[3] Oslo Metropolitan University, Oslo, Norway
anisy@oslomet.no
[4] Oslo Metropolitan University, Kristiansand, Norway

Abstract. State representation learning aims to capture latent factors of an environment. Although some researchers realize the connections between masked image modeling and contrastive representation learning, the effort is focused on using masks as an augmentation technique to represent the latent generative factors better. Partially observable environments in reinforcement learning have not yet been carefully studied using unsupervised state representation learning methods.

In this article, we create an unsupervised state representation learning scheme for partially observable states. We conducted our experiment on a previous Atari 2600 framework designed to evaluate representation learning models. A contrastive method called Spatiotemporal DeepInfomax (ST-DIM) has shown state-of-the-art performance on this benchmark but remains inferior to its supervised counterpart. Our approach improves ST-DIM when the environment is not fully observable and achieves higher F1 scores and accuracy scores than the supervised learning counterpart. The mean accuracy score averaged over categories of our approach is ∼66%, compared to ∼38% of supervised learning. The mean F1 score is ∼64% to ∼33%. The code can be found on https://github.com/mengli11235/MST_DIM.

Keywords: State representation Learning · Contrastive learning

1 Introduction

Deep representation learning is a machine learning (ML) type that focuses on learning useful data representations. These representations can be learned using deep neural networks (NNs) and transferred to a variety of downstream computer vision (CV), and natural language processing (NLP) tasks [7,15]. Deep representation learning includes autoencoders [14], generative models [9], contrastive methods [11,20] and transformer models [6].

© The Author(s), under exclusive license to Springer Nature Switzerland AG 2023
N. Tsapatsoulis et al. (Eds.): CAIP 2023, LNCS 14185, pp. 212–222, 2023.
https://doi.org/10.1007/978-3-031-44240-7_21

State representation learning (SRL) [1,13,18] is a particular field of representation learning where the state observations are commonly seen in the reinforcement learning (RL) setup. Agents can interact with the environment, which itself changes accordingly throughout interactions. RL is a well-established ML field that solves the Markov decision process (MDP) [21]. Traditional RL methods such as Q-learning [26] have evolved through adopting NNs [19]. Moreover, convolutional neural networks (CNNs) are deployed in environments with image inputs, and RL agents can learn from raw pixels.

Partially observable Markov decision processes (PODMPs) [3,23] are MDPs where an agent can only observe a limited part of the environment, not the full state. Recently, there have been some developments in decoupling SRL from RL [10,16,17,22]. More improvements by using SRL have been reported in partially observable environments than in fully observable ones. However, it is not clear how the POMDP state is captured and preserved by representations.

This paper designs an unsupervised representation learning scheme for partially observable environments. This method extends ST-DIM [1] and introduces an unsupervised pretraining setting suitable to partially observable Atari Games. Different pretraining hyper-parameter choices are also discussed in our ablation study. Our contribution is summarized as follows: (1) We propose MST-DIM, a contrastive method suitable to pretrain data collected in a partially observable environment. (2) We test our method on the SRL benchmark using 20 Atari 2600 games and compare the results with the ST-DIM and supervised methods. (3) Should the percentages of the observable parts of states be the same in pretraining and in probing? Extensive evaluations are conducted to examine what is needed for SRL in order to let the model accurately predict the ground truth labels.

2   Related Work

Self-supervised Learning. Self-supervised learning learns useful representations from unlabeled data, which can be used in various downstream tasks. The methodology has played an important role in NLP [6] and CV fields. Contrastive Predictive Coding (CPC) [20] learns predictive representations by capturing the information that is maximally useful to predict future (spatial or temporal) samples. SimCLR [4] provides a simple yet effective framework for contrastive learning. Momentum Contrast (MoCo) keeps dynamic dictionaries for contrastive learning [11]. Self-supervised Vision Transformers [5] study the usage of ViTs ([8]) on MoCo. SRL benefits from those paradigms by having a low dimensional state space that can learn a control policy more efficiently [18].

Contrastive Representations for RL. Contrastive Unsupervised Representations for RL (CURL) [16] is an RL pipeline that extracts high-level features using an auxiliary contrastive loss, which can be combined with on-policy or off-policy RL algorithms. Masked Contrastive Representation Learning (M-CURL) [27] improves the data efficiency in CURL by considering the correlation among consecutive inputs and using masks to help the transformer module learn to reconstruct the features of the ground truth. The loss is defined as a sum of the RL loss and masked contrastive loss, and the transformer module is discarded during inference. M-CURL reportedly outperforms CURL on 21 out of 26 environments from Atari 2600 Games.

Representation Learning in POMDPs. Predictions of Bootstrapped Latents (PBL) [10] is an RL algorithm designed for the multitask setting. PBL is trained by predicting future latent observations from partial histories and the current states from latent observations. Histories in POMDPs are typically compressed into a current agent state using NNs [23]. Agents trained with PBL achieve significantly higher human normalized scores than baseline methods in the partially observable DMLab 30 environments, but the gap is at most minimal in fully observable environments. Augmented Temporal Contrast (ATC) [22] associates temporally close pairs of observations and also shows its usefulness in POMDPs.

3   Method

ST-DIM [1] is a method that captures the latent generative factors through maximizing mutual information lower-bound estimate over consecutive observations x_t and x_{t+1} given a set of cross-episode observations $\chi = \{x_1, x_2, ..., x_n\}$, originated from agents interacting with RL environments. It uses infoNCE [20] that maximizes Eq. 1 as the mutual information estimator between patches as Deep InfoMax (DIM) [12] does.

$$\mathcal{I}_{NCE}(\{(x_i, y_i)\}_{i=1}^N) = \sum_{i=1}^N log \frac{exp \, f(x_i, y_i)}{\sum_{j=1}^N exp \, f(x_i, y_j)} \tag{1}$$

For any i, (x_i, y_i) is called positive examples from the joint distribution $p(x, y)$ and (x_i, y_j) from the product of marginals $p(x)p(y)$ is called negative examples for any $i \neq j$. Meanwhile, $f(x, y)$ is a score function, i.e., a bilinear layer.

ST-DIM utilizes both the global-local (Eq. 2) and local-local objective (Eq. 3). An illustration of the global-local contrastive task is also shown in Fig. 1. The difference between the local-local and global-local tasks is that an additional MLP is used to extract the global features.

$$\mathcal{L}_{GL} = \sum_{m=1}^M \sum_{n=1}^N -log \frac{exp \, g_{m,n}(x_t, x_{t+1})}{\sum_{x_{t*} \in X_{next}} exp \, g_{m,n}(x_t, x_{t*})} \tag{2}$$

$$\mathcal{L}_{LL} = \sum_{m=1}^M \sum_{n=1}^N -log \frac{exp \, f_{m,n}(x_t, x_{t+1})}{\sum_{x_{t*} \in X_{next}} exp \, f_{m,n}(x_t, x_{t*})} \tag{3}$$

Here, M and N are the height and width, $g_{m,n}(x_t, x_{t+1}) = \phi(x_t)^T W_g \phi_{m,n}(x_{t+1})$ and $\phi(m, n)$ is the local feature vector produced by convolutional layers in the representation encoder ϕ at the location (m, n). On the other hand, $f_{m,n}(x_t, x_{t+1}) = \phi_{m,n}(x_t)^T W_l \phi_{m,n}(x_{t+1})$. Observations x_t and x_{t+1}

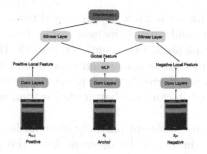

Fig. 1. An illustration of the global-local contrastive task in ST-DIM. For the local-local contrastive task, we discard the MLP and use the local feature of the anchor.

are temporally adjacent, whereas x_{t*} is a randomly sampled observation from the minibatch.

In order to fit ST-DIM into partially observable environments, we propose MST-DIM and define random masks k_t for each consecutive pair (x_t, x_{t+1}) that is drawn from a binomial distribution $\mathbb{K}$. Therefore, Eq. 2 and Eq. 3 are modified as Eq. 4 and Eq. 5:

$$\mathcal{L}_{MGL} = \sum_{m=1}^{M} \sum_{n=1}^{N} -log \frac{exp \, g_{m,n}(x_t k_t, x_{t+1})}{\sum_{x_{t*} \in X_{next}} exp \, g_{m,n}(x_t k_t, x_{t*})} \tag{4}$$

$$\mathcal{L}_{MLL} = \sum_{m=1}^{M} \sum_{n=1}^{N} -log \frac{exp \, f_{m,n}(x_t k_t, x_{t+1})}{\sum_{x_{t*} \in X_{next}} exp \, f_{m,n}(x_t k_t, x_{t*})} \tag{5}$$

Meanwhile, we can tune the probability of masking in $\mathbb{K}$ for both the pre-training and probing. For example, a masking ratio of 0.4 means that 40% of the full observation is not visible to the agent. As a result, our method not only allows pretraining in partially observable environments, but is also capable of pretraining even though the dataset comes from a different $\mathbb{K}$ distribution.

4   Experimental Details

Our experiment is conducted among 20 Atari games of Arcade Learning Environment (ALE). Performances are evaluated by probe accuracy and F1 scores for each game. Because ALE does not directly provide ground truth information, ST-DIM has been conducted on the newly designed Atari Annotated RAM Interface (AtariARI) [1] that exposes the state variables from the source code [24] in 22 games. State variables are categorized as agent localization (Agent Loc.), small object localization (Small Loc.), other localization (Other Loc.), score/clock/lives/display (Score/.../Display), and miscellaneous (Misc.). Detailed descriptions of states for each game across categories can be found in the original paper [1]. We also summarize probe accuracy and F1 scores across those state categories for each game in our experiment. Not all categories are available for each game, and we only include results from applicable ones.

Due to practical implementation issues, we exclude Berzerk, Riverraid and Yars Revenge and include Battle Zone in our experiment, making a total number of 20 games. Trajectories collected by random agents are used in our experiment, as ST-DIM [1] suggested it can be a better choice than using trajectories from PPO agents.

For pretraining, we use different partially observable setups. To verify if the masking ratio in pretraining can be different from the probing, five types of pretraining images have been considered in our experiment, as illustrated by Fig. 2. The images can be original, 20% masked, 40% masked, 60% masked, or 80% masked.

We follow the same probing protocol as ST-DIM and focus on the explicitness, i.e., how well the latent generative factors can be recovered. This is done by training a linear classifier that predicts the state variables using the learned representations. We keep the hyper-parameters the same as ST-DIM to make our experiment comparable. A short list of hyper-parameters is shown in Table 1. Setting the entropy threshold removes large objects that have low entropy from the labels. The encoder architecture is the same as in ST-DIM, as illustrated by Fig. 3.

Table 1. Parameter Choices

Hyper-parameter	Value
Image Size	160×210
Batch Size	64
Learning Rate	$3e{-}4$
Entropy Threshold	0.6
Pretraining Steps	80000
Probe Training Steps	35000
Probe Testing Steps	10000

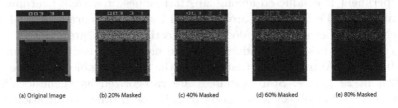

(a) Original Image   (b) 20% Masked   (c) 40% Masked   (d) 60% Masked   (e) 80% Masked

Fig. 2. The original image is masked by different percentages of random noise.

Fig. 3. Architecture of the encoder.

Table 2. Probe F1 scores of each game averaged across categories

Games	Observable	Non-obs.	Supervised	Pretrain	Ratio 0.2	Ratio 0.6	Ratio 0.8
Asteroids	**0.46**	0.39	0.39	**0.45**	**0.45**	0.44	0.44
Battle Zone	**0.5**	0.29	0.28	**0.45**	0.39	0.41	0.38
Bowling	**0.96**	0.29	0.29	**0.9**	0.72	0.85	0.63
Boxing	**0.59**	0.11	0.1	**0.53**	0.38	0.43	0.2
Breakout	**0.87**	0.37	0.37	**0.85**	0.83	**0.85**	0.29
Demon Attack	**0.66**	0.46	0.45	**0.64**	0.6	0.63	0.57
Freeway	**0.81**	0.03	0.03	**0.27**	**0.27**	0.1	0.05
Frostbite	**0.72**	0.33	0.34	**0.7**	0.65	0.66	0.58
Hero	**0.92**	0.57	0.58	**0.9**	0.87	0.88	0.84
Ms Pacman	**0.7**	0.35	0.36	**0.69**	0.64	0.68	0.62
Montezuma Revenge	**0.77**	0.54	0.53	**0.75**	0.74	0.74	0.71
Pitfall	**0.68**	0.24	0.25	**0.62**	0.53	0.6	0.54
Pong	**0.81**	0.13	0.13	**0.71**	0.69	0.65	0.42
Private Eye	**0.88**	0.5	0.49	**0.84**	0.81	0.82	0.68
Qbert	**0.72**	0.47	0.47	**0.71**	0.69	**0.71**	0.69
Seaquest	**0.64**	0.38	0.37	**0.62**	0.59	0.61	0.54
Space Invaders	**0.56**	0.45	0.44	0.56	0.55	**0.57**	0.56
Tennis	**0.6**	0.13	0.13	**0.48**	0.34	0.4	0.23
Venture	**0.55**	0.39	0.4	**0.54**	0.53	0.53	0.52
Video Pinball	**0.62**	0.29	0.3	0.62	0.57	**0.63**	0.6
Mean	**0.7**	0.34	0.33	**0.64**	0.59	0.61	0.5

5   Results

In this section, we demonstrate the performance of unsupervised representation learning in the partially observable reinforcement learning environment. Table 2 shows the F1 scores for each game and Table 3 shows the accuracy. "Observable" represents the setting where the probing is implemented with full observations. "Non-obs." is the ST-DIM setting where the pretraining is with full observations, but the probing are with partial observations. "Supervised" is the setting where no pretraining is included but the model is trained and tested only in probing using the supervised manner. "Ratio" indicates the masking ratio in probing,

Table 3. Probe accuracy scores of each game averaged across categories

Games	Observable	Non-obs.	Supervised	Pretrain	Ratio 0.2	Ratio 0.6	Ratio 0.8
Asteroids	**0.5**	0.46	0.46	**0.5**	**0.5**	**0.5**	0.49
Battle Zone	**0.52**	0.36	0.35	**0.48**	0.44	0.45	0.44
Bowling	**0.96**	0.36	0.36	**0.91**	0.73	0.85	0.66
Boxing	**0.59**	0.14	0.13	**0.54**	0.39	0.44	0.22
Breakout	**0.88**	0.41	0.41	**0.86**	0.84	**0.86**	0.37
Demon Attack	**0.66**	0.47	0.47	**0.65**	0.6	0.64	0.58
Freeway	**0.81**	0.06	0.06	**0.3**	**0.3**	0.15	0.09
Frostbite	**0.73**	0.38	0.38	**0.7**	0.66	0.67	0.59
Hero	**0.92**	0.59	0.59	**0.9**	0.88	0.88	0.84
Ms Pacman	**0.71**	0.4	0.4	**0.7**	0.66	0.69	0.65
Montezuma Revenge	**0.77**	0.55	0.54	**0.76**	0.74	0.74	0.72
Pitfall	**0.69**	0.3	0.3	**0.64**	0.55	0.62	0.57
Pong	**0.82**	0.21	0.21	**0.73**	0.7	0.67	0.47
Private Eye	**0.88**	0.52	0.51	**0.84**	0.81	0.83	0.68
Qbert	**0.73**	0.51	0.51	**0.72**	0.7	0.71	0.69
Seaquest	**0.66**	0.46	0.45	**0.63**	0.61	**0.63**	0.57
Space Invaders	**0.57**	0.48	0.47	**0.59**	0.57	**0.59**	0.58
Tennis	**0.61**	0.22	0.22	**0.51**	0.39	0.44	0.29
Venture	**0.56**	0.41	0.42	**0.55**	0.54	0.54	0.53
Video Pinball	**0.63**	0.31	0.32	0.62	0.57	**0.63**	0.61
Mean	**0.71**	0.38	0.38	**0.66**	0.61	0.63	0.53

e.g., ratio 0.2 equals that 20% part of each observation in probing is not visible. By default, the masking ratio in probing is set to 0.4.

It is obvious that the model is capable of predicting the state variables the most in fully observable environments, as the observations in probing are not masked by noise. The rest results are all from models trained and tested with masked observations for probing. The performance deteriorates considerably if the model still uses ST-DIM and pretrains on full observations. Supervised training also exhibits the same characteristic and obtains similar results with ST-DIM. On the other hand, MST-DIM achieves significantly higher accuracy and F1 scores by taking advantage of masked pretraining. Pretraining with a different masking ratio has also shown improvements over ST-DIM. Using masking ratios 0.2 and 0.6 in pretraining yields slightly inferior results than the default masking ratio of 0.4. Surprisingly, using a masking ratio of 0.8 still improves the ST-DIM despite most of the images being masked in this setting.

The mean accuracy score (0.66) and F1 score (0.64) of MST-DIM are slightly worse than the accuracy score (0.71) and F1 score (0.7) under the fully observable setup. However, these results considerably exceed those of supervised learning (0.38 and 0.33) and ST-DIM (0.38 and 0.34) under the same partially observable setup. For the other three masking ratios, a ratio of 0.6 achieves the highest accuracy (0.63) and F1 scores (0.61), a ratio of 0.2 achieves slightly lower scores

Table 4. Probe F1 scores of different ground truth categories averaged across all games

Categories	Observable	Non-obs.	Supervised	Pretrain	Ratio 0.2	Ratio 0.6	Ratio 0.8
Agent Loc	**0.58**	0.26	0.26	**0.52**	0.48	0.5	0.41
Misc.	**0.73**	0.48	0.48	**0.72**	0.68	0.7	0.61
Other Loc.	**0.64**	0.34	0.34	**0.59**	0.56	0.54	0.47
Score/.../Display	**0.9**	0.42	0.42	**0.86**	0.77	0.83	0.7
Small Loc.	**0.53**	0.21	0.21	**0.47**	0.42	0.44	0.28

Table 5. Probe accuracy scores of different ground truth categories

Categories	Observable	Non-obs.	Supervised	Pretrain	Ratio 0.2	Ratio 0.6	Ratio 0.8
Agent Loc	**0.59**	0.32	0.32	**0.54**	0.5	0.52	0.44
Misc.	**0.74**	0.52	0.52	**0.73**	0.69	0.71	0.64
Other Loc.	**0.65**	0.38	0.38	**0.59**	0.58	0.55	0.49
Score/.../Display	**0.9**	0.44	0.44	**0.87**	0.78	0.84	0.71
Small Loc.	**0.55**	0.29	0.29	**0.5**	0.46	0.47	0.34

(0.61 and 0.59), and a ratio of 0.8 obtains the worst accuracy and F1 scores (0.53 and 0.5).

Meanwhile, Table 4 and Table 5 show the results for each category averaged over games. It is clear that MST-DIM still performs the best category-wise in partially observable environments, and achieves scores that is slightly worse than ST-DIM that is probed under fully observable environments. A different masking ratio in pretraining still enhances the model's capability across games in probing tasks, and even a masking ratio (0.8) that is remote from the probing masking ratio (0.4) can facilitate achieving better scores for each ground truth category.

6 Discussion

It was found that there was a sizable gap between the performances of ST-DIM and supervised training by [1]. However, their difference is trivial under our partially observable setting. Meanwhile, MST-DIM has demonstrated better performance than both of them. The reason might be that ST-DIM and supervised methods do not possess better initializations, and yield similarly deteriorated results in partially observable environments.

On the other hand, Randomly initialized CNNs can perform reasonably well in probing tasks. Their scores are only slightly lower than those of generative methods in [1], because random CNNs are considered a strong prior in Atari games and can capture the inductive bias [2, 25].

Different masking ratios in pretraining have shown to be effective, even for a large masking ratio that generates visually invisible images. Although the closer the pretraining masking ratio is, the more accurate the probing prediction can be, the masking ratio in pretraining is not required to be the same. The results indicate that unsupervised pretraining can learn reliable latent generative factors from a different data distribution. Unlike in fully observable environments, this is strong evidence that contrastive methods can play a key role in strengthening model capabilities in partially observable environments for downstream tasks.

The results of small object localization in Tables 4 and 5 are highlighted in ST-DIM because generative methods typically do not penalize enough for not modeling the pixels making up small objects. The local-local contrastive task in ST-DIM is specialized in capturing local representation. In our experiment, it is clear that the performances of ST-DIM and the supervised method have dropped significantly in partially observable experiments because small objects with few pixels can be easily masked out completely. On the other hand, MST-DIM overcomes this problem by masked pretraining and is close to achieving the same level of performance (0.47 to 0.53 for F1 scores and 0.5 to 0.55 in accuracy scores). However, MST-DIM has suffered from pretraining with a masking ratio of 0.8, which masks most of the image.

In some games, such as boxing, easy-to-learn features might saturate the objective and let contrastive methods fail. For example, contrastive methods other than ST-DIM fail to model features besides the clock in boxing [1]. This is also a problem in partially observable environments and causes ST-DIM, supervised method, and MST-DIM with a masking ratio of 0.8 to perform worse. On the other hand, MST-DIM with a masking ratio close to 0.4 exhibits robustness as ST-DIM in fully observable environments.

For the study of different masking ratios, we observe that a masking ratio that is slightly higher than one of the underlying observations obtains the best accuracy and F1 scores when the original ratio is not available. Thus, it suggests that a higher masking ratio facilitates unsupervised representation learning in partially observable environments. If we were to choose between decreasing or increasing the ratio with the same amount in pretraining, increasing the number could be a reasonable choice.

7   Conclusion

We propose MST-DIM in this paper to deal with partially observable environments through pretraining. MST-DIM is a contrastive method based on an estimate of mutual information bound and uses masking in unsupervised pretraining to ensure the agent can learn reliable latent generative factors. Experiments are conducted using a benchmark of unsupervised learning on the annotated interface of Atari 2600 games. MST-DIM shows the benefit of using unsupervised representation learning in partially observable environments by achieving higher accuracy and F1 scores than ST-DIM and supervised learning.

For future work, it would be interesting to directly apply MST-DIM to RL environments and evaluate its performance using RL baselines. Designing an auxiliary contrastive loss in RL is typical, but the implementation details can vary among different research. Exploiting the weight initialization of pretrained representation encoders that resembles more to CV probing tasks can also be an intriguing topic.

Recognizing small objects can be a challenging task in partially observable environments. ST-DIM deploys the local-local contrastive task to reliably learn the representations of small objects. However, it still suffers from information loss and obtains worse results in partially observable environments. MST-DIM deals with this issue and achieves scores close to ST-DIM under the fully observable setup. It still remains to be studied how to recognize small objects where the environment is almost invisible, and information loss is severe.

Acknowledgements. This work was performed on the [ML node] resource, owned by the University of Oslo, and operated by the Department for Research Computing at USIT, the University of Oslo IT-department. http://www.hpc.uio.no/.

References

1. Anand, A., Racah, E., Ozair, S., Bengio, Y., Côté, M.A., Hjelm, R.D.: Unsupervised state representation learning in atari. In: Advances in Neural Information Processing Systems, vol. 32 (2019)
2. Burda, Y., Edwards, H., Pathak, D., Storkey, A., Darrell, T., Efros, A.A.: Large-scale study of curiosity-driven learning. arXiv preprint arXiv:1808.04355 (2018)
3. Cassandra, A.R., Kaelbling, L.P., Littman, M.L.: Acting optimally in partially observable stochastic domains. In: AAAI, vol. 94, pp. 1023–1028 (1994)
4. Chen, T., Kornblith, S., Norouzi, M., Hinton, G.: A simple framework for contrastive learning of visual representations. In: International Conference on Machine Learning, pp. 1597–1607. PMLR (2020)
5. Chen, X., Xie, S., He, K.: An empirical study of training self-supervised vision transformers. In: Proceedings of the IEEE/CVF International Conference on Computer Vision, pp. 9640–9649 (2021)
6. Devlin, J., Chang, M.W., Lee, K., Toutanova, K.: BERT: pre-training of deep bidirectional transformers for language understanding. arXiv preprint arXiv:1810.04805 (2018)
7. Doersch, C., Zisserman, A.: Multi-task self-supervised visual learning. In: Proceedings of the IEEE International Conference on Computer Vision, pp. 2051–2060 (2017)
8. Dosovitskiy, A., et al.: An image is worth 16×16 words: transformers for image recognition at scale. arXiv preprint arXiv:2010.11929 (2020)
9. Gregor, K., Danihelka, I., Graves, A., Rezende, D., Wierstra, D.: DRAW: a recurrent neural network for image generation. In: International Conference on Machine Learning, pp. 1462–1471. PMLR (2015)
10. Guo, Z.D., et al.: Bootstrap latent-predictive representations for multitask reinforcement learning. In: International Conference on Machine Learning, pp. 3875–3886. PMLR (2020)
11. He, K., Fan, H., Wu, Y., Xie, S., Girshick, R.: Momentum contrast for unsupervised visual representation learning. In: Proceedings of the IEEE/CVF Conference on Computer Vision and Pattern Recognition, pp. 9729–9738 (2020)
12. Hjelm, R.D., et al.: Learning deep representations by mutual information estimation and maximization. arXiv preprint arXiv:1808.06670 (2018)
13. Jonschkowski, R., Brock, O.: Learning state representations with robotic priors. Auton. Robot. **39**(3), 407–428 (2015). https://doi.org/10.1007/s10514-015-9459-7

14. Kingma, D.P., Welling, M.: Auto-encoding variational Bayes. arXiv preprint arXiv:1312.6114 (2013)
15. Kolesnikov, A., Zhai, X., Beyer, L.: Revisiting self-supervised visual representation learning. In: Proceedings of the IEEE/CVF Conference on Computer Vision and Pattern Recognition, pp. 1920–1929 (2019)
16. Laskin, M., Srinivas, A., Abbeel, P.: CURL: contrastive unsupervised representations for reinforcement learning. In: International Conference on Machine Learning, pp. 5639–5650. PMLR (2020)
17. Lee, K.H., et al.: Predictive information accelerates learning in RL. Adv. Neural. Inf. Process. Syst. **33**, 11890–11901 (2020)
18. Lesort, T., Díaz-Rodríguez, N., Goudou, J.F., Filliat, D.: State representation learning for control: an overview. Neural Netw. **108**, 379–392 (2018)
19. Mnih, V., et al.: Playing atari with deep reinforcement learning (2013)
20. Oord, A.V.D., Li, Y., Vinyals, O.: Representation learning with contrastive predictive coding. arXiv preprint arXiv:1807.03748 (2018)
21. Puterman, M.L.: Markov decision processes. Handbooks Oper. Res. Management Sci. **2**, 331–434 (1990)
22. Stooke, A., Lee, K., Abbeel, P., Laskin, M.: Decoupling representation learning from reinforcement learning. In: International Conference on Machine Learning, pp. 9870–9879. PMLR (2021)
23. Sutton, R.S., Barto, A.G.: Reinforcement Learning: An Introduction. MIT Press, Cambridge (2018)
24. Taylor, L.N., Whalen, Z.: Playing the Past: History and Nostalgia in Video Games. JSTOR (2008)
25. Ulyanov, D., Vedaldi, A., Lempitsky, V.: Deep image prior. In: Proceedings of the IEEE Conference on Computer Vision and Pattern Recognition, pp. 9446–9454 (2018)
26. Watkins, C.J., Dayan, P.: Q-learning. Mach. Learn. **8**(3–4), 279–292 (1992)
27. Zhu, J., et al.: Masked contrastive representation learning for reinforcement learning. IEEE Trans. Pattern Anal. Mach. Intell. **45**(3), 3421–3433 (2022)

Structural Analysis of the Additive Noise Impact on the α-tree

Baptiste Esteban$^{(\boxtimes)}$, Guillaume Tochon, Edwin Carlinet, and Didier Verna

EPITA Research Laboratory, 14-16 rue Pasteur, Le Kremlin-Bicêtre, France
`baptiste.esteban@lrde.epita.fr`

Abstract. Hierarchical representations are very convenient tools when working with images. Among them, the α-tree is the basis of several powerful hierarchies used for various applications such as image simplification, object detection, or segmentation. However, it has been demonstrated that these tasks are very sensitive to the presence of noise in images. While the quality of some α-tree applications has been studied, including some with noisy images, the noise impact on the whole structure has been little investigated. Thus, in this paper, we examine the structure of α-trees built on images in the presence of noise with respect to the noise level. We compare its effects on constant and natural images, with different kinds of content, and we demonstrate the relation between the noise level and the distribution of every α-tree node depth. Furthermore, we extend this study to the node persistence under a given energy criterion, and we propose a novel energy definition that allows assessing the robustness of a region to the noise. We finally observe that the choice of the energy has a great impact on the tree structure.

Keywords: α-tree · noise analysis · persistent hierarchy

1 Introduction

Hierarchical representations are powerful tools for several image processing tasks. They are divided into two categories [1]: *inclusion hierarchies* and *partitioning hierarchies*. Inclusion hierarchies, such as the max-tree [2] or the tree of shapes [3], describe the relation of the connected components of an image. In another hand, partitioning hierarchies stack different image partitions whose regions are obtained with a given criterion. They include the α-tree and the ω-tree [4], the hierarchical watersheds [5], and the binary partition trees [6]. However, despite their division, there exist some links between the different categories [7]. In this article, we focus on the α-tree, which is used for numerous tasks such as segmentation, simplification [8], or attribute profiles [9].

To evaluate the quality of these hierarchies, a set of metrics such as the quality of regions and contours in the context of horizontal and optimal cut, is proposed and applied to hierarchical watersheds [10]. However, this evaluation does not

© The Author(s), under exclusive license to Springer Nature Switzerland AG 2023
N. Tsapatsoulis et al. (Eds.): CAIP 2023, LNCS 14185, pp. 223–232, 2023.
https://doi.org/10.1007/978-3-031-44240-7_22

take into account the case where a hierarchy is built on a noisy image. The impact of the noise on hierarchies applied to attribute profiles is investigated in [11], where the superiority of inclusion trees and the ω-tree compared to the α-tree is demonstrated for such applications. Finally, the tree structure is investigate in [12] to estimate its size and reduce the amount of memory allocation in the context of an efficient α-tree construction algorithm. Nonetheless, the impact of the noise on its structure has not been really studied.

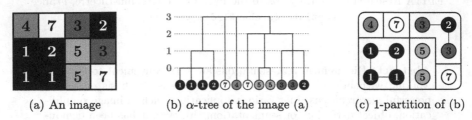

(a) An image   (b) α-tree of the image (a)   (c) 1-partition of (b)

Fig. 1: Illustration of the α-tree representation.

Our objective is to study the relation between the level of the noise corrupting an image and its impact on the structure of the tree. To this aim, we focus on the evolution of some attributes computed on the α-trees built on images corrupted by some noise with respect to its level. The first attribute is the depth of every node in the tree, particularly their statistical distribution. The second attribute originates from the scale-set theory [13] and yields the notion of persistent nodes according to a given energy criterion. Using these attributes, we highlight the relation between the structure of the tree and the noise level, and we propose a novel energy criterion, relying on the values of a region of the tree and the gradient at its contour, in order to assert the robustness of a region to the noise.

This article is structured as follows: in Sect. 2, we recall the definition of the α-tree and explain how to obtain the persistence of a node when constrained to a particular energy. Then, we study the impact of the noise on the structure of the tree in Sect. 3. We extend this study to the node persistence in Sect. 4. Finally, we conclude and give the perspectives of this work in Sect. 5.

2   Hierarchical Representations

2.1   The α-tree Representation

Let $f : \Omega \rightarrow I$ be an image defined on a domain Ω and whose values belong to I. Two points $p, q \in \Omega$ are α-connected if there exists a path of m consecutive points $(p \rightarrow q) = (x_0 = p, ..., x_{m-1} = q)$ according to an adjacency relationship such that for every two consecutive points x_i and x_{i+1} of this path, $w(f(x_i), f(x_{i+1})) \leq \alpha$, with w a dissimilarity measure between two pixel values. An α-connected component is a connected component composed of α-connected points. Thus, a 0-connected component is a flat zone. An α-partition α-P is a partition composed of disjoint α-connected components whose union is Ω. An α-tree $\mathcal{T}_\alpha$ is the tree representation of the hierarchy $\mathcal{H}_\alpha = (0\text{-P}, ..., (m-1)\text{-P})$ composed of m α-partitions. Each node of $\mathcal{T}_\alpha$ represents an α-connected component and its parent represents the fusion of this node with all its siblings. Finally, a cut ζ is a set of disjoint regions $(R_\alpha)_i$ represented by the nodes of $\mathcal{T}_\alpha$ whose union is Ω. A particular case of cut is the *horizontal cut* at a given level t which results in an α-partition with $\alpha = t$.

By applying these notions to graphs, and by the links between different hierarchical representations on edge-weighted graphs [7], the α-tree is the min-tree [2] of the minimum spanning tree of a graph, such as an adjacency graph of an image. This link leads to an efficient construction procedure based on the Kruskal algorithm [14]. Furthermore, there exist more efficient algorithms such as one based on flooding [12] or a parallel version of the α-tree construction [15].

An example of α-tree is illustrated in Fig. 1. It is built on the image in Fig. 1a and displayed in Fig. 1b as a dendrogram. In this representation, each pixel is represented by a leaf of the tree and each inner node represents the fusion of different sets of pixels. Finally, a partition of the α-tree is given in Fig. 1c.

2.2 Persistent Hierarchies

Each region R of a partitioning hierarchy appears in the tree for a given continuous set of scale values associated with the hierarchy. This set is called *interval of persistence* and is defined by $\Lambda(R) = [\lambda^+(R), \lambda^-(R)[$, where $\lambda^+(R)$ is the *scale of appearance* of R and $\lambda^-(R)$ is its *scale of disappearance*. Thus, for each region R_α represented by a node r_α of an α-tree $\mathcal{T}_\alpha$, $\lambda^+(R_\alpha)$ is the value α associated with r_α and $\lambda^-(R_\alpha)$ is the value α of the parent of r_α. The scale of disappearance of the root is a particular case where $\lambda^-(\Omega) = +\infty$.

There exist several image processing approaches relying on energy minimization for different tasks such as segmentation or denoising. Guigues *et al.* [13] propose to apply energy minimization to hierarchical representations to obtain a cut ζ^*, which is optimal according to a separable energy of the form:

$$E_\lambda(\zeta^*) = \sum_{R_i \in \zeta^*} D(R_i) + \lambda \sum_{R_i \in \zeta^*} C(R_i) \qquad (1)$$

with $D(R_i)$ a data-fidelity term to R_i, $C(R_i)$ a regularization term and λ a parameter of this energy. When λ is varying from low value to high value, this produces different cuts whose regions are evolving from fine to coarse. Therefore, this parameter may be seen as a scale parameter, and it is possible to obtain an interval of persistence using a functional dynamic programming problem [13] by subjecting an energy of the form $E_r = D(r) + \lambda C(r)$ to a node r. This reveals some *non-persistent* nodes, with $\lambda^-(r) \leq \lambda^+(r)$, which are removed from the hierarchy, leading to a *persistent hierarchy*.

3   Noise Impact on the Tree Structure

In the following, an image corrupted by an additive Gaussian noise is defined by $f_\sigma = f + n_\sigma$ with n_σ the values of the additive noise drawn from a normal law $\mathcal{N}(0, \sigma^2)$ where σ^2 is the variance of the noise. A particular case of f is the constant image f_c such that $\forall p, f_c(p) = c$, and its noisy version is denoted by $f_{c,\sigma}$. For all the experiments performed in this paper, the set of pixel values I is included or equal to $[\![0-255]\!]$.

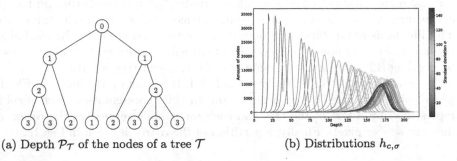

(a) Depth $\mathcal{P}_\mathcal{T}$ of the nodes of a tree $\mathcal{T}$ (b) Distributions $h_{c,\sigma}$

Fig. 2: The depth attribute and its representation as histograms for $f_{c,\sigma}$. (Color figure online)

3.1   Study on a Noisy Constant Image

We propose here to evaluate the impact of the noise on a tree $\mathcal{T}$ by studying the *depth* $\mathcal{P}_\mathcal{T}(r)$ of each node r, defined by

$$\mathcal{P}_\mathcal{T}(r) = \begin{cases} 0 & \text{if } r \text{ is the root of } \mathcal{T} \\ \mathcal{P}(r_p) + 1 & \text{else} \end{cases} \tag{2}$$

with r_p the parent node of r in $\mathcal{T}$. This attribute is illustrated in Fig. 2a, representing a tree whose labels in blue are the depth value of each node. The depth distribution of $\mathcal{T}$ is studied by observing its histogram h, whose values are defined by $h(d) = |\{r \in \mathcal{T} \mid \mathcal{P}_\mathcal{T}(r) = d\}|$ for a particular $d \in \mathcal{P}_\mathcal{T}$. The mode $m(h)$ of the distribution h and its empirical mean $\mu(h)$ are used throughout this paper. They are respectively obtained by $m(h) = \text{argmax}_{d \in \mathcal{P}_\mathcal{T}} h(d)$ and $\mu(h) = \frac{1}{|h|} \sum_{d \in \mathcal{P}_\mathcal{T}} h(d)$. The depth distributions obtained from the α-trees built on f_σ and $f_{c,\sigma}$ are respectively denoted by h_σ and $h_{c,\sigma}$.

In this part, the depth distributions are obtained from α-trees built on images containing only noise, without any texture information, in order to observe the evolution of the tree structure in the presence of noise with respect to its level. To this aim, the distributions $h_{c,\sigma}$ are built from α-trees constructed on constant images $f_{c,\sigma}$, with $c = 127$, which have been corrupted with noise whose level σ is varying from 1 to 150. The resulting distributions $h_{c,\sigma}$ are displayed in Fig. 2b, where they are represented by plots whose color corresponds to the noise level σ of the image on which the α-tree is built and depicted by the color bar.

By examining these distributions, the evolution of the tree structure related to the noise level corrupting the image is studied. First, while the noise level increases, the depth distribution becomes a tailed distribution for nodes with a low depth. These nodes are α-connected components resulting from the fusion of another component and a small region, usually of size 1, which have an intensity significantly different from their surrounding pixel values. Then, the mode of the distributions increases while the noise level grows up to some high level ($\sigma \approx 100$), beyond which this mode decreases slowly. This is due to the clipping of values to the limits of I during the noising process of the image, creating new flat zones.

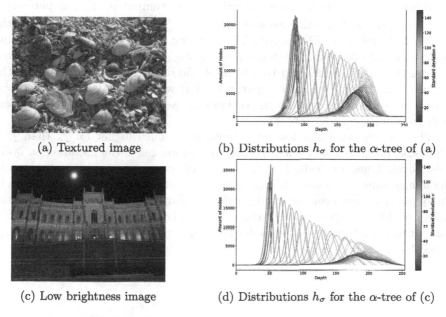

(a) Textured image (b) Distributions h_σ for the α-tree of (a)

(c) Low brightness image (d) Distributions h_σ for the α-tree of (c)

Fig. 3: Distributions h_σ on different kind of images.

3.2 Comparison with Natural Images

In this section, 150 natural images of size 720×540 from the database of Laurent CONDAT[1] are used to take into account different characteristics likely to be impacted by the noise such as a high texture or a low brightness. Examples of images are displayed in Fig. 3a and 3c, with their respective depth distributions h_σ in Fig. 3b and 3d. These distributions are obtained by the same process as previously described and using the same noise level ranges.

---

[1] https://lcondat.github.io/imagebase.html.

These distributions have similar behaviors as the ones in Fig. 2b. Their mode increases up to some noise level, and then decreases slowly. Then, the variance of each distribution is increasing as the noise level becomes high. However, there also are several differences between the distributions of tree depth obtained from $f_{c,\sigma}$ and f_σ, and between the natural images. First, the distribution modes, at low noise levels, are higher for h_σ than for $h_{c,\sigma}$. This is due to the content of the natural images which, conversely to the constant image, has some texture. Consequently, for very small σ values, the image content is still prevailing. Finally, the distributions h_σ in Fig. 3d with high σ values have a higher variance than the distributions in Fig. 3b. This demonstrates the impact of the noise on α-trees built on images with low brightness.

The analysis of the noise impact is then extended to the whole image database. For this purpose, an α-tree is built on each image and the empirical mean $\mu(h_\sigma)$ of the depth distribution h_σ is computed. This is performed $N = 10$ times to obtain the average $\mathcal{M}(\sigma) = \frac{1}{N} \sum_{i=0}^{N-1} \mu((h_\sigma)_i)$, with $(h_\sigma)_i$ the ith depth distribution. This process is carried out for several noise levels varying between 1 and 150, resulting in the plots in Fig. 4. Each dashed plot is related to a particular image, leading to a total of 150 dashed plots. Furthermore, the red plot results from the same experiment, but with $f_{c,\sigma}$, to compare the noise impact on the structure of an α-tree built on a pure noisy image and α-trees built from images with content.

The average $\mathcal{M}(\sigma)$, at low noise levels σ, is much higher for f_σ than $f_{c,\sigma}$. This observation is true for a large majority of images in the database on every noise level. Thus, we deduce that, in spite of the noise corrupting the image, the image content has still an impact on the depth distribution of the nodes in the α-tree, as it has been observed previously. Furthermore, for every image, the values of $\mathcal{M}(\sigma)$ is decreasing starting from a given high noise level. This may come from the clipping of image values during the noising process, as previously noted for all kind of images.

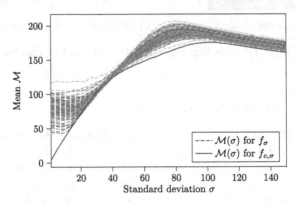

Fig. 4: Comparison between h_σ from all the images from the base and $h_{c,\sigma}$

4 Impact of the Noise on Nodes Persistence

In this section, the α-trees constructed from noisy images are transformed into persistent hierarchies using a particular energy criterion. Two different energies are utilized for this purpose. First, the piecewise constant Mumford-Shah functional [16] is employed since it is widely used in image simplification applications using hierarchical representations of images. It is defined by

$$E_{\mathrm{ms},r_\alpha}(\lambda) = \sum_{p \in R_\alpha} (f(p) - \tilde{f}(p))^2 + \lambda \, |\partial R_\alpha| \tag{3}$$

where $\tilde{f}$ is the average intensity of the values in the region R_α and ∂R_α is the set of elements in the contours of R_α. Besides, we propose to modify the Mumford-Shah functional to use the sum of gradient values in the contour of R_α instead of the length of its contour. This functional, denoted by E_{cs,r_α}, is defined by

$$E_{\mathrm{cs},r_\alpha}(\lambda) = \sum_{p \in R_\alpha} (f(p) - \tilde{f}(p))^2 + \lambda \sum_{p \in \partial R_\alpha} g(p) \tag{4}$$

with g the set of contour values computed using the dissimilarity function w between two adjacent pixel values of the image from which the α-tree is built. This change of regularization term is proposed because a region with a small variance and a high gradient along its contour is most likely to be contrasted relatively to its adjacent regions, and therefore prone to be less affected by the noise in the image on which the α-tree is built.

To compare the usage of these functionals, but also to evaluate the impact of the noise on the persistence of the nodes, the percentages of non-persistent nodes using these energies E_{ms,r_α} and E_{cs,r_α} are computed on an α-tree built on the image in Fig. 3a and are displayed on Fig. 5. These plots have a similar behavior: when the noise level increases, the amount of non-persistent nodes is growing. Additionally, a greater amount of non-persistent nodes is observed when E_{cs,r_α}

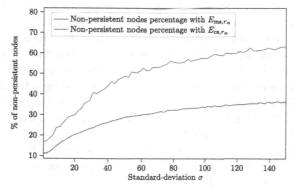

Fig. 5: Non-persistent nodes percentage related to the noise level σ

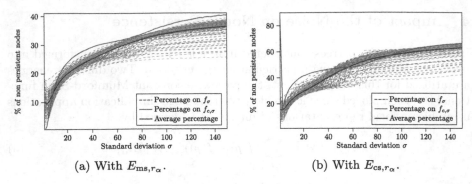

(a) With E_{ms,r_α}.   (b) With E_{cs,r_α}.

Fig. 6: Evolution of the amount of non-persistent nodes with respect to the noise level. (Color figure online)

is used as an energy criterion than E_{ms,r_α}, and this difference is twice as large for E_{cs,r_α} at high noise levels.

The evolution of the plots of non-persistent nodes percentage is confirmed on all the images from the database with E_{ms,r_α} and E_{cs,r_α} in Fig. 6a and 6b respectively. In this figure, the average percentage of non-persistent nodes is displayed as the blue plot. Furthermore, the red line represents the percentage of non-persistent nodes on the constant image $f_{c,\sigma}$. On the two figures, the red plot has a different behavior: with E_{ms,r_α}, the amount of non-persistent nodes is close to 0%, whereas with E_{cs,r_α}, it is near 80%. This observation suggests that using E_{cs,r_α} as an energy criterion instead of E_{ms,r_α} in the presence of noise is more relevant. Furthermore, this is enforced due to the fact that when σ is increasing, the amount of non-persistent nodes on a tree built on $f_{c,\sigma}$ gets closer to the average percentage when E_{cs,r_α} is used.

5   Conclusion and Perspectives

To conclude this article, we have shown that there exists a relationship between the noise level degrading the image and the distribution of the depth attribute computed from the α-tree built on the noisy image. Furthermore, on natural images, we observed that the content of the image has an effect on the depth distributions: for low noise levels, the impact of noise on the α-tree is negligible, and at a high noise level, the brightness impacts the variance of the distribution. Finally, we have noticed that the choice of the functional used to obtain persistent nodes affects the amount of non-persistent nodes in the hierarchy.

Our work is different from the previous approaches to evaluate the quality of the hierarchies since our objective is to investigate the relation between the noise level and the tree structure, but the results obtained here may be used to develop new methodologies to make such assessments on noisy images, taking into account the various levels.

We plan to extend this work to other kinds of noise, but also to generalize our study to different partitioning hierarchies such as the ω-tree, the binary partition trees, or the hierarchical watersheds, but also to inclusion hierarchies. Finally, these results open new perspectives in terms of applications. For example, it may be convenient to use the resulting relation to measure them. Furthermore, noise level estimation is not the only perspective this paper opens: segmentations using optimal cut could be improved in the presence of noise or new denoising methods could be developed.

References

1. Bosilj, P., Kijak, E., Lefèvre, S.: Partition and inclusion hierarchies of images: a comprehensive survey. J. Imaging **4**(2), 33 (2018). https://doi.org/10.3390/jimaging4020033
2. Salembier, P., Oliveras, A., Garrido, L.: Antiextensive connected operators for image and sequence processing. IEEE Trans. Image Process. **7**(4), 555–570 (1998). https://doi.org/10.1109/83.663500
3. Monasse, P., Guichard, F.: Fast computation of a contrast-invariant image representation. IEEE Trans. Image Process. **9**(5), 860–872 (2000)
4. Soille, P.: Constrained connectivity for hierarchical image partitioning and simplification. IEEE Trans. Pattern Anal. Mach. Intell. **30**(7), 1132–1145 (2008). https://doi.org/10.1109/TPAMI.2007.70817
5. Cousty, J., Najman, L.: Incremental algorithm for hierarchical minimum spanning forests and saliency of watershed cuts. In: Soille, P., Pesaresi, M., Ouzounis, G.K. (eds.) Mathematical Morphology and Its Applications to Image and Signal Processing. LNCS, vol. 6671, pp. 272–283. Springer, Heidelberg (2011). https://doi.org/10.1007/978-3-642-21569-8_24
6. Salembier, P., Garrido, L.: Binary partition tree as an efficient representation for image processing, segmentation, and information retrieval. IEEE Trans. Image Process. **9**(4), 561–576 (2000). https://doi.org/10.1109/83.841934
7. Cousty, J., Najman, L., Perret, B.: Constructive links between some morphological hierarchies on edge-weighted graphs. In: Hendriks, C.L.L., Borgefors, G., Strand, R. (eds.) ISMM 2013. LNCS, vol. 7883, pp. 86–97. Springer, Heidelberg (2013). https://doi.org/10.1007/978-3-642-38294-9_8
8. Perret, B., Cousty, J., Ferzoli Guimarães, S.J., Kenmochi, Y., Najman, L.: Removing non-significant regions in hierarchical clustering and segmentation. Pattern Recogn. Lett. **128**, 433–439 (2019). https://doi.org/10.1016/j.patrec.2019.10.008
9. Bosilj, P., Damodaran, B.B., Aptoula, E., Mura, M.D., Lefèvre, S.: Attribute profiles from partitioning trees. In: Angulo, J., Velasco-Forero, S., Meyer, F. (eds.) ISMM 2017. LNCS, vol. 10225, pp. 381–392. Springer, Cham (2017). https://doi.org/10.1007/978-3-319-57240-6_31
10. Perret, B., Cousty, J., Guimarães, S.J.F., Maia, D.S.: Evaluation of hierarchical watersheds. IEEE Trans. Image Process. **27**(4), 1676–1688 (2018). https://doi.org/10.1109/TIP.2017.2779604
11. Koç, S.G., Aptoula, E., Bosilj, P., Damodaran, B.B., Dalla Mura, M., Lefevre, S.: A comparative noise robustness study of tree representations for attribute profile construction. In: 2017 25th Signal Processing and Communications Applications Conference (SIU), pp. 1–4. IEEE (2017). https://doi.org/10.1109/SIU.2017.7960159

12. You, J., Trager, S.C., Wilkinson, M.H.F.: A fast, memory-efficient alpha-tree algorithm using flooding and tree size estimation. In: Burgeth, B., Kleefeld, A., Naegel, B., Passat, N., Perret, B. (eds.) ISMM 2019. LNCS, vol. 11564, pp. 256–267. Springer, Cham (2019). https://doi.org/10.1007/978-3-030-20867-7_20

13. Guigues, L., Cocquerez, J.P., Le Men, H.: Scale-sets image analysis. Int. J. Comput. Vision **68**(3), 289–317 (2006). https://doi.org/10.1007/s11263-005-6299-0

14. Najman, L., Cousty, J., Perret, B.: Playing with Kruskal: algorithms for morphological trees in edge-weighted graphs. In: Hendriks, C.L.L., Borgefors, G., Strand, R. (eds.) ISMM 2013. LNCS, vol. 7883, pp. 135–146. Springer, Heidelberg (2013). https://doi.org/10.1007/978-3-642-38294-9_12

15. Havel, J., Merciol, F., Lefèvre, S.: Efficient tree construction for multiscale image representation and processing. J. Real-Time Image Proc. **16**(4), 1129–1146 (2016). https://doi.org/10.1007/s11554-016-0604-0

16. Mumford, D., Shah, J.: Optimal approximations by piecewise smooth functions and associated variational problems. Commun. Pure Appl. Math. **42**(5), 577–685 (1989). https://doi.org/10.1002/cpa.3160420503

Augmented Reality for Indoor Localization and Navigation: The Case of UNIPI AR Experience

Dionysios Koulouris, Andreas Menychtas, and Ilias Maglogiannis(✉)

University of Piraeus, 80, M. Karaoli & A. Dimitriou Street, 18534 Piraeus, Greece
{dnkoulouris,amenychtas,imaglo}@unipi.gr

Abstract. Indoor localization and navigation is a common problem mostly in large buildings where multiple floors, rooms and corridors may generate a struggling experience for the visitor. The complex internal environment, the composite architectural designs and the interference of objects and people in crowded areas, make the adoption of generic solutions hard to implement and apply, while their performance and the provided user experience do not meet the typical operational requirements. Different ways to achieve indoor localization are examined, but all require either static interventions (QR codes) or installing IoT sensors. In this work we present an AR Navigation System solution which utilizes a mobile device's ability to exploit Augmented Reality (AR) for indoor localization and mapping. At the core of the system is a hybrid platform (cloud/edge), which enables the generate immersive AR navigation experiences. Key contribution of this work is the use of the aforementioned platform for introducing an AR "checkpoint" navigation system which integrates our algorithms for indoor localization, path planning, point of interest visualization and device interoperability. A prototype of the overall solution has already been implemented and it is deployed at the University of Piraeus for evaluation from students, personnel and visitors.

Keywords: Augmented Reality · Hybrid Cloud · Computer Vision · Indoor Localization

1 Introduction

The evolution of edge and mobile devices and the related technologies, in both hardware and software level, enables the execution of even heavier Machine Learning tasks on the edge providing new possibilities for research and innovation. Smartphones are nowadays the mainstream computing paradigm for users of all types, and their commodity hardware incorporates advanced capabilities for communication with other systems and interacting with the physical environment [3]. In parallel, the advancements in Computer Vision and the extensive

N. Tsapatsoulis et al. (Eds.): CAIP 2023, LNCS 14185, pp. 233–243, 2023.
https://doi.org/10.1007/978-3-031-44240-7_23

use of Machine Learning technologies create new opportunities in all application domains by exploiting the capabilities and the performance of the hardware, especially when the operations are performed locally. Augmented Reality (AR) is a technological area which benefited from these advancements and in its recent form, offers to users of smartphones means for interacting with the physical world by utilizing raw data from a mobile device's sensors. Use cases of AR can be found in a variety of scientific fields, from architecture and engineering [2] to health and education [14]. The proposed solution is based on the extraction of the features of a front scene using pattern recognition to identify surfaces on which virtual Anchors are placed. After the system is trained, it is able to discover these Anchors in runtime and translate them to points of interest which can be used for localization and indoor guidance. AR also supports user interactivity by creating a series of indoor waypoints to indicate a path, or other information, introducing an innovative navigation system which can adapted to support different scenarios and applications [22].

The rest of the paper is structured as follows: Sect. 2 highlights related works and studies on the field. In Sect. 3, the technological foundation is presented along with the overview of the system architecture and implementation. Results from the system in practice are demonstrated in Sect. 4. A discussion of the evaluation of the system is presented in Sect. 5 while Sect. 6 concludes the work.

2   Related Work

Traditional mobile navigation methods retrieve the position of the device either by cellular network [16] or via satellite using GPS [7]. While these methods perform good giving driving, cycling or walking directions, they lose precision when indoors. To overcome this limitation, solutions utilizing static hardware attached to a building are introduced. Adam Satan's system uses Bluetooth Beacons which emit radio frequency signals identified by the device before using Dijkstra algorithm to find the shortest path [18]. Following the same concept, but using WiFi signal instead of Bluetooth, indoor navigation was achieved in COEX complex in Scoul [6]. An approach was to identify landmarks and create magnetic maps for multiple corridors of a floor in a building using a phone's built-in magnetometer [5]. All aforementioned examples require modifications and sensor installations in order to produce the desired result. Another proposal, which does not require any kind of sensor installation, is navigation by estimating steps using accelerometer and 5G signals [19]. Keeping aligned with the using-onboard-sensors-only approach, more integrated hardware can be utilized and combined, such as the device's camera. At this point the term AR will be introduced. AR in comparison with Virtual Reality (VR), captures the outside world and interacts with the area in front by attaching and visualizing augmented information [1]. Generic implementation of AR gamification techniques with physical activity goal and combined with AR navigation can also be found in Nature-Based solutions [13], where the user is navigated through a park's attractions. Target indication in facility maintenance operations is another proof-of-concept scenario of AR's [11] localization ability, along with freight car routing [21]. In combination with WiFi/Bluetooth Low Energy signals, Jehn-Ruey Jiang et al. introduced an AR indoor navigation framework [8] which is applicable in both AR for mobile and VR glasses. The scientific base behind these solutions is a combination of feature extraction from a series of images with data retrieved from device sensors, called Simultaneous Localization and Mapping (SLAM). SLAM is identified as a problem [4] with solutions in robotics [20] and more recently in combination with AR [17]. The Googles ARCore Library facilitates indoor space recognition by utilizing SLAM in such a way that enables a device to identify locations previously recorded by other devices. Features from the device's camera feed are recorded, processed and stored to the cloud. Then, they are retrieved by other devices which compare them to what they are recording at runtime [15]. Such feature extraction techniques are used by handheld PCs to identify similar locations in an image database and display location-related information [10] or used in a simulated physical shopping mall environment by utilizing the Vuforia engine [9].

3 Design and Implementation

3.1 Background Technologies

For a better understanding of the applied computer vision concepts and technologies, a brief introduction and description regarding the required terminology is following:

Augmented Reality: An immersive human-machine-interaction experience is achieved without the need of additional hardware. By utilizing onboard camera and IMU sensors, the phone's video feed can be supplemented with additional augmented information such as labels, images, markers and other kinds of multimedia. A marker's position remains attached at the predefined location regardless of any device movement or environment change. All items attached to a surface are generally referred to as *Anchors* in AR terminology. In order to attach an Anchor to the scene, the area needs to be scanned using specific software that implements SLAM.

SLAM and Cloud Anchors: Local area identification and localization is achieved by extracting features of an image feed along with data from device IMU sensors. At first, the area around the device needs to be slowly and steadily scanned. While scanning, the SLAM algorithm parses the camera frame feed and extracts feature points from each frame. SLAM algorithms are optimized to focus on certain and dense segments of each image to achieve better data processing. Extracted features are combined with data from the IMU sensors to determine the exact distance, rotation and orientation of the recorded frames. Segments of the feed that have a confident amount of features offer the ability to attach Anchors to the scene, considering that the nearby features of an Anchor can be easily recognized once the device reaches that spot. Cloud Anchors functionality gets use of a SLAM output as a base to store Anchor locations for remote use. Goal of Cloud Anchors is the ability to preview Anchors that were placed by another device in the past. Hence, feature points in the range of an Anchor are captured and stored in a cloud database. By providing a camera feed from the same area and comparing the current extracted features with the database, the exact position of an Anchor can be precisely estimated. Limitation of the aforementioned capability is the bounded amount of Cloud Anchors that can be searched at the same time. ARCore Cloud Anchors implementation, which is used in the current work, allows up to 20 simultaneous Anchor scans. Needs to be mentioned, though, that once an Anchor is attached, it is removed from the scanning stack, allowing for an additional Anchor to be scanned.

3.2 Methodology

To address the requirements of developing an AR navigation system, a set of algorithms and techniques, aiming at achieving indoor localization, performing efficient path planning and visualizing the guidance system are designed and implemented.

Indoor Positioning and Key Anchors: A plausible observation arising from the Cloud Anchor functionality is the ability to achieve indoor positioning. If information about a location is related to an Anchor instance, the nearest Anchor identified by the device leads to the knowledge of the current position. Having multiple Anchors acting as reference points in a complex space, we can introduce a new term, Key Anchors. Such Anchors do not contain any visual information and are rather used to determine the device's position at the area.

Routing: Apart from identifying the device's position, Cloud Anchors can be used for a variety of other use cases. Our proposed system prompts the user to follow an on-screen visualized path by using Anchors as route checkpoints. Routing entities are categorized as: *ArPaths*, *ArRooms* and *ArRoutes*. These entities are referring to relations between Anchors and locations, offering a state-of-the-art solution to the AR routing problem. An *ArPath* entity contains a list of Anchors that lead from a starting point to a gateway point. The order of the list defines the flow of the navigation. A gateway point is a special Anchor which includes references to the next ArPaths that begin from there. The *ArRoom* entity corresponds to a room of a building and includes ArPaths along with a set of additional satellite Anchors. Finally, the *ArRoute* entity acts as a connecting pole between paths and indicates the final gateway of the route. Once a gateway is reached it is first checked if this is the final point. Otherwise, the first path of the ArRoute that is included in this gateway's next ArPaths is shown. This naive approach achieves a completely modular functionality which is tested under real scenarios showing successful results. Following the flow of this algorithm, a device can be navigated through different rooms, corridors and stories of the same building with the least required Cloud Anchors downloaded.

Navigation Elements Placement Algorithm: To overcome the possible long distance between two checkpoints, a series of helper Anchors is programmatically placed following our Navigation Elements Placement (NEP) algorithm. NEP locations are generated by

(a) subtracting the first Anchor's transformation vector from the second to get the angle
(b) getting the distance between these vectors
(c) programmatically attaching an Anchor following the line of the subtracted angle every 0.2 m, which is our interval until the distance is reached

3.3 System Overview

The proposed AR indoor navigation system ingrates the aforementioned algorithms, manages their parameters and offers a client application which is accessible by the end-users. The system consists of two main elements:

A. **Hybrid AR Platform**: A unified framework which includes a client platform and requires integration of a client library. Is responsible for handling AR related information and consists of three modules: *Creator Module, Administrator Module, Backend Service* and a *Query Engine.*
B. **Player Module**, a subsystem which can be integrated to any third-party mobile application.

The users, which have the client application installed into their mobile devices, are able to reach their selected destination guided by on-screen AR instructions, without the need of additional hardware interventions. AR components are configured to identify the specific area and initialize the routing algorithm. Configuration of the system's functionality is performed through limited access applications which are responsible for content creation and management.

3.4 Implementation

Figure 1 highlights the architecture of the proposed system. All applications follow the object oriented programming design principles and are built using Flutter, a cross platform development environment. For AR services, *ARCore* platform and its *Cloud Anchors* environment is selected due to its ability of retrieving and sharing feature maps between both Android and iOS, resulting, thus, in seamless integration and interoperability.

The key advantage of the *Hybrid AR Platform* approach is that AR operations are separated from client applications, and are integrated into them through a software library.

The platform's *Creator module* is an application that hosts Anchors to the cloud and supplementary manages other system aspects and parameters. Hosting functionality is performed by initializing an AR session which allows Anchor placement at the front scene. Anchors are uploaded to the Cloud and their references along with other metadata are stored in the database. Additionally,

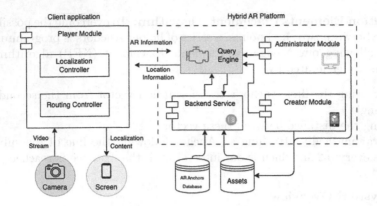

Fig. 1. System Architecture

this module modifies an Anchor's mesh position, location and orientation. An extended version of the *Creator Module*, without AR capabilities but with the ability to upload 3D model files and better manage the related content, is the *Administrator module*. This web application creates and manages instances of routing entities, modifies other administrative parameters that affect the workflow of the Query Engine and globally performs changes to all system configuration. A backend in AR applications was introduced to monitor physical activity via AR exergames [12]. The platform's *Backend service* is an extension of the aforementioned implementation, managing the storage of information regarding Anchors, Routes, Paths, Rooms and the assets related to them. The *Query Engine* acts as the interface of the platform. It is retrieving AR information and producing Localization material which is then transmitted to the *Player Module*.

The *Player module* can be integrated into any third-party application. The integrated *Localization Controller* searches for nearby Key Anchors and identifies the user's current position by communicating with the platform's *Query Engine*. At the same time, the *Routing Controller* interprets the routing algorithm starting from the current location towards the destination. Each time the *Routing Controller* retrieves new Anchors, they are transported to the AR screen in order to be visualized. In addition, this controller indicates that a user has either reached at a gateway or at a destination by returning this information to the *Routing Controller*.

4   Results

4.1   System in Practice

All previously demonstrated technologies, concepts and algorithms have been implemented in a state-of-the-art application which is not only a proof-of-concept prototype, but an end-user product. "UNIPI: AR Experience" application is available to download for both Android and iOS[1] and the innovative AR integration is in the initial release phase at the university. When opening the app, users can select their destination which lies under a 2-level categorization. The first level refers to the building where the navigation will take place and the second to the type of destination.

Currently there are two buildings supported, "Central" and "Venentokleio", and for each building two types of routes, "Faculty" and "Classrooms" which refer to directions towards faculty offices and classrooms respectively. An additional route type called "Erasmus" is available only in "Central" building providing directions to Erasmus-related rooms. Users have to tap the Category and then the desired destination.

Fig. 2. System in practice

Starting point can either be selected via the next screen's list, or the user is able to scan the area in front, in order for the Key Anchor system to identify his current location. After a while, arrows are displayed in the user's screen showing the direction he has to follow, as demonstrated in Fig. 2. The case of a floor difference between the route's endpoints is also covered by navigating the user to either the elevator or the stairs, and then indicate to them the next floor via on-screen dialog. While in the navigation phase, additional AR related content containing localized information may be displayed on the user's AR screen.

4.2   Experimentation

Most important aspect of such an application is the time required for a device to first localize itself and then correctly display the desired checkpoints at their precise locations. We concluded that two metrics are important and attempted to be optimized: duration of first Anchor identification and Anchor displacement error. Two Anchor hosting methods were used, Method 1: hosting each Anchor

---

[1] https://unipi-ar-experience.web.app/.

in an individual AR session and Method 2: hosting all Anchors in the same session. For each test we compared the results to the Anchor hosting method that was used, using two devices: an iPhone SE 2020 and a Huawei H20 Pro. Table 1 demonstrates results of the metrics and is clearly indicated why we finally selected Method 2 for the route recording process. In a single AR session, the surrounding feature points are more than one time visited and are more precisely recorded, thus resulting in better SLAM.

Table 1. Session hosting

Device	Duration (s)	Displacement (cm)	Hosting session
iPhone SE 2020	4.32	22.6	Individual
Huawei H20 Pro	6.01	30.1	Individual
iPhone SE 2020	2.99	12.4	Same
Huawei H20 Pro	4.24	21.9	Same

Additionally, 100 tests were performed to find the percentage of successful navigations for the "Erasmus Office" route using the iPhone SE 2020 device.

Table 2. Success rate per missed Anchors

Anchors missed	Tests performed	Destination reached
0	58	100% (58)
1	24	83.3% (20)
2	8	25% (6)
3	6	50% (1)
4+	4	0% (0)

Table 2 indicates the number of successful tests compared to their missing Anchors. 58% of the tests had no missing Anchors while tests with one, two or even three Anchors still showed a successful navigation, resulting in the final 85% of successful navigations. Routing algorithm is developed in such a way that if a checkpoint is not recognized, but the next one is, navigation will proceed to the next checkpoint overcoming the current.

5   Discussion

A significant limitation of our system is the requirement of ARCore compatible devices[2] Concerning the efficiency of the SLAM, if a corridor or place does

---

[2] ARCore compatible devices: https://developers.google.com/ar/devices.

not contain any special characteristic rather than plain walls or is filled with people, localization will take longer to process. Needs to be noted, though, that the aforementioned limitations are directly bound to the quality of the Anchor placement procedure.

Low GPS/Cellular coverage or the lack of precision in small displacements is a deterrent factor of using these technologies while installation of transmitters (sensors) can be expensive and slow down the integration of such a system. Although existing studies try to follow a SLAM oriented direction, there are many occurring limitations, obstacles and restrictions this work is overcoming. Other works are either proof-of-concept prototypes with limited functionality, have no user-tester friendly experience and do not meet the hardware independence standards. The between-checkpoint-distancing problem, which occurred not only in our development process, but also indicated as an issue in other published works, is finally solved using our NEP algorithm. Moreover, instead of using Dijkstra or other shortest path algorithms, the proposed system follows a multi-floor-centric model with support for all use cases a visitor will create. Our state-of-the-art routing algorithm introducing the "room to gateway" model ensures that the correct path will be presented while optimizing the use of AR resources to the least required.

6 Conclusion

Advancements in Computer Vision technologies along with the evolution of microprocessors, sensors and cameras form a rich set of assets which facilitate the implementation of innovative solutions for indoor localization and navigation. The proposed solution not only improves and expands the AR Anchor "checkpoint" navigation approach, but also introduces a new routing algorithm, offers interoperability and platform independence.

Future extensions of this work may include a wider system usage monitoring. Moreover, other cross platform AR frameworks can be considered (e.g. Unity AR Foundation) and compared with the current implementation. SLAM's environmental understanding provides indication of a device's deviation from a route path. For people with special needs and particularly the visually impaired, a voice command module indicating directions and deviations is a possible future proposal. AR navigation systems can be experimented in other scenarios with limited signal coverage and short distances between targets (e.g. in a museum or hospital). Considering the route creation procedure, an extension of the system is expected to further automate this process, and possibly eliminate completely the need of an experienced system administrator, either by integrating this functionality to an AI tool which will be integrated into the Creator Module.

The case of "UNIPI: AR Experience" highlights the development process of a complete functional system with a *Hybrid AR Platform* and client application, able to apply in real conditions providing satisfactory results while maintaining the cost and interventions at the lowest level.

Acknowledgements. This work has been partly supported by the University of Piraeus Research Center.

References

1. Arena, F., Collotta, M., Pau, G., Termine, F.: An overview of augmented reality. Computers **11**(2), 28 (2022)
2. Chi, H.L., Kang, S.C., Wang, X.: Research trends and opportunities of augmented reality applications in architecture, engineering, and construction. Autom. Constr. **33**, 116–122 (2013)
3. Davidson, P., Piché, R.: A survey of selected indoor positioning methods for smartphones. IEEE Commun. Surv. Tutorials **19**(2), 1347–1370 (2016)
4. Durrant-Whyte, H., Bailey, T.: Simultaneous localization and mapping: Part I. IEEE Robot. Autom. Mag. **13**(2), 99–110 (2006)
5. Gozick, B., Subbu, K.P., Dantu, R., Maeshiro, T.: Magnetic maps for indoor navigation. IEEE Trans. Instrum. Meas. **60**(12), 3883–3891 (2011). https://doi.org/10.1109/TIM.2011.2147690
6. Han, D., Jung, S., Lee, M., Yoon, G.: Building a practical Wi-Fi-based indoor navigation system. IEEE Pervasive Comput. **13**(2), 72–79 (2014)
7. Ishikawa, T., Fujiwara, H., Imai, O., Okabe, A.: Wayfinding with a GPS-based mobile navigation system: a comparison with maps and direct experience. J. Environ. Psychol. **28**(1), 74–82 (2008)
8. Jiang, J.R., Subakti, H.: An indoor location-based augmented reality framework. Sensors **23**(3), 1370 (2023)
9. Kasprzak, S., Komninos, A., Barrie, P.: Feature-based indoor navigation using augmented reality. In: 2013 9th International Conference on Intelligent Environments, pp. 100–107 (2013). https://doi.org/10.1109/IE.2013.51
10. Kim, J., Jun, H.: Vision-based location positioning using augmented reality for indoor navigation. IEEE Trans. Consum. Electron. **54**(3), 954–962 (2008). https://doi.org/10.1109/TCE.2008.4637573
11. Koch, C., Neges, M., König, M., Abramovici, M.: Natural markers for augmented reality-based indoor navigation and facility maintenance. Autom. Constr. **48**, 18–30 (2014)
12. Koulouris, D., Menychtas, A., Maglogiannis, I.: An IoT-enabled platform for the assessment of physical and mental activities utilizing augmented reality exergaming. Sensors **22**(9), 3181 (2022)
13. Koulouris, D., Pardos, A., Gallos, P., Menychtas, A., Maglogiannis, I.: Integrating AR and IoT services into mHealth applications for promoting wellbeing. In: 2022 18th International Conference on Wireless and Mobile Computing, Networking and Communications (WiMob), pp. 148–153. IEEE (2022)
14. Lampropoulos, G., Keramopoulos, E., Diamantaras, K., Evangelidis, G.: Augmented reality and gamification in education: a systematic literature review of research, applications, and empirical studies. Appl. Sci. **12**(13), 6809 (2022)
15. Lanham, M.: Learn ARCore-Fundamentals of Google ARCore: Learn to Build Augmented Reality Apps for Android, Unity, and the Web with Google ARCore 1.0. Packt Publishing Ltd., Birmingham (2018)
16. del Peral-Rosado, J.A., Raulefs, R., López-Salcedo, J.A., Seco-Granados, G.: Survey of cellular mobile radio localization methods: from 1G to 5G. IEEE Commun. Surv. Tutorials **20**(2), 1124–1148 (2017)

17. Reitmayr, G., et al.: Simultaneous localization and mapping for augmented reality. In: 2010 International Symposium on Ubiquitous Virtual Reality, pp. 5–8 (2010). https://doi.org/10.1109/ISUVR.2010.12

18. Satan, A.: Bluetooth-based indoor navigation mobile system. In: 2018 19th International Carpathian Control Conference (ICCC), pp. 332–337. IEEE (2018)

19. Schuldt, C., Shoushtari, H., Hellweg, N., Sternberg, H.: L5IN: overview of an indoor navigation pilot project. Remote Sens. **13**(4), 624 (2021)

20. Somlyai, L., Vámossy, Z.: ISVD-based advanced simultaneous localization and mapping (SLAM) algorithm for mobile robots. Machines **10**(7), 519 (2022)

21. Yi, B., Sun, R., Long, L., Song, Y., Zhang, Y.: From coarse to fine: an augmented reality-based dynamic inspection method for visualized railway routing of freight cars. Meas. Sci. Technol. **33**(5), 055013 (2022)

22. Zhang, H., et al.: Visual indoor navigation using mobile augmented reality. In: Magnenat-Thalmann, N., et al. (eds.) Advances in Computer Graphics: 39th Computer Graphics International Conference, CGI 2022, Virtual Event, 12–16 September 2022, Proceedings, pp. 145–156. Springer, Cham (2023). https://doi.org/10.1007/978-3-031-23473-6_12

A Benchmark and Investigation of Deep-Learning-Based Techniques for Detecting Natural Disasters in Aerial Images

Demetris Shianios(✉), Christos Kyrkou, and Panayiotis S. Kolios

KIOS Research and Innovation Center of Excellence, University of Cyprus, Nicosia,
Cyprus
{shianios.demetris,kyrkou.christos,kolios.panayiotis}@ucy.ac.cy
https://www.kios.ucy.ac.cy/

Abstract. Rapid emergency response and early detection of hazards
caused by natural disasters are critical to preserving the lives of those
in danger. Deep learning can aid emergency response authorities by
automating UAV-based real-time disaster recognition. In this work, we
provide an extended dataset for aerial disaster recognition and present
a comprehensive investigation of popular Convolutional Neural Network
models using transfer learning. In addition, we propose a new lightweight
model, referred to as *DiRecNet*, that provides the best trade-off between
accuracy and inference speed. We introduce a tunable metric that combines speed and accuracy to choose the best model based on application
requirements. Lastly, we used the Grad-CAM explainability algorithm to
investigate which models focus on human-aligned features. The experimental results show that the proposed model achieves a weighted F1-
Score of 96.15% on four classes in the test set. When utilizing metrics
that consider both inference time and accuracy, our model surpasses
other pre-trained CNNs, offering a more efficient and precise solution for
disaster recognition. This research provides a foundation for developing
more specialized models within the computer vision community.

Keywords: Natural Disasters Recognition · Image Classification ·
UAV (Unmanned Aerial Vehicle) · Deep Learning · Benchmark ·
Grad-CAM

1 Introduction

Natural disasters have been on the rise worldwide in recent years, with ecological
and socioeconomic consequences. According to the United Nations Office for
Disaster Risk Reduction, there were 7,348 disaster incidents between 2000 and
2019, resulting in 1,23 million deaths and US $3 trillion in economic losses [22].
The World Meteorological Organization, claims that over the last 50 years, a

© The Author(s), under exclusive license to Springer Nature Switzerland AG 2023
N. Tsapatsoulis et al. (Eds.): CAIP 2023, LNCS 14185, pp. 244–254, 2023.
https://doi.org/10.1007/978-3-031-44240-7_24

disaster related to weather, climate, or water hazard has occurred every day, killing 115 people and inflicting US $202 million in losses [4].

Unmanned Aerial Vehicles (UAVs) such as drones have emerged as effective tools for the early identification of these disasters due to their low cost, wide coverage area, and low risk to personnel. However, on-board processing presents its own set of issues, due to limited computational resources and low-power limits imposed by UAVs. As a result, the operational performance of the underlying computer vision algorithm is critical for autonomous UAVs to detect disasters in real-time. With the combination of Deep Learning, drones can be used for disaster classification, which can quickly and accurately identify affected areas, assess damage severity, and prioritize response efforts.

One crucial aspect of the successful implementation of deep learning models is the availability of a sufficient amount of dataset, which plays a significant role in their overall performance. However, gathering data, in the event of an emergency, is time-consuming and expensive, as it frequently involves human data processing and expert evaluation. The potential for evaluating deep learning models in such situations is constrained by the dearth of comprehensive datasets related to natural disasters. Furthermore, while there has been considerable research on algorithms for natural disaster detection in aerial images, explainable AI has not been extensively investigated for this domain in the existing literature. By providing an explainable visual representation of the image regions on which the model is focusing, image explainability algorithms can help emergency responders quickly identify the location and extent of a natural disaster, allowing them to respond more effectively and efficiently.

This work addresses these gaps by extending aerial image datasets for disaster recognition, including four classes; normal, earthquakes, floods, and wildfires encompassing a total of 16,723 images. We propose the DiRecNet CNN model and compared it to widely known pre trained models such as EfficientNet-B0 [21], MobileNet-V2 [17] ResNet50 [8], VGG16 [19], DenseNet121 [9], Inception-ResNetV2 [20] NASNetMobile [23] and Xception [5] using transfer learning. The proposed CNN achieved a weighted F1-score of 96.15% in the test set and outperformed other pre-trained CNNs when considering inference time. In our study, we also conducted experiments on the explainability of the image using Gradient-weighted Class Activation (Grad-Cam) technique, with the objective of improving the explainability of the model. Using Grad-CAM, we better understood common failures or errors by emphasizing the significant areas of an image that contribute to a certain prediction. Overall, CNN-based deep learning models exhibit strong potential for real-time natural disaster detection.

2   Background and Related Work

Several innovative solutions have been developed for visual disaster recognition in recent years, which can be crucial for rapid response operations. Gadhavi et al. [7] proposed a model that uses transfer learning to recognize natural disasters using a video dataset. Aamir et al. [1] developed a binary model to detect the existence of a disaster and a classification model to identify different types of disasters. Agrawal and Meleet [2] fine-tuned the ResNet-50 model for disaster recognition and tested it on real-time and pre-recorded videos. Alam et al. [3] used transfer learning with various pre-trained CNN models to classify the MEDIC dataset. Li et al. [14] used YOLOv3 for detection and various neural networks, including VGG, ResNet, and MobileNet, for classification on the LADI dataset [15].

The current state-of-the-art methods for disaster detection typically focus on identifying a single type of disaster. Some recent techniques aim for multi-class disaster detection, but their models are too large and have too many parameters for effective execution on unmanned aerial vehicles (UAVs) onboard hardware. Therefore, developing custom models that are tailored to the specific constraints and requirements of embedded systems on drones is crucial to achieving efficient and effective disaster recognition. It should be noted that most existing models may not incorporate explainable AI techniques, which can limit their usefulness in providing valuable insights to first responders in the field.

Previous studies have suffered from a lack of diversity in their datasets, some containing limited images or not aligning well with UAV viewpoints. Our work aims to address these limitations and establish a benchmark. Moreover, the lack of aerial perspective images in current datasets hinders natural disaster recognition. Some datasets focus exclusively on a single type of disaster, failing to represent the full spectrum of real-world scenarios. Geographic or temporal bias can further compromise representativeness, as certain datasets can draw from a restricted range of locations or events. Our proposed methodology aims to mitigate the limitations of biased datasets by incorporating diverse aerial imagery and promoting transparency in the decision-making process of our models. Furthermore, our model is optimized for deployment in embedded systems, such as drones, and achieves a favourable balance between speed and accuracy.

3 Proposed Approach

3.1 Dataset for Disaster Recognition Using UAVs

Our aim was to create a benchmark for aerial natural disaster recognition suitable for UAV applications. To do so we start initially from the AIDER database [12,13] which had a similar purpose but a smaller number of images per disaster class which can result in overfitting, and poor generalization. In addition to these samples, we extracted images as frames of videos downloaded from YouTube searched using queries like "aerial" + "disaster", "flood", "collapsed building".

The data collection process involved scanning images to match the visual perspective of the UAV, and filtering out any irrelevant images, such as those that were blurred or not related to the disaster. The mean resolution ($width \times height$) for each class is; earthquake 667×1018, flood 595×884, normal 553×395, wildfire 1557×834. Overall, the images collected belong to commonly occurring natural disasters, earthquakes/collapsed buildings, floods, and wildfire/fire with an additional class, the normal case. Normal images do not reflect events, disasters, or any other aspects that could be related to catastrophic events. Figure 1

Fig. 1. Overview of aerial images from the Database.

Table 1. Proportion of images in each class within the train, validation, and test set.

	Earthquakes	Floods	Wildfire/Fire	Normal	Total
Train	1927	4063	3509	3900	13399
Validation	239	505	439	487	1670
Test	239	502	436	477	1654
Total	2405	5070	4384	4864	**16723**

shows samples from the dataset, while the summary of the data is explained in the Table 1. As a result, our contribution compared to the state-of-the-art is a newer, larger dataset containing a set of images of natural disasters that are also suitable for use in UAV applications for aerial disaster recognition.

3.2 Disaster Recognition Network Architecture

To enhance the operation of a UAV in emergency response, it is necessary to have lightweight algorithms that provide a good trade off of complexity and accuracy. To this end and to motivate more work towards this area, we proposed the design of a custom CNN designed from scratch to be efficient by tailoring the use of convolutional layers and kernel sizes.

The custom CNN called *DiRecNet* consists of four main blocks, making it feasible for the model to learn hierarchical feature representations without reducing the feature map resolution too much. On the first two blocks, we use normal convolutional layers to extract richer low level features, while on the last two blocks we utilized separable convolutions to account for the fact that the channel size increases and has more efficient computations with a reduced number of operations and parameters.

In more detail, the model first passes the scaled images onto two consecutive normal convolutional layers. The former with a kernel size of 7×7 pixels and 16 filters, while the latter with 5×5 pixels and 16 filters. This follows modern network trends that apply larger kernels [16]. The smaller channel number is used to offset the larger kernel size. Batch normalization is applied just after these convolutions, with a max-pooling operation of stride 2×2 after that. The data points are then passed to the next block of two convolutional layers with kernel size of 3×3. The first convolution involves 32 filters, while the second has 64 convolution filters. Again, batch normalization is applied before the next max pooling layer. The third block involves two separable convolutions with 128 and 256 filters respectively and 3 × 3 size, followed by a batch normalization layer. A max-pooling operation is also applied with a pool size of 2 × 2. The last block is designed with two identical separable convolutions of the 512 filter and the size 3 × 3. Finally, a global average pooling layer is applied to flatten the features. These are then passed to a fully connected layer of 1024 neurons, before a dropout of 0.7. Another fully connected layer is applied with 512 neurons with a dropout of 0.5. The last layer of the model is a fully connected layer of size 4 as the number of classes. An overview of the model is depicted in Fig. 2.

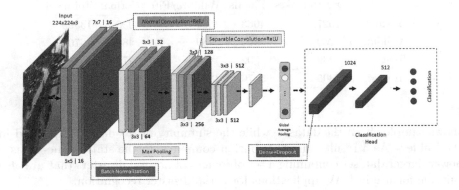

Fig. 2. Proposed Convolutional Neural Network Architecture.

3.3   Baseline Designs

To provide a useful benchmark for the constructed dataset, we compare the performance of various CNN models. We use transfer learning approach to modify and fine-tune CNNs trained on the ImageNet large scale dataset [11] to perform image disaster recognition. The transfer learning CNN models investigated in this work are: EfficientNet-B0 [21], MobileNet-V2 [17], ResNet-50 [8], VGG-16 [19], DenseNet-121 [9], InceptionResNet-V2 [20], NASNetMobile [23] and Xception [5]. These models capture a wide range of architectural design choices.

During the experiments, we freeze some layers of the pre-trained models and add some others to be trained. Specifically, in our experiments, we remove the last fully connected (FC) layer of each model and Global Average Pooling (GAP) was attached. On top of that, we added three fully connected layers with two dropouts in between. In general, the classification head architecture attached to the transfer learning models is the same as in the proposed model. For each pre-trained model, a pre-processing function was implemented using the TensorFlow library to standardize the input images based on the ImageNet dataset [6].

3.4   Data Pre-processing and Training Process

The images in our data collection were scaled to $224 \times 224 \times 3$ and standardized for DiRecNet therefore to change the distribution to have a mean of zero and a standard deviation of one. Random augmentations were applied to expand the diversity of the dataset and combat overfitting. Specifically, we applied rotation, zoom, horizontal shift, vertical shift, horizontal flip, and shear. We experimented with different color spaces, but chose RGB for the final experiments. We used slightly different training regimes for the pre-trained models and the DiRecNet model. The pre-trained models were frozen until the feature extraction layer, before attaching the global average pooling layer and fully connected layers. This implies that the initial layer weights are fixed and cannot be changed so as to preserve learned features. Then they were fine-tuned for 40 epochs with a learning rate of $1e-3$ and weight initialization based on ImageNet ILSVRC Challenge [11]. On the contrary, the proposed DiRecNet was trained from scratch for 300 epochs, with a reduced learning rate of $1e-4$. The batch size was set to 32, and Adam optimizer was selected for both DiRecNet and pre-trained models.

Table 2. Performance evaluations for disaster predictions.

Models	PARAMS (M)	Weighted F1 (%)	FPS (1/s)	Score 1 Biased FPS	Score 1 Biased F1	Score 1 Balanced	Score 2
EfficientNet-B0 [21]	5.89	95.82	11.72	0.74	0.82	0.78	819.64
MobileNet-V2 [17]	4.10	93.77	**15.37**	**0.90**	0.77	0.84	259.57
ResNet50 [8]	26.21	**96.98**	6.87	0.47	0.77	0.62	1073.61
VGG16 [19]	15.77	94.50	5.22	0.00	0.55	0.42	146.22
DenseNet101 [9]	8.61	95.07	7.46	0.45	0.65	0.55	310.21
InceptionResNet [20]	54.43	88.09	5.48	0.12	0.11	0.11	1.81
NASNetMobile [23]	5.88	90.65	12.96	0.66	0.49	0.57	25.18
Xception [5]	23.49	92.44	5.48	0.25	0.42	0.33	36.81
DiRecNet (Proposed)	**1.53**	96.15	14.05	0.89	**0.91**	**0.90**	**1235.12**

3.5   Explainability Through Grad-CAM

Understanding how a deep learning model works and why it predicts a specific classification outcome is highly important for critical applications such as emergency management. Consequently, we move beyond the "black box" of CNN predictions and acquire a deeper understanding of how these models arrive at their decisions. This was achieved through experimentation with an explainable AI technique, known as Gradient-weighted Class Activation Mapping (Grad-CAM) [18]. The algorithm creates a coarse localization map that highlights key areas in the image for class prediction, by using the gradients of each target as they flow into the final convolutional layer. In this way, we can identify classes that are more challenging for the different models and understand whether additional context is needed and whether current state-of-the-art methods are suitable for the application of disaster recognition.

4   Experimental Evaluation and Results

4.1   Configuration and Evaluation Metrics

The experiments were carried out on the Linux operating system using the Tesla V100 Graphics Processor Unit, with 64 GB RAM and CUDA version 10.2. We use TensorFlow[1] 2.4.1 as the deep learning framework along with Python [2] version 3.8.0. To evaluate the performance of the models, we investigated two key performance indicators. These are the weighted F1 score and frames per second (FPS). This is particularly important because both performance and speed are crucial to detect natural disasters in real-time.

We then formulated a parametrizable score function as shown in Eq. 1 in a way to allow for choosing the trade-off between accuracy and speed. By setting the λ value, we can identify the model that performs best for a particular setting. In this work, we have chosen λ to be 0.7 to bias towards more accurate models, and 0.3 to bias towards speed. Additionally, to provide a more extensive evaluation we benchmark the models using a modified version of the scoring formula proposed in [10] for evaluating the combined effect of speed and accuracy as shown in Eq. 2, where we set the normalizing constant C to $1e27$.

$$\text{Score1} = \lambda \times F1_{\text{norm}} + (1 - \lambda) \times FPS_{\text{norm}} \tag{1}$$

$$\text{Score2} = \frac{2^{\text{F1}} \times \text{FPS}}{C} \tag{2}$$

However, prior to this, since the values of FPS and F1 have different ranges, we normalize them across all models by using the formula in Eq. 3, where values in x are squeezed into the range $[a, b]$ where a was set to 0.1 and b at 1, thus making the variables comparable to each other.

$$x_{norm} = (b - a)\frac{x - min(x)}{max(x) - min(x)} + a \tag{3}$$

---

[1] http://www.tensorflow.org.
[2] http://www.python.org.

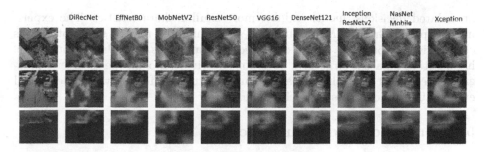

Fig. 3. Results of Grad-Cam algorithm for the different models. The heat-maps show that the classification's importance is dominated by the pixels associated with the disastrous occurrence.

4.2   Disaster Classification Evaluation

The general evaluation of the disaster classification performance of the models is shown in Table 2. In summary, the models' weighted F1-Score ranges between 88% and 97%. ResNet-50 demonstrates optimal performance in terms of accuracy, while MobileNet-V2 exhibits the highest FPS, rendering it appropriate for processing multiple streams concurrently. By evaluating the performance of the models using a balanced approach that considers both speed and accuracy ($\lambda = 0.5$) according to the metric score in Eq. 1, our proposed model surpasses other models, achieving a score of 0.9, with MobileNet-V2 ranking second at 0.84. When biasing for FPS or F1, the proposed model remains the first or a very close second. Specifically, when prioritizing FPS ($\lambda = 0.3$), MobileNet-V2 achieves a score of 0.9, while the proposed model reaches 0.89. Conversely, when emphasizing F1, the proposed model leads with a score of 0.91, followed by EfficientNET-B0 at 0.82. Additionally, with respect to the metric presented in Eq. 2, the proposed model demonstrates superior performance compared to other methods. The proposed model achieves an overall score of 1235.12, while the second-best performing model, ResNet50, achieves a score of 1073.61. This shows that the heterogeneous design of mixing normal and separable convolutions provides a well-balanced solution with fewer parameters than other models.

4.3   Gram-CAM Evaluation

We interpret the decision of each model using Grad-CAM. In Fig. 3, all models predict the right class, and the heat-map produced by Grad-Cam is displayed. First, comparing the pre-trained models, we observe that the majority create a coarse grain heat map except for the VGG model. In contrast, while the proposed model correctly predicts the disaster type, it does so with a much sparser heat map. For example, in the collapsed building image, the region focuses more on the rubble rather than the building structure, while in the flood image, the model seems to distinguish the flood class based on the presence of surrounding buildings. In most pre-trained models, larger regions are emphasized, but for fire-related decisions, models exhibit more similar characteristics. The experiment exposed Grad-CAM's limitations, as highlighted regions may not always clarify disaster presence, like in collapsed building cases. In collapsed buildings, highlighting adjacent structures does not effectively explain the disaster's presence. We expect that this research can drive more efforts toward specialized explainability techniques for such applications.

5 Conclusion and Future Work

In this work, we presented a new larger dataset, offering 16,723 images, for aerial image recognition of disasters. We have explored the direct application of various existing CNN pre-trained models on this dataset to provide an initial benchmark. More importantly, we have shown that a heterogeneous CNN with mixed normal and separable convolutions can provide adequate trade-off between accuracy and speed and can thus be an optimal choice for these kinds of applications. Through this process, we have formulated a tunable metric to evaluate models. Based on the various scoring schemes, the proposed model still outperforms traditional pre-trained CNNs. Lastly, the gradient-weighted class activation mapping (Grad-CAM) method was used to visualize the input regions crucial for class predictions, demonstrating that different models provide a varying degree of granularity in explanations.

The experimental findings indicate that we were able to obtain classification outcomes that offered promising results for real-time disaster recognition from aerial images. Those initial results are encouraging, but there are still some challenges. Further, improvements and further investigation on more lightweight models are possible based on the experiments in this paper. Furthermore, an approach for multi-task scenarios where classification is combined with segmentation to provide more localized and precise identification of disasters is desired. Finally, it is worth investigating non-supervised approaches, since data for emergency management applications are scarce and difficult to annotate.

Acknowledgements. This work is supported by the European Union Civil Protection Call for proposals UCPM-2022-KN grant agreement No 101101704 (COLLARIS Network). The work is partially supported by the European Union's Horizon 2020 research and innovation program under grant agreement No 739551 (KIOS CoE - TEAMING) and from the Republic of Cyprus through the Deputy Ministry of Research, Innovation and Digital Policy.

References

1. Aamir, M., et al.: Natural disasters intensity analysis and classification based on multispectral images using multi-layered deep convolutional neural network. Sensors **21**(8), 2648 (2021)
2. Agrawal, T., Meleet, M., et al.: Classification of natural disaster using satellite & drone images with CNN using transfer learning. In: 2021 International Conference on Innovative Computing, Intelligent Communication and Smart Electrical Systems (ICSES), pp. 1–5. IEEE (2021)

3. Alam, F., et al.: MEDIC: a multi-task learning dataset for disaster image classification. arXiv preprint arXiv:2108.12828 (2021)
4. Association, W.M., et al.: WMO Atlas of mortality and economic losses from weather, climate and water extremes (1970–2019). Technical report (2021)
5. Chollet, F.: Xception: deep learning with depthwise separable convolutions. In: Proceedings of the IEEE Conference on Computer Vision and Pattern Recognition, pp. 1251–1258 (2017)
6. Deng, J., Dong, W., Socher, R., Li, L.J., Li, K., Fei-Fei, L.: ImageNet: a large-scale hierarchical image database. In: 2009 IEEE Conference on Computer Vision and Pattern Recognition, pp. 248–255. IEEE (2009)
7. Gadhavi, V.B., Degadwala, S., Vyas, D.: Transfer learning approach for recognizing natural disasters video. In: 2022 Second International Conference on Artificial Intelligence and Smart Energy (ICAIS), pp. 793–798. IEEE (2022)
8. He, K., Zhang, X., Ren, S., Sun, J.: Deep residual learning for image recognition. In: Proceedings of the IEEE Conference on Computer Vision and Pattern Recognition, pp. 770–778 (2016)
9. Huang, G., Liu, Z., Van Der Maaten, L., Weinberger, K.Q.: Densely connected convolutional networks. In: Proceedings of the IEEE Conference on Computer Vision and Pattern Recognition, pp. 4700–4708 (2017)
10. Ignatov, A., Malivenko, G., Timofte, R.: Fast and accurate quantized camera scene detection on smartphones, mobile AI 2021 challenge: Report. In: Proceedings of the IEEE/CVF Conference on Computer Vision and Pattern Recognition, pp. 2558–2568 (2021)
11. Krizhevsky, A., Sutskever, I., Hinton, G.E.: ImageNet classification with deep convolutional neural networks. Commun. ACM 60(6), 84–90 (2017)
12. Kyrkou, C., Theocharides, T.: Deep-learning-based aerial image classification for emergency response applications using unmanned aerial vehicles. In: 2019 IEEE/CVF Conference on Computer Vision and Pattern Recognition Workshops (CVPRW), pp. 517–525 (2019). https://doi.org/10.1109/CVPRW.2019.00077
13. Kyrkou, C., Theocharides, T.: EmergencyNet: efficient aerial image classification for drone-based emergency monitoring using atrous convolutional feature fusion. IEEE J. Sel. Topics Appl. Earth Observ. Remote Sens. 13, 1687–1699 (2020). https://doi.org/10.1109/JSTARS.2020.2969809
14. Li, Y., Wang, H., Sun, S., Buckles, B.: Integrating multiple deep learning models to classify disaster scene videos (2020)
15. Liu, J., Strohschein, D., Samsi, S., Weinert, A.: Large scale organization and inference of an imagery dataset for public safety. In: 2019 IEEE High Performance Extreme Computing Conference (HPEC), pp. 1–6, September 2019. https://doi.org/10.1109/HPEC.2019.8916437
16. Liu, Z., Mao, H., Wu, C.Y., Feichtenhofer, C., Darrell, T., Xie, S.: A ConvNet for the 2020s. In: Proceedings of the IEEE/CVF Conference on Computer Vision and Pattern Recognition (CVPR), pp. 11976–11986, June 2022
17. Sandler, M., Howard, A., Zhu, M., Zhmoginov, A., Chen, L.C.: MobileNetV2: inverted residuals and linear bottlenecks. In: Proceedings of the IEEE Conference on Computer Vision and Pattern Recognition, pp. 4510–4520 (2018)
18. Selvaraju, R.R., Cogswell, M., Das, A., Vedantam, R., Parikh, D., Batra, D.: Grad-CAM: visual explanations from deep networks via gradient-based localization. In: Proceedings of the IEEE International Conference on Computer Vision, pp. 618–626 (2017)
19. Simonyan, K., Zisserman, A.: Very deep convolutional networks for large-scale image recognition. arXiv preprint arXiv:1409.1556 (2014)

20. Szegedy, C., Ioffe, S., Vanhoucke, V., Alemi, A.A.: Inception-v4, inception-ResNet and the impact of residual connections on learning. In: Thirty-First AAAI Conference on Artificial Intelligence (2017)
21. Tan, M., Le, Q.: EfficientNet: rethinking model scaling for convolutional neural networks. In: International Conference on Machine Learning, pp. 6105–6114. PMLR (2019)
22. Yaghmaei, N.: Human Cost of Disasters: An Overview of the Last 20 Years, 2000–2019. UN Office for Disaster Risk Reduction (2020)
23. Zoph, B., Vasudevan, V., Shlens, J., Le, Q.V.: Learning transferable architectures for scalable image recognition. In: Proceedings of the IEEE Conference on Computer Vision and Pattern Recognition, pp. 8697–8710 (2018)

Perceptual Light Field Image Coding with CTU Level Bit Allocation

Panqi Jin[1], Gangyi Jiang[1(✉)], Yeyao Chen[1], Zhidi Jiang[2], and Mei Yu[1]

[1] Faculty of Information Science and Engineering, Ningbo University, Ningbo, China
jiangganyi@126.com
[2] College of Science and Technology, Ningbo University, Ningbo, China

Abstract. Light field imaging simultaneously records the position and direction information of light in scene, as one of the important techniques for digital media. The amount of light field image (LFI) data is huge, it needs to be effectively compressed. In this paper, a perceptual LFI coding method with coding tree unit (CTU) level bit allocation strategy is proposed. To remove angular redundancy, a hybrid coding framework with joint deep learning reconstruction networks is constructed. At the encoder side, only four corner sub-aperture images (SAIs) are compressed with new CTU level bit allocation, a complete SAIs array is reconstructed by a LFI angular super-resolution network at the decoder side. To remove perceptual redundancy, we design a CTU level bit allocation strategy with the assumption of perceptual consistency, considering the characteristics of the human visual system in the bit allocation process. Experimental results show that for the proposed method with the designed CTU level bit allocation strategy, an average BD-BR savings of 13.676% in Y-PPSNR metric and 2.045% in VSI metric can be achieved. Compared with the high efficiency video coding (HEVC) intra coding model, the proposed method can achieve an average BD-BR savings of over 90%.

Keywords. Light Field Image · Perceptual Coding · Light Field Reconstruction

1 Introduction

Light field imaging can simultaneously record the intensity and direction information of light in a scene [1]. Light field images (LFIs) have many applications, such as refocusing [2], 3D reconstruction [3], and multi view display [4]. But the rich scene information makes the data volume of LFIs much larger than 2D images of the same resolution. Therefore, efficient compression of LFI is crucial for its applications.

Generally, LFI compression methods can be mainly divided into the traditional encoder based approach and the view synthesis based approach. The former directly uses or improves existing encoders to compress LFIs, for example, treating LFI's sub-aperture images (SAIs) as pseudo video sequence (PVS), and compressing the PVS with video encoders [5]. LFI's spatial and angular redundancies are removed through intra and inter prediction of the video encoder. Monteiro et al. [6] improved high efficiency video coding (HEVC) and used a prediction method combining local linear embedding and

© The Author(s), under exclusive license to Springer Nature Switzerland AG 2023
N. Tsapatsoulis et al. (Eds.): CAIP 2023, LNCS 14185, pp. 255–264, 2023.
https://doi.org/10.1007/978-3-031-44240-7_25

self-similarity for LFI compression. Ahmad et al. [7] proposed a coding method using the multi-view extension of HEVC to explore the correlation between SAIs. These methods can remove most of the data redundancy, but encoding all the data results in limited encoding efficiency.

For the latter (view synthesis based approach), only a subset of SAIs is selected for encoding, and the rest of SAIs will be synthesized at the decoder side. Bakir et al. [8] compressed sparsely sampled SAIs, and used the LF Dual Discriminator GAN at the decoder side to synthesize discarded SAIs. Hedayati et al. [9] used JPEG to compress the central SAI and designed a deep learning network that includes quality enhancement and depth estimation to reconstruct the SAIs array. Huang et al. [10] compressed the selected SAIs and the disparity maps corresponding to the unselected SAIs, and rendered the unselected SAIs at the decoder side. Liu et al. [11] compressed eight selected SAIs and constituted multi-disparity geometry to reflect abundant disparity characteristics; then, synthesizing remaining LFI's SAIs using the multi-stream view reconstruction network at the decoder side. These methods improve encoding efficiency through sparse sampling and view synthesis. However, the selected SAIs are generally coded with video coding techniques. The intra frame-based coding tree unit (CTU) level bit allocation algorithms for existing video coders do not fully consider the visual perception characteristics. This leads to perceptual redundancy in the compressed SAI subset. Due to the fact that the SAIs in the subset will be used as references at the decoder side, this perceptual redundancy will be further transmitted to the synthesized SAIs.

Therefore, in this paper, a perceptual LFI coding method with a new CTU level allocation strategy is proposed to improve LFI coding efficiency. The experimental results show that the effect of bit allocation is maintained in synthesized SAIs. At the same bit rate, the proposed method achieved better subjective quality and structural consistency in the salient regions.

2   The Proposed Method

In this paper, a perceptual LFI coding method with new CTU level bit allocation strategy is proposed, and its framework is shown in Fig. 1. At the encoder side, the original LFI L_{org} is sparsely sampled, and the SAIs at four corner positions are selected to form a subset of SAIs S_{sel}, which are arranged into PVS for input into HEVC. At the same time, the depth map I_D and saliency map I_S of the central SAI I_C are extracted separately through deep learning networks. Subsequently, I_C, I_D and I_S are input into the proposed bit allocation model to calculate the bit weight for each CTU. The complete set of weights W is input into HEVC to guide the target bit rate allocation at the CTU level. At the decoder side, the decoded SAIs set S'_{sel} is input into the LFI angular super-resolution network to recover the dropped SAIs. Finally, the complete reconstructed LFI L_{rec} consist of a synthesized SAIs set S'_{unsel} and S'_{sel}.

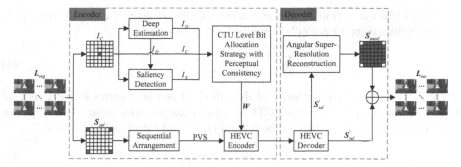

Fig. 1. The framework of the proposed LFI perceptual coding method.

2.1 Designed CTU Level Bit Allocation Strategy with Perceptual Consistency

The Assumption of Perceptual Consistency

There is a high content similarity between SAIs with different angular coordinates. Taking a 7×7 SAIs array as an example, Fig. 2 shows the residuals between I_C and other angular positional SAIs of the LFI *Fountain_&_Vincent_1*. Whether they are far away or adjacent, the residual between them is small. Therefore, the assumption of perceptual consistency for SAIs array is proposed, stating that the visual sensitive regions of SAIs with different angular coordinates are basically the same. Based on this assumption, each scene only needs to use I_C to calculate the weight of bit allocation once, rather than independently calculating for all selected SAIs. It is very meaningful for improving encoding speed.

(a)   (b)

Fig. 2. The residual maps. (a) The residual between the SAIs located at (4,4) and (4,3). (b) The residual between the SAIs located at (4,4) and (1,1). (Here, pixel values are magnified by 4 times for visualization).

Calculation and Allocation of CTU Level Bit Weight

Initial Bit Weight Calculation

Compared to flat regions, complex texture regions have more complex prediction modes and deeper block depth. Generally, complex texture regions require more bit rate consumption to achieve the same quality as flat regions. In addition, studies have shown that humans pay more attention to complex texture regions than flat regions. Therefore, texture complexity is used as the initial bit weight for each CTU. CTUs with complex textures are given larger initial weights, while flat CTUs are given smaller initial weights. The initial bit weight for each CTU is calculated as follows:

$$T_i = \sum_{x=1}^{M-1} \sum_{y=1}^{N-1} G_i(x, y) + c \tag{1}$$

where T_i is the texture complexity of the i-th CTU and also serves as the initial bit weight. M and N are the size of the CTU. c is a constant to avoid an initial bit weight of 0. $G_i(x, y)$ is the gradient value of the pixel at (x, y), and calculated as follows:

$$G_i(x, y) = |p_i(x, y) - p_i(x + 1, y)| + |p_i(x, y) - p_i(x, y + 1)| \tag{2}$$

where $P_i(x, y)$ is the pixel value at (x, y), $| \cdot |$ denotes an absolute value operation. The calculation is performed on the Y component of the image.

Weight Adjustment of Visual Sensitive Regions
When human eye observes images, the visual sensitivity of different regions varies. Regions with higher visual sensitivity should be assigned more bits. In the proposed method, the foreground region and the salient object region are considered as high visual sensitivity regions, and the bit weights of the CTU in these regions are adjusted. Firstly, the depth map I_D and saliency map I_S of I_C are obtained using deep learning networks [12] and [13]. Secondly, I_D and I_S are binarized to obtain the foreground mask and salient object mask. Then, the masks are employed to calculate the foreground density ρ_D and salient density ρ_S of each CTU, respectively. The calculation is expressed as follows:

$$\rho = \sum CTU / (M \times N) \tag{3}$$

where $\sum CTU$ is the number of pixels with the value of 1 in the binary mask corresponding to the CTU, and $M \times N$ is the size of the CTU. If $\rho_D > 0.5$, the CTU belongs to the foreground region, and similarly, if $\rho_S > 0.5$, the CTU belongs to the salient region. Finally, the bit weights of visual sensitive regions are adjusted based on the judgment results, and the calculation is expressed as follows:

$$W_i = \begin{cases} T_i, \; if \; \rho_D < 0.5 \; \& \; \rho_S < 0.5 \\ T_i \times \alpha, \; if \; \rho_D > 0.5 \; \& \; \rho_S < 0.5 \\ T_i \times \beta, \; if \; \rho_D < 0.5 \; \& \; \rho_S > 0.5 \\ T_i \times \alpha \times \beta, \; if \; \rho_D > 0.5 \; \& \; \rho_S > 0.5 \end{cases} \tag{4}$$

where α and β are weight adjustment factors used for the foreground and salient regions, respectively, to increase the bit weights of CTUs belonging to these regions. Based on extensive experiments, α and β are taken as 1.1 and 1.5, respectively. W_i is the final bit weight of the i-th CTU, used for allocating the target bit.

CTU Level Target Bit Allocation
After calculating the bit weights of all CTUs, the target bit is allocated for each CTU, and the calculation is expressed as follows:

$$R_i = \frac{(R_p - R_h - R_c) \times W_i}{\sum_{k=i}^{N_c} W_K} \tag{5}$$

where R_i is the target bit of the i-th CTU, R_p is the total target bits of the current frame, R_h is the actual consumption bits of frame header information encoding, R_c is the actual consumption bits of the encoded CTU and N_c is the total number of CTUs in the current frame. After allocating all the bits, QP is calculated based on $R - \lambda$ and $QP - \lambda$ model [14].

2.2 Decoding and Reconstruction

In the proposed method, only the selected SAIs set S_{sel} is compressed and transmitted, while the remaining SAIs are synthesized at the decoder side. The network and pre trained model in [15] are selected for LFI reconstruction. Specifically, S'_{sel} is fed into the angular super-resolution network to reconstruct complete LFI, and represented as:

$$L' = f(S'_{sel}) \qquad (6)$$

where L' is the LFI output by the network, and it is already a complete SAIs array, and $f(\cdot)$ denotes the angular super-resolution network.

Finally, the reconstructed LFI L_{rec} is obtained as follows:

$$L_{rec} = S'_{sel} + S'_{unsel}, S'_{unsel} \in L' \qquad (7)$$

where S'_{unsel} is the set of SAIs from L' except for the four corner positions. The SAI at the four corner positions still uses S'_{sel} to minimize the reconstruction distortion caused by the angular super-resolution network.

3 Experimental Results and Analyses

3.1 Experimental Setup

The proposed method is tested on the commonly used EPFL light field database [16], which provides multiple scenes captured by a Lytro Illum camera. Here, the MATLAB light field toolbox [17] is adopted to decode the RAW light field data into a SAIs array, with angular and spatial resolutions are 15×15 and 434×625, respectively. Figure 3 shows the SAI thumbnails corresponding to the scenes used in this paper. In specific experiments, the central 7×7 SAIs array is selected, and the spatial resolution of each SAI is cropped to 432×624 to meet the requirements of the encoder for encoding block size. In addition, the SAIs in S_{sel} are arranged into PVS and converted into the format of 4:2:0 YUV. Due to only comparing intra encoding mode, the arrangement order of PVS will not affect the final performance.

The proposed bit allocation method is implemented using the HEVC reference software (HM16.20). Specifically, the PVS is encoded with All Intra coding structure. The size of the CTU is set to 64×64, and the maximum division depth is set to 4. Rate Control and LCU Level Rate Control are set to 1. Besides, the target bitrate of each sequence is collected under the platform of HM16.20 with fixed QPs (*i.e.*, QP = 22, 27, 32, 37, respectively).

Fig. 3. SAI   thumbnails: *Caution_Bees,   Danger_de_Mort,   Fountain_&_Vincent_1,*
Stone_Pillars_Outside, Sophie_&_Vincent_on_a_Bench, Sophie_Krios_&_Vincent.

Perceptual Peak Signal to Noise Ratio (PPSNR) [18] and Visual Saliency induced
Index (VSI) [19] are adopted as the perceptual quality metrics. Between them, PPSNR
is a quality metric that only targets salient region, and calculated as follows:

$$PPSNR = 10\log_{10} \times \frac{255^2}{\frac{1}{L \times H} \sum_{x=1}^{L} \sum_{y=1}^{H} (I(x, y) - I'(x, y))^2 \times \delta(x, y)} \qquad (8)$$

where $\delta(x, y) = 1$ indicates the salient region, and $\delta(x, y) = 0$ indicates the non-salient
region

Note that it is meaningful to calculate PSNR only for salient regions, as these regions
are more susceptible to attention and have a greater impact on perceived quality. However,
when the total bitrate is fixed, the increase of the bitrate in the salient region will inevitably
be accompanied by the decrease of the bitrate in the non-salient region. Therefore, this
paper also adopts VSI to evaluate the global quality of images. VSI considers the visual
saliency and has been validated to be in line with human perception [19].

This paper measures encoding performance by calculating Bjontegaard Delta bitrate
(BD-BR) [20]. A negative BD-BR value indicates that under the same quality, the proposed method can save more bitrate compared to the benchmark method, while conversely, it means consuming more bitrate. The bitrate is measured in bit per pixel (bpp)
and calculated as follows:

$$bpp = \frac{R_{LF}}{x \times y \times u \times v} \qquad (9)$$

where R_{LF} denotes the size of the bitstream, $x \times y$ and $u \times v$ are the spatial and angular
resolutions of the LFI, respectively. In addition, the quality of each LFI is represented
by the average quality of all SAIs.

Here, two compression methods are used for comparison to evaluate the effectiveness
of the proposed method. The abbreviations for these methods are as follows:

- *HM*: Encode all SAIs on HM16.20. Except for the target bitrate collected when
  encoding 49 SAIs. The other configurations are consistent with the ones described
  earlier.
- *HM&ASR*: It can be seen as a version of the proposed method using HM's rate
  allocation strategy. Specifically, only four corner SAIs are encoded, and the remaining
  SAIs are synthesized by an angular super-resolution network.

3.2 Rate-Distortion Performance

Table 1 gives the Bjøntegaard metrics [20] of the proposed method with *HM* and *HM&ASR* as the baselines, respectively. Y-PPSNR indicates to the average PPSNR metric for all SAIs calculated on the Y component. Compared with the *HM* method, the proposed method achieves average BD-BR savings of 90.305% in the Y-PPSNR metric and 90.825% in the VSI metric, respectively. This is mainly due to the sparse encoding, which saves a lot of bitrates. Compared to the *HM&ASR* method, the proposed method achieves an average BD-BR savings of 13.676% in the Y-PPSNR metric. This indicates that the proposed bit allocation method significantly improves the visual quality of salient regions. In addition, the proposed bit allocation method effectively balances the bitrates of non-salient regions, thereby improving the global quality of the image. This can be reflected in the average BD-BR savings of 2.045% in the VSI metric.

Table 1. The BD-BR comparison of the proposed method with *HM* and *HM&ASR* methods as baselines, respectively.

Scenes	*Proposed* vs *HM*		*Proposed* vs *HM&ASR*	
	BD-BR (Y-PPSNR)	BD-BR (VSI)	BD-BR (Y-PPSNR)	BD-BR (VSI)
101	−91.494%	−90.551%	−17.490%	−2.477%
102	−91.283%	−90.538%	−10.982%	−0.635%
103	−88.590%	−90.152%	−14.895%	−0.998%
104	−91.728%	−91.482%	−23.650%	−4.545%
105	−88.552%	−90.843%	−13.245%	−3.162%
106	−90.182%	−91.381%	−1.795%	−0.451%
Avg	**−90.305%**	**−90.825%**	**−13.676%**	**−2.045%**

Figure 4 show the visual comparison results of the decoded central SAI, where the red box is taken from the salient region of the image and the blue box is taken from non-salient region, and the PSNR values of these regions are given. It can be found that the proposed method maintains better details in salient regions, such as the eye details. Correspondingly, the quality of the proposed method has decreased in non-salient regions. However, this has a small impact on the overall perceived quality, as these regions have a low level of attention. Moreover, in the proposed method, the central SAI is not encoded, but synthesized by the decoder side. The experimental results indicate that the designed bit allocation strategy not only affects S_{sel}, but also affects S'_{unsel}, thereby generating results with better visual quality.

Fig. 4. Comparison of the decoded central SAI of *Sophie_&_Vincent_on_a_Bench* (105). The number in the sub-figure indicates the PSNR of the region. Here, 0.324bpp for *HM* methods, 0.026bpp for *HM&ASR* method and the proposed method.

Fig. 5. Comparison of the EPI consistency of salient regions of *Danger_de_Mort* (102), *Fountain_&_Vincent_1* (103), *Stone_Pillars_Outside* (104). Unit: PSNR/bpp.

3.3 Structural Consistency of Reconstruction

The structural consistency of LFIs is considered key to techniques such as refocusing and depth inference. Epipolar Plane Images (EPIs) contain parallax changes and object occlusion information, and the continuity of their polar lines can well reflect the structural consistency of the LFI. Hence, Fig. 5 shows the EPIs in the salient regions extracted from the decoded results. It can be observed that the proposed method achieves higher PSNR and visual quality at lower bitrates. The HM method independently encodes each SAI, consuming large bitrates while damaging structural consistency, resulting in significant distortion on the EPI. The HM&ASR method saves bits through sparse encoding, but also introduces reconstruction distortion generated by deep learning networks. In contrast, the proposed method increases the bitrates of the salient regions by reallocating the CTU level bit, thereby improving the quality of the regions, and at the same time enhancing the structural consistency of the salient regions.

4 Conclusions

This paper presents a perceptual light field image (LFI) coding method with coding tree unit (CTU) level bit allocation strategy. At the encoder side, the four corner sub-aperture images (SAIs) are compressed. In order to remove the perceptual redundancy, a CTU level bit allocation strategy with perceptual consistency is proposed. Firstly, the texture features of each CTU of central SAI are extracted as the initial bit weight. Then, the bit weight of CTU belonging to foreground and salient regions are adjusted to obtain the final bit weight. Finally, the calculated weights are employed to allocate the target bit of each CTU. At the decoder side, the complete SAIs array is reconstructed by the LFI angular super-resolution network. The experimental results show that the proposed method can effectively improve the quality of the salient regions and the overall image at the same bitrate, while maintaining better structural consistency of the salient regions.

This work was supported in part by the Natural Science Foundation of China under Grant Nos. 62271276, 62071266 and 61931022, in part by the Natural Science Foundation of Ningbo under Grant No. 202003N4088, and in part by Science and Technology Innovation 2025 Major Project of Ningbo under Grant No. 2022Z076.

References

1. Xiang, J., Jiang, G., Yu, M., Jiang, Z., Ho, Y.-S.: No-reference light field image quality assessment using four-dimensional sparse transform. IEEE Trans. Multimedia **25**, 457–472 (2023)
2. Yang, N., et al.: Detection method of rice blast based on 4D light field refocusing depth information fusion. Comput. Electron. Agric. **205**, 107614 (2023)
3. Yuan, L., Gao, J., Wang, X. and Cui, H.: Research on 3D reconstruction technology based on the fusion of polarization imaging and light field depth information. In: 2022 7th International Conference on Intelligent Computing and Signal Processing (ICSP), pp. 1792–1797. IEEE, Xi'an, China (2022)
4. Shen, S., Xing, S., Sang, X., Yan, B., Chen, Y.: Virtual stereo content rendering technology review for light-field display. Displays **76**, 102320 (2022)
5. Dai, F., Zhang, J., Ma, Y. and Zhang, Y.: Lenselet image compression scheme based on subaperture images streaming. In: 2015 IEEE International Conference on Image Processing (ICIP), pp. 4733–4737. IEEE, Quebec City, QC, Canada (2015)
6. Monteiro, R., Lucas, L., Conti, C., et al.: Light field HEVC-based image coding using locally linear embedding and self-similarity compensated prediction. In: 2016 IEEE International Conference on Multimedia & Expo Workshops (ICMEW), pp. 1–4. IEEE, Seattle, WA, USA (2016)
7. Ahmad, W., Olsson, R., Sjöström, M.: Interpreting plenoptic images as multi-view sequences for improved compression. In: 2017 IEEE International Conference on Image Processing (ICIP), pp. 4557–4561. IEEE, Beijing, China (2017)
8. Bakir, N., Hamidouche, W., Fezza, S.A., Samrouth, K., Déforges, O.: Light field image coding using VVC standard and view synthesis based on dual discriminator GAN. IEEE Trans. Multimedia **23**, 2972–2985 (2021)
9. Hedayati, E., Havens, T.C., Bos, J.P.: Light field compression by residual CNN-assisted JPEG. In: 2021 International Joint Conference on Neural Networks (IJCNN), pp. 1–9. IEEE, Shenzhen, China (2021)

10. Huang, X., An, P., Chen, Y., Liu, D., Shen, L.: Low bitrate light field compression with geometry and content consistency. IEEE Trans. Multimedia **24**, 152–165 (2022)
11. Liu, D., Huang, Y., Fang, Y., Zuo, Y., An, P.: Multi-Stream Dense View Reconstruction Network for Light Field Image Compression. IEEE Transactions on Multimedia, early access (2022)
12. Miangoleh, S.M.H., Dille, S., Mai, L., Paris, S., Aksoy, Y.: Boosting monocular depth estimation models to high-resolution via content-adaptive multi-resolution merging. In: 2021 IEEE/CVF Conference on Computer Vision and Pattern Recognition (CVPR), pp. 9680–9689. IEEE, Nashville, TN, USA (2021)
13. Wang, F., Pan, J., Xu, S., Tang, J.: Learning discriminative cross-modality features for RGB-D saliency detection. IEEE Trans. Image Process. **31**, 1285–1297 (2022)
14. Li, B., Li, H., Li, L., Zhang, J.: λ domain rate control algorithm for high efficiency video coding. IEEE Trans. Image Process. **23**(9), 3841–3854 (2014)
15. Wang, Y., et al.: Disentangling light fields for super-resolution and disparity estimation. IEEE Trans. Pattern Anal. Mach. Intell. **45**(1), 425–443 (2023)
16. EPFL dataset. https://www.epfl.ch/labs/mmspg/downloads/epfl-light-field-image-dataset/. Accessed 28 April 2023
17. Dansereau, D.G., Pizarro, O., Williams, S.B.: Decoding, calibration and rectification for lenselet-based plenoptic cameras. In: 2013 IEEE Conference on Computer Vision and Pattern Recognition, pp. 1027–1034. IEEE, Portland, OR, USA (2013)
18. Majid, M., Owais, M., Anwar, S.M.: Visual saliency based redundancy allocation in HEVC compatible multiple description video coding. Multimed. Tools Appl. **77**, 20955–20977 (2018)
19. Zhang, L., Shen, Y., Li, H.: VSI: a visual saliency-induced index for perceptual image quality assessment. IEEE Trans. Image Process. **23**(10), 4270–4281 (2014)
20. Bjontegaard, G.: Calculation of average PSNR differences between RD-curves. ITU SG16 Doc. VCEG-M33 (2001)

A Comparative Performance Assessment of Different Video Codecs

Ioanna Valiandi[1]([✉]), Andreas S. Panayides[1][iD], Efthyvoulos Kyriacou[2][iD], Constantinos S. Pattichis[3,4][iD], and Marios S. Pattichis[5][iD]

[1] VIDEOMICS Group, CYENS Centre of Excellence, 1016 Nicosia, Cyprus
{i.valiandi,a.panayides}@cyens.org.cy
[2] Department of Electrical Engineering, Computer Engineering and Informatics,
Cyprus University of Technology, 3036 Limassol, Cyprus
[3] Department of Computer Science, University of Cyprus, 1678 Nicosia, Cyprus
[4] HealthXR Group, CYENS Centre of Excellence, 1016 Nicosia, Cyprus
[5] Department of Electrical and Computer Engineering, University of New Mexico,
Albuquerque, NM 87131-0001, USA

Abstract. Video streaming applications have witnessed widespread adoption over the past decades due to the rising demand for real-time and on-demand video content across different application domains. As a result, video streaming has become the dominant source of internet traffic, while the abundance of video-driven applications will likely lead to a further increase in the near future, enabled by associated advances in video devices' capabilities. In that context, there is a strong need to develop efficient compression and video delivery algorithms to accommodate future growth. To this end, this study presents a comparative performance evaluation of six different video codecs. More specifically, we compare the performance of the Versatile Video Coding (VVC) standard developed by the Joint Video Experts Team (JVET) and the AV1 codec developed by the Alliance for Open Media (AOM). Additionally, we assess the capacity of the newly released UVG-266 VVC encoder available from the Ultra Video Group, along with the Essential Video Coding (EVC) standard's reference implementation. Finally, we include in our experiments the most popular High Efficiency Video Coding (HEVC) implementation, namely x265, together with the VP9 codec. Experimental evaluation based on three general-purpose video datasets (768×432 and 3840×2160 video resolutions) and one ultrasound video dataset (560×448 video resolution) demonstrates that VVC outperforms all rival codecs to date, especially as video resolution increases, followed by AV1.

Keywords: Video Streaming · Video Coding Standards · Video compression · Video quality · Performance comparison

This study is partly funded by the project 'Atherorisk' "Identification of unstable carotid plaques associated with symptoms using ultrasonic image analysis and plaque motion analysis", code: Excellence/0421/0292, funded by the Research and Innovation Foundation, the Republic of Cyprus.

1   Introduction

It is estimated that 720,000 h of video are shared online daily [1] with video traffic significantly surpassing 82% of all internet traffic [2]. High video traffic demands are both enabled and driven by associated advances in video compression and wired/ wireless networks achieving significant bandwidth availability. At the same time, video delivery protocols such as HTTP Adaptive Streaming (HAS), including Dynamic Adaptive Streaming over HTTP (MPEG-DASH) and HTTP Live Streaming (HLS), have revolutionized the video streaming industry. Moreover, high-caliber video rendering devices materialize the notion of anywhere, anytime, and any-device, ubiquitous video streaming. As a result, new and traditional video sources and applications have seen widespread acceptance and market penetration. A non-exhaustive list includes mobile gaming, mixed and extended reality (XR), and healthcare applications, on the one hand, and teleconferencing and live streaming events, including sports, news, and entertainment, on the other, accounting for a sizeable portion of the most popular applications [3].

Versatile Video Encoding (VVC)/H.266 standard [4], the successor of the High Efficiency Video Coding (HEVC)/ H.265 standard, was developed by JVET to recapture the best encoding efficiency to date, which was previously claimed by the AV1 of the Alliance of Open Media (AOM) [5,6]. Both codecs target ultra-high-definition (4K and beyond) video encoding, with a particular interest towards mobile, real-time 360° video streaming and mixed/ extended reality applications [7,8]. However, in this video compression efficiency pursue, complexity is often overlooked resulting in computationally expensive tools that are not real-time friendly. The latter is especially true for video compression standards' reference implementations. To mitigate this phenomenon, optimized, standards-compliant open-source implementations emerge, that typically provide a trade-off between complexity and efficiency. Such can be considered the recently released UVG-266 codec, being a VVC/H.266 standard's implementation licensed under 3-clause BSD [9], or the earlier x265 implementation of the HEVC/ H.265 standard. Moreover, in response to the ever increasing computational complexity but also the associated intellectual property, Essential Video Coding (EVC) [10] was developed by the ISO/IEC Moving Picture Experts Group (MPEG) [11], followed by its open source implementation, namely the extra-fast Essential Video Encoder (XEVE) [10].

The continuously evolving video codecs development landscape depicted in Fig. 1, necessitates for a fair and unbiased comparison across the range of underlying application scenarios that involve different content, and may impose different limitations and/ or activate (and use) different and often specific video coding tools. This study aims to provide an objective and reproducible comparative assessment of the currently dominant video compression standards. More specifically, to provide a fair comparison of the VVC (both its reference implementation and UVG-266) and AV1 codecs, along with both its predecessors, namely the x265 implementation [12] and VP9 codec [13], respectively, as well and the recently released XEVE codec.

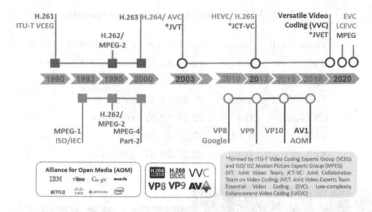

Fig. 1. Video Coding Standards [18]

2 Methodology

In the present section, we describe the methodology used to perform a comparative performance evaluation of the investigated video coding standards and corresponding codecs. The video datasets used in this work are first introduced (see Table 1), followed by the experimental encoding setup (see Table 2). Finally, the objective video quality assessment (VQA) approach and metrics are provided.

2.1 Video Datasets

Three video datasets were used in the context of the present study as depicted in Table 1. The first two datasets consist of general-purpose videos, while the third one includes ultrasound videos of the common carotid artery (CCA). More specifically, the first one comes from the SJTU 4K Video Sequence Dataset [14] and consists of five 4K (3840 × 2160) ultra-high definition (UHD) video sequences at 30 frames per second (fps), out of a total of 15 videos parting the dataset. The second one is abstracted from the Netflix video dataset [15,16], comprising of 10 selected videos with a video resolution of 768 × 432, of which seven have a frame rate of 25 fps and three have a frame rate of 50 fps. Finally, the third dataset consists of ten CCA ultrasound videos with a resolution of 560 × 448 and with

Table 1. Video Datasets Characteristics.

Dataset Name	No. Videos	Video Resolution	Frame Rate	Duration
SJTU 4K Dataset	5	3840 × 2160	30	10
Netflix Dataset I	7	768 × 432	25	10
Netflix Dataset II	3	768 × 432	50	10
CCA Dataset	10	560 × 448	40	10

Table 2. Video codecs and coding parameters.

Video Codec	Version	QP Range	Preset Profile
VVC	1.8	22,27,32,37	Random Access
x265	3.3	22,27,32,37	placebo
SVT-AV1	1.4.1	27,35,46,55	preset 8
UVG-266	0.4	22,27,32,37	veryslow
VP9	1.13	27,35,46,55	best
XEVE	0.4.3	22,27,32,37	placebo

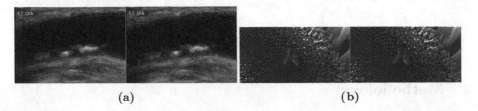

(a)   (b)

Fig. 2. (a) Left: Compressed CCA video with x265 codec, Right: Original CCA video (560 × 448), (b) Left: Compressed Netflix video with AV1 codec, Right: Original Netflix video (768 × 432)

a frame rate of 40 fps. All selected videos are 10 s long and are in yuv420p raw format. A representative sample of the incorporated video content appears in Fig. 2. Overall, the goal is to investigate low to ultra-high definition video resolutions with varying frame rates and different content, in order to better validate the examined codecs' video coding tools capabilities under different setups.

2.2 Experimental Setup

The selected encoding parameters per investigated video codec are depicted in Table 2. The experimental setup was prepared in accordance with the relevant literature to enable a fair comparison of the video codecs involved [3,17,18]. Selected quantization parameters for constant quality encoding comprised of 27, 35, 46, 55 for AV1 and VP9 codecs, while matching QPs of 22, 27, 32, 37 were selected for VVC, UVG-266, XEVE, and x265 codecs. The objective here was to accommodate a broad spectrum of representative bandwidths as suggested by the literature. To support random access for VVC, an intra frame was inserted every 32 frames for 25 fps and 30 fps videos and every 48 frames for 50 fps videos. Likewise, the same intra-update was used for all the other video codecs. Default preset parameters for encoding were set at Random Access for VVC, -preset 8 and -best for AV1 and VP9, respectively, -placebo for x265 and -slower for both UVG-266 and XEVE. The latest reference software versions available on March 2023 were used for each codec (see Table 2).

2.3   Video Quality Assessment

The importance of objective and subjective video quality assessment and the approach followed in the current study are detailed next.

1. Objective Video Quality Assessment

Peak to Signal Noise Ratio (PSNR)

Peak Signal to Noise Ratio (PSNR) is still one of the most widely used VQA metrics, especially for video compression comparison studies, despite not correlating particularly well with subjective quality. To compensate for this shortcoming, a popular alternative has prevailed over the past decade, which favors the luma component (PSNR Y), which captures the intensity of the monochrome signal over the color ones (PSNR U and PSNR V) [17]. $PSNR_{611}$ has demonstrated superior correlation to the actual video's perceptual quality [19]:

$$PSNR_{611} = \frac{6 * PSNRY + PSNRU + PSNRV}{8} \tag{1}$$

2. Subjective Video Quality Assessment

Compression is a very sensitive process and therefore subjective VQA must be employed, to quantify the validity of objective, computerized VQA methods and verify that the objective scores correlate sufficiently to what the human eye actually perceives. Various subjective VQA methods exist, including displaying compressed videos randomly, with the original video being rendered at the beginning of each evaluation session, or even during the session, to try and minimize biases. Another popular approach, which is typically used to compare video coding standards performance, is to render videos that were compressed with the same encoding parameters side by side and ask evaluators to determine which video has the highest quality. Alternative approaches include rendering together videos that are compressed to the same bitrate or exhibit similar VQA scores (i.e. PSNR ratings). The latter methods allow to deduct the superiority of one codec over the other [20]. Examples of such evaluations are presented in Fig. 2, depicting (a) a CCA video (560 × 448) compressed using a QP of 27 and the x265 codec and (b) a video abstracted from the Netflix dataset (768 × 432), compressed using a QP of 55 and the AV1 codec. The right video in each case corresponds to the original, uncompressed video, to facilitate comparison. As evident is both displayed cases, the compressed videos suffer from degradation in video quality compared to the original videos.

3. BD-Rate Bjodegraad Metric

The Bjontegaard Delta (BD-rate) metric [21] is a more formal, numbers-only analysis, typically used for codec comparisons. The metric essentially computes the bitrate demands reduction for equivalent perceptual quality (measured in terns of a VQA metric, here $PSNR_{611}$) of one codec over the other.

This method creates rate-distortion curves that compute how each technology "distorts" at the various data rates while providing a combined score for luma and chrominance assessment. Rate-distortion curves are produced with a corresponding number of samples that matches with a third-order polynomial. Then, the distance between the two curves is calculated, capturing the average bitrate difference for equivalent objective video quality between the examined codecs.

3   Results

In this section we provide a comprehensive comparative evaluation of the six investigated video codecs per examined video dataset. The experimental evaluation was performed using a 64-bit Windows 10 (v.22 H2) machine, consisting of a 12th Gen Intel(R) Core(TM) i9-12900K (16 cores, 3.20 GHz). Objective VQA was based on PSNR scores that are computed during the encoding process. In other words, we relied on the integrated PSNR computations implemented by each investigated video codec, which were then post-processed to compute the $PSNR_{611}$. Moreover, BD-Rate results are further given to demonstrate the bitrate demands reductions for equivalent objective video quality of the more efficient video compression standards compared to their earlier, or less-performing counterparts.

1. **Objective Video Quality Assessment**

   BD-Rate results for all examined video codecs categorized per investigated video dataset appear in Table 3 and Table 4. Similarly, the corresponding rate-distortion curves are given in Fig. 3 and Fig. 4. Here, it is worth noting that the depicted results are averaged over the entire video dataset(s) taking into consideration all four compression levels depicted in the experimental evaluation setup. As expected, VVC, the most recent video compression standard, significantly outperforms all rival video compression standards, including its recent

Table 3. BD-RATE (a) Netflix video dataset I: 768 × 432 @25 Hz (b) Netflix video dataset II: 768 × 432 @50 Hz

	Bitrate Savings Relative to						Bitrate Savings Relative to				
	SVT-AV1	UVG-266	x265	XEVE	VP9		SVT-AV1	UVG-266	x265	XEVE	VP9
VVC	43,4	44,7	44,9	47,9	62,6	VVC	38,5	34,9	50,2	46,9	59,9
SVT-AV1		4,1	3,9	8	32,3	SVT-AV1		−6,8*	16	14,6	33,7
UVG-266			−0,2*	2,4	27,6	UVG-266			19,3	17,3	35,3
x265				4,3	28,6	x265				−1,5*	19,9
XEVE					25,9	XEVE					20,9

(a)   (b)

Table 4. BD-Rate (a) SJTU 4K Dataset: 3840×2160 @30 Hz (b) CCA Dataset: 560×448 @40 Hz

Bitrate Savings Relative to						Bitrate Savings Relative to				
	SVT-AV1	UVG-266	x265	XEVE	VP9		SVT-AV1	UVG-266	x265	XEVE	VP9
VVC	43,9	40,4	47,6	49,5	49,3	VVC	34	35,3	36,3	45,4	58,4
SVT-AV1		-7,2*	3,8	8,9	11,8	SVT-AV1		4,2	12,4	16,8	41,9
UVG-266			12,1	16,1	17,9	UVG-266			12,5	17,9	42,6
x265				4,1	6,1	x265				4,2	31,9
XEVE					2,5	XEVE					30,5

(a)   (b)

* *Negative numbers indicate that the encoding standard depicted on the leftmost column demands higher bitrate compared to the encoding standard depicted on the 2nd row. For example in Table 3 (a) UVG-266 vs x265 = −0.2, which translates to UVG-266 demanding 0.2% higher bitrate compared to x265 for equivalent $PSNR_{611}$ ratings*

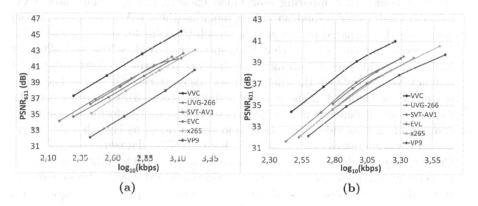

(a)   (b)

Fig. 3. Rate-distortion curves ($PSNR_{611}$ vs log (bitrate)) of mean dataset values of (a) Netflix Dataset I 768×432 @25 fps and (b) Netflix Dataset II 768×432 @50 fps

open-source UVG-266 implementation. Indicatively, VVC achieves bitrate demands reductions for equivalent $PSNR_{611}$ quality that extend over 40% for all compared video codecs and datasets, besides AV1 and UVG for Netflix dataset II and AV1, UVG, and x265 for CCA ultrasound video dataset. AV1 and UVG-266 are the next best performing codecs, achieving comparable performance between them, interchangeably and marginally outperforming each other, depending on the underlying dataset's video content, resolution, and frame rate. Likewise, the x265 and XEVE codecs are closely ranked, with the former receiving slightly favorable performance rankings in all scenarios but the Netflix II video dataset. At the lowest performing end, we can find the earlier VP9 codec. However, as discussed later, VP9 is an excellent choice

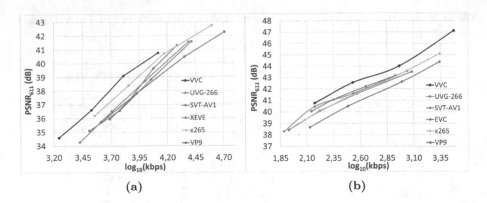

Fig. 4. Rate-distortion curves ($PSNR_{611}$ vs log (bitrate)) of mean dataset values of
(a) SJTU 4K Dataset 3840 × 2160 @30 fps (b) CCA Dataset 560 × 448@40 fps

when considering the trade-off between performance and complexity.

When it comes to comparing how video codecs, and especially how VVC behaves when lower resolution videos (such as the CCA ultrasound videos) are involved, compared to higher video resolutions (as for example the SJTU 4K videos), one can observe that VVC gains over AV1, UVG, and x265 are increased as video resolution increases. This is also true for Netflix dataset I but not Netflix dataset II, which is more likely attributed to the low number of videos included in the particular dataset (only 3), that constitute the dataset content-dependent. Compared to XEVE, the performance gains are comparable across video resolutions and frame rates, as is with VP9, where actually less increases are documented for the SJTU dataset.

Clearly, larger-scale comparison studies are needed to draw robust and definitive conclusion, including substantial subjective video quality assessment sessions. However the documented trends in the present paper are aligned with the collective findings of the recent literature.

2. Encoding Time Assessment

The goal in the present result section is to demonstrate the trade-off between compression performance and time-efficiency of the investigated video codecs. Figure 5 shows the encoding time (in seconds) consumed by each video codec to compress videos parting a dataset using constant quality encoding. In particular, for VVC, UVG-266, XEVE, and x265 the average encoding time is calculated for a quantization parameter of 27, while a matching QP of 35 was used for encoders AV1 and VP9. A key observation emanates from the fact that VVC is excluded from the depicted graphs. The latter is due to the 10x time requirements of VVC, which would render the figure axis unbalanced and incomprehensible. Another important finding relates to the encoding time necessary to encode 4K videos, as in the case of the SJTU dataset. The significant amount of time compared to much lower-resolution datasets is depicted in Fig. 5(b) where the SJTU dataset

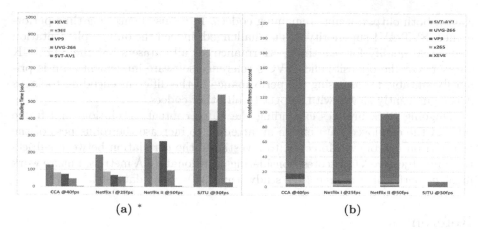

Fig. 5. (a) Encoding Time in seconds *The encoding time values of the SJTU dataset are displayed at 50% of their original values, to facilitate all datasets' results depiction on the same plot. Likewise, the maximum bound for the encoding time axis was set to 1000, despite the XEVE value of the SJTU dataset that extends up to 2389 s* (b) Average Encoding Speed in Frames per Second

has the lowest encoding speed in terms of frames per second compared to the other datasets. In fact, SJTU dataset's encoding time requirements were divided by 2 in Fig. 5(a), in order to depict the results more clearly and in the same plot. For the same reason, the maximum bound for the encoding time axis was set to 1000 s. Here, it is important to note that the XEVE value for the SJTU dataset extends up to 2389 s. Overall, SVT-AV1 is the fastest encoder among the examined ones, achieving orders of magnitude lower encoding times or higher encoded frames in one second. UVG-266 is the 2nd best performing encoder in terms of speed for all datasets but the SJTU one, where VP9 demonstrated better performance. In that sequence, VP9 is better than x265 and XEVE in all occasions but the Netflix II dataset. XEVE is the worst performing codec, 2nd only to VVC, which is not depicted here. Clearly, despite the documented trends, more datasets of diverse video content, resolutions, and frame rates, are required to unambiguously capture the performance of all video codecs with respect to the aforementioned video dataset characteristics.

4   Discussion and Concluding Remarks

The present study reinforced the superiority of the VVC encoding standard in terms of compression efficiency, following a comprehensive comparative evaluation study that examined recent and established video coding standards across multiple video datasets of different video characteristics and content, including general-purpose and clinical videos. The latter findings were computed using both traditional rate-distortion curves, employing PSNR metrics, but also BD-rate computations. SVT-AV1 and UVG-266 achieved similar compression efficiency, both outperforming remaining codecs. In terms of encoding time performance, SVT-AV1 superiority was unchallenged, indeed the only implementation that could qualify for real-time performance for all datasets but the SJTU 4K dataset. On the opposite end, VVC's reference software implementation is primarily suitable for assessing the performance of the different encoding tools, as it is significantly slower with respect to all other codecs.

Ongoing work involves expanding the video content, resolution, and frame rate, of the employed datasets, in an attempt to increase the robustness of the comparison outcomes. Moreover, to investigate the correlation between subjective and objective VQA scores, considering additional VQA metrics. Future work involves performing a large-scale study using 360° video datasets.

References

1. Dootson, P.: 3.2 Billion Images and 720,000 Hours of Video are Shared Online Daily. Can You Sort Real from Fake? https://www.qut.edu.au/study/business/insights/3.2-billion-images-and-720000-hours-of-video-are-shared-onlinedaily.-can-you-sort-real-from-fake
2. Cisco, Cisco visual networking index: Forecast and trends, 2018–2023, White Paper (2020)
3. Esakki, G., Panayides, A.S., Teeparthi, S., Pattichis, M.S.: A comparative performance evaluation of VP9, X265, SVT-AV1, VVC codecs leveraging the VMAF perceptual quality metric. In: Proceedings of SPIE 11510, Applications of Digital Image Processing XLIII, August 2020. https://doi.org/10.1117/12.2567392
4. Versatile Video Coding (VVC). https://jvet.hhi.fraunhofer.de/
5. Encoder design for SVT-AV1 Scalable Video Technology for AV1 Encoder. https://gitlab.com/AOMediaCodec/SVT-AV1. Accessed Apr 2023
6. Alliance for Open Media. https://aomedia.org/
7. Mahmoud, M., et al.: A survey on optimizing mobile delivery of 360° videos: edge caching and multicasting. IEEE Access **11**, 68925–68942 (2023). https://doi.org/10.1109/ACCESS.2023.3292335
8. Mahmoud, M., et al.: A review of deep learning solutions in 360° video streaming. In: 2023 12th International Conference on Modern Circuits and Systems Technologies (MOCAST), Athens, Greece, pp. 1–4 (2023). https://doi.org/10.1109/MOCAST57943.2023.10176729
9. An open-source VVC encoder licensed under 3-clause BSD proposed by Ultra Video Group. https://github.com/ultravideo/UVG-266
10. The eXtra-fast Essential Video Encoder (XEVE) is an open source and fast MPEG-5 EVC encoder. https://github.com/mpeg5/xeve
11. Moving Picture Experts Group - MPEG-5. https://mpeg.chiariglione.org/standards/mpeg-5. Accessed Mar 2023
12. X265 Video Codec. https://www.videolan.org/developers/x265.html
13. VP9 Video Codec. https://www.webmproject.org/vp9/
14. SJTU 4K Video Sequence Dataset. https://medialab.sjtu.edu.cn/post/sjtu-4k-video-sequences/
15. UT Live Video Quality Assessment Database. http://live.ece.utexas.edu/research/quality/live_video.html

16. Seshadrinathan, K., Soundararajan, R., Bovik, A.C., Cormack, L.K.: Study of subjective and objective quality assessment of video. IEEE Trans. Image Process. **19**(6), 1427–1441 (2010)
17. Esakki, G., Panayides, A.S., Jalta, V., Pattichis, M.S.: Adaptive video encoding for different video codecs. IEEE Access **9**, 68720–68736 (2021). https://doi.org/10.1109/ACCESS.2021.3077313
18. Panayides, A.S., Pattichis, M.S., Pantziaris, M., Constantinides, A.G., Pattichis, C.S.: The battle of the video codecs in the healthcare domain - a comparative performance evaluation study leveraging VVC and AV1. IEEE Access **8**, 11469–11481 (2020). https://doi.org/10.1109/ACCESS.2020.2965325
19. Ohm, J.-R., Sullivan, G.J., Schwarz, H., Tan, T.K., Wiegand, T.: Comparison of the coding efficiency of video coding standards-Including high efficiency video coding (HEVC). IEEE Trans. Circuits Syst. Video Technol. **22**(12), 1669–1684 (2012)
20. Panayides, A., et al.: Atherosclerotic plaque ultrasound video encoding, wireless transmission, and quality assessment using H.264. IEEE Trans. Inf. Technol. Biomed. **15**(3), 387–397 (2011). https://doi.org/10.1109/TITB.2011.2105882
21. Bjøntegaar, G.: Improvements of the BD-Rate Model, document ITU-T SG16 Q.6 VCEG-AI11, July 2008

Author Index

Printed in the United States
by Baker & Taylor Publisher Services